Praise for *Banking in Asia: Acquiring a Profit Mindset (2nd edition)*

"Asia's banking industry is an industry in transition. In the midst of this transition comes this important book, with the key message that there are considerable profits to be made in banking in Asia, if managers acquire a profit mindset. Contained in this book is the wisdom that McKinsey consultants have been sharing with leading banks in Asia, now available to a general readership.

This book should also be essential reading for policy-makers throughout Asia. The volume does a great service by clearly explaining the fundamental economic and demographic shifts under way in the region, and their impact on the banking sector. Policy-makers who do not heed the trends outlined in this book risk undermining the ability of local financial institutions to adapt to change, restricting the flow of capital to the most dynamic sectors of the economy and impeding growth."

David K.P. Li
Chairman and Chief Executive Officer, Bank of East Asia

"With details on the complementary roles played by the public and private sectors to overcome the 1997-1998 Financial Crisis in Korea, this book provides invaluable lessons to other markets facing similar problems. Furthermore, by emphasizing the importance of private sector leadership, the book raises the awareness of business leaders in Korea's financial sector to the critical roles that they can play to complete the change journey that began in 1998."

Duk-hoon Lee
Chairman and Chief Executive Officer, Woori Bank

"*Acquiring a Profit Mindset* is the key to being successful in today's very demanding and unpredictable business environment!"

Takahiro Moriguchi
Deputy President, Bank of Tokyo-Mitsubishi

"A profit mindset is fundamental to the revival of not only the Japanese banking industry, but also the whole economy. This book highlights the key elements of the formula for future success in Asia:
- Shift from seeking stability to welcoming discontinuity
- "Shrink to grow" by shifting management resources away from corporate customers to retail customers and SMEs
- Shift from a "do-everything" approach to greater specialization and customer-centric practices"

Masamoto Yashiro
Chairman & President, Shinsei Bank

BANKING IN ASIA

Acquiring a Profit Mindset

(2nd edition)

BANKING IN ASIA
Acquiring a Profit Mindset

(2nd edition)

Tab Bowers
Greg Gibb
Jeffrey Wong
and

members of McKinsey & Company's
Asia Financial Institutions and
Corporate Finance & Strategy practices

John Wiley & Sons (Asia) Pte Ltd

This publication is designed to provide accurate and authoritative information in regard to the subject
matter covered. It is sold with the understanding that the publisher is not engaged in rendering
professional services. If professional advice or other expert assistance is required, the services of a
competent professional person should be sought.

Other Wiley Editorial Offices

John Wiley & Sons, Inc., 111 River Street, Hoboken, NJ 07030, USA
John Wiley & Sons Ltd, The Atrium, Southern Gate, Chichester PO19 8SQ, England
John Wiley & Sons (Canada) Ltd, 22 Worcester Road, Rexdale, Ontario M9W 1L1, Canada
John Wiley & Sons Australia Ltd, 33 Park Road (PO Box 1226), Milton, Queensland 4064, Australia
Wiley-VCH, Pappelallee 3, 69469 Weinheim, Germany

Library of Congress Cataloging-in Publication Data:
ISBN: 0-470-82099-3

Typeset in 10.5/13 points, Minion by Linographic Services Pte Ltd
Printed in Singapore by Saik Wah Press Pte Ltd
10 9 8 7 6 5 4 3 2 1

Contents

Foreword

In Asia, a lot can change in five years. In 1998, when authors from McKinsey & Company wrote the first edition of this book (*Banking in Asia: The End of Entitlement*), Korea and Southeast Asia were in the midst of the financial crisis and China was a market only at the edge of most banks' radar screens. Today, Korea is regarded as one of the best reformed banking markets in Asia, and China is the hot topic in global and local boardrooms.

The landscape of Asian banking has shifted rapidly and it will continue to do so. The pace of change in Asia presents difficult questions for bankers and investors: Will Asia and its banks reform quickly enough to escape another crisis? Where are the sustainable opportunities for long-term profits? How can Asian financial institutions build new skills to compete? Can foreign players really build local leadership positions on the back of recent liberalizations? And finally, how should mergers, acquisitions, and alliances be executed to advance successful strategies?

These questions, asked often by our clients and colleagues, are the inspiration for this book. Asia provides growth opportunities that are unlikely to be matched by maturing banking markets around the world. Yet, successfully capturing profits from Asia will only be possible for domestic and global banks that adopt a new mindset: A mindset that goes beyond just identifying new market strategies and embodies a willingness to change the daily behaviors of bank tellers and board members alike. The title to this second edition *Banking in Asia: Acquiring a Profit Mindset* highlights the core challenge for banks operating in Asia – most must start from a clean sheet in how they perceive themselves and the evolution of the markets around them.

This second edition is far from a mere update of the first. The pace of change, alterations in line up of competitors, and shifts in regulation have compelled us to write from a clean sheet and fully update our estimates of market sizes and growth potential. Our objective has been to look beyond day-to-day headlines, drawing lessons from our client work and research, to paint a picture of how Asian banking is likely to evolve in the coming decade, and what it will take for local and global banks to capture the most attractive opportunities.

Our focus is on the most significant geographic markets in Asia, namely Japan, Korea, India, China, Taiwan, Hong Kong, Singapore, Malaysia, Thailand, Indonesia, and the Philippines. To aid regional comparisons, we have crafted chapters that provide a regional perspective of Asia's core banking business lines, specifically, personal financial services, retail and institutional asset management, and corporate banking. And in recognition of the growing importance that mergers, acquisitions, and alliances play in realizing strategic ambitions across an increasingly liberalized Asia, we have added chapters to this edition that focus on the success factors in executing domestic merger and acquisition (M&A), cross-border M&A, and international alliances.

Although much of the content of this book is drawn from our experience as McKinsey consultants to financial services clients around the world, the views expressed in this book are ours and do not necessarily reflect those of McKinsey & Company. We hope that you will enjoy reading this edition.

Tab Bowers
Greg Gibb
Jeffrey Wong
and members of McKinsey & Company's Asia Financial Institutions
and Corporate Finance & Strategy practices

About the Contributors

The authors and core research team are members of McKinsey & Company, based in offices all over Asia.

TAB BOWERS is a Director based in Tokyo. He joined the New York Office in 1987 and serves leading Western and Asian financial institutions on their most pressing strategy, alliance, and marketing issues. He leads the Financial Institutions Practice in Asia and has worked with financial services clients in New York, California, and across Asia. He is fluent in Japanese and has lived in Japan for a total of 10 years. Tab led the development of *Banking in Asia: Acquiring a Profit Mindset* and wrote the chapter on Japan. Tab writes frequently and was a co-author of *Collaborating to Compete*, 1993, and *Banking in Asia: The End of Entitlement*, 1999.

GREG GIBB, a Principal based in Taiwan, is a core member of the Corporate Finance and Financial Institutions practices in Asia. During his 12 years with the firm, of which 10 years have been in Asia, he has served local and international financial institutions primarily across Greater China. He is fluent in Mandarin. Greg co-led the development of *Banking in Asia: Acquiring a Profit Mindset* and wrote the chapter on Taiwan. Greg was also the co-author of *Banking in Asia: The End of Entitlement*, 1999.

JEFFREY WONG is a Consultant with the Asia Corporate Finance & Strategy Practice, based in Shanghai. Since 1999, he has served several leading Asian and global financial institutions on strategic and policy issues. Jeffrey was the project manager for *Banking in Asia: Acquiring a Profit Mindset*, overseeing all research and analyses, as well as the lead author for the chapters on Personal Financial Services, China, and Hong Kong.

FABRICE DESMARESCAUX is a Principal based in Singapore and leads the Southeast Asian team of the Financial Institutions Practice. During his five years with the firm, he has served financial institutions in every major Southeast Asian market. Fabrice is the lead author for the chapters on Southeast Asia and Singapore.

CHRIS BESHOURI is an Associate Principal of the Asia Financial Institutions Practice, based in Manila. During his six years with the firm, he has served financial institutions and central banks, as well as multilateral institutions such as the IFC and ADB in Southeast Asia and Korea. Chris is the lead author for the chapter on Corporate Banking.

OLIVIER DE DEMANDOLX is a Consultant with the Asia Corporate Finance & Strategy Practice, based in Hong Kong. During his seven years with the firm, of which four years have been in Asia, he has served domestic and global financial institutions across Asia on MA&A and strategic partnership transactions. Olivier is the lead author for the chapter on International Alliances.

NICOLAS LEUNG, a Principal based in Hong Kong, is the Head of Asia Corporate Finance & Strategy Practice, based in Hong Kong. During his 10 years with the firm, he has served many financial institutions in Europe and Asia on strategy and MA&A. Nicolas is the lead author for the chapter on Domestic Consolidation.

MAYANK PAREKH is a Principal based in Singapore. He leads the Southeast Asian team of the Corporate Finance & Strategy Practice. During his seven years with the firm, he has advised local banks on MA&A strategies, global banks on M&A entry into Asia, and government agencies on bank asset restructuring. Mayank is the lead author for the chapter on Cross-Border M&A.

JAEHONG PARK is a Principal of the Asia Financial Institutions Practice, based in Seoul. During his eight years with the firm, he has served retail banks, life & non-life insurance carriers, and credit card issuers on various strategic and operational issues. Jaehong is the lead author for the chapter on Korea.

EMMANUEL PITSILIS is a Principal of the Asia Financial Institutions Practice, based in Hong Kong. During his nine years with the firm, he has served financial institutions in Asia, Europe, and the United States. Emmanuel is the lead author for the chapter on Asset Management.

CHRISTIAN RAUBACH is a Principal of the Asia Financial Institutions Practice, based in Seoul. During his six years with the firm, he has served retail and private banks, as well as private equity firms in Europe, Greater China, Southeast Asia, and Korea on credit risk management and wealth management issues. Christian is the co-author for the chapter on Personal Financial Services.

JOYDEEP SENGUPTA, a Principal based in Delhi, leads the Financial Institutions Practice in India. During his eight years with the firm, he has served financial institutions in Asia and Europe on retail and wholesale banking issues. He has also served central banks in Asia on banking sector reforms. Joydeep is the lead author for the chapter on India.

The Research and Analytics Team comprises three core members (from left to right): **ANGELI CHANSRICHAWLA**, a Senior Research Analyst from the Asia Corporate Finance and Strategy Practice, based in Hong Kong; **ROHIT KAPOOR**, a Research Analyst from McKinsey Knowledge Center, specializing in financial institutions, based in India; and **PATRICIA WHONG**, a Senior Information Analyst in Greater China's Financial Institutions Practice, based in Hong Kong. This team worked tirelessly to develop the comprehensive fact base that appears throughout this book.

ALEJANDRO REYES, the sole member of the group of contributors who is not from McKinsey, edited this book. He drew on his extensive experience as a reporter, writer and editor in Asia for more than 15 years (most of them with *Asiaweek* magazine in Hong Kong) to help crystalize our perspectives.

Acknowledgements

Besides the contributions of the core group of authors and research team, we received additional support and research from our colleagues in McKinsey, in particular, Jinwook Joung and Joshua Crossman from the Seoul office on the Korea chapter; Sandeep Sabharwal from the Delhi office on the India chapter; Arnab Datta from the Mumbai office on the Corporate Banking chapter; and Diaan-Yi Lin from the Singapore office on the Cross-Border M&A chapter. Special thanks go to Emi Kuroda and Ayami Hamakawa from the Tokyo office and John Shao from the Taipei office, for their contributions to the core research team during the course of this effort.

The authors and research team depended further upon the research and information services provided by Romy Buchari, Chester Chen, Haoshan Chen, Suchart Chiracharasporn, Jiyoung Chung, Antonette Consuelo, Shalini Goenka, Cecilia Ho, Asako Iijima, Hyunjoo Lee, Zhenyu Li, Sawitree Limvongsakul, Fritzie Medina, Ajay Nahar, Haruko Nishida, Michelle Perez, Bismo Prakoso, Amit Sachdeva, Supriya Sahai, Serene Tan, Suvidha Vasudeva, Bhaskar Verma, Celena Yew and Suejin Youn. Compilation of the charts called upon the talents of many visual aids professionals in McKinsey offices, in particular, Priscilla Pun from the Hong Kong office.

We received helpful comments, input and feedback from our colleagues in the firm: David Von Emloh and George Nast from the Shanghai office on the China chapter and Dr. Klass Reineke and Henri Guedeney from the Singapore office and Nicholas Kukrika from the Bangkok office on the Singapore and Southeast Asia chapters.

Michiyo Kawabata, Kmay Lin, and Pansy Kwok must not be forgotten for their untiring administrative support needed to coordinate all the working sessions conducted across Asia over the course of the project.

Last but not least, Dominic Casserley must be acknowledged for pioneering the original idea of writing a book to address the pressing issues that define banking across Asia.

1

Acquiring a Profit Mindset: Nurturing the Seeds, Managing the Weeds

The smoke from erupting fireworks obscured the talking head on the three floating cinema-sized screens. The beaming face belonged to the CEO of one of Taiwan's leading banks. After warmly welcoming his employees to the exhibition center in the outskirts of Taipei for their annual Chinese New Year party, he wished them good fortune in the Goat Year. Over the next four hours, the crowd would cheer on as colleagues performed electrifying musical numbers replete with exuberant dance routines, blinding strobes, and a dry-ice mist billowing across the stage. A trio of local celebrities turned up. And, of course, there was the popular lucky draw. Among the prizes: more than $30,000 in cash and a new car.

Few banks in Asia could stir such excitement and camaraderie among their staff. The purpose of the elaborate celebration was to send a rousing message: We thank you for your hard work and the past year's strong financial performance and hope you will do even better in 2003.

The optimism on show at the gala stood in marked contrast to the doom and gloom in 1998 when McKinsey & Company's financial institutions team in Asia wrote *Banking in Asia: The End of Entitlement,* the first edition of this book. Is there reason to be upbeat? While much of the crisis-hit region and many of its banks have continued to languish, a handful of

---

Note: All prices are in US dollars unless otherwise stated.

aggressive local and international banks has taken advantage of falling market barriers to move resolutely forward. This select group of leaders has employed best practices to attack non-performing loans (NPLs), instituted strong sales cultures, launched innovative products, upgraded its credit capabilities, and boldly embraced mergers and acquisitions (M&A). In short, they have begun to specialize more and no longer indiscriminately grow assets.

Yet six years since the crisis, doubts about Asia and its banks still linger. Have financial institutions and regulators made enough progress to prevent another meltdown? Do the underlying fundamentals of customer demand point to a bright future? Is it possible to make significant profits?

In 1996, Asian banks outside Japan accounted for 11 percent of the profits of the world's top 1,000 banks. By 2001, this figure had fallen to 8 percent, with the global economy much weakened. While the profits of the world's top 1,000 banks outside Asia grew an average of 18 percent a year between 1996 and 2001, the Asian banks in the top 1,000, excluding Japan's, eked out only 6 percent annual growth in profits. In the same period, Japanese banks in the top 1,000 went from generating $7 billion in profits in 1996 to bleeding $50 billion in losses by 2001.

The stock prices of Asian banks in contrast to those of their global counterparts reflect this relative stagnation (see Exhibit 1.1). By all measures of financial health, virtually all of Asia's banks have failed to rebound to pre-crisis levels. The overhang of NPLs and their drag on earnings are a persistent problem for most. Because of this and the region's protracted recovery, many multinational institutions have substantially lowered Asia's importance in their global strategies. Are they right to do so?

We believe that financial institutions that write off Asia risk foregoing one of the largest growth markets of the coming decade. Retail banking alone is expected to add approximately $180 billion in new revenues over the rest of this decade, as much new growth as occurred in the United States in the boom period between 1994 and 2001 (see Exhibit 1.2). As a result, revenues from personal financial services will reach $390 billion by 2010, nearly the size of the US personal financial services market in the late 1990s. China, of course, is set to be a major banking market. By 2010, close to 100 million Chinese are expected to sign up for their first credit card, creating the third-biggest market in the world (in terms of card holders) after the United States and Japan. While many big international investors may dismiss Asia as a small pond, our forecasts suggest that there are enormous opportunities to catch.

What is particularly exciting is that both local and global players will be able to tap into this surge in Asian growth. All banking markets in Asia – with the exception of China and Malaysia – are now open to majority foreign

Exhibit 1.1 Banking sector share prices

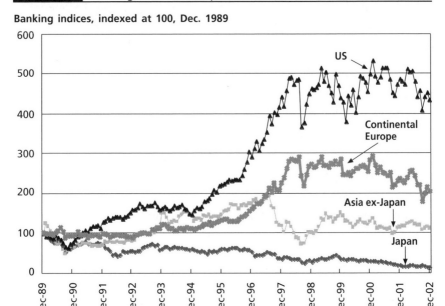

Banking indices, indexed at 100, Dec. 1989

Source: Datastream; McKinsey analysis

Exhibit 1.2 Asian banking long-term growth potential

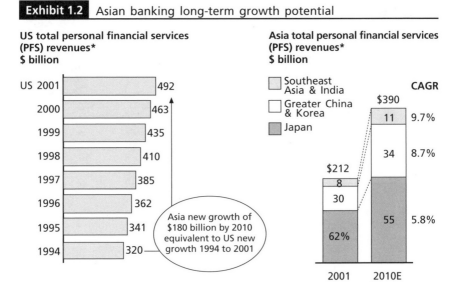

US total personal financial services (PFS) revenues*
$ billion

US 2001	492
2000	463
1999	435
1998	410
1997	385
1996	362
1995	341
1994	320

Asia new growth of $180 billion by 2010 equivalent to US new growth 1994 to 2001

Asia total personal financial services (PFS) revenues*
$ billion

☐ Southeast Asia & India
☐ Greater China & Korea
▨ Japan

CAGR

* Includes all retail deposit, credit, and investment product revenues sold through banks

Source: McKinsey analysis

ownership. This is a significant change from before the crisis when foreign majority control was only possible in Japan, Hong Kong, and Indonesia.

The underlying structure of Asian banking markets today is indeed more dynamic than it has ever been. Only 246 of the top 500 banks in 2000 were on that list in 1997 (see Exhibit 1.3). More open competition, fewer business boundaries, the rise of domestic M&A, and increased access to foreign capital are planting the seeds for stronger players to grow and rise to the top. They are forming the foundation for more resilient and rational banking markets across Asia.

To spot these seeds of new growth that need to be nurtured, bankers must look beneath what seems on the surface to be a messy or even forbidding landscape. The budding opportunities lie in six "mega-trends" that will drive much of the growth in Asia's banking markets: the rise of the modern consumer; the aging population; a growing concentration of wealth; a likely doubling of the "bankable" population; the emergence of powerful small and medium-sized enterprises; and Asia's fascination with new technologies that could lead to major competitive disruptions. Be it in India or Japan, banks that are able to position themselves well in anticipation of these trends stand to benefit from growth rates that the saturated banking markets in developed economies are unlikely to match.

While the seeds of opportunity are there, no player can afford to ignore the pernicious "weeds" that can stymie growth. There are five such weeds:

Exhibit 1.3   Top 500 Asian financial institutions: 2000 versus 1997

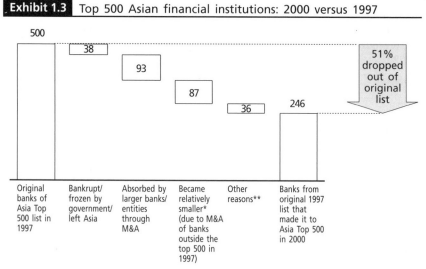

* Minimum asset value of $2,235 million in 2000 compared to $402 million in 1997
** Reclassification of entity by Bankscope to non-bank, etc.
Source: Bankscope

- The growing stock of NPLs that continue to weaken financial systems and impose a tax on economic growth;
- Inefficient, underdeveloped domestic capital markets that do not yet provide a meaningful alternative to intermediate capital flows;
- The lack of true markets for corporate control that would allow the full pursuit of strategic M&A;
- Powerful domestic political interests that are unwilling to take the pain of transforming the financial sector, thus keeping weak banks alive and, as a result, spoiling overall market margins; and
- Slow progress in instituting the changes to corporate governance required to promote greater transparency and real accountability to shareholders.

The growth opportunities in Asia are among the biggest and potentially most lucrative anywhere. But the interplay between the seeds of gain and the weeds of pain means that while possible profits may be huge, uncertainty is high. Because there are so many drivers of change in motion at the same time, Asia remains a "high-beta" environment. Financial institutions that wish to make money in this volatile region need to take a very different approach from how they compete in more mature, stable markets such as the United States or Europe. Deep insight into the true, underlying drivers of market growth is essential. Once players identify where the attractive opportunities are, they must place sufficiently large "bets," with downside risks properly managed. They should avoid linear plans with inflexible targets and proactively expect volatility.

But above all, banks will need a new mindset to win. This entails accepting that the traditional corporate businesses that make up 70 percent of bank balance sheets have to shrink and that retail banking will drive profits for the next decade. It requires the foresight to build new standardized, low-cost processes that can serve millions of customers through revamped distribution networks. And it means plucking up the courage to abandon legacy personnel policies that protect poor performers and prevent banks from building highly effective sales-oriented cultures.

To acquire a profit mindset, local and international banks alike have to take advantage of Asia's inherent market volatility and deepen market presence through mergers, acquisitions, and alliances. Banks that create country strategies that take into account intra-regional influences and opportunities will succeed. The leading players will adopt more collaborative approaches, both to resolving market challenges such as NPLs and to building new, shared utilities such as credit bureaus that will help expand financial services within each market.

In addition, local banks in particular will have to drop their fixation with universal banking. Instead of creating "one-stop shops" designed to meet all the needs of all their customers, they must focus more on building specialized market positions and business models. They have to adopt customer-centric structures, reconstituting and centralizing the management of their largely independent branches.

For foreign players to adopt the profit mindset, they must give up the old strategy of "flag-planting." Instead of collecting a string of outposts, they should make heavier, well-considered bets in selected Asian markets to generate material profits on their global balance sheets. They will have to overcome their longstanding organizational inability to develop and execute a coherent, long-term vision. Asia, after all, cannot be won in three years.

Still, the opportunities in Asian banking and the freedom to pursue them are greater than ever before. In the coming decade, the winners will be those banks that plant firmly in their organizations the mindset that allows them to manage the dangerous weeds and grow new, lucrative businesses from the seeds of profit that have already been sown across the region.

SEEDS OF OPPORTUNITY

Look beyond the market volatility and the NPLs and the enormous growth opportunities of Asia's banking markets come into sharper focus. This is a highly diverse region, with some of the poorest and richest people in the world. All the economies are in the throes of major transition, each at a different stage of development. A common mistake investors make is to take a simple snapshot view of Asia. But such an approach presents a static picture that belies the deep forces of change reshaping the requirements for success and profitability in banking.

Consider Starbucks, the icon of the global coffee culture, and its expansion in Asia. At the end of March 2003, the Seattle-based company had nearly 6,500 stores around the world, with just over 20 percent outside North America, including about 900 in Asia, the Middle East, Australia, and New Zealand. It aims eventually to have 25,000 locations altogether, of which 6,000 are expected to be in the Asia-Pacific region.

Asia is obviously a critical market for Starbucks. Its aggressive plans are based on the belief that tastes in this tea-drinking region are shifting rapidly and even converging. The popularity of Starbucks from Seoul to Singapore indicates too that the spending power of consumers is increasing substantially and the demand for global brands among the residents of Asia's top 50 cities is rising fast.

The Starbucks phenomenon is part of a much bigger story. Fundamental shifts in demographics, income distribution, family structures, values, and attitudes are working out across Asia. Much of this is taking place quietly – either under the surface or out in the open, but just not easily discerned. That young Asians are embracing the coffee culture may not mean anything of itself, but it is evidence of major socioeconomic changes afoot. We have pinpointed six mega-trends that are reshaping the underlying economies in Asia. Their cumulative force will drive future growth and profits in banking in the region.

The rise of the modern consumer: Many banks have yet to wake up to the fact that the needs of Asia's consumers are changing. Bankers in most markets cling to the traditional profile of a good customer – the hard-working saver who puts money away for a rainy day. In contrast, those who borrow to enhance their lifestyles are considered irresponsible individuals, credit risks who are best avoided.

While Asian consumers themselves generally share this view, perceptions are quickly changing. McKinsey's annual personal financial services survey has shown that Asians have become more open to credit in recent years. In 2001, 52 percent of the 4,000 respondents said it is reasonable to borrow money for purposes other than a mortgage. Among consumers under 40 years of age, 58 percent were amenable to personal borrowing.

This new attitude is reflected in the tremendous growth of unsecured personal finance. From 1995 to 2001, credit card receivables roughly tripled in Asia excluding Japan, which registered a 50 percent increase. By 2010, McKinsey estimates that unsecured consumer credit balances in the whole region will grow to about $5 trillion, more than double 2001 levels.

That a third of Citibank's global profits and two-thirds of its profits from operations in Asia are drawn from consumer finance underscores the emergence of the modern Asian consumer. The same young people that Starbucks is betting on are seeking out financial institutions that can cater to their lifestyles and spending patterns. Those players that hope to ride the rise of the consumer culture in Asia will need to change their perception of what constitutes a good customer, and foster emotional connections between customer and brand. In short, they must replicate the appeal of Starbucks.

The aging population: Except for Japan, Asia's populations are considerably younger than in most of the developed world. But this is set to change dramatically over the next two decades. By 2020, 12 percent of Asians will be 65 years old or over, compared to 7 percent in 2001. In Japan, where the population has begun shrinking, the number of retirees is expected to equal the number of working adults by the middle of this century – an unprecedented occurrence (see Exhibit 1.4).

The impact of the aging of Asia is already being felt. In a 2001 McKinsey survey,[1] two-thirds of respondents were concerned that they would not have

---

1   McKinsey Asia Personal Financial Services Survey (PFS) 2001.

Exhibit 1.4 Asia's aging will be most dramatic in Japan

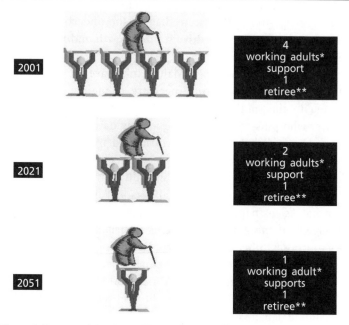

<table>
<tr><td>2001</td><td>4 working adults* support 1 retiree**</td></tr>
<tr><td>2021</td><td>2 working adults* support 1 retiree**</td></tr>
<tr><td>2051</td><td>1 working adult* supports 1 retiree**</td></tr>
</table>

* Working adults are adults from 15 to 64 years of age
** Retirees are adults 65 years old and above

Source: Data up to 2021 from Asian Demographics; data in 2051 from McKinsey estimates

enough savings to fund their retirement. Behind their worries is the growing recognition that they cannot rely on their children – today's modern consumers – to provide for them. This is particularly the case in China where years of the one-child policy have rendered it virtually impossible for families to support themselves, their new lifestyles, and their parents too. Across Asia, filial piety is eroding with urbanization, shrinking families, consumerism, and greater economic pressures.

But concerns extend beyond the breakdown of traditional family structures. In the decade leading up to 2001, Asia's highly volatile stock markets have performed poorly, while equity mutual funds in the United States and Europe have generated double-digit returns and outpaced real estate and interest rate investments (see Exhibit 1.5).

Governments in both developing and developed economies in Asia are recognizing the threat posed by an emerging pension crisis and pushing through legislation to launch mandatory defined-contribution savings plans. But such schemes may not meet the immediate needs of the half billion Asians now between the ages of 45 and 65.

Exhibit 1.5 Financial returns across asset classes in Asian markets and the US: 1991–2001

	Annualized returns %			Asset class performance	
	Equities	Residential real estate	Time deposits	Best performing	Worst performing
Japan	−7.5	−2.7	1.6	Time deposits	Equities
Singapore	3.0	5.8	3.4	Real estate	Equities
Hong Kong	10.3	1.5	5.7	Equities	Real estate
Taiwan	1.6	−1.8	6.7	Time deposits	Real estate
Korea**	1.3	−1.7	9.6	Time deposits	Equities
Indonesia***	4.1	4.5	17.5	Time deposits	Equities
Thailand***	−11.3	2.9	7.8	Time deposits	Equities
Malaysia	2.2	4.8	6.6	Time deposits	Equities
India	5.3	n/a	10.4	Time deposits	Equities
Philippines****	−12.0	n/a	10.3	Time deposits	Equities
United States	12.2	10.6	5.1	Equities	Time deposits

* Returns represent price returns of major indices not including dividends
** Real estate is represented by general property prices and not only residential real estate values
*** 1992–2001
**** 1993–2001

Source: Datastream, Bank of Japan, Japan Real Estate Institute, Monetary Authority of Singapore, Urban Redevelopment Authority, Info Winner Database, Sinyi Realty, Bank of Korea, Korea Land Corporation, Bank Indonesia, Bank of Thailand, Bank Negara Malaysia, Valuation Department (Malaysia), National Council of Real Estate Investment Fiduciaries (US)

An enormous opportunity exists for banks to build on their trusted images to distribute a far greater range of investment and protection products than they do today. With more than half of the net savings of Asian households held in low-yielding bank deposits, banks are uniquely positioned to advise customers on preparing for the future. They will have to provide a range of domestic and international investment and protection products that will help customers weather the volatility of the markets. They will also need to work through new channels such as financial consultants that are able to offer more sophisticated approaches to investment planning.

A growing concentration of wealth: Aside from Singapore, Korea, and Japan, which have managed to build relatively egalitarian societies founded on large middle classes, most Asian economies are marked by a wide disparity of income. And in many of them, the gap is growing, resulting in the formation of a narrow segment of affluent consumers that are the main drivers of new banking opportunities.

China offers the most striking example of this polarization in income. Less than 1 percent of urban households accounts for half of total deposits. *Datamonitor* estimated that China had up to two million households with over $100,000 in liquid assets in 2001 – more than anywhere else in Asia except Japan. According to *Asian Demographics,* the top 10 percent of income earners in China's cities accounted for at least 20 percent of total income in 2001. By 2010, this segment is expected to generate more than 30 percent of total income. In McKinsey's experience, it is not uncommon for the top 100 clients of a Chinese securities firm to have an average of $10 million in liquid investments.

This pattern of growing wealth concentration is evident across much of Asia. The explosive growth of UBS' private banking operations in the region is a testament to this burgeoning opportunity. In 2002, UBS was believed to be managing for its high-net-worth Asian clients approximately $50 billion in assets, estimated to be more than double what the bank was handling in 1997. While local banks are unlikely to capture much of the private banking money that flows offshore, the growing affluent class that has more than $100,000 to invest is very important to them. In our experience, the top 5–10 percent of individual customers often account for more than 50 percent of profits generated by local branch networks in Asia. Banks that can build a dominant position in the top cities and differentiate their services to attract affluent customers will be rewarded with significant growth.

The doubling of the bankable market: While much of Asia's new wealth will be in the hands of a few, overall income levels will continue to rise, with hundreds of millions of people beginning to earn more than they need to subsist. When an individual's income approaches $1,000 a year, this person usually needs a basic bank account in which to deposit savings and for receiving and making payments. We estimated that for 2001 there would have been about 300 million bank account holders in Asia. By 2010, an additional 300 million individuals are expected to pass the $1,000 income mark, effectively doubling the "bankable" population in the region.

The Asian countries with the biggest populations – China and India – will together account for more than 70 percent of all new accounts, with about 20 percent in Southeast Asia, excluding Singapore. Roughly a third of the new accounts will be opened in Asia's 50 biggest cities, where about 300 million people live. By 2020, these urban areas will be home to more than 500 million people.

The implications of this growth have not been lost on Citibank. Take India, where at the start of 2003 the bank had 20 branches in 15 cities, up from seven branches in five cities in 1996. Citibank is expanding to parts of Asia where even well-traveled businessmen have never been. But to capture the lion's share of new customers will also require reaching into rural areas. And because these accounts will have relatively low balances, to generate profits, banks must adopt a low-cost business model that relies more on remote services than branches.

Is it possible to make money on the mass banking market? The experience of Standard Bank in South Africa suggests that it is. In the 1990s, Standard Bank developed a simple set of banking services, delivered mostly through ATMs and the phone, which could be profitable with relatively low balances. Banks in Asia that can redesign their processes to be as efficient should be able to find profitable growth in this large, untapped market segment. Indeed, while the majority of players fight it out for the favor of Asia's affluent, some banks would do very well to pursue the less well-to-do.

The emergence of small and medium-sized enterprises (SMEs): The Asian economic growth model of the 1980s and 1990s favored the formation of large corporations. Government-directed lending to Korea's *chaebol*, Japan's *keiretsu*, China's state-owned enterprises, and the politically well-connected business groups of Southeast Asia created unwieldy empires that simply piled up debt faster than profits. Banks were coaxed into accepting that these behemoths were too big to fail. But the financial crisis of 1997 showed otherwise.

The SMEs have been generally ignored. While they are often unable to secure adequate credit and services from banks, SMEs play a significant role in many economies and are growing in importance. In China, private and foreign SMEs generate a large share of new jobs, while the state-owned enterprises are laying off workers. In Taiwan and Hong Kong, SMEs have been among the first to relocate operations to the mainland to take advantage of lower labor costs and the rapidly growing domestic market. And in debt-ridden Indonesia, while many large corporations are still saddled with foreign debt payments, many SMEs have found new sources of profits.

In the United States, where SMEs have reasonable access to credit, they account for 50 percent of GDP. Asia's SMEs generated half that level of output in 2001 (see Exhibit 1.6). One Asian banker joked that the reason there are so many Starbucks outlets in Asia is because SMEs are so cost efficient that they do not have suitable offices for customer meetings and hence arrange conferences over coffee. Nimbleness comes at a price.

In the coming decade, SMEs will be better positioned to respond to new challenges and opportunities as Asia is more closely integrated with the global economy. This is not to say that these businesses are without credit risk. But properly managed banks in the United States and Europe have demonstrated that SMEs can be a very profitable segment of the economy to serve, often offering superior returns to the large corporations that command razor-thin margins. Banks that recast their value propositions, service models, and credit risk processes to tap the SME market will be able to take advantage of the fundamental shift in the underlying corporate economics of the region.

Asia's fascination with technology: Asia's love for gadgets could spawn breakthrough distribution and service strategies. Imagine if a bank could allow customers to make payments to each other directly over their mobile phones. Imagine if a customer could get approval for a personal loan remotely without ever meeting a bank officer or filling out a paper application. Any bank that conducts most of its business using new

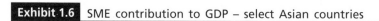

Exhibit 1.6 SME contribution to GDP – select Asian countries

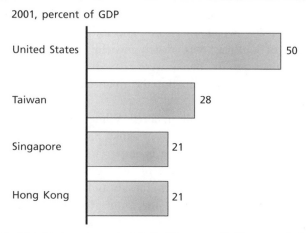

2001, percent of GDP

United States	50
Taiwan	28
Singapore	21
Hong Kong	21

Source: Central banks; government statistical bureaus; McKinsey analysis

technologies could offer unparalleled customer convenience and save millions of dollars in branch network expenses.

In fact, some financial service providers in Asia are already doing the once unimaginable. Chinatrust Commercial Bank in Taiwan allows customers to transfer funds to each other over their i-mode phones. Japan's leading consumer finance companies handle a majority of their loan applications through automated kiosks. These machines scan in documents and deliver a video image of the prospective borrower back to a loan approval center where a customer service representative makes an assessment.

Of course, such examples are not representative of how banking is conducted in Asia. Most transactions are carried out in oversized branches in expensive locations, with little or no centralized processing. Yet many of Asia's urban centers have some of the highest rates of mobile phone ownership anywhere. Internet service is widely available. Notably, Korea boasts the highest home broadband penetration in the world. In the coming decade, the infrastructure will be in place for innovative Asian banks to leapfrog to new business models that may redefine the economics of many traditional banking services.

The six mega-trends outlined above underscore that for banks to pursue the significant growth opportunities in Asia, they must focus on the consumer and the lower end of the corporate market. This demands a much higher degree of service differentiation than banks practice today. The complex business models necessary to penetrate the urban affluent segment profitably are entirely different from the low-cost platforms banks must have to reach out to rural customers earning disposable income for the first time. The product design, credit skills, and brand-building needed to attract the modern consumer are distinct from the capabilities and market positioning required to earn the confidence of aging savers.

As the sources of profits in Asian banking are shifting, banks too must reinvent themselves. For most, embracing such wholesale change – nurturing the seeds of opportunity while managing around the troublesome weeds – will be as big a challenge as surviving the 1997 financial crisis.

WEEDS OF MARKET VOLATILITY

In 2000, New York-based private equity fund Ripplewood Holdings led a consortium that invested $1.2 billion to buy Long-Term Credit Bank of Japan, a once-formidable institution that had been driven to bankruptcy. The new owners hired the former head of Citibank Japan and a fresh management team to launch a turnaround. Over the next two years, the revamped bank – now called Shinsei Bank – moved aggressively to instill best practices in credit pricing and recall loans to higher credit risks in a bid to clean up its portfolio. Large Japanese banks, fearing that Shinsei's actions would trigger a series of corporate defaults, lobbied the government to bring the maverick to heel, working behind closed doors to ostracize Shinsei from the tightly knit banking community. In 2002, Shinsei was one of the few Japanese banks to make a profit, but it faces major obstacles as it attempts to break away from the pack of poor performers.

Undeniably, for Asian banks to realize their full potential they have to take significant risks. The fundamentals behind growth in the region are real. But still present are the same structural deficiencies that created the conditions that led to the 1997 financial crisis and have kept Japan's economy moribund for over a decade. These factors are deeply rooted in how capital is intermediated within Asian economies, the low level of transparency that is available to investors, and the limited independence of central banks, bank boards, and regulators. The problems are complex and interconnected. Addressing one without simultaneously fixing the others could lead Asia to relapse into crisis.

While laissez faire purists would argue that stable, efficient markets are created by removing or limiting the influence of the State, Asia's structural problems are so deep that governments must play a role in setting the new foundations for success. But this will take time. Meanwhile, many of the poor lending practices typical of capital intermediation in the region will continue, leading to boom–bust credit cycles in banking markets.

To succeed in such an environment, banks must plan for market uncertainty and volatility. At a minimum, they must redirect portfolios away from higher risk large corporations and focus on earning fee income from businesses that enhance returns without further taxing balance sheets.

Strong players also need to develop strategies to capitalize on the downturns that will plague Asia's banking markets over the coming years. To be prepared for unexpected market shifts, banks must build up their reserves and sketch out in advance the M&A moves they will make in troubled times. By doing so, strong players can leverage volatility to consolidate their leadership, pouncing ahead while rivals scramble to survive. Devising strategies that anticipate the recurrence of cycles marks a clear departure from the past, when plans assumed fast, linear growth. As the Shinsei case highlights, however, even the best laid plans require boldness and patience to succeed. Determining the right timing to act requires a careful reading of the market landscape, particularly the intertwined weeds that threaten opportunity growth.

For banks to cope with market volatility and build leading positions, they must work around five such weeds:

A growing stock of NPLs: While the bad loans have been a major scourge of banks across Asia, the larger problem rests in the new flow of NPLs that continue to emerge even in reformed markets such as Korea and laggards such as Japan and much of Southeast Asia. From our experience even in booming economies such as China, as much as 5–8 percent of loans go sour within the first year of issuance.

The failure to stem new losses by improving credit processes and addressing the backlog of NPLs is taxing balance sheets, shutting off the flow of new capital, and restraining underlying economic growth. Consequently, the potential for social unrest is rising in the most populated economies where about 7 percent nominal annual growth is required to keep employment levels steady. Given that Asia will remain in a boom–bust cycle over the coming decade, banks playing to win have little choice but to build up reserves to ride out gathering storms.

Underdeveloped capital markets: NPLs continue to pile up in part because most of Asia's capital markets lack the depth to offer an alternative means to channel funds to the real economy. The resulting high market volatility deters the formation of deep pockets of institutional capital through domestic pension funds and the investments of wealthy individuals. This in turn hinders the creation of efficient markets to price and allocate risk. The lack of domestic institutional pools of capital also prevents the formation of bond markets that could offer an alternative for the medium- and long-term financing of corporations and large, public-sector infrastructure projects.

All this means that the demand for bank-intermediated capital will persist and the related structural risks will remain. Asia's capital markets will deepen as governments gradually put in place mandatory pension schemes that pool capital. In the interim, the volatility of bank-led capital deployment will continue to be a problem.

The lack of a true market for corporate control: Leading banks will be able to consolidate their positions during downturns only if the market for corporate control is freed up further. On the surface, Asia's banking markets appear to be going through dramatic restructuring, often driven by mergers and acquisitions. In many markets, the number of banks has dropped dramatically and asset concentration in the largest institutions has risen significantly since the crisis of 1997 (see Exhibit 1.7). But there has been little real improvement in the efficiency and effectiveness of the banking system.

Despite laws that allow and even encourage consolidation, M&A activity in most markets is orchestrated by the government. Banks that should naturally be acquisition targets in a downturn often use political connections to fend off possible attacks or slow the speed of consolidation. This results in "zombie" financial institutions operating in the market, sometimes with little change beyond a new name slapped onto several old entities that have been stapled together. These banks have few incentives to address their problems and are a tax on industry-wide profits, as they do not properly

Exhibit 1.7	Change in Asian banking market structures*

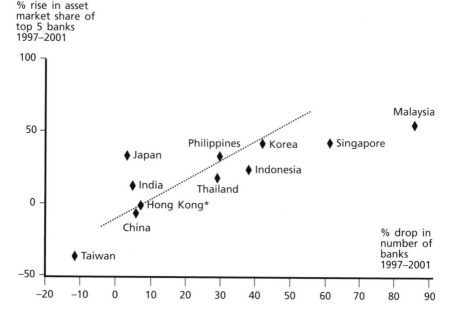

% rise in asset
market share of
top 5 banks
1997–2001

* Commercial banks only. The locally incorporated sister banks of the Bank of China
  (BOC) Group are considered one entity

Source: Central banks; Bankscope; McKinsey analysis

price risks. They also block stronger players from gaining superior scale through M&A. Banks looking to capitalize on market volatility must convince regulators that the creation of stronger banks at the expense of weaker ones is in the interest of the underlying economy.

The lack of political will to restructure: The reluctance on the part of some governments to let certain M&A transactions occur reveals the weak political will to pursue broad financial-sector restructuring. When a private-sector player is to take over a government-controlled bank, the chief obstacle is usually concern over the large number of civil servants who could lose their jobs. Any comprehensive restructuring would include efforts to prevent new bad loans by turning off the liquidity tap to technically bankrupt financial institutions, and, in turn, to debt-ridden corporations. This could be a politically painful measure, resulting in substantially higher unemployment. Because political will is stronger in some markets than in others, regulatory policy in Asia is inconsistent.

Complicating matters is the limited scope that bank regulators have in pursuing necessary restructuring. In 2002, Taiwan's finance minister tried to close down rural credit cooperatives whose NPLs surpassed 40 percent of total loans. When farmers called a protest march through the streets of Taipei, President Chen Shui-bian abandoned the plan, traveled south to apologize to farmers, and accepted his minister's resignation. Without adequate independence on the part of the government to see through policy, the speed of change, consolidation, and recapitalization will be haphazard.

Slow progress in improving transparency and corporate governance: To be sure, there are no easy ways for governments to reform the banking sector and yet maintain economic stability. Even if all poorly performing banks and corporations were shut down immediately, the underlying corporate economy in Asia's markets lacks sufficient transparency to redirect capital with confidence. Less than 15 percent of top companies in Asia carry any credit rating. Corporate disclosure remains more of a carefully manipulated art than a rigorous science.

In addition, corporate governance typically lacks the checks and balances to ensure rational economic choices and protect the interests of minority shareholders. If there is one thread that runs through the many challenges facing Asia's banks, it is that transparency and best practices in corporate governance are essential for capital to be properly channeled and for market economies to expand. Banks must strengthen the independence of their boards and set up mechanisms to share information on creditors.

Banks too must take into consideration other powerful forces shaping Asia's economies. Possibly the most important is the rise of China. Over the next decade, as Hong Kong and Taiwan integrate more deeply with the mainland, the Chinese economy could drive much of the growth in Asia (see Exhibit 1.8). It could rob neighbors of opportunities by sucking in investment and commerce that might otherwise go to them. China's growing share of foreign direct investments (FDI) and trade suggests that other emerging economies, particularly the highly indebted Southeast Asian countries, are losing capital that they need to sustain recovery. The rush by manufacturers in Hong Kong, Taiwan, Japan, and, to a lesser extent, Korea to relocate factories to China to remain competitive in export markets is putting further pressure on the domestic banks in these economies, which must deal with a shrinking customer base.

While a surging China presents a formidable challenge for other Asian economies, a weak China could be even more of a headache, depriving the region of its strongest source of economic growth. As the mainland integrates more closely with the rest of the world, new risks could emerge. One stark example: the spread of the severe acute respiratory syndrome (SARS) virus from southern China in early 2003. A sharp downturn in the Chinese economy or social unrest could also spill over. If its neighbors become too dependent on China, risk and volatility in the region could increase. China is like a turbocharger that works in both forward and reverse. While it can

Exhibit 1.8 China: A primary driver of economic growth in Asia

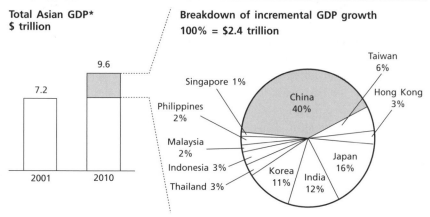

Total Asian GDP*
$ trillion

Breakdown of incremental GDP growth
100% = $2.4 trillion

* At 2001 prices
Source: Global Insight; McKinsey analysis

power much of the banking growth in Asia, it can also make a downturn more severe. The key is to keep this powerful engine engaged in forward, running as smoothly as possible at a manageable speed.

Because Asia is largely a collection of emerging markets, it is not surprising that the region is likely to experience both rapid growth and high volatility. And while the more mature markets – Japan, Hong Kong, Korea, Singapore, and Taiwan – are as rich as, or even wealthier than, many of the developed countries in North America and Europe, their underlying economies are strongly affected by how their neighbors are doing.

Many of the banking structures and practices in Asia's developed markets are still woefully inadequate, typical of what we might expect in emerging economies. While this may be a controversial point to make, it should not come as a surprise. Even in the region's richest economies, bank markets have until very recently been an important tool of state-managed development efforts. Banks operated in protected environments where money could be made without having to adopt global best practices to compete. The financial crisis changed this.

Looking ahead, Asia's banks must fundamentally reshape their operations and ways of doing business to capture the opportunities open to them. The way to succeed is to acquire the mindset necessary to meet the challenge.

ACQUIRING A PROFIT MINDSET

To say that Asia's banks have not been pursuing profits may be a little unfair. However, it is true that they have generally competed on volume, often to the detriment of accuracy in asset pricing and credit risk assessment.

International banks, for their part, typically believed that they had to take whatever path they could into the region's growing markets even if the paybacks were minimal. Given the enormous opportunities post-crisis Asia offers, as well as its many pitfalls, it is time for bankers to put profit-focused strategies at the top of their agendas.

While local and international players start from different positions owing to regulations that protected domestic banks, the playing field is gradually leveling. Given this context, both types of institution would do well to adopt a profit mindset, which would entail pursuing certain strategies.

Capitalize on market downturns through a "plant-and-pounce" strategy: Asia's growth will be anything but linear. While there is significant pent-up demand for financial products and services, anomalies in the market will result in boom–bust cycles. To capitalize on this market volatility, a local or international bank should adopt a "plant-and-pounce" strategy, planting itself in high-potential areas either on its own or through alliances. When a downturn weakens the competition and lowers valuations, or when rapid product and pricing deregulation takes place in a particular market, the player would be ready to pounce aggressively through mergers and acquisitions. Rather than fear market discontinuities or distress, the winners in the coming decade will be those that are prepared to face adversity and sudden change with confidence and quick action.

The leading banks of the future will plan rigorously and meticulously for market troughs. Most players did not bother with "trough planning" in the past. The mindset shift from seeking stability to welcoming discontinuity requires that competitors develop multiple scenarios for their target markets and invest in maintaining a full-time M&A team that is constantly scanning the landscape for natural partners and takeover opportunities to pursue when a market disruption occurs.

Target retail and SME profits: To act decisively requires a razor-sharp focus on where profit opportunities lie. This is the second element of the new mindset that both local and foreign players should adopt. For most banks in Asia, the strongest growth and most attractive profits over the long term will lie in retail banking, and serving small and medium-sized enterprises. To focus on these businesses would require a major shift in direction for the many banks that derive a majority of their revenue – albeit with poor returns – from mid- to large-sized corporations.

International banks need to be willing to make large, long-term investments in select markets to gain access to front-line retail distribution. Many local players, meanwhile, have to pursue a "shrink-to-grow" strategy, shifting management resources and capital away from established corporate clients to customers previously given low priority: consumers and small businesses. Because it will take time to ramp up retail banking operations, many banks would have to forego top-line growth in the short run in exchange for higher, long-term profits. To make this leap of faith, management must be convinced that catering to retail customers and SMEs is where the hefty returns are.

Focus on key cities and regions: A fresh, objective look at the facts can lead to real insight. Sometimes this requires a Copernican shift in mindset. For local or foreign bankers navigating Asia's volatile markets, this means developing a broader geographic view built on two assumptions: first, that regional economic integration will continue, and second, that the most robust growth will be in the top 50 cities.

National borders no longer define banking markets. In North Asia, in particular, corporate interests are quickly flowing across borders as businesses in Hong Kong, Taiwan, Japan, and Korea move to China in search of lower manufacturing costs and a large domestic market. Local and international banks that fail to cater to these flows will lose the ability to serve their customers' most pressing financial needs. Equally, banks that operate in several Asian markets, but do not reckon on converging consumer tastes, risk missing opportunities to leverage product knowledge and operating scale from one market to the next. A nation-based focus could also dilute growth. Many retail opportunities, for example, will be concentrated in only a handful of fast-emerging mega-cities within any given country.

Banks aiming to grow rapidly must redraw their maps to highlight cross-border customer flows, the most attractive cities, and low-cost locations where back-office operations from one or more markets may be centralized to amplify scale synergies. For a majority of local banks, becoming a full-scale regional player in the coming decade is not a realistic option. Still, as economies are more integrated, regional trends will have a direct impact on domestic markets and clients. Hence, they cannot be ignored in setting even domestic strategies.

Cooperate to compete: This particular mantra is counterintuitive. Yet for banks to succeed, they must find more ways to cooperate with each other. To pursue many of the challenges and opportunities in Asia's markets requires the cohesive efforts of leading market players. NPLs, for example, can only be properly addressed if leading banks pool their efforts to restructure loans. One bank acting alone usually does not have sufficient share of one customer's debt to make a difference. Similarly, if banks are to realize the full potential of the consumer credit business, they must share data through credit bureaus so that lending to individuals is prudently distributed.

With competition intensifying in fragmented markets, the natural inclination of most banks would be to avoid cooperation. Traditionally, local and international banks have tended to view all competitors alike since there was little difference among what they offered customers. But as aggressive banks develop specialties, it will be in their medium-term interest to find ways to increase cooperation with each other and with regulators.

Beyond the four common strategies that would propel the mindset shift among local and international players, there are additional changes in approach, organization, and operations that each group of banks must take. Local players must switch from focusing on building asset volume and playing "across the board" to extracting sustainable profits by developing deep insight into select customer segments and product categories. International players, meanwhile, should move from being superficial niche players, or "flag-planters," across the region to becoming embedded local competitors in specific markets where they can extract material profits that make a meaningful contribution to their global returns.

LOCAL BANKS: MANAGING FOR PERFORMANCE

Most of Asia's domestic banks were set up either by governments to foster economic development or by leading conglomerates or family groups as a source of capital for related corporate interests. As such, the core goal of these financial institutions was not to generate strong shareholder returns. This changed after the 1997 financial crisis as banks have had to look to new investors to recapitalize balance sheets.

But the legacy mindset is not easily shaken off. Perhaps most difficult to abandon is the fixation with growing asset volume, customer numbers, and branch networks. Compounding this challenge is the fact that few banks have a real understanding of the underlying economics of products and customers.

In the last 20 years, most banks have focused on "land-grabbing" for business. More branches meant more customers, while more deposits and expanding liquidity pools meant a greater scope to lend. As regulatory boundaries melt away, allowing banks to move into the insurance and securities businesses, most players are inclined to move rapidly into these new areas. Ask top bankers to explain their vision and most will say that they aspire to turn their institution into a universal bank that provides a broad repertoire of services to a wide range of customers. The quest for business volume is still very much alive.

Most banks will fail to realize those ambitions. Banking markets are too fragmented and skill gaps too large for a universal banking strategy to succeed. Instead, all but the largest local banks will have to become more specialized to survive and prosper. Over the rest of this decade, the successful local players will be those that invest in deepening their skills in two or three retail and wholesale segments. Only by limiting their scope can they develop a distinctive understanding of evolving customer needs, risks, and economics to exploit those deep insights to extract superior profits over the competition. With many product categories expected to grow rapidly, the traditional do-everything approach makes no sense.

Banks seeking to be more focused will need to adapt their organizations for greater specialization. Most institutions in Asia are organized along functional lines: credit, operations (including branches), information technology, human resources, and auditing. Each division often supports a broad range of customers and, as a result, lacks the specialization needed to meet the demands of distinct customer segments. In the future, banks will become more customer-centric. For example, a bank may set up three business units: wealth management for the affluent, mass-market retail banking, and services for large corporations and SMEs. Supporting functions such as marketing and credit would then be shaped around these distinct customer groups, allowing the bank to build superior market insight to design tailored products and better control segment-specific risk.

A major barrier to specialization is the branch network. Often branches operate as relatively independent entities with little or no ability to provide specific solutions to meet the needs of particular customers. Most branch managers prefer the easy life, simply processing customer transactions through expensive mini-operation centers contained within each branch. Instead, branches must become primarily sales platforms housing specialized sales forces aimed at the priority customer segments, with a basic capability to serve the broad customer base. These sales forces must be managed centrally or regionally to build the requisite expertise to cater to specific customer groups. A more centralized approach allows banks to better leverage data-mining skills to spot customer trends that can then be acted upon across the entire portfolio.

Increased customer specialization should result in much higher revenue per customer. In Asia, the average bank product holding per customer is between 1 and 1.5. In the United States and Europe, the more customer-centric banks achieve average product holdings of between 2 and 3 for retail and wholesale customers. Best practice players such as Wells Fargo boast an average product cross-sell rate in excess of 4 for their select retail customers.

Simply specializing their strategic focus and structure will not be enough to put local banks on a winning track. The deeper challenge lies in changing mindsets and behaviors to reflect external market realities. Getting somebody to change what they have done daily for two decades requires both incentives and consequences. This is where most banks in Asia that are seeking to change fail.

First, many do not adequately define the drivers of customer profitability that can guide employee behavior. Second, even when the appropriate measures of desired performance have been specified and applied, banks resist asking poor performers to depart. The tacit understanding has long been that if you are a loyal and hardworking employee, you will have a job. Removing staff that cannot survive in a more specialized, profit-oriented environment breaks this unspoken covenant. But if those not up to standard are not dealt with, the strong performers soon figure out that there is no need to work so hard. Once this happens, a bank's profit hopes soon unravel.

Managing for performance starts at the top. The chief executive must shift from the traditional obsession with volume to targeting specific customer segments and products that earn higher returns. A command-and-control organization must give way to an entrepreneurial customer-focused structure. Independent branch networks must be reconstituted into centralized sales groups. And a culture that rewards people for pursuing profitable growth must become the norm. Local banks that acquire the profit mindset will be in a better position to ride out market volatility. They will extract more synergy from acquisitions and become leaders at home, with the potential to have the scale and skills to be a regional player.

INTERNATIONAL BANKS: AIMING FOR MATERIAL IMPACT

In the past, because of regulatory restrictions, international banks could do relatively little to build material banking businesses. Among the handful of foreign financial institutions that generate at least $100 million in annual profits from Asia – HSBC, Citibank, and Standard Chartered, for example – most have been deeply embedded in the region for a hundred years or more. They entered before barriers went up. The vast majority of the several hundred foreign players that have entered Asia in the last two or three decades have had to play a limited "outsider" game in certain retail, wholesale, and private banking products. Most have little to show for it. In fact, we believe that the vast majority fail to make money, particularly on a risk-adjusted basis.

This has naturally soured many international financial institutions on the region's banking markets. Many question if Asia should be a priority. Much of course has changed since the financial crisis in 1997. With the exception of Malaysia and China, all of the region's banking markets are now technically open to foreign majority ownership. And both cross-border M&A and product alliances have become common. International M&A activities, including Asian banks crossing into new markets, have increased eightfold from $1.6 billion in 1997 to $12.5 billion in 2001. But the experiences have been mixed. For example, due to a severe downturn in the Japanese equity market, Merrill Lynch lost several hundred million dollars following its 1998 acquisition of Yamaichi Securities' retail brokerage network. This led some to question whether it is possible to build a profitable business in markets where the structural weeds have overgrown.

We believe that over the long term, the benefits of the seeds of opportunity will outweigh the risks posed by the weeds. In fact, foreign financial institutions have the benefit of choice over many local banks. An Indonesian bank, for example, has little choice but to ride out the highs and lows of its home market. A foreign player can pick its target markets, the timing of entry, and how it moves in.

Banks seeking growth opportunities outside the increasingly saturated developed markets could be well served by actively exploiting Asia's volatility. But to succeed, instead of flag-planting across the region, banks will have to place heavier bets in selected markets. The new profit mindset among foreign players, particularly those wishing to build retail businesses, will require setting out a range of options that would enable them eventually to gain direct access to selected markets.

In China, one of the fastest growing economies in the region, market access is restricted. A minority stake in a local bank or joint venture can lead to deeper market understanding. In this emerging giant, foreign players would do well to pursue several options as the long-term outcome of minority ownership is unclear. Foreign banks may need to forge several partnerships to gain access to the most attractive cities or product categories. The risk of relying on gradual organic growth is that other foreign competitors willing to make bolder moves could jump ahead.

In more developed markets such as Korea and Taiwan, it is possible to buy a local bank outright, but such an investment would be substantial and the risks associated with NPLs high. Beyond specific product plays, these markets are generally too competitive for foreign banks to grow a meaningful business organically. For those seeking to deepen their understanding of these markets and build their presence, a compromise would be to secure a series of product-focused joint ventures with leading players. The banking markets of North Asia are the biggest in the region and offer the most medium-term potential to foreign specialists such as consumer finance mono-lines.

To put the relative importance of North Asia's banking markets into perspective, consider that bank assets in Taiwan in 2001 stood at $682 billion, more than double India's and 50 percent bigger than all of Southeast Asia's combined, excluding Singapore's. For this reason, the small Southeast Asian markets are a low priority for foreign players. But because of the low level of competition and high margins, foreign banks often extract more profits from Southeast Asia than they do from North Asia. In some product segments such as credit cards, international players have been able to capture over half of the market through a combination of organic and inorganic growth (see

Exhibit 1.9). Acquisitions or alliances, at least in focused businesses, will remain an attractive medium-term option for some. Southeast Asia will never produce enormous profits in the long run, but its markets could be a good source of returns while banks wait for bigger opportunities, say in China, to materialize.

Exhibit 1.9 International players' credit card market share

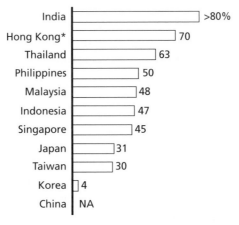

International players' share of credit card receivables – 2001

India	>80%
Hong Kong*	70
Thailand	63
Philippines	50
Malaysia	48
Indonesia	47
Singapore	45
Japan	31
Taiwan	30
Korea	4
China	NA

* Global banks such as HSBC and Standard Chartered Bank are not considered local banks in this analysis for consistency

Source: Annual reports; Lafferty; McKinsey analysis

Any acquisition or alliance concluded by a foreign bank entails a significant migration of resources to transfer skills. Most international players can only afford to select certain markets on which to concentrate. Many lack a long-term perspective and are unable to place bold bets. Senior management stationed back at headquarters in Europe or the United States blow hot and cold on Asia, depending on the latest headlines – hot when China announces astounding growth, cold when North Korea tests a missile. Managers posted in the region usually lack the clout at home to make the case for a major acquisition or alliance. The revolving door at the regional HQ means that institutional knowledge so painstakingly built up is quickly lost.

Simply put, for foreign financial institutions to make a viable play for selected Asian markets, the region must become a central topic on their boards' agenda over the long term. This may be done by basing senior management in Asia or cultivating senior Asian managers to play a role on the global board. Building a solid perspective on Asia into the bank's leadership is integral to the new profit mindset a foreign player must adopt.

Even with the strategies we have outlined, only a handful of new global players will extract material profits from Asia. That is good news for local banks, but a disappointment for the many international banks searching for new avenues of growth. Still, we believe that the presence of just a few global players in each market would be sufficient to boost local competition. The products, business models, and marketing approaches that they bring raise the bar for everyone.

❊ ❊ ❊

Few markets in the world offer growth prospects equal to Asia's. But this region is not for the faint of heart. Setbacks are inevitable as banks try to leapfrog into the twenty-first century. The winners of this decade will be those that find ways to exploit the seeds of change while actively – sometimes opportunistically – taking advantage of the weeds that interfere with the smooth growth paths that all players naturally wish for.

For most banks, this means recasting their strategies around a new profit mindset. These fresh approaches require greater anticipation of the future, broader geographic thinking, increased willingness to cooperate, bigger bets to exploit market discontinuities and freedom, and more often than not, the construction of more specialized business models. The heart of this challenge is to change the mindset of thousands of bankers. Successes should be celebrated – possibly with an extravagant New Year's party – but it is more important for bank managers to show leadership and to pluck up the courage to reshape the core of their organizations to match the realities of Asia's dynamic banking markets.

PART 1

GEOGRAPHIC MARKETS:

WHICH BETS AND WHERE

2

Japan: To Win, Dare to be Different

Macroeconomics

- GDP ($bn)[1]   4,155
- GDP per capital ($)   32,687
- PPP GDP per capita ($)   25,766
- Exports ($bn/% of GDP)   384/9
- Imports ($bn/% of GDP)   313/8
- FDI inflow ($bn/% of GDP)   6.2/0.1
- FDI outflow ($bn/% of GDP)   38.5/0.9
- Foreign currency reserves ($bn/% of GDP)   347/8
- External debt ($bn/% of GDP)   766/18
- NPL of banks ($bn/% of total net loans)   346/9
- National government borrowing
  ($bn/% of GDP/% external)   5,099/123/0
- Top 3 trading partners   US, China, Taiwan
- Number of corporates in Global Top 500[2]   88

Socioeconomics

- Population (mn)   127
- Number of households (mn)   47
- Average household income ($)   60,135
- Number of households earning >US$100K p.a. (mn)   4
- Mobile phones/100 population   57
- Internet subscribers/100 population   40
- Urbanization (% of population)   79
- % of population with university degrees   14.9
- % of population above 65 years old in 2001
  and 2021   18/29

Capital Markets

- Number of listed corporations   3,476
- Equity market capitalization ($bn/% of GDP)   2,265/55
- Trading volume ($bn/% of market cap)   1,835/81
- Debt market capitalization ($bn/% of GDP)   1,623/39
- Equity underwriting[3] ($bn/% of GDP)   18/0.4
- Debt underwriting[3] ($bn/% of GDP)   61/1.5
- M&A ($bn/% of GDP)   53/1.3
- Retail assets under management ($bn)   265
- Institutional assets under management ($bn)   1,786

Banking Markets

- Total loans of all financial institutions, including
  non-banks ($bn/% of GDP)   12,545/302
- Total deposits of all financial institutions, including
  non-banks ($bn/% of GDP)   9,627/232
- Mortgages ($bn/% of GDP)   1,500/36
- Personal loans ($bn/% of GDP)   477/11
- Credit card receivables ($bn/% of GDP)   45/1
- Credit cards per person above 15   1.10
- Credit card spend as % of household total spend   9
- Foreign ownership limit in 1997 and 2002[4] (%)   100/100
- Number of banks in Global Top 1,000 in 1997 and 2001   53/87
- Number of ATMs/1,000 population   0.60
- Number of branches/1,000 population   0.12
- Number of banking employees/1,000 population   2.63

---

[1] At 2001 prices
[2] *The Fortune Global 500*: July 22, 2002
[3] Average from 1995–2001
[4] For investments >10%, approval from Financial Services Agency is required

Note: All figures as of December 2001 unless otherwise indicated

Japan's Financial Landscape

Types	Number of institutions, 1997	Number of institutions, 2002	Percent of total assets 2001	Top 3 players
Local ordinary bank	154	153	36	• Mizuho • Sumitomo Mitsui Banking Corp. • UFJ Holdings
Foreign ordinary bank	102	82	2	• BNP Paribas • Citibank • Deutsche Bank
Long-term financial institution	3	0	0	• n/a
Financial institution for small business	823	618	7	• Shinkin Central • Shoko Chukin Bank • Federation of Labor Banks
Financial institution for agriculture and fishery	3,317	1,899	3	• Norinchukin Bank • JA Aichi • JA Hyogo
Public financial institution	11	9	35	• Postal Savings Department • Housing Loan Corporation • Finance Corporation for Municipal Enterprises
Money lender and others*	31,760**	29,041**	17	• Takefuji • Acom • Promise
Total	**36,170**	**31,802**	**$12,363bn**	

*   Others include dealer broker, investment trust, etc.
** Only refers to money lenders.

With over $5.2 billion in net worth, Yasuo Takei is the second-highest ranking Japanese on *Forbes* magazine's list of the wealthiest people in 2002 – behind Nobutada Saji, whose family controls beverage-maker Suntory. Of the dozen billionaires from Japan in the ranking, Takei is one of four who made their fortunes by creating financial empires. Surprisingly, these tycoons did not accumulate wealth by shrewdly investing in start-up companies or buying out struggling corporate giants. Takei and the three others in this elite club made their money in one narrow slice of Japan's huge financial market: consumer finance.

Ironically, this segment of the market had been completely ignored by Japanese banks until recently. They dismissed it as too risky and undignified a business, more appropriate for a loan shark. But as the market boomed in the late 1980s and into the 1990s, consumer finance became a mass-market product. Total customers surpassed 10 million, while firms like Takei's Takefuji reaped enormous profits. That Japan's big banks missed what turned out to be a highly profitable opportunity underscores their strategic paralysis. Over the last several years, more nimble, innovative, and daring players including foreign firms have swooped in to capture the major growth opportunities in the financial sector and almost all of the profits. Japan's banking giants have begun to stir – a little. Realignments have created some of the largest financial groups in the world under newly permitted holding companies. The grim realities of the market have also forced specialty institutions, such as trust and long-term credit banks, into restructuring – mainly through their acquisition by larger groups. The jury is still out, however, as to whether these moves will help the leading banks overcome organizational and cultural challenges and begin to grow again.

All signs point to continuing stagnation and value destruction in the old retail and commercial banking businesses of the major banks. But these problems, combined with the pressures exerted by macroeconomic and demographic forces, will lead to the emergence of a new set of attractive opportunities, mostly outside traditional banking product markets. These will include off-balance sheet asset management products, bancassurance (insurance products provided through banks), and asset finance products for corporations.

While a few of the old guard might struggle out of the mud and rise up to the challenges, the majority will falter badly in the face of new competition. Specialized players, such as retail credit providers, financial advisors, and middle market-focused investment and wholesale banks, will be tough opponents. Also in the game will be foreign groups that have already created or bought significant businesses, as well as aggressive domestic non-bank companies that see banking profit streams as a way to enhance their core business. The battle for the spoils in Asia's wealthiest market will certainly be intense.

RICHES LOCKED IN A STAGNANT MARKET

A dozen years after the bubble economy began to collapse, Japan is still in a confused state. One of the biggest and most important financial markets in the world, it is one of the most difficult to tap profitably. With a few interesting exceptions, the underlying banking markets have been stagnant and devoid of growth opportunities since the beginning of the 1990s. Yet wherever one looks, Japan remains a market of staggering wealth and potential. Whatever the merits of Asia's other economies, Japan consistently demands attention if only for its scale and breadth.

Japan generates the second-largest GDP in the world with over $4 trillion in annual output. Despite more than a decade of stagnation, this economic powerhouse still possesses the biggest pool of personal wealth in Asia. Average levels of affluence rival those of the US and Western Europe. Total personal financial assets, excluding real estate, amount to over $11 trillion and continue to grow at over $300 billion a year as the rapidly aging population saves over 15 percent of its income. Average household income at $60,000 is roughly 30 percent higher than in Hong Kong, the next wealthiest market in Asia.

By a wide margin, Japan has the largest financial product markets in Asia. Even after almost five years of asset contraction, banks in Japan hold more debt on their balance sheets – close to $4 trillion – than banks anywhere else in the world. The life insurance market is also the largest on the planet with total premium income of $400 billion, equivalent to $3,200 annually for every man, woman and child in the country. The pension market accounts for 90 percent of all retirement assets in Asia. Forty-five percent of Japan's $2.4 trillion in pension assets are managed by life insurers, trust banks, and other private asset managers. Even if other countries achieve growth rates that average two or three times that of Japan, it will be many decades before their financial product markets rival the scale of this giant.

The basis for all of this wealth was created in the incredible 40 years between 1945 and the economic bubble of the late 1980s. Since then, Japan has been in decline, struggling to find ways to address its non-performing loan (NPL) problems, restructure its institutions, and put itself back on a growth path. In 2002, real estate prices were 75 percent off their peaks and still declining at 5–6 percent a year. Major banking product markets, such as corporate lending, were contracting 5 percent or more annually. Financial institutions were earning low returns and destroying huge amounts of shareholder value. Total bad debts written off by the 20 largest banks in the

10 years from 1992 to 2002 amounted to $600 billion, which was equivalent to 130 percent of pre-provision operating profits during the same period.

Although Japanese banks still occupy three of the top 10 positions among all banks globally in terms of total assets, a comparison by market capitalization paints a more accurate picture (see Exhibit 2.1). The most valuable Japanese bank – Bank of Tokyo-Mitsubishi – had only $36 billion in total market capitalization at the end of fiscal year 2001, ranking it just 19 in the world. By the end of 2002, the total shareholder value of the top four Japanese bank groups, with a 70 percent share of the Japanese market, was less than half the market capitalization of Citigroup.

This value crisis is even more dramatic when comparing the premiums to book value commanded by Japanese banks with those of their foreign counterparts. Since 1990, leading global banks such as Citigroup, HSBC, and Deutsche Bank have increased their book values impressively, while major Japanese banks have languished. Japanese institutions have done little beyond combining their businesses. Most trade at share prices barely above book

Exhibit 2.1	Strategic control map of top 5 Japanese banks relative to global banks

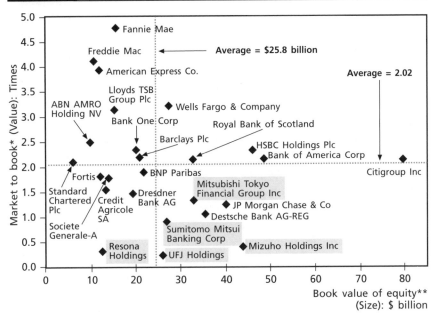

* Market capitalization as of Sept. 15, 2002 (30 days average); book value of common equity as of end FY 2001
** Book value of common equity is equal to shareholders' equity less minority interest, and preferred equity

Source: Bloomberg; Datastream; McKinsey analysis

value. Several have seen their total market values drop significantly. This decline has forced these much weakened banks to close down overseas operations and restrict themselves almost entirely to domestic competition.

Despite the persistent problems plaguing the banking system, several types of players have succeeded in building robust, profitable financial businesses in the post-bubble period. At the top of this list are the consumer finance players. These entrepreneurial firms such as Takefuji and Acom aim to meet a very specific need: short-term, unsecured credit for below-average income consumers, usually young adult males. Armed with an aggressive, focused mindset, these companies consistently generated handsome cash flow and profits through the post-bubble decline of the 1990s.

The power of customer service

In 2001, Japan's most profitable retail financial services businesses were not banks but consumer finance companies. The top four – Takefuji, Acom, Promise, and Aiful – generated pre-tax profits of $3.6 billion and an after-tax ROE of 11 percent. According to *The Consumer Credit Monthly,* the quartet commanded 60 percent of the $80 billion market. By providing credit to those who could not get it from banks or others, these new kids on the block fundamentally transformed consumer lending in Japan.

At the end of the 1990s, unsecured consumer finance was perhaps the only retail financial business in Japan that could be considered world-class. Appreciating that Japanese consumers are embarrassed to apply for credit, these companies locate shops on upper floors. Unmanned kiosks accept credit applications, while video cameras collect the face-to-face 'information' – the type of clothing and accessories worn by the applicant, for example – needed for a credit risk assessment. Customers can perform all their transactions through the ATM. They can also conveniently repay loans by electronic transfer from regular bank accounts.

By 2001, despite interest rates averaging 26 percent, 10 million Japanese consumers, including a quarter of all 20–45-year-olds, had taken out a consumer finance loan at least once. These are clearly attractive mass-market products, not sub-standard offerings from shady operators. Taking out a loan is convenient, easy, and private. When dealing with banks, customers had gotten used to suffering in silence. The consumer finance companies have shown that poor service does not have to be the norm.

There are similar innovators in other sectors, even in the depressed corporate banking market. Invariably, these are players who have minimized reliance on on-balance sheet corporate lending. Basic corporate loans have very low profit margins because the market is saturated. Domestic securities and leasing firms, such as Orix, have become increasingly skilled at asset-specific financing products that can be funded through the capital markets, rather than relying entirely on their own balance sheets.

Global investment banks have also prospered in Japan by exploiting their superior skills and networks to capture the most lucrative segments of the advisory and capital markets businesses. They also have natural advantages in cross-border equity and debt issuance deals. Although foreign investors only hold about 14 percent of all Tokyo-listed equity, they often account for a third or more of daily stock exchange trading. This transaction flow gives the foreign investment banks disproportionate power in the trading business and helps them to attract business from domestic institutional investors. As a result, there have been periods when global banks were the top traders in Japan, such as in the Fall of 1998 when Morgan Stanley accounted for the largest volume share for a few months.

ADRIFT IN A SEA OF DEBT

In spite of its problems, Japan's banking system is still one of the most expansive. The combination of an economy with a GDP of $4 trillion and a bank-dominated financial system has created some of the largest banks in the world as measured by assets. The scale of these institutions is staggering, given that almost 90 percent of their assets and operations are in their home country. To be sure, they have contributed to Japan's lingering economic malaise. Japan has been drifting in and out of recession for more than a decade. Repeated attempts to stimulate the economy through fiscal spending have had little impact. In the Fall of 2002, the Nikkei stock market index touched a 19-year low.

At the center of these troubles is a sea of bad debt. The bubble economy of the 1980s that peaked in 1991 had created a one-time $1.5 trillion surge in bank debt, linked mainly to the overheated real estate market. The stagnant economy and lack of bold measures to write off inappropriate loans meant that a decade later the excess debt persisted on the banks' books. According to official estimates in the Fall of 2002, bad debts amounted to approximately $360 billion (some analysts say the real figure is $1 trillion or even higher) or about 9 percent of GDP. Compare this to about 1 percent of GDP in the case of the United States at the time of its savings and loan crisis in the 1980s. The problem in Japan is at least 10 times as big. At the end of 2002, Japanese regulators were admitting that bank estimates of the size of the bad debts were not accurate.

Concerns about the consequences of Japan's enormous debt have been heightened by corporate failures such as the sudden collapse of Mycal, the fourth-largest supermarket chain. Banks had consistently given Mycal a good credit rating. But in the summer of 2001, Mycal was unable to meet bond obligations. It filed for bankruptcy, leaving banks with over $3 billion in non-performing loans.

Despite the worries, few consider it likely that Japan could suffer a serious financial meltdown, as many other East Asian nations did in 1997–98. Unlike most of its neighbors, Japan has a vast reserve of wealth locked up in low-productivity deposits and postal savings accounts – wealth that could be leveraged to work off bad debt. But will Japan make the tough decisions necessary to mobilize its immense wealth, clean up the bad debt, and get its economy back on track? Whatever happens, in the end Japan's taxpayers are going to have to foot a large portion of the bill for cleaning up the mess. How this will be done is unclear, but there are a few alternatives.

IS CRISIS INEVITABLE?

After six years of painful stagnation, the government in 1996 realized it had little choice but to deregulate the financial industry. In December that year, it launched the "Big Bang" in the hope that unleashing competitive forces would reinvigorate the financial industry and, in turn, spur the economy to grow again. The reforms were designed to overhaul the financial markets in just five years – much more quickly than reform efforts in other countries. The goal was to change the financial system from one focused on banks, bank debt, and corporate customers, to one that would disintermediate banks and unlock retail investors' wealth. To that end, the government relaxed the rules on product and price competition, market entry, and distribution channels.

Although the reforms were broad and expectations high, their real impact has been only modest. Their implementation was hampered by weakness in Japan's economy and the inability of the banks to make true progress in resolving their bad debt problems. The banking system has remained gridlocked by a vicious circle of interlinked problems. Writing off and resolving bad debts depend on the ability of the economy to absorb the impact of restructuring in the corporate sector. No one is willing to accept the near-term pain – higher unemployment and the collapse of wages – required to put the economic and financial systems back on solid footing.

So how will Japan get out of its hole? There are two possible paths: either the economy regains enough growth to allow the banks to work out their problems on their own, or there is a significant economic and financial disruption – a crisis – that upsets the status quo and leads to sizable losses in value for many players. While both scenarios are possible, the passage of time is increasing the odds of a painful adjustment.

The Japanese government desperately wants to achieve the first outcome. For policymakers, the moves other countries have employed to induce rapid restructuring of their financial systems – forced asset sales, tightening of capital requirements to reduce lending capacity, and setting up national scale "bad banks" that can buy and hold NPLs, among other measures – are too disruptive. Instead, politicians and bureaucrats are convinced that the country has the wealth and "social patience" to grow the economy slowly and allow banks to earn their way back to health gradually.

But if a catastrophe is to occur, it would likely involve several elements such as bankruptcies, the nationalization of major banks, and a severe loss of confidence in the currency. Although counter intuitive in the deflationary environment of the early years of the twenty-first century, there is also a growing chance that a meltdown would be accompanied, or quickly followed, by a period of high inflation.

Japan has a self-contained financial system with enough wealth to resolve its own problems if it slips into crisis. The quandary stumping its leaders is how to find a politically palatable way to mobilize Japan's wealth to bail out the banking system. Although the government could reallocate assets through massive tax increases, it would be extremely hard to create the necessary consensus to do so. Inflation, on the other hand, could be launched through excess fiscal spending and supportive action by the central bank, such as by increasing the direct purchase of government bonds and private-sector securities.

A period of sustained inflation of five years or more would significantly reduce debt. It would be much easier for banks to increase loan spreads, and it would help life insurers suffering under the heavy obligations of guaranteed interest rate products. There is a risk, of course, of rampant price increases. Also, the yen would likely depreciate, potentially leading to friction with trading partners. But as other options fade, this is a risk that Japanese officials and politicians may be increasingly willing to take.

WAVE OF OPPORTUNITIES

Even with all Japan's problems, most Japanese regard the possibility of economic crisis and high inflation as remote. With the economy in deflation for several years, hopes are fading that the government will be able to re-ignite growth soon. The financial system will stay shaky for some time. While many traditional banking product segments will remain unattractive for years to come, new opportunities are emerging. The challenge for players in the market is to know where to look.

Many of the opportunities will be outside the traditional core banking product set. It is essential to focus on the truly lucrative opportunities and avoid everything else. An important first step in devising a strategy is to understand the fundamental drivers of change over the coming decades. Key among these is Japan's shifting demographic and social structure. The average age of the population is increasing faster than in other industrialized nations. Without a dramatic reversal in fertility rates or a surge in immigrants, Japan's population will decline from 125 million in 2000 to less than 115 million by 2020. By then, traditional families with children will drop from 40 percent to less than a third of all households. And the rapid aging of the population will lead to a combined annual deficit in the pension and national health insurance systems of about $300 billion, roughly doubling the total annual government deficit in 2002.

All this compounds the country's debt problem and adds to the already severe stress on the fiscal and financial systems. The pressures and likely disruptions will force the restructuring of key banking and insurance markets, resulting in the elimination of some traditional players. At the same time, demand will grow for new and better financial products and services to meet the changing needs of the population. While it is difficult to predict when opportunities will emerge or how big they will turn out to be, they could prove lucrative for players poised to take advantage.

Consumer credit: The boom in unsecured lending

Traditionally, retail banking was a steady and profitable business line that most Japanese banks took for granted. Even though retail banking businesses earned about $30 billion a year in pre-write-off operating profits through the 1990s, banks viewed individual customers as little more than a low-cost source of funding. In recent years, ultra-low interest rates have driven profits out of traditional deposit and payment products. Banks were forced to turn to credit products, especially home mortgages, to maintain retail profits.

This model, however, is not sustainable. The mortgage market will face growing profit pressures from many sides. The government will gradually reduce its holdings of residential loans through the public housing agency, now standing at 40 percent of total mortgages. Still, competition will be intense among the major city and regional banks that have huge excess liabilities due to swelling deposits and a lack of sound corporate lending opportunities in their markets. Over the medium term, the absolute demand for mortgages will drop as people start families later and the population begins to shrink. Finally, securitization is likely to increase, facilitated by government moves to standardize mortgage products. All of these forces will put downward pressure on mortgage profits for traditional bank players.

Specialized mortgage players may emerge and a few investment banks may make profits by trading mortgage-backed securities, but this market is not likely to be a major contributor of retail bank profits.

Unlike mortgages, spreads of unsecured consumer credit are likely to remain attractive for at least the next decade. We estimate that total unsecured lending balances in Japan will grow by over one-third between 2002 and 2010 as middle-market consumers turn more actively to a range of products to support their daily lifestyles. This trend will be reinforced as Japanese in their twenties and thirties, who are heavy credit users, enter their higher earning and spending years. All told, we expect unsecured consumer credit balances to grow from $420 billion in 2001 to $560 billion by 2010, generating roughly $50 billion in pre-tax profits.

Most of the opportunities will be in consumer finance loans of various types. Running up large revolving balances on credit cards has not been popular. Such spending makes up only about 6 percent of unsecured consumer credit balances in Japan. Although credit card usage is likely to increase for payment purposes, there is little indication that consumers will change their behavior and begin running up sizable interest-bearing balances. The market for other forms of short-term consumer finance loans, however, is changing and will provide many different opportunities in the years ahead.

The core market for traditional consumer finance companies, such as Takefuji and Aiful, is getting saturated and growth is slowing. This market consists mainly of young males who borrow from one or two of these short-term lenders. Banks are allying with leading consumer finance companies to target a new higher income "super-prime" segment by offering unsecured loans carrying 15–17 percent interest rates. Another potential opportunity is to build a nationwide franchise targeting "sub-prime" borrowers with slightly higher interest rates and rigorous credit management. Currently this segment is dominated by a collection of regional players that are beginning to consolidate to build up scale.

Perhaps the most attractive consumer finance opportunity is "cashing." This is typically marketed as a cash advance feature on a regular credit card. Interest rates range from 18–22 percent. Because the card is usually issued under a broader middle-market brand such as a major department store or general merchandise chain, middle-class consumers feel more comfortable taking out these loans than going to a traditional consumer finance company. Successfully driving cashing balances can generate a significant profit stream for a credit card offering. In 2001, troubled department store group Daiei made over 40 percent of its total operating profits from its credit card, practically all of which came from the cashing business.

Retail asset management: Preserving wealth for retirement

Japan remains an extremely affluent country despite the economic problems it has experienced during much of the 1990s. In 2001, about 9 percent of all Japanese households had an annual income of more than $100,000. By far, this is the largest concentration of high-income households in Asia (see Exhibit 2.2). Even assuming aggressive growth rates for other countries across the region, Japan will continue to have the lion's share of wealthy individuals through to the end of the decade.

The scale of the pool of accumulated wealth and its relatively even spread across Japanese society are also impressive. In 2001, over 12 million households, a remarkable 25 percent of the total, had more than $100,000 in savings and investments, while less than 1 percent had more than $1 million (not counting real estate). But for all the accumulated wealth, this remains a market of savers, not investors. The Japanese still keep most of their money in low-risk, low-return investments, though many are beginning to dabble in the new higher return products that have emerged since deregulation. As of 2002, about 63 percent of all personal financial assets (excluding corporate and public pensions) were invested in very safe, low-return retail bank or post office accounts, or similar deposits. A further 22 percent went into

| **Exhibit 2.2** | **Number of households with annual income >$100,000** |

Thousands	**2001**	**% of total households**	**2010**	5,500	**% of total households**
Japan	4,132	8.9			10.8
China (urban)*	710	0.5	1,400		0.7
India (urban)*	489	0.9	870		1.3
South Korea*	244	1.7	440		2.7
Taiwan	224	3.4	400		5.3
Hong Kong	186	9.1	400		16.9
Indonesia*	122	0.2	220		0.4
Singapore	44	4.6	90		7.9
Thailand*	41	0.2	70		0.4
Philippines*	36	0.2	70		0.4
Malaysia*	25	0.5	50		0.7

* Rough estimates

Source: Asian Demographics; National Council of Applied Economic Research (India); McKinsey analysis

savings-type life insurance products, while the remaining 15 percent was in higher risk securities and mutual funds.

Yet moderate-risk investment products, most of them offered by Western asset managers, have started to draw considerable interest. In 1997, for example, Goldman Sachs launched a family of limited-risk, international fixed-income mutual funds (known as investment trusts in Japan) that attracted an amazing $7 billion in assets in less than 18 months – reaching well over $10 billion in total assets under management. Later in 1999 and 2000, Fidelity attracted a similar surge in assets into a collection of Japanese equity funds. These successes, however, are limited and often tainted by the subsequent outflow of funds when market conditions turned sour, suggesting that retail investor and distribution channel attitudes have yet to really change.

In addition to a rich and dynamic set of asset management products to meet retirement needs, a radical reform of distribution channels is required. Until 1998, sales of retail mutual funds were the exclusive preserve of Japanese securities houses and investment trust companies. Consequently, the top four securities houses – Nomura, Nikko, Daiwa, and Yamaichi (before its closure) – alone controlled about 75 percent of the market. Retail investors had no choice but to deal with these providers and have been frustrated at the limited products and channels available to them. Customers of securities brokers have felt especially ill served by managers who turn over their entire accounts year after year.

The entry in 1998 of banks and insurers into the retail mutual fund market provided some relief for frustrated investors by triggering an explosion of new products and outlets. By December of that year, every major domestic bank had lined up an impressive series of offerings to compete with brokers and each other. And leading global asset managers – Fidelity, UBS, Deutsche Bank, and Mellon-Dreyfus, among others – scrambled to enter or expand their positions, mainly by pairing up with leading banks that could provide distribution. As a result, by 2002, banks had succeeded in capturing close to 30 percent of all new retail mutual fund sales in Japan.

Going forward, there is an opportunity to capture significant market share by investing in more effective channels that can deliver trustworthy products and advice. Wealth management advice is also needed in different forms, priced in different ways for the needs of specific segments of retail investors. Players that can provide valuable alternatives to the traditional sales push approach of retail brokers will be able to build new franchises. At the high end, there is a need for full-service advisory services, such as private banking, which is still not well understood by most wealthy individuals. Lower cost product and investment advice delivered through both branches and remote channels such as call centers and the Internet are also missing in the market. Japan has no equivalent to Charles Schwab.

There are also opportunities to develop highly specific product-channel businesses, such as selling variable annuities through banks. Bancassurance was deregulated in 2001 and 2002 for an initial set of products, including annuities. Although this is a new business for banks, they are likely to have significant success selling some forms of insurance in the years ahead. Insurance companies have had a range of fundamental product, channel, and reputation challenges that reduced total premiums in the market by 14 percent between 1995 and 2001. This trend is set to continue for traditional insurance products over the next few decades. Banks stand a very good chance of capitalizing on these difficulties to gain a significant share in insurance, especially in investment- and retirement-related products.

Asset finance and restructuring: Advising corporations

The steadily deteriorating loan spreads and massive write-offs that created net losses in recent years will gradually be brought under control by the major banks in the coming decades. Accomplishing this, however, would only generate ROEs of about 5–7 percent on these corporate portfolios. To achieve acceptable profit levels, banks will have to expand direct capital market and advisory fee services. In particular, asset finance, mergers and acquisitions (M&A), and restructuring businesses will be the most attractive as much of corporate Japan goes through fundamental reorganization.

From 2000 to 2001, total outstanding corporate loans shrunk by 4 percent in US dollar terms. By 2002, average loan spreads finally showed signs of reversing their downward trend with Sumitomo-Mitsui Bank announcing that they had succeeded in increasing prices by an average of 10 basis points. According to the Bank of Japan, about half of the approximately $4 trillion total debt held by Japanese banks was in corporate loans, which generated an estimated $35 billion in pre-write-off operating profits.

To turn these gross cash flows from corporate banking into net profits, however, Japanese banks must overcome significant challenges. First, they will need to bring credit-loss levels and loan pricing in line with those of other developed economies. This will require a complete reworking of bank-loan underwriting processes and risk-management controls. Average spreads need to increase from roughly 125 basis points for large- and medium-sized borrowers to at least 250 basis points. There is also an urgent need to collect more loans from borrowers who are in arrears and write off losses more aggressively. Achieving this has been extremely difficult in Japan's moribund economy, but the lack of quick action by the banks is only compounding the problem. The banks must also increase returns on assets or equity by generating much higher fees and capital market income.

The major domestic banks have shown the ability to make gains with basic capital markets products. By 1997, after only five years in the business, they had captured a 40 percent share of debt underwriting for major corporates. (Until 2000, banks were not allowed to own full-service securities firms that could do equity underwriting. The four major bank groups all now have such securities subsidiaries in their holding companies.) While long-term relationships worked in the banks' favor, their success has largely been thanks to aggressive pricing against incumbent securities firms too wounded to respond. In the second half of the 1990s, the leading domestic securities brokers were plagued by extended market losses and a series of internal scandals. With the exception of proprietary gains, Japanese banks have not, however, generated sustained profits in their capital market businesses.

Over the rest of this decade, the demand for corporate finance is likely to remain muted. Rather, companies will increasingly need to restructure their businesses and find new ways to finance their assets. Approximately 20–30 percent of all corporate assets could be refinanced during this period as companies strive to reduce the debt on their balance sheets and change their relationships with banks. This will lead to growing markets in securitization of a wide range of assets, non-recourse real estate lending, M&A and restructuring advisory services, and financing for acquisitions and leveraged and management buyouts. More specialized derivative products, such as credit derivatives, are likely to see high growth rates in this environment.

Although these markets are inherently volatile, going up and down dramatically from year to year, they are growing. M&A and advisory services are expected to more than double to over $1.5 billion in revenues by 2010. Acquisition and other forms of restructuring finance such as real estate sale-lease backs should grow from roughly $5 billion in 2001 to reach at least $15 billion in assets and $300 million in revenues by 2010. Finally, the already sizable securitization markets are likely to grow dramatically, but will swing largely with the fluctuating demand for real estate-related products. Assuming that both commercial and residential mortgage-backed securities markets open up as expected, total securitized issuance could exceed $200 billion by 2010.

By 2002, the early asset finance and restructuring opportunities were already emerging. Although the overall debt and equity markets were down, restructuring deals were increasing among some of Japan's leading corporate and financial conglomerates. Several began selling or spinning off divisions that were losing money or deemed not to be part of their core strategy. Examples include Hitachi's spin-off of its huge semiconductor business into two joint ventures with Mitsubishi Electric and NEC; retailing giant Seiyu's sale of up to 67 percent of its equity to Wal-Mart; and Nissan Motor's takeover by, and integration into, Renault's global business.

Major changes in Japan usually take a very long time to initiate – much longer than in most other societies. But once accepted, transformations can proceed with surprising speed. When industry leaders begin to manage their total business portfolios based on profitability and unload businesses that do not fit with overall corporate objectives, restructuring can proceed more quickly. The expected unbundling of major conglomerates such as Hitachi, Toshiba, Mitsubishi Electric, and Nissan Motors is already leading to a marked increase in banking opportunities.

Lessons for the rest of Asia

In the early 1990s Japan was still widely regarded as an example of how a dynamic economy and banking system could create incredible wealth and power in relatively few years. It was a model for the rest of Asia to emulate. A decade later, its neighbors are trying to figure out how to avoid the traps into which their idol had fallen. So what lessons should bankers draw from Japan's journey? Here are three:

First, even in systems burdened with overriding problems such as crippling bad debts, pockets of wealth creation still exist. In Japan, the most stunning example is consumer finance. Through the best years and the worst, the major shift in public attitudes toward credit continued to drive profitable growth in the consumer credit markets. Bankers should note that the vast majority of these profits were captured by non-bank institutions willing to create businesses tailored to meet the unique preferences of Japanese consumers.

Second, failure to deal with bad debts can quickly change the fundamental nature of the problem. If banks had acted decisively in the early 1990s to write off NPLs, change pricing to reflect risks, and reduce lending to weak borrowers, they would have been able to withstand the losses and put their core economics back on track. By avoiding action, the banks let the problem fester and grow so large that they no longer have the resources to resolve it. This only exacerbated Japan's overall economic troubles. The NPLs became a macroeconomic headache and a tricky political issue. The scale of restructuring required and fears of high unemployment have fueled fierce resistance in the ruling Liberal Democratic Party to any strong measures to bring NPLs down to manageable levels.

Finally, to build a sustainable international business, it is not enough to follow your customers overseas. In the 1970s and 1980s, Japanese banks aggressively entered markets abroad in an effort to serve their manufacturing clients around the world. By the mid-1990s, Japan was the largest foreign lender across Asia, with the four top banking groups extending over $100 billion in loans and operating branches in most of the major cities in the region. The Asian financial crisis and shifting fortunes at home revealed that these banks had actually built little more than lending businesses focused on Japanese customers. By 2002, total loans in Asia made by Japan's top four mega-banks had shrunk to half their peak. Obviously, Japanese banks had not bothered to penetrate local markets. With many of their clients doing the same, they retreated to their island home.

<hr>

Small businesses: Better access to capital

Nearly 99 percent of Japan's 2.4 million companies fall in the small to medium-sized category, defined as having less than $1 million in paid-up book capital. Lending to these companies made up 56 percent of all Japanese bank lending in 1998, though they account for only half of total sales and a third of operating profits. Small and mid-sized business customers need and value broad-based relationships with their bankers. Indeed, the average Japanese middle-market company borrows slightly more than 80 percent of its capital from banks, with most of the rest in equity held by its customers, suppliers, and often, the founder's family.

These traditional relationships are under pressure as banks tighten credit standards for small businesses to improve their own profitability. From 2001 to 2002, lenders raised average interest rates by as much as 5 percent, forcing small companies to look for alternative capital sources and, in some cases, driving them to bankruptcy. According to the Bank of Japan, bank lending to small and medium-sized businesses declined by 18 percent from 1995 to 2002, when banks had a total of $1.6 trillion in outstanding loans to these companies.

Small and medium-sized companies will remain under strong profit pressure through the rest of this decade. Their profitability will eventually rebound, but the market for banking services to these companies is likely to contract first before expanding again. In the meantime, significant inefficiencies need to be driven out of below-scale manufacturers, overlapping distribution layers, and unsophisticated service operations. The surge in unemployment that began in 1997 signaled that this restructuring was under way. After years of hovering around 2 percent, the unemployment rate reached 5.4 percent in 2002.

Amid the gloom of this credit crunch, opportunities exist to differentially provide capital at risk-based prices. Underwriting standards for small businesses are not refined and services are provided through the banks' branch networks. Better priced lending services provided through lower cost channels and more centralized underwriting centers are a potentially attractive opportunity. In 2002, a few leading banks such as Sumitomo-Mitsui and Bank of Fukuoka had already announced small business services offered through new multi-channel structures.

Pension funds: Quality products, improved skills

Most bankers in Japan have their eyes on pension and other institutional asset management services. This business had been reserved for domestic life insurers and trust banks until the mid-1990s, at which point commercial banks, securities companies, and foreign financial institutions were given the right to set up institutional asset management subsidiaries. With the entry of these new competitors, some of the market shifted to investment management companies and foreign funds. Despite the terrible returns on funds managed by life insurers and trust banks, these incumbents still controlled more than 70 percent of the total institutional asset management market in 2002.

The Japanese institutional money market is a "good news/bad news" market for new entrants. The good news is that since the 1990s it has been one of Japan's fastest growing financial services markets. With the population aging, assets under management in pension funds are growing at more than 8 percent a year. The bad news is that the average fees and profits from this business have been very poor. Fees are typically half those of other developed markets, averaging only 20–30 basis points, or less.

The story is somewhat better for skilled specialist managers, especially Western firms, that are able to command significantly higher fees and accumulate funds several times faster than the market's underlying growth rate. Leaders in the market, such as Barclays Nikko Global Investors and JP Morgan Chase, have built up scale businesses that are generating attractive profit streams. That notwithstanding, many foreign players that have accumulated $5–10 billion in assets under management have yet to reach the break-even point due to the high service costs associated with operating in Japan.

Over the next decade, the opportunities will be promising for skilled fund managers that can reach a minimum scale of about $10 billion in assets under management. Total pension assets in Japan will continue to grow at 6–8 percent a year, although a one-time dip will occur in 2003 as government regulations allow some small pension funds to close. Major pension funds are continuing to shift assets away from very low return life insurers toward asset managers with better performance records. From the mid-1990s through 2002, life insurers on average lost 10 percent of their pension funds under management each year. Better performing fund managers are commanding higher fees and are disproportionately attracting more assets. Pension consultants are also exercising more influence in the selection of fund managers. The market still needs to change structurally and to move from balanced mandates, where one manager is given funds to invest in a broad range of asset classes, to asset class-specific mandates.

One wild card is the introduction of defined-contribution pension plans, which began in 2001. Unfortunately, the initial plan structure approved by the government restricts tax-advantaged contributions to very low levels. It is possible that this will be revised in coming years as the need for more flexible pension products becomes more acute. This could provide another boost to the total size of the market and would play to the strengths of more skilled fund managers and distributors.

DARING TO BE DIFFERENT IN TOUGH TIMES

Mining the riches of Japan is a bit like extracting oil from Alaska's North Slope – while the opportunities are substantial, they have to be captured in a harsh environment. In the seemingly barren landscape, it is the persistent innovators willing to try different approaches and fully commit their resources that ultimately reap attractive profits. Even for the strong, it is important to judge the conditions carefully. Innovators who place large bets at the wrong time could get caught in turbulent weather that might bring them crashing down.

Winners will come in many forms. Incumbent Japanese banks have major advantages that will help them capture opportunities in the coming years. But they first need to isolate their problem businesses and, perhaps more importantly, overcome entrenched mindsets that often block bold action. Foreign banks need to remain committed to the market and be willing to increase their bets when opportunities arise, especially if Japan goes through a major crisis. Non-bank players often have significant customer, brand, and financial assets that can be leveraged to enter Japan's banking markets. Most, however, need to think much more clearly about how to create profits, rather than simply accumulate accounts. In short, there are many opportunities, but taking advantage of them requires insightful strategies, full commitment over a sustained period, and a true profit mindset.

Mega-banks: The enemy is the mindset

The traditional post-war role of major banks at the center of Japan's power structure is gone forever. Since the 1950s, the country's 12 biggest banks – the nine original so-called city banks and the three long-term credit banks –

dominated the major *keiretsu*, or industrial groups, through their cross shareholdings, extensive loans, and corporate relationships. A dozen years of inaction since the economic bubble of the early 1990s, a huge bad debt burden, and the growing international strength of Japan's leading industrial companies have permanently reduced the influence of the banks. Although these institutions still channel much of Japan's capital flows, they no longer hold sway over the top corporations and carry little weight in international banking circles.

Ironically, at least a couple of the remaining five mega-banks – if they can avoid sinking under the weight of their legacy debt problems – are still well positioned to capture a large share of the most attractive opportunities. The best brands such as Bank of Tokyo-Mitsubishi, which is part of the Mitsubishi Tokyo Financial Group (MTFG), continue to command respect. This "flight to quality" can be seen in their stock prices and market capitalization. The strong are clearly outperforming the weak amid the uncertainty of Japan's financial markets. These leaders employ some of the best talent in the financial sector and enjoy dominant retail distribution networks and deep relationships with major companies.

Yet these institutions are in serious trouble. For them to dig their way out of the hole they are in will require drastic action. First, they must correct fundamental problems in their core businesses. Without uncharacteristically bold action, their core banking products will continue to suffer low profitability for years to come. Even putting aside the existing NPLs, commercial banking in Japan does not produce attractive enough returns due to an over-reliance on uneconomically priced loans. To generate profits, commercial loan spreads need to be roughly double today's average of 125 basis points. Tough decisions must be made to stop rolling over loans to the roughly 20 percent of corporations that have not made principal payments in over a decade. From those companies in arrears on all interest payments as well, banks have to demand rigorous restructuring plans that generate positive cash flow and repay loans in reasonable time. Pricing and fees for retail customers also need to be improved dramatically. Eighty percent of retail accounts lose money. And banks can never generate enough sales of other products, such as mortgages or credit cards, to break even.

Second, each of the mega-banks must split the old legacy bank products and operations from new organizations targeting promising product opportunities. The scale of the problems they face is too big and the inertia too strong for the existing organizations to pursue new opportunities effectively while trying to restructure their existing businesses. Organizational structures, incentives, information systems, and career path options for employees have changed little over the past 30 years, and are inextricably tied to the traditional products and business lines. Effectively capturing new opportunities requires the freedom to design highly competitive products, channels, and marketing approaches, practically impossible to do through existing bank infrastructures.

Third, once they create separate organizations, the mega-banks need to set out new, more differentiated revenue streams from their huge existing corporate and retail customer bases. Profitably serving customers will mean building best-in-class skills in a limited number of areas. For example, for corporate customers, one or two banks may become strong enough in capital market products, M&A, and restructuring advisory services to compete with the best securities companies in the market. A few other banks may build cash management and payment capabilities on a national, or even global, scale. Yet others may excel at custodian services and trust processing. The mistake will be to believe that they can continue to do all of these businesses well. This will only lead to the mega-banks falling even further behind the leading US and European players, and continuing to depress profits in the Japanese market.

Finally, the mega-banks need to aggressively tackle their biggest enemy: the mindset of their organizations. We have discussed the required changes described above with many senior Japanese bankers. The majority of them agree that these remedies are essential. Unfortunately, to date they have not been able to overcome the organizational and cultural resistance to change in their institutions. They persistently view themselves as infallible powerbrokers – both within the banking system and in the economy overall. These delusions prevent most of them from accepting inevitable decline and taking appropriate action. Besides, even if a manager fights the system and is proven right, there is little chance of reward through accelerated promotion or higher compensation. A maverick would be ostracized. Not surprisingly, most senior managers prefer to keep a low profile – and coast.

Still, the strongest mega-bank groups are in the best position to win in Japan's post-deregulation financial system. They have vast resources and employ some of the nation's brightest people. Moreover, they remain at the center of their industrial groups, and retain a certain degree of both direct and indirect management influence over many of the big corporations and even some of the smaller banks and non-bank financial institutions within their groups. All of these factors will continue to work in the banks' favor, but not all of the institutions will necessarily make the cut. Only those that have the will to restructure quickly and adopt new ways of operating will make it in a more competitive world.

Regional banks: Stronger franchises

If the mega-banks have ruled the banking system and Japan's economy from their city strongholds, the regional banks have been the lords of the countryside. Historically, these second-tier commercial banks have provided an extended distribution network throughout the rural areas. As of 2002, the 129 regional banks held more than $2 trillion in assets and operated 13,000-plus branches. Many of these banks have been solid financially and maintain both product and management links to some of the mega-banks.

Within this broad group, there is a small number of banks that are well positioned to emerge as winners. These leading banks have relatively robust balance sheets, strong local positions – often with 25–40 percent share of the market – and are proactive, progressive leaders who aspire to build broader franchises. Some of these players operate close to Tokyo. The Bank of Yokohama, Chiba Bank, Joyo Bank, and Shizuoka Bank are examples. Others such as Bank of Fukuoka and Hiroshima Bank operate in Japan's mid-sized cities. The consolidation of the mega-banks, deregulation that now permits the selling of investment products and insurance, and encouragement by the Financial Services Agency to acquire weaker institutions, are driving the regional players to restructure. They are moving more aggressively than the mega-banks, taking advantage of their distance from the policymakers in Tokyo, who have always favored the big players.

The leading regional banks have to meet several challenges if they are to become true winners. One of the most fundamental is to deal with an overhang of excess liabilities created by the intersection of the traditional preference among the Japanese for bank deposits over other investments and the shortage of attractive lending opportunities (see Exhibit 2.3).

To address this issue, the regional players urgently need to access off-balance sheet investment products and develop the requisite sales and marketing facility. Although Japanese asset managers have some of these capabilities, American and European firms often have better products and more extensive marketing skills. Leading regional banks will be well served by structuring effective alliances with best-in-class foreign retail funds manufacturers, wealth managers, and insurance players with expertise in key products like annuities.

Improving cost efficiency and achieving sufficient competitive scale are also necessary to becoming a long-term winner. Restructuring is already emerging on two fronts. First, several of the regional banks have begun to root out the cost inefficiencies embedded in their functionally integrated structures. Moves to slash costs include outsourcing those functions such as information-processing in which the banks lack critical scale, and aggressively reduce purchasing costs. Second, we are beginning to see a push for geographic scale. We have already seen a few "in-market" acquisitions of small players by stronger players, such as Bank of Fukuoka. Some banks are also forging tie-ups across regions. Such alliances could lead to complete mergers and result in the emergence of super-regional banks with more cost-

Exhibit 2.3 Imbalance of deposits and loans in Japanese regional banks

$ billion; end March 2001

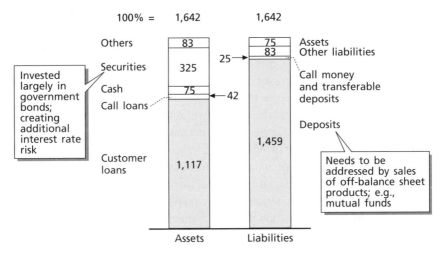

Source: Financial statements of leading regional banks; McKinsey analysis

efficient, large-scale operations covering natural markets such as economically linked semi-rural areas or the vicinities outside the larger urban centers.

Finally, regional banks need to overhaul their basic approach to distribution. As they move to reduce costs and reach customers beyond their traditional geographic boundaries, they need to fundamentally rethink how different types of customers access their banks. Retail, small business, and even middle-market corporate customers can be segregated and served more cost-effectively – and often at higher levels of service – with a better mix of branch, direct sales, and remote channels. Early work by regional leaders such as Suruga and Fukuoka is demonstrating that, when properly pursued, the distribution channel revolution that we have seen in other developed markets can yield equally impressive results in Japan.

The foreign insiders: Building new business models

For the rest of this decade, Japan's banking and financial markets will remain predominantly the domain of domestic institutions. Only a very small percentage of total bank assets are in the hands of foreigners. Yet foreign players wanting to build positions in Japan will have unprecedented opportunities to do so. Japanese bankruptcies, business exits, alliances, and the general turmoil in the financial markets are creating once-in-a-lifetime chances for foreign players. Foreign entrants into Japan's financial markets have two options: Try to become insiders and build customer businesses in what is a highly relationship-driven market, or differentiate themselves from the domestic pack by offering niche products and services.

So far, only a handful of foreign institutions, most notably Citibank and AIG, have managed to establish an early and enduring presence. Although both of these players from the United States have made large acquisitions, they spent decades building their core businesses in Japan organically. A key factor in their success is the pressure for change that they put on the system. Citibank pushed the Ministry of Finance to allow it to provide a more complete set of innovative retail banking services and to be the first bank in Japan to operate its ATMs 24 hours a day. AIG, meanwhile, persuaded the government through trade talks to open the insurance sector to foreign players and helped carve out the so-called third sector of insurance products, which includes profitable niche offerings such as personal injury and medical insurance.

Our experience has shown that any foreign player who hopes to succeed in Japan and build a major position needs to demonstrate this sort of persistence. Such effort often pays off handsomely. By the late 1990s, Citibank was considered one of the most innovative leaders in the market. Its appeal as a stable yet bold competitor was amply demonstrated when the number of its new accounts grew 40 percent, even with confidence dipping as the Asian financial crisis unfolded in late 1997 and early 1998. Its experience, knowledge, and existing platforms also allowed it to make several important mergers and acquisitions that dramatically increased its overall position.

In Japan, aggressive management and a dose of luck are necessary ingredients for a successful acquisition. Perhaps the most dramatic example of this is Merrill Lynch's 1998 takeover of bankrupt Yamaichi Securities, Japan's fourth-largest brokerage. After four years and over $1 billion in losses, Merrill was forced to downsize the operation to roughly 20 percent of what it had been. Although many factors were at work, the plain and simple problem was that the market for retail securities and wealth management contracted. At the same time, Merrill was not aggressive enough in reducing costs, hoping in vain that the market would pick up. Merrill's basic service offering was not necessarily wrong for Japan, but the timing and execution did not work.

In addition to managing the economics of the acquired business, foreigners buying into the Japanese market almost always face a second challenge: building a new business in parallel to restructuring the acquired old. With the possible exception of consumer finance companies, there are almost no financial businesses that can be bought in Japan and then simply managed better to generate sustainable profits. Any acquired business will benefit from repair, but after initial restructuring, it has to be used to create a more profitable business. This means that buyers need to commit double the resources to improve management, bring in new products, build new channels, and invest in the brand, among other priorities. Without this level of commitment, those hunting for an opportunity in Japan should resist the temptation to cut that "once-in-a-lifetime" deal.

Foreign niche players: Searching for access

The majority of foreign players have opted for the second way to enter Japan's financial services sector: leveraging their global capabilities to build a niche business. These companies have typically chosen a limited market niche such as foreign investment funds or specialized insurance products. Often, they have tried to gain distribution and market access through someone else's retail network or their own limited institutional network, delivering leading-edge skills or world-class products. Some players are also trying to create a Japanese component of a truly global business.

In asset management, for example, some foreign players with strong products have linked up with local or other foreign players that had distribution capabilities. There are several good examples. In 1997, Putnam allied with Nippon Life Insurance to manage institutional funds and develop mutual funds for the insurer's retail customer base. This alliance has since evolved into the distribution of annuity life insurance products through banks. Putnam provides funds management and marketing support for the bank channel, while Nippon Life provides the domestic insurance structure for the product. Entering the market in 1999, The Hartford insurance company rapidly expanded to become within three years the largest provider of variable annuities in Japan, driven by a successful distribution alliance with Nikko Securities and new relationships with the Bank of Tokyo-Mitsubishi and the Bank of Yokohama.

Relying on a partner's distribution network can also be risky. One of the most dramatic examples of this was Goldman Sachs' 1997 success in attracting close to $10 billion in assets into a family of retail mutual funds, distributed almost entirely through major Japanese securities brokers. Although Goldman clearly came up with the right product for the market at that time – a multi-currency, high-quality, fixed-income fund with currency risk protection – it succeeded mainly because it worked well with the local brokers. Goldman invested significant time and resources educating front-line salespeople about the value of the product for retail investors. To build a longer term brand franchise, Goldman also invested heavily in mass-media advertising. Unfortunately, all of this began falling apart in 2000 when market preferences shifted to equity products. Brokers encouraged retail investors to unload Goldman's fixed income offerings. The result: a 50 percent drop in Goldman's assets under management.

Many niche markets in Japan are likely to be very attractive throughout this decade. Some of these can be profitably tackled with well-structured alliances or joint ventures. Domestic players lack world-class skills and products in lucrative market segments. Among them: equity and credit derivatives, securitization, investment banking advisory services such as for M&A, and some types of investment products. Locals would be relatively open to alliances that provide access to these capabilities. Profit margins for many of these products and services are likely to remain attractive, at least until these niches go through periods of extended growth.

But profitability does not last forever. When the niche is commoditized, meaning it is no longer such a specialized product or value-added service, the joint venture may lose its vitality. Japanese institutions will have much less need for an overseas partner once they learn the core skills and upgrade their own capabilities. Foreign investors must take care to think through the end game of any link-up and strengthen the ties through the introduction of fresh products or skills. They also need to consider what they would be left with should the alliance dissolve. Opportunities are attractive, but shifts in markets and partnerships mean that senior management has to keep a close eye on the business as it evolves.

3

South Korea: From Basket Case to Case Study

Macroeconomics

- GDP[1] ($bn)   423
- GDP per capital ($)   8,905
- PPP GDP per capita ($)   18,741
- Exports ($bn/% of GDP)   151/36
- Imports ($bn/% of GDP)   138/33
- FDI inflow ($bn/% of GDP)   3.2/1
- FDI outflow ($bn/% of GDP)   2.6/0.6
- Foreign currency reserves ($bn/% of GDP)   96/23
- External debt ($bn/% of GDP)   115/27
- NPL of banks ($bn/% of total net loans)   8/4
- National government borrowing
  ($bn/% of GDP/% external)   66/16/9
- Top 3 trading partners   US, Japan, China
- Number of corporates in Global Top 500[2]   12

Socioeconomics

- Population (mn)   47
- Number of households (mn)   14
- Average urban household income ($)   22,923
- Number of households earning >$100K p.a. (mn)   0.24
- Mobile phones/100 population   69
- Internet subscribers/100 population   51
- Urbanization (% of population)   80
- % of population with university degrees   24
- % of population above 65 years old in 2001
  and 2021   8/16

Capital Markets

- Number of listed corporations   688
- Equity market capitalization ($bn/% of GDP)   194/46
- Trading volume ($bn/% of market cap)   381/196
- Debt market capitalization ($bn/% of GDP)   255/60
- Equity underwriting[3] ($bn/% of GDP)   7/2
- Debt underwriting[3] ($bn/% of GDP)   24/6
- M&A ($bn/% of GDP)   18/4
- Retail assets under management ($bn)   43
- Institutional assets under management ($bn)   116

Banking Markets

- Total loans of all financial institutions, including non-banks ($bn/% of GDP)   636/151
- Total deposits of all financial institutions, including non-banks ($bn/% of GDP) 625/148
- Mortgages ($bn/% of GDP)   60/14
- Personal loans ($bn/% of GDP)   190/45
- Credit card receivables[4] ($bn/% of GDP)   24/6
- Credit cards per person above 15   1.47
- Credit card spend as % of household total spend   83
- Foreign ownership limit in 1997 and 2002[5] (%)   4/100
- Number of banks in Global Top 1,000 in 1997 and 2001   20/15
- Number of ATMs/1,000 population   0.27
- Number of branches/1,000 population   0.10
- Number of banking employees/1,000 population   1.86

---

[1] At 2001 prices
[2] *The Fortune Global 500*: July 22, 2002
[3] Average from 1995–2001
[4] Exclude card loans and cash advance only cards
[5] For investments >10%, approval from government is required

Note: All figures as of December 2001 unless otherwise indicated

South Korea's Financial Landscape

Types	Number of institutions, 1997	Number of institutions, 2002	Percent of total assets 2001	Top 3 players
Government national commercial bank	0	2	14	• Chohung Bank • Woori Bank
Private national commercial bank	16	6	40	• Kookmin Bank • Korea First Bank • Korea Exchange Bank
Government regional commercial bank	0	2	2	• Kwangju Bank • Kyongnam Bank
Private regional commercial bank	10	4	4	• Daegu Bank • Pusan Bank • Cheju Bank
Government specialized bank	7	5	28	• Industrial Bank of Korea • Korea Development Bank • Export-Import Bank of Korea
Foreign commercial bank	52	41	6	• Citibank • HSBC • JP Morgan Chase
Merchant bank (local + foreign)	30	3	1	• Woori Investment Bank • Korea French Banking Corporation • Kumho Investment Bank
Private mutual savings	231	122	2	• Hansol Mutual Savings Bank • Jeil Mutual Savings Bank • Korea Mutual Savings Bank
Private credit union	1,666	1,268	3	• n/a
Total	**2,012**	**1,453**	**$701bn**	

South Koreans will always remember June 2002 as the summer their nation became a football power. They successfully hosted the World Cup with Japan and, against the odds, made it to the last four, a feat no other Asian country had ever accomplished. But almost unnoticed in the euphoria of that month was the robust state of the nation's finances. Less than four years after the devastation of the Asian economic crisis, South Korea has emerged as a case study of how to restructure a national economy. Buried in the sports hoopla of that June was the startling news that GDP had expanded 5.7 percent in the first quarter, and that the credit rating of the major banks had leapfrogged from junk status to investment grade.

What did South Korea do right? Its recipe for recovery is one that the rest of Asia would have done well to follow. The government had the will to break tradition and give away power. It imposed strict capital requirements on banks, forcing those who could not meet them to exit the business or supply new funds. The authorities took a firm stance against unions to make the labor market more flexible. Once the State provided the proper environment, the private sector stepped up and took the lead on restructuring. There was decisive action on non-performing loans and against overstaffing in companies. Performance management systems were put in place.

Still, after all the hard work, South Korea is not yet on a secure, stable development path. There is a sense across this land of 47 million people that they still have a long way to go. The World Cup had not been won and the economic miracle has yet to be completed. The banking system, in particular, is struggling toward full rehabilitation. Non-performing loans and assets, for example, remain a major problem that, if not satisfactorily resolved, could undo much of the progress made so far.

The government did the initial spadework, then the private sector did its part by shaking up bank management, refocusing on the bottom line, improving corporate governance, and embarking on mergers. The challenge now is for the government to resolve remaining issues and trust the private sector to drive change. The main preconditions for success include action on the overhang of potential non-performing assets, the continued shift of bank ownership from public to private hands, and flexibility in labor management.

Assuming restructuring continues, the South Korean economy is expected to expand significantly over the rest of this decade, with the personal financial services market outpacing it by five to 10 percentage points. Credit cards and personal loans will be major drivers, but that depends on the acquisition of institutional risk management skills and systems development. Investment products such as mutual funds and related wealth management services could be next-generation boosters – if capital market reforms, including consolidation in pension funds, are to proceed.

THE STATE AS WHITE KNIGHT

The roots of South Korea's 1997–98 financial crisis are well known. In the 1960s the State began using the banks to funnel scarce capital to conglomerates, known as *chaebol*, in accordance with a series of five-year economic development plans. All that the banking sector had to do was collect retail deposits and lend the money to the *chaebol*. The system worked while the economy was small enough not to attract the attention of global competitors, simple enough so that bureaucrats could micro-manage its development, and clean enough so that politicians could base policy decisions on purely economic considerations.

Success changed the ground rules. The country was forced to reform its protectionist policies so South Korean-made textiles, chemicals, steel, ships, automobiles, and semiconductors could retain access to the global marketplace. But the *chaebol* continued their time-honored practice of generating growth via increasing inputs instead of enhancing productivity. Their profitability had been seriously eroded by the early 1990s. Yet, the banks continued to feed their appetite for capital because no one could afford to see them go bankrupt. Many were already under pressure from new competition, high-risk foreign-exchange trading, internal corruption, and business scandals. There were industry-wide concerns as well, among them inadequate and fragmented regulatory supervision, poor profitability resulting from excessive industry fragmentation, and insufficient credit-risk assessment and management skills.

When push came to shove, however, the government was surprisingly quick to admit the need for change. By April 1, 1998, it had created the Financial Supervisory Commission (FSC), a ministry-level agency reporting directly to the country's president. In one stroke, the various regulatory bodies were consolidated into a single organization responsible for banking, securities, and insurance. At the same time, the government formed the Korean Asset Management Corporation (KAMCO) to take over the non-performing assets of failing financial institutions.

All banks were directed to provide plans to meet the minimum capital requirement of 8 percent. Based on its assessment of the proposals, the FSC shut down or merged with better performers: 14 of the 26 commercial banks, including regional banks. For the first time, foreigners were allowed to acquire closed institutions. Newbridge Capital and Carlyle Capital of the United States became majority shareholders of Korea First Bank and KorAm Bank, respectively. Joint ventures were also encouraged. Goldman Sachs bought a stake in Kookmin Bank while ING became a major shareholder of Housing & Commercial Bank (H&CB). German insurance group Allianz invested in Hana Bank, and Commerzbank, also from Germany, bought shares in Korea Exchange Bank.

The FSC sought to strengthen corporate governance by mandating the appointment of outside directors, among other directives. It banned the use of book value in accounting for security instruments issued in-house. Whenever the government had to inject capital to maintain solvency, it implemented strict performance requirements. The management team at Chohung Bank was removed in 1998 and Peace Bank was consolidated into Hanvit Bank in 2001, when they failed to follow through with the agreed restructuring milestones.

The government also tackled problems at the *chaebol*. Banking could again be at risk if nothing was done about the leverage ratios of South Korean companies, which stood at an average of more than 400 percent. An ultimatum was sent out: Bring down the leverage to below 200 percent or face bankruptcy as loans would not be extended. The directive brought results. But the impact could have been maximized and distortions in the capital markets minimized if the government used interest-coverage ratio rather than leverage ratio in determining sustainable debt levels.

THE PRIVATE SECTOR WEIGHS IN

It was clear that even after the government-led consolidation and clean-up of non-performing loans (NPLs), many financial institutions, including a number of banks, would not survive the next five years without significant strategic and operational change. To their credit, management rose to the challenge. Many old-line CEOs at national retail banks were shunted off to a titular role. From 1998 to 2001, the majority of national retail banks had named a new generation of executives committed to transforming their institutions. These CEOs sought to break the bureaucratic culture that stifled productivity, pursued profits instead of government favor, and embraced global standards of governance and performance. Kim Jung-tae of Kookmin Bank, formerly H&CB, is the best-practice example of the new style of leadership (see sidebar).

❧✦❧

Lessons in transformation

Kim Jung-tae is not shirking from challenging convention – and fighting the government. The CEO of Kookmin Bank recruited foreign talent while letting go of a third of the existing workforce. He introduced performance-based compensation, and then shared the risk by taking compensation only in the form of options. His salary is a token 1 won (less than one US cent) a year. Despite accusations that he was being unpatriotic, he reduced the bank's exposure to the now-bankrupt Daewoo group, the only bank to do so in 1998. In 2001 Kim did the unthinkable. He held his ground against government pressure to extend troubled semiconductor manufacturer Hynix additional lines of credit, a signal to everyone that the historic ties between the government, banks, and business had finally been broken.

It had been a frenetic four years for the 24-year veteran of the securities industry (see Exhibit 3.1). Brought in by the board of H&CB in 1998, Kim hit the ground running by tackling the bank's NPLs. Before he came on board, 8 percent of H&CB's portfolio was not being serviced, a shocking state of affairs given its monopoly on residential mortgages. Within 18 months, the new CEO took a $435 million write-down and increased loan-loss provisions from 2 percent to 8 percent. NPLs fell to 2.9 percent of total.

To keep it that way, Kim systematically reduced the bank's exposure to troubled companies. So when Daewoo and other *chaebol* went bankrupt in 1999 and 2000, H&CB was not as badly affected as its competitors, especially since the workforce cuts of 1998 had also strengthened the bottom line. Kim also pushed H&CB to follow stringent international accounting standards. One measure of his success: H&CB became the first bank to list on the New York Stock Exchange. By 2000 H&CB was boasting a return on equity of 23 percent – from minus 8 percent in 1998 – while reducing the cost–income ratio to 29.9 percent from 47 percent. Kim was just getting started. The following year he led a merger of H&CB with Kookmin Bank to create South Korea's largest mass retail lender. It was as head of the enlarged entity that he asserted banking independence by declining new loans to Hynix. Kim also played hard ball with the competition. In early 2002 several leading banks raised interest rates on time deposit certificates. Kookmin refused to follow suit, arguing that the move was a shortsighted attempt to artificially increase bank assets during merger discussions. When $1.86 billion left Kookmin, however, the bank raised interest rates too and lowered loan rates for good measure. The rival banks have since begun cutting back on deposit rates.

The new Kookmin Bank has laid out a clear road map for the future. It is expanding its wealth management products by developing higher margin affluent and private banking services, and sourcing from alliances with foreign players like ING. The bank is doing this without raising costs through a sustained focus on streamlining its retail channel, reducing its management overhead, and improving its back office IT systems (helped by a healthy bump in revenue). Kookmin aims to transform itself into an integrated provider of financial services, no mean goal considering that its primary products three years ago were time deposits and mortgages.

Kim completed a negotiation with labor unions to extend performance-based compensation from the managerial ranks to the entire workforce. He can point to the stock market's verdict on the bank's performance to buttress his case. On the day Kim joined H&CB, its stock was trading at approximately $2.30 per share. At its peak in 2002, Kookmin Bank was valued at $54.35 a share. He may be a one-cent CEO, but Kim earned good money on his well-deserved stock options.

The new managers have not hesitated to acquire other banks or let themselves be acquired in pursuit of sustainable profitability, even without prodding from the government. Kim led the way in 2001 by merging H&CB with Kookmin Bank, creating a giant nearly twice the size of its nearest competitor. At the end of 2001, Kookmin had $133.7 billion in assets, compared with $72.4 billion for second-largest Woori Bank (merger of Woori, Kyoungnam, and Kwangju), $44.1 billion for Shinhan Bank (merger of Shinhan and Cheju), $43.8 billion for Chohung, $43.3 billion for Korea Exchange Bank, and $36.7 billion for Hana Bank. In 2002, no. 6 Hana tendered an offer with government approval for the struggling Seoulbank, while Shinhan made an offer for the government's stake in Chohung Bank. The merger of Hana and Seoulbank at the end of 2002 pushed the combined entity to no. 3 in Korea.

Some questions have been raised about the merger and acquisitions (M&A) spree. Are banks sacrificing profitability in their fixation on sheer size? Banks like Kookmin and Hana counter that they have clear plans to maximize shareholder returns. The mergers go beyond physical integration. They identify sources of synergy and ways to leverage a larger customer base through initiatives such as cross-selling of non-banking products. If these plans are implemented as structured, the consolidation could produce not only bigger banks, but also larger payouts for shareholders and employees.

NOW FOR THE HARD PART

South Korea's restructuring efforts have had impressive results. The banking sector's overall return on assets was 0.8 percent in 2001, from minus 2.5 percent in 1998. Return on equity was 16.5 percent compared with minus 42.7 percent in 1998. The BIS ratio is an adequate 10.7 percent. The

Exhibit 3.1 Reform driven by CEO Kim Jung-tae

Market capitalization
$ million

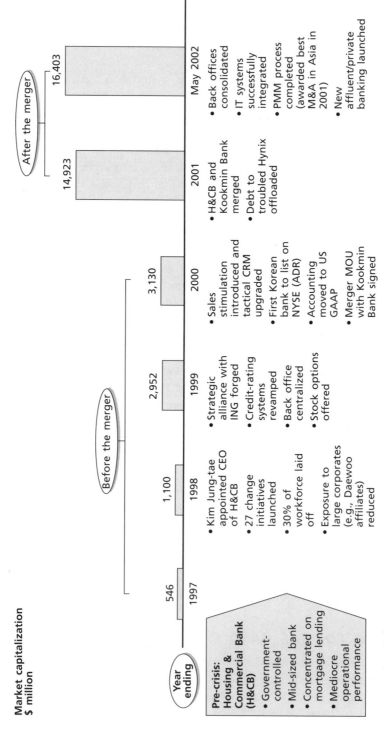

After the merger

16,403   14,923

May 2002   2001

- Back offices consolidated
- IT systems successfully integrated
- PMM process completed (awarded best M&A in Asia in 2001)
- New affluent/private banking launched

- H&CB and Kookmin Bank merged
- Debt to troubled Hynix offloaded

3,130   2,952   1,100   546

2000   1999   1998   1997

Before the merger

- Sales stimulation introduced and tactical CRM upgraded
- First Korean bank to list on NYSE (ADR)
- Accounting moved to US GAAP
- Merger MOU with Kookmin Bank signed

- Strategic alliance with ING forged
- Credit-rating systems revamped
- Back office centralized
- Stock options offered

- Kim Jung-tae appointed CEO of H&CB
- 27 change initiatives launched
- 30% of workforce laid off
- Exposure to large corporates (e.g., Daewoo affiliates) reduced

Year ending

Pre-crisis: Housing & Commercial Bank (H&CB)
- Government-controlled
- Mid-sized bank
- Concentrated on mortgage lending
- Mediocre operational performance

Source: Bloomberg; press releases

ratio of NPLs to total loans outstanding was reduced to 3.3 percent in 2001, and that is reckoned under a definition of NPLs that is more stringent than the international norm. The level of NPLs was reported at 6 percent in 1998, but that was when the banks had leeway to define what a non-performing loan was. These solid numbers persuaded international rating agencies such as S&P and Moody's to restore the investment grades of major banks like Kookmin, Shinhan, and Woori in 2002.

But much more is needed to preserve and extend these gains. First, banks should continue increasing their capital base and the government should defuse a potential explosion in new NPLs. The banks still have exposure to put options embedded in the NPLs they sold to KAMCO. These are not reflected in their balance sheets. A strong capital base will help them deal with any fallout should circumstances require them to settle these options. More disturbing, some 30 percent of South Korea's manufacturing companies cannot meet interest expenses from current earnings despite low interest rates. We believe the government should inject new money as soon as possible to deal with this problem once and for all. South Korea should learn from the expensive mistake of Mexico, which had to infuse more money into the banking system because it did not act early enough.

Second, the government needs to clean up the non-performing assets of investment trust companies or ITCs. South Korea's clean-up had stopped short of the ITC sector. In the past, the government pressured the ITCs to purchase and keep corporate junk bonds to prevent troubled companies from going under or to support the stock market. Many ITCs continue to hold non-performing assets that they cannot write off for fear of going bankrupt themselves. In the meantime, they must pay guaranteed returns to their clients. The government hopes the ITCs can still earn adequate profits, but that may be wishful thinking given the current market situation. South Korea must clean up the ITC sector now and bring in sounder institutions to manage the capital markets.

Third, the government should help to sell non-viable credit card companies as quickly as possible, in the form of business entities or asset portfolios before the credit crunch causes a more serious economic downturn. Since mid-2002, credit card delinquency and charge-off rates have been rapidly growing, increasing the additional capital required to revive ailing credit card companies to a range of five to 10 trillion won ($4–8 billion). Some credit card companies are likely to fail in raising the required funds from shareholders and the market. If those companies keep going unchecked for a long time, they will limit credit approvals, putting more downward pressure on private consumption and the economy, further aggravating the credit crunch. Hence, the government should immediately take action. Small-sized credit companies should be sold in the form of asset portfolios and large companies (if they are too large for asset portfolio sales), should be sold in the form of business entities. Only by doing so, the government will be able to prevent the entire economy from being caught in a vicious cycle and spiraling into a massive downturn.

Fourth, bank ownership must be returned to the private sector. Due to its inevitable intervention right after the financial crisis, the government owns significant stakes in many banks. It denies interfering with bank operations, but it is a well-known fact that political influence and relationships still determine the designation and tenure of top managers. The average length of service by a bank CEO today is less than three years, too short to make lasting changes. Full privatization will not only eliminate politics and promote merit-based appointments, it will also naturally lead to the elimination of government intervention in corporate lending decisions.

Fifth, the government should provide an environment for more flexible labor management. Because salaries are among the biggest cost components in banking, reducing headcount is one of the primary reasons for industry consolidations. But labor laws and regulations often tie management's hands, not only in hiring and firing, but also in terms of compensation. A strong government commitment to support a flexible labor structure is vital to bring the South Korean banking sector's competitiveness to a truly global level.

Finally, banks themselves should exert more effort to establish a performance-oriented culture. This is an important priority not just in South Korea, but across Asia. Only a very few players in the region – Kookmin is one – are taking the appropriate steps in earnest. Banks should junk promotions based on tenure, which offer no incentive for people to excel and erect barriers to attracting new talent. Generalists should not fill technical posts in such areas as risk management, customer relations management, and product creation. Specialists should be given the opportunity to advance and be recognized based on merit.

WHERE THE GROWTH OPPORTUNITIES ARE

If South Korea's public and private sectors succeed in nurturing financial reforms going forward, we see tremendous potential in personal financial services (see Exhibit 3.2). Credit card usage is already skyrocketing, powered mainly by utilization of cash advances. Mutual funds and asset management services may be ready to take off as the merging banks cross-sell products using their expanded customer bases and improve their marketing, back office, and IT systems.

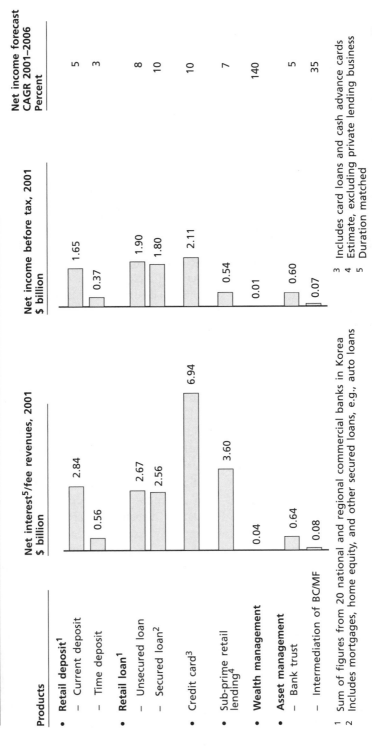

Exhibit 3.2 Assessment of attractiveness by retail banking products

Products	Net interest[5]/fee revenues, 2001 $ billion	Net income before tax, 2001 $ billion	Net income forecast CAGR 2001–2006 Percent
Retail deposit[1]			
– Current deposit	2.84	1.65	5
– Time deposit	0.56	0.37	3
Retail loan[1]			
– Unsecured loan	2.67	1.90	8
– Secured loan[2]	2.56	1.80	10
Credit card[3]	6.94	2.11	10
Sub-prime retail lending[4]	3.60	0.54	7
Wealth management	0.04	0.01	140
Asset management			
– Bank trust	0.64	0.60	5
– Intermediation of BC/MF	0.08	0.07	35

1 Sum of figures from 20 national and regional commercial banks in Korea
2 Includes mortgages, home equity, and other secured loans, e.g., auto loans
3 Includes card loans and cash advance cards
4 Estimate, excluding private lending business
5 Duration matched

Source: Bank of Korea; Financial Supervisory Commission; Korea Development Institution; Salomon Smith Barney; Datamonitor; Korea Life Insurance Association; The Korea Federation of Banks; Economist Intelligence Unit; Global Insight; Korea Institute of Finance; press releases; expert interviews; McKinsey analysis

Credit cards: Still up for grabs

The growth of the South Korean credit card market has been nothing short of phenomenal. Historically, annual usage had grown with GDP. This changed in 2000 when real credit card penetration, excluding card loans and cash advance cards, almost doubled. The number of real credit cards issued per capita increased from 0.8 at the beginning of 2000 to about 1.5 toward the end of 2002. Credit card usage jumped nearly four times to about $300 billion in the same period. The government was the prime mover. In 1998, to bring the cash-based underground economy above ground, it began offering tax credits to consumers who used credit cards and penalized retailers who did not allow card purchases.

The initiative came as consumers began buying again after the 1997–98 crisis. South Korea's economy was recovering more rapidly than expected, boosting the people's confidence and helping change their "savings-first" mentality to a "spend-first" mindset. As usage rose, credit card issuers aggressively marketed their cards, extending their franchise from the affluent to the mass-market, and on to sub-prime customers. Suddenly, people who could not borrow from banks had access to cash through their credit card's cash advance facility. By the end of 2001, cash advances from credit cards totaled more than $180 billion, representing about 60 percent of all credit card transaction volume, nearly 3–4 times the levels in developed markets such as the United States, Hong Kong, and Singapore.

Credit card delinquency rose to a record 9.4 percent, twice the level in the United States, in the first half of 2002. Not surprising given South Korea's undeveloped credit-scoring system and the lack of discrimination on the part of issuers in their drive to attract customers, including those likely to default. Mindful that prime rates were at historic lows, account holders who were not delinquent became increasingly vocal about the high interest rates they had to pay. The card companies were forced to make concessions. The government also stepped in. Regulators directed increases in loan-loss provisions and limited credit card company assets from cash advances and card loans to 50 percent of their total assets, down from 60 percent in 2001. As a result, the high margins that South Korean card companies and those focusing on other forms of unsecured personal lending have enjoyed are likely to come under significant pressure.

If the current trend continues, the charge-off rate of the entire credit card business will rise above 10 percent at the end of 2003. The charge-off rate might reach 13 percent unless the situation turns for the better in the third or fourth quarter of 2003. With charge-off rate at 13 percent, the capital required to normalize the credit card business may go up to 10 trillion won ($8 billion). Some mono-line players are likely to fail in raising funds from shareholders and the market. If the failure of some credit card companies is not properly addressed in the second half of 2003, these credit card companies are likely to lower credit limit and restrict credit approval, and the credit crunch could become even more serious.

Do South Korea's credit card issuers have a gloomy future? No, credit card has a positive future. A look at advanced markets reveals that the credit card business has credit cycles. Once the business bottoms out, profitability substantially improves. In addition, there still exists growth potential as the growth to date has been primarily driven by cash advances. Revolving credit has been limited relative to advanced markets. To be sure, the credit card business will not see all players profitable as it did in the past. The current credit correction process will determine future winners and losers. While the credit card market has room for further growth, the broader unsecured personal finance market is rapidly reaching maturity. By 2002 South Koreans were carrying as much personal unsecured debt as the Americans (adjusting for the income-level differential between the United States and South Korea).

For credit card companies to prepare for the new challenges, they must work on four fronts: tighten risk management; move to risk-based pricing; introduce sophisticated customer relationship management, or CRM; and consolidate for economies of scale. As of the end of 2002 none of the industry leaders had demonstrated best practice in these areas. It is important for card companies looking to enter or expand in the South Korean market to gradually build a meaningful scoring system to screen out potential deadbeats. As the market gets saturated, micro-segmentation to target the most attractive customers with risk-based pricing will be the key to profitable growth. Market leaders like Samsung, LG, and Kookmin have all announced plans to develop their credit-scoring and CRM capabilities. While they certainly have an early lead, the credit cards business in South Korea is still very much anyone's game.

Mortgages: Intense competition

In 1999, mortgage lending in South Korea started to accelerate, soaring above 10 percent growth in each of the next three years. Driving factors included deregulation and the strategic shift by banks from corporate to consumer lending. Overall consumer lending as a percentage of bank assets increased from 35.1 percent in 2000 to 42.9 percent in the first quarter of 2002. Yet total mortgage lending, excluding home equity loans, has remained at only 13 percent of GDP, compared to more than 40 percent in the United States or Hong Kong. There is certainly room for growth. Mortgage lending relative to output is far behind where the United States was when it was at the same GDP-per-capita level. In 2001 the loan-to-market-value ratio in the United States was more than 70 percent. In South Korea, it was about 50 percent.

But South Korea's mortgage/home equity industry is so fiercely competitive that the interest rate on new loans barely covers the total cost, including the risk premium. Banks have to be extremely sophisticated with their pricing strategy to turn a profit. At the same time, they should relentlessly lower funding and operating costs to secure a price advantage over competitors.

Sub-prime lending: High interest rates

For banks, another potential growth area is the high-risk unsecured consumer lending market. There has been a deluge of companies catering to this segment after the government eliminated the 40 percent cap on annual interest on any type of loan in 1998. Taking advantage of more relaxed policies regarding foreign ownership, Japanese consumer finance companies have entered the South Korean market to provide small loans (usually less than $1,000) "on the spot and in less than 20 minutes." If a customer gives out the phone numbers of several relatives, loans of less than $1,650 are approved immediately. Though interest rates can be as high as 150 percent a year, unsecured lending has grown into an $833 million business. Many local black market lenders have gone above ground to join the Japanese players, along with foreign firms such as Citibank.

But the rapidly increasing pile of consumer credit debt has prompted the government to take a second look at sub-prime lending. There have been horror stories about acts of violence by collection agencies, and how an initially small loan grew to an unmanageable size due to extremely high interest rates. A new law has been passed capping interest rates on consumer loans at 60 percent a year. Consumer finance companies must now have a minimum capital size. Restrictions have been placed on their ability to openly market their products to customers. To encourage stronger players, banks have been allowed to enter the sub-prime market by forming a consumer finance subsidiary.

It is unclear if a 60 percent interest rate can justify the sizable investment banks will need to enter the unsecured personal loan market. A centralized credit bureau will be essential, not to mention a segment-specific risk management system. We do not believe that a cap is the answer to the problem of excessive interest rates. If legitimate consumer finance companies close shop, high-risk customers in need of cash will be forced to go to the underground economy. The best course is to trust that competition will bring down interest rates.

Asset and wealth management: The next battleground

As the South Korean economy develops and the population ages, the number of high-income households is expected to grow. Affluent customers are already demanding sophisticated advisory service for their long-term investments. However, the available tools are still heavily skewed to time deposits and real estate. In the past, long-term capital had gone to property rather than capital markets, which had been highly volatile and speculative. An investment in the Korea Composite Stock Price Index (KOSPI) at the start of 1975 would have returned less than 10 percent, including dividend income, by the end of 2001. Buying real estate in metropolitan areas would have yielded a return of over 200 percent during the same period. There was nothing productive to justify these stellar real estate returns. There simply was no alternative long-term investment tool for people to put their money.

The past does not have to be the future. First, the fundamentals of South Korean corporations are actually not so weak as to justify the recent value destruction in the capital market. According to McKinsey projections, the South Korean capital market is undervalued by 40 percent. This implies that the KOSPI should have reached 1,600 points at the end of 2001, providing our hypothetical long-term investor with a return of over 100 percent, not just 10 percent. Had this been the case, it is not too much to assume that the real estate price increase would have been much less.

Second, there are positive trends that are improving corporate governance (see sidebar). Doubts about the commitment of South Korean companies to protect minority shareholders is one of the reasons for the steep discount in share valuations. Meanwhile, corporations taking serious steps to improve earnings, including many enterprises bought by foreigners during the crisis, have seen their stock prices rise.

Improving corporate governance

Corporate governance and shareholder protection in South Korea have improved since the mid-1990s, but as with many other aspects of the economy, they are still not up to global standards. Corporate governance reform began to gain momentum in 1995 and 1996 – prior to the crisis – when both the securities and company laws were significantly revised. However, there remained many issues concerning transparency and board oversight, and when the *chaebol* were shaken by the crisis of 1997, many of the questionable management and accounting practices were exposed.

Specifically, the intricate network of cross-holdings and subsidiaries created numerous conflicts of interest. It is difficult to escape the conclusion that the arrangement was designed to ensure that the founding family retained control of the business. The network also had the disadvantage (or benefit, depending on which side of the table you sat) of being able to obscure which divisions were being subsidized by their higher performing siblings.

The financing that the *chaebol* received from the banks also had little oversight. Unlike Germany, a country that also relies more heavily on corporate lending than the equity markets, banks did not manage the credit risk of their largest customers. They did not cut off credit when it was clear that the investments were losing propositions. The banks had no influence on the *chaebol*'s decision-making. Neither did institutional investors, which were either the subsidiaries of the banks or the *chaebol* themselves.

A number of corporate governance reforms were enacted in 1998 and 1999. The minimum number of outsiders named to the board of directors (and those in audit committees) was increased. Intra-group guarantees were eliminated. The minimum number of shares a stakeholder could own in order to assert his or her rights was lowered. Quarterly reports were made a requirement. The fiduciary duty of directors was made explicit.

However, additional reforms are yet to be made, including measures to strengthen the practical authority of the board of directors, ensuring fairness in related-party transactions, and removing de facto barriers that prevent shareholders from challenging corporate decisions. Legislation removing barriers to class-action lawsuits by shareholders was tied up in the legislature through 2002. Prospects for passage look cloudy before national elections in 2003, even though both stock markets support the bill.

Third, if the government is willing, there is a significant source of long-term investment that can help improve stock valuations. This is the national pension system, which currently has $63 billion in assets. Privatizing the management of this pile of capital would be one way of funneling some of the funds into the market and insulating the decisions from politics. Introducing a corporate pension system in the form of defined contributions can be a force for good as well. It can potentially match the amount of money currently invested in the national pension fund.

World Bank research has found evidence of a positive correlation between the availability of long-term financing and capital market development. Chile is the poster country here. After the government privatized the management of its national pension plan, equity returns surpassed all other investment tools. The accumulation and supply of significantly large long-term investments stabilized and strengthened the capital markets. As seen in the developed markets, institutional investors (such as the California Public Employees' Retirement System, or CalPERS) play a significant role in facilitating good corporate governance and ensuring that good companies obtain long-term financing for growth.

When all these pieces fall in place, we believe that asset management services will take off and create a huge market in South Korea. When the defined-contribution system was introduced in the United States, for example, the sale of mutual funds increased. Demand for wealth management and advisory services was stimulated, eventually creating a market of more than $480 billion in assets under management. Most South Korean financial institutions, including banks, are now building business systems to provide such advisory services, to be ready for the time when pension fund reforms and the development of capital markets create the ultimate high-income market.

SME loans: New growth engine

Although difficult to grasp at first, commercial bankers eventually realize that every default quickly negates any profit from operations. So they work to reduce the burden of NPLs, not only lowering risk but also improving profitability in the process because previous loan-loss provisions can be clawed back. But as discussed earlier, at the end of 2000, more than 40 percent of listed companies in South Korea were not sufficiently profitable to pay their interest expense, raising the specter of a new round of NPL problems (see Exhibit 3.3).

So what is a banker to do? Everyone seems to have hit on an alternative growth engine: small and medium-sized enterprises (SMEs). When the *chaebol* reigned supreme, these entities did not have ready access to credit. Today, the dynamics of this relatively new market can be simply summarized as a fight for market share by corporate and retail banks. In the past two years, South Korean banks have increased their SME loans by 14.7 percent, from $69.6 billion in 1999 to $79.8 billion by the end of 2001.

Because of its size, one SME does not pose the same amount of risk that a single *chaebol* does. The trade-off is the danger of over-serving these smaller customers via costly delivery models using the relationship-oriented corporate sales approach or the marketing-heavy approach of retail banking. Success in this market will be determined by appropriate refinements of the business model applied to these customers, especially in the areas of credit risk management and cost-of-delivery. Retail banks not weighed down by NPLs and pre-NPL issues would seem to have the advantage in winning the battle for the SMEs. But the larger reach and bigger resources of corporate

Exhibit 3.3 Many Korean large corporates are still unsustainable

Interest coverage ratio*	Number of listed companies,** 2000	Total debt, 2000	
	100% = 585	100% = US$270 bn	
More than 200			
S&P "BBB" rating requires 290	36.4	34.7	• ~40% of companies will not be sustainable in the long run
100–200	21.2	23.4	• These companies represent 42% of debt outstanding
50–100	14.0	18.0	
0–50	9.9	15.1	
Less than 0%	18.5	8.8	

* Based on EBIT/interest expense
** Companies analyzed account for 61 percent of the economy based on revenue size

Source: McKinsey analysis

banks, their NPL problems notwithstanding, can still help them dominate this segment.

FUTURE TRENDS

In the next few years, the South Korean financial service industry will experience rapid consolidation. The government's increasingly relaxed policy on business convergence will encourage the creation of integrated financial service providers with banks at the core. The likely scenario: no more than two to three behemoths dominating the market with a few product specialists with strong spikes managing to bolster their growth. Foreign investments in the South Korean banking industry have taken on several forms, but the likely winners are those that focus on niche markets, including product or customer segments with high growth and profit potential.

Intra-industry consolidation will continue

The traditional banking sector has gone through considerable consolidation, with the number of nationwide banks decreasing from 16 in 1997 to nine at the end of 2002. The ranks of regional banks have been cut from 17 to 10 over the same period. As a result, capacity has been substantially trimmed and the overall management performance sector has improved significantly since 1998. For example, the industry's average net interest margin rose from 2.52 percent in 1998 to 3.04 percent in 2001, while the average cost-to-income ratio declined from 62.5 percent to 39.3 percent.

Initially, the government was the main driver of bank mergers. But the private sector has begun consolidating on its own in an effort to secure competitiveness through economies of scale and of scope. Kookmin Bank and H&CB started the trend in 2001. Securities brokerages are also testing the M&A waters. Their numbers had soared after government deregulation in 1997, but intense competition has resulted in significant falls in brokerage commissions. A merger can ensure survival and bring economies of scale in research, marketing, and IT systems. But the difficulties should not be underestimated, given the clout of labor unions and potential customer attrition. Brokers closely watched the merger in 2002 of Shinhan and Good Morning Securities. Most companies are happy with the increase in margins a consolidation brings, but do not want to lead the effort.

On the insurance front, consolidation is expected to be limited because the life and non-life areas are already considerably concentrated. The top three companies took up nearly 80 percent of the life insurance market as of the end of 2001, and around 60 percent of the non-life insurance segment. Mergers and acquisitions will proceed among small players, but consolidation among the majors that can have potentially large repercussions seems unlikely.

Dominant integrated services providers will emerge

After intra-industry consolidation, the next logical step is industry convergence. For South Korea, the model is Europe. Until 1980, the Continent's financial sector had been segregated into well-defined segments, which is the case with South Korea today. But the birth of the European Union and more recently the advent of the euro are spurring consolidation and convergence, resulting in the emergence of integrated financial service providers. In 1997 bancassurance and universal banking entities accounted for 40 percent of the retail and commercial banking market, and close to 20 percent of the insurance sector. Integrated service providers are expected to dominate Europe's financial landscape going forward.

Given the government's deregulation bent, it seems only a matter of time for similar conglomerations to emerge in South Korea. The key factor driving financial convergence is the customer's need for one-stop shopping, multi-channel convenience and comprehensive financial advice offerings. South Korea is already developing the infrastructure to make these services possible, including customer relationship management skills and financial planning tools backed by advances in technology that continuously upgrade customer experiences.

The question is not whether the integrated services model will succeed, but which type of financial institutions would be the main winner in the

Exhibit 3.4 Wealthy Korean customers trust banks more than the other financial institutions

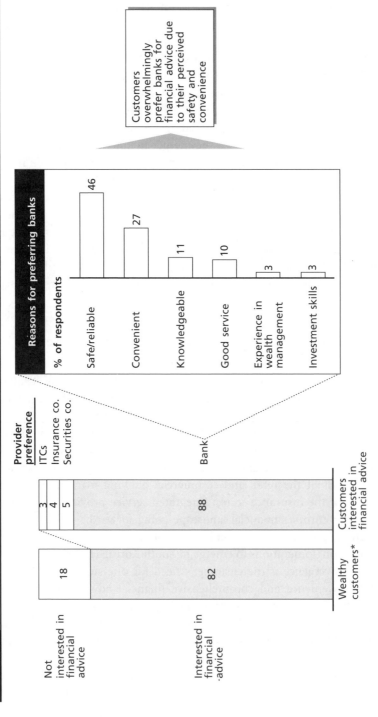

* Customers holding more than $300,000 in financial assets

Source: Wealthy Customer Survey, 2002; McKinsey analysis

convergence trend. Banks in South Korea have earned the trust of most financial customers (see Exhibit 3.4), so bank-driven integrated financial service providers would seem to have an edge. However, it will take some time for this model to fully realize its potential because of government restrictions on banks engaging in non-banking activities and the banks' own lack of cross-selling capabilities at the branch level. The development speed and success of bank-driven integrated financial service providers will depend on how deregulation in business convergence evolves and to what extent banks improve their cross-selling capabilities.

The emergence of an integrated services model is most visible in bancassurance. Foreign-based insurance companies have already begun building and strengthening cooperation with domestic banks, such as the strategic alliances struck by Allianz and ING with Hana Bank and Kookmin Bank, respectively. Shinhan Bank has also launched a joint corporation in the bancassurance arena. Given strong customer trust in South Korean banks, the training and granting of proper incentives to bank tellers could give rise to a powerful bancassurance sector, which will in turn also bring about realignment in the insurance sector.

Any bank with a limited distribution network and customer base will be handicapped when regulators finally allow convergence. This early, banks should be seriously working on these issues through mergers or acquisitions (M&A). Moreover, they should decide where and how to build strong in-house capabilities, and must put significant effort into besting competitors in the area in which they decide to specialize. Combining average or below-average businesses is not a value-creating exercise. What will distinguish the successful integrated financial services provider will be excellence in core areas such as distribution, operations, and risk management.

Kookmin Bank and the financial institutions under the Samsung Group look most likely to emerge as powerful integrated financial services providers (see Exhibit 3.5). Kookmin has built an extensive customer base and distribution network, and has won customer trust. The bank has also demonstrated outstanding performance vis-à-vis the competition in major product categories, including credit cards. The Samsung Group has also earned market trust because of the quality of its services, and has maintained a leading position in all product and service areas in the non-banking sector for retaining and expanding customer relationships. There is a key drawback: Samsung does not yet own a bank to serve as the core of the integrated financial services provider it may launch.

Shinhan Bank and the Woori Financial Group have also adopted the integrated services model as their long-term strategic direction. They have already transformed their organizational structures along the lines of a financial holding company. However, both need to overcome various

Exhibit 3.5 2–3 leading players likely to dominate the Korean financial service industry

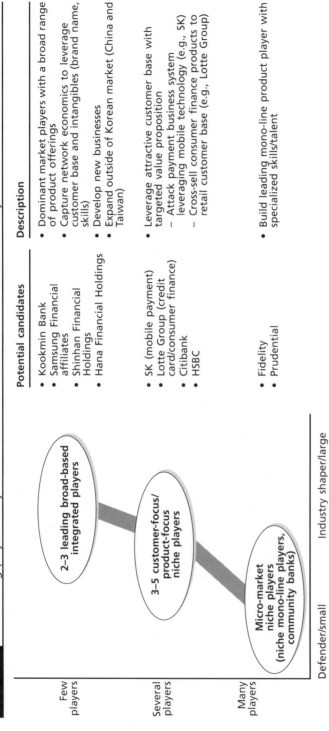

	Potential candidates	Description
2–3 leading broad-based integrated players	• Kookmin Bank • Samsung Financial affiliates • Shinhan Financial Holdings • Hana Financial Holdings	• Dominant market players with a broad range of product offerings • Capture network economics to leverage customer base and intangibles (brand name, skills) • Develop new businesses • Expand outside of Korean market (China and Taiwan)

3–5 customer-focus/ product-focus niche players	• SK (mobile payment)
	• Lotte Group (credit card/consumer finance)
	• Citibank
	• HSBC
		• Leverage attractive customer base with targeted value proposition
		  – Attack payment business system leveraging mobile technology (e.g., SK)
		  – Cross-sell consumer finance products to retail customer base (e.g., Lotte Group)

Micro-market niche players (niche mono-line players, community banks)	• Fidelity • Prudential	• Build leading mono-line product player with specialized skills/talent

Few players

Several players

Many players

Defender/small   Industry shaper/large

Market capitalization (size)

Source: McKinsey analysis

challenges if they are to become winners. They need to further strengthen their network and brand-building campaigns, and work harder to convince the market that their plans will generate true value instead of just promote a name.

Specialists with core competencies will survive

The emergence of integrated financial services providers does not necessarily ring the death toll for other types of financial companies in South Korea. There are highly successful specialists in other places where the convergence trend is under way. In Europe, for example, MLP is a leader in wealth management, while Abbey National is a provider of choice in traditional banking and mortgages. Specialists such as Fidelity in asset management, Visa and MasterCard in credit-card processing, and Charles Schwab in securities brokering have a significant presence worldwide. The main reason for their success is that they wisely concentrated on shoring up their competitiveness in their core skills, instead of trying to be all things to everyone and ending up selling inferior proprietary products to their existing customers.

Two segments particularly lend themselves to product specialization in South Korea: credit cards and asset management. In credit cards, the success factors include CRM and marketing capabilities, credit risk management and alliance-building skills. Mono-line credit card issuers in South Korea excel in the above areas because they are more flexible than banks in recruiting and retaining people with the necessary skills. The human resources policies and systems at many banks are still geared toward generalists rather than specialists, contributing to their laggard performance in credit cards.

LG Card has increased market share from 10 percent in 1996 to 24 percent in 2001. Fellow mono-line player Samsung Card has also seen its share rise to 23 percent from 13 percent in the same period. In contrast, the consortium of bank credit card businesses known as BC suffered a drop in market share from 42 percent to 32 percent. Local mono-line players are expected to make more gains going forward, but their competitive advantage is not big enough to label them as sure winners. The banks could still get their human resources act together, and global specialists such as GE Capital, MBNA, and Capital One are seeking to enter the South Korean market.

In asset management, the key success factors are innovative product development, fund management skills, and a strong performance-oriented culture. Again, the banks are at a disadvantage here. They do have existing trust units that develop asset management products (different from US trust units that focus on the custody business). But conservatism reigns here like in the rest of the organization. Domestic investment trust companies (ITCs, which manage products akin to mutual funds) have more innovative mindsets than banks, but these companies have yet to recover the public's trust. Some ITCs became insolvent when the corporate bonds they invested in became worthless as the issuing *chaebol* went bankrupt.

All this plays into the hands of new players, including foreigners like Franklin Templeton and Schroders, which are steadily increasing their assets under management in South Korea. Fidelity, UBS Asset Management, and Merrill Lynch Investment are also making inroads. Sustainable success, however, will depend on the development of South Korea's capital markets.

Product-centered, niche-focused foreign investment will thrive

Foreign investment will likely come in three forms. The first model takes as its goal the build-up of product-development capabilities in areas with high potential for profit or growth. At the same time, it also aims to create cross-selling platforms through strategic investments in banks with extensive distribution networks. The second model takes as its strategy the injection of capital in companies under pressure from industry consolidation and convergence. It focuses on restructuring and turning around the acquired assets so they can be sold at a profit. The third model is a straightforward investment in an existing wealth management operation focused on high net worth or upper affluent customers. The investor does not need to spend heavily on infrastructure because one is already in place.

Two examples of the first model are ING's investment in Kookmin Bank and Allianz's involvement in Hana Bank. Interestingly, the two foreign investors have a lot in common. They are building up their ability to tailor bancassurance and asset management products for South Korea on the basis of their in-depth know-how. They have also chosen to gain access to an extensive customer base and distribution network by buying into the consolidation leaders of the retail and commercial banking sector. The returns from this investment will come not only from the volume sale of bancassurance and asset management products leveraging on the distribution networks of strategic partners. The foreigners can also gain from improved stock valuations when their partners become integrated financial services providers. The price-to-earnings ratios of South Korean retail and commercial banks with ROEs of 15–20 percent currently hover around six to seven times earnings. Similar performers in Asia and Europe trade at up to 15–20 times earnings.

The second model is represented by Carlyle's purchase of KorAm Bank and Newbridge's investment in Korea First Bank. These acquisitions were made after the financial crisis, when bank values had plummeted. The two private equity firms operated on the assumption that they could turn the banks around by improving decision-making, focusing management's energies on maximizing market value, and promoting transparency in corporate governance. They have succeeded to an extent, but neither Carlyle nor Newbridge has succeeded in improving the bottom line enough to allow them to sell out at a premium.

For example, Korea First Bank succeeded in trimming its branch network, but failed to persuade the labor unions to sanction job cuts. The result: a cost-to-income ratio higher than 70 percent as the same number of employees staff fewer offices. It remains to be seen whether private equity firms could ever realize the hefty financial gains they envision. They may succeed if they find a way to work around the unions. Otherwise, they may have to find a buyer willing to take the assets off their hands at the same price they paid for them.

The third model is the route chosen by Goldman Sachs and Credit Suisse First Boston (CSFB) in investment banking, Citibank and HSBC in banking services targeted at affluent customers, and Merrill Lynch in wealth management. Goldman and CSFB are already reaping gains from large-sized direct financing, a corporate segment that local players have not yet entered. South Korean investment bankers do not have the capital and talent to go head to head with the foreigners. Citibank and HSBC are making some headway, but extending their reach beyond the major urban areas has been difficult. Local banks with the desired distribution networks are priced too highly. HSBC showed keen interest when the government tried to sell Seoulbank on the cheap, but the deal did not push through. Merrill Lynch and Citibank are moving aggressively in the wealth management area, but winners here are hard to call because many domestic banks are also entering the race.

Which foreign investment model has the best chances of succeeding? The most promising would seem to be the strategy of cementing exclusive alliances with a local bank and leveraging on its distribution and customer networks. The acquire-rehabilitate-and-sell model could pay off only if the foreign investor has put in place a strong enough management team that can work effectively with the unions. The third model can potentially bring handsome returns, but the investor must be prepared to see little or no profits while the capital markets remain undeveloped. It could take at least three to four years for South Korea's pension program to be reformed and harnessed in the cause of asset management.

The longevity of joint ventures between foreign players and domestic ones is never guaranteed. For now, local banks are reaching out, eager to tap the expertise that international institutions can bring. But once a South Korean partner builds up its own skills and capabilities, it may decide that it has little need for an ally from overseas. Foreign investors have to keep this in mind as they manage their partnerships and aim to become a case study for success in this critical Asian market.

The flurry of foreign investor interest in Korea is testament to the depth of its economic restructuring since the 1997 crisis. The crucial question is whether reforms will continue, further unleashing competitive forces. In February 2003, human rights lawyer Roh Moo-hyun took over as president from veteran politician Kim Dae-jung. Roh's plate has been full: the crisis over North Korea's nuclear weapons program, a profits-reporting scandal at conglomerate SK Group, and liquidity troubles at local credit card companies. He has also had to deal with the effects of the war in Iraq, the spread of the SARS virus in Asia, and the flagging global economy.

The government insists that it will push ahead with reforms. Korea has little choice. "Over the past five years, a social consensus has evolved that the only way to advance is to continue to reform," Deputy Prime Minister Kim Jin-pyo told the *Financial Times* newspaper in April. "This consensus is unshakeable, whoever is in government." That may be so. Still, there is much to do. Having transformed itself from basket case to case study, Korea has some way to go before it can be labeled a real success story.

4

India: Market of Extremes

Macroeconomics

- GDP[1] ($bn)   488
- GDP per capital ($)   472
- PPP GDP per capita ($)   3,042
- Exports ($bn/% of GDP)   45/9
- Imports ($bn/% of GDP)   55/11
- FDI inflow ($bn/% of GDP)   3.4/0.7
- FDI outflow ($bn/% of GDP)   0.04/0
- Foreign currency reserves ($bn/% of GDP)   71/15
- External debt ($bn/% of GDP)   94/19
- NPL of banks ($bn/% of total net loans)   14/11
- National government borrowing
  ($bn/% of GDP/% external)   275/56/5
- Top 3 trading partners   US, U.K., Belgium
- Number of corporates in Global Top 500[2]   1

Socioeconomics

- Population (mn)   1,034
- Number of households (mn)   181
- Average urban household income[3] ($)   4,721
- Number of households earning >$100K p.a.[3] (mn)   0.48
- Mobile phones/100 population   0.5
- Internet subscribers/100 population   0.8
- Urbanization (% of population)   33
- % of population with university degrees   2
- % of population above 65 years old in 2001
  and 2021   6/10

Capital Markets

- Number of listed corporations   5,795
- Equity market capitalization[4] ($bn/% of GDP)   118/24
- Trading volume ($bn/% of market cap)   243/206
- Debt market capitalization ($bn/% of GDP)   6/1.2
- Equity underwriting[5] ($bn/% of GDP)   1/0.2
- Debt underwriting[5] ($bn/% of GDP)   9/2
- M&A ($bn/% of GDP)   4/0.8
- Retail assets under management ($bn)   15
- Institutional assets under management ($bn)   6

Banking Markets

- Total loans of all financial institutions, including non-banks ($bn/% of GDP)   168/34
- Total deposits of all financial institutions, including non-banks ($bn/% of GDP) 263/54
- Mortgages ($bn/% of GDP)   8/2
- Personal loans ($bn/% of GDP)   7/2
- Credit card receivables ($bn/% of GDP)   0.5/0
- Credit cards per person above 15   0.01
- Credit card spend as % of household total spend   1
- Foreign ownership limit in 1997 and 2002[6] (%)   26/49
- Number of banks in Global Top 1,000 in 1997 and 2001   7/3
- Number of ATMs/1,000 urban population   0.007
- Number of branches/1,000 urban population   0.15
- Number of banking employees/1,000 urban population   2.56

---

[1] At 2001 prices
[2] *The Fortune Global 500*: July 22, 2002
[3] Based on estimates from National Council of Applied Economic Research
[4] Based on Mumbai Stock Exchange
[5] Average from 1995–2001
[6] Since February 2003, the government allowed up to 74 percent foreign ownership, except for
     public sector banks (limited to 20 percent)

Note: All figures as of December 2001 unless otherwise indicated

India's Financial Landscape

Types	Number of institutions, 1997	Number of institutions, 2002	Percent of total assets 2001	Top 3 players
Government full license bank	27	27	61	• State Bank of India • Punjab National Bank • Bank of Baroda
Private full license bank	34	31	14	• ICICI Bank • HDFC Bank • Uti Bank
Foreign bank	38	42	6	• Citibank • HSBC • Standard Chartered Bank
Term lending institution*	8	7	10	• IDBI • NABARD • IFCI
Non-banking financial company (NBFC)	41,494	37,339**	3**	• Reliance Capital • Tata Finance • Sundaram Finance
Regional rural bank	196	196	1	• n/a
Cooperative bank	n/a	2,487	5	• Gujarat State Cooperative Bank • Saraswat Cooperative Bank • Madhya Pradesh Rajya Sahakari Bank
Total excluding cooperative banks	**41,797**	**37.642**	**$373bn**	

* Exclude state level institutions
** 2000 figures

In 2001, when broadcaster CNBC named India's K.V. Kamath, CEO of ICICI Bank, as its first Asian Business Leader of the Year, many were surprised by the choice. The judges had considered dozens of corporate chiefs from over 10 countries. If they had wanted to recognize a financier, the selectors could easily have given the award to a more famous figure from one of the big banks in Hong Kong or Singapore. In the end, they picked Kamath for transforming ICICI from "a term lending institution into a technology-driven, customer-centric, virtual universal bank," explained economist Lester Thurow, a member of the panel, when the choice was announced.

Tribute well deserved. Only a decade since its establishment, ICICI Bank has emerged as India's largest private-sector bank and its second-biggest commercial bank. Along the way, Kamath has significantly driven up shareholder value – ICICI's share price rose by an average of 24.9 percent a year from October 1997 to October 2002. ICICI and other new privately owned Indian banks such as HDFC Bank that are aspiring to be world-class have been helped by three key factors: a significant rise in personal income driven by average real GDP growth of 6.1 percent over the last 10 years; a benign regulatory environment that promotes competition; and with few exceptions, the inability of incumbent public-sector and old private-sector banks to adapt to market liberalization.

All this suggests that India's banking sector, though still relatively small by global standards, could hold significant opportunities. After all, for many foreign players, India is already a major target market. Citibank and Standard Chartered Bank, together, account for more than half of all credit card receivables and personal loans drawn. This possibly translates into an annual profit of about $30–50 million each. Already, about one-tenth of Standard Chartered Bank's revenues come from its India operations. "In the medium term, China will be huge for us, but our short-term focus is on India," Mervyn Davies, chief executive of the London-based bank, told reporters in late 2002. "Today you're limited as to what you can do in China; in India, you're not."

⚜

India versus China: The great debate

Investors looking for opportunities in Asia often ask themselves which economy is more attractive – India or China? Many will go into both markets. But then which should be the priority? The two countries are both large, each accounting for about one-fifth of the world's population. China is the world's sixth-largest economy, while India is the 13th. Both are among the fastest growing in the world. Since China joined the World

Trade Organization (WTO) in 2001, both are now full members of the global trading club. One key difference: While China has seen the ranks of its middle class swell in recent years, official figures indicate that India's personal income growth has been concentrated at the top end of the social spectrum. Many India watchers, however, strenuously dispute this, arguing that substantial under-reporting of personal income has meant that the size of India's middle class has been grossly underestimated.

As far as banking goes, China lags. In some ways, the Chinese banking industry resembles India's before the implementation of reforms. State-owned banks dominate, interest rates are tightly controlled by the central bank, and a capital market culture has yet to develop. Foreign banks, which account for less than 2 percent of total banking assets, face many restrictions. Non-performing loans (NPLs) are officially stated at 25 percent of total loans but could be as high as 50 percent.

To meet its WTO commitments, China will have to open its banking sector to foreign investors over the coming years. Foreign banks, for example, will be able to do local currency business with Chinese corporations in 2004 and with retail customers in 2007. But the pace of liberalization will be gradual as the central bank can be expected to wield tight control on the issuing of licenses to operate and open new branches, and the granting of permission for foreign investors to take stakes in domestic banks.

In contrast, foreign banks enjoy a great deal of freedom in India. In the past five years, Citibank and HSBC have rapidly widened their branch networks, while other players such as Standard Chartered Bank, ABN AMRO Bank, and ING have grown their businesses significantly. Most are planning further expansion.

Is India the better bet? Not necessarily. With over $2 trillion in assets, China's banking sector is nearly six-fold larger than India's. Not surprising, since China's GDP is 2.5 times India's output. Compare banking penetration as measured by the ratio of banking assets to GDP: 1.6 in China; 0.6 in India. Moreover, the Chinese banking sector is growing at 12 percent a year in US dollar terms, compared to 9 percent in India.

China and India are both long-term growth stories. The potential appears to be far higher in China, although it could easily take a decade or more for a foreign bank to make profits. India's banking sector, on the other hand, is already fairly open to foreign participation, but it is smaller – only the 12th largest in the world. To be sure, the pace of reform in India is likely to accelerate over the next few years, providing even greater freedom for foreign players. However, China is also liberalizing and will remain the bigger market. Still, new growth opportunities are likely to ripen much sooner in India.

Yet that sort of hype cannot change the fact that, like China, India will take some time to reach its full potential. While the banking sector is far more efficient and competitive than it was a decade ago, it is still in the throes of a wrenching, reform-driven transformation. The majority of the old-guard private-sector and state-owned banks continue to perform poorly and are badly in need of restructuring. Although they account for over 80 percent of total banking assets, their combined profitability, measured by ROA, is a paltry 0.4 percent. Most still focus on serving value-destroying, commodity-based industries, which were hardest hit by the liberalization of trade in the 1990s.

The dinosaur banks have been caught in a vicious circle as the lack of capital and talent prevents them from investing in the technological and operational improvements needed to keep up with the new breed of high-performing banks.

Also holding them back is the persistent problem of NPLs, 90 percent of which are held by the old-guard institutions (see Exhibit 4.1). NPLs are officially at 12 percent of all loans but international rating agencies estimate that the real figure is more than twice that. The key reasons for the high level of bad debts – capital misallocation, poor governance, and ineffective regulations – are problems that still need to be comprehensively addressed.

Another reason why growth opportunities in India's banking sector may still be limited is that, according to official figures, the country has a relatively small middle class, with much of the population still poor. There is much debate about this. Many India analysts strongly argue that substantial under-reporting of income means that the real size of the middle class is significantly larger than official numbers suggest. According to an estimate by India's National Council of Applied Economic Research, 47 percent of the total 181 million households have an annual income of at least $2,500.

While it may be difficult to reliably determine exactly how big India's middle class is, what is clear is that economic reforms in recent years led to a significant increase in overall personal income, with the most robust growth among the richest segments of the population. The middle income segment, defined as households with an annual income between $2,500 and $16,000, grew by 65 percent between 1994 and 2002 to reach 39 million. Meanwhile, households with income between $16,000 and $100,000 grew by 142 percent to 3.3 million and those with income greater than $100,000 grew by nearly 137 percent to 374,000.

| **Exhibit 4.1** | Reported gross NPLS in the Indian financial sector |

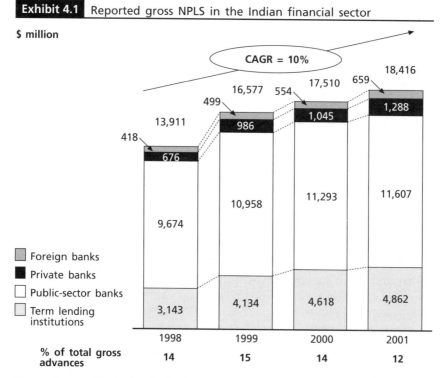

Source: Reserve Bank of India (RBI); annual reports; recovery specialist interviews

What all this means is that for now, banks may not have all that many lucrative alternatives when it comes to choosing a winning strategy in India – target the very rich with wealth management services, go for the mass market with low-cost deposit accounts and micro-credit, or do both. There may be some middle income consumer opportunities such as mortgages and credit cards, and niche plays such as corporate banking that may grow fast and prove profitable, but they may take some time to become major businesses. For now, in approaching the Indian market, banks would do well to aim high or low – and not expect too much from the middle.

In short, banking in India is a sector of extremes: nimble new attackers compete with lumbering veterans that still dominate; opportunities for growth tend mainly to be at the high and low ends of the market. Over the next few years, there is likely to be enhanced competition and significant consolidation as the high-performing players leverage their strong capital base and the conducive regulatory environment to capture the value-creating opportunities through inorganic growth. It is against this backdrop that both current players and prospective investors will need to assess their strategic position.

THE IMPACT OF LIBERALIZATION

India's financial sector is dominated by public-sector institutions that were created after India's independence in 1947. Facing little external competition, they thrived in the tightly controlled economy as they focused on fulfilling the State's social agenda of promoting rapid industrialization and bringing financial services to the rural masses. Economic reforms in early 1990s brought gradual competition in the form of new private and foreign players. Planned development gave way to liberalization.

The transformation started when the central bank – the Reserve Bank of India (RBI) – introduced stringent asset classification, income recognition, and capital adequacy requirements to modernize the banking sector and align it with international standards. The RBI followed up by allowing more foreign banks and domestic private players to establish operations. As a result, 19 foreign institutions and nine new Indian private-sector banks started greenfield operations between 1992 and 1998. Today, although these new banks account for only 14 percent of total assets, they have managed to capture 25 percent of the sector's profits. The commercial banking segment now includes 100 banks with some 52,000 branches and an asset base of $296 billion. The 27 public-sector banks continue to dominate, with nearly 80 percent of total assets and 95 percent of branches.

The capital markets too were liberalized. Until the mid-1980s, the state-sponsored Unit Trust of India was the only mutual fund in the country. But growth in the nascent capital markets led to several public-sector banks and financial institutions – State Bank of India, Canara Bank, and Life Insurance Corporation of India, among them – to enter the business through newly floated mutual fund subsidiaries. In 1993 the sector opened further to private and foreign participation. The number of players increased to over 30. UTI tried to stall an accelerated decline in its market share by promoting assured-return schemes, but its market share progressively declined to less than 50 percent due to the strong competition. Several mutual fund subsidiaries of public-sector banks have suffered losses due to poor performance and either wound up or sold out to other strategic investors. Their loss has been the private sector's gain. With strong competition in the mutual fund sector, the stage is now set for consolidation.

Enter the new attackers

The biggest beneficiaries of banking sector reforms have been the new private-sector and foreign banks. These players have leveraged the favorable regulatory environment to expand their operations and franchises, capturing a disproportionate share of profits as a result.

When the RBI invited applications for new bank licenses, it wanted to create a new cadre of private-sector players that would be technology savvy and able to cater to a level of customer service that Indians had never known. Consider this: Until the mid-1990s, not a single one of the old-guard banks offered its customers ATM and telebanking facilities. There were only 60 ATMs in the country, nearly all of them belonging to foreign banks. Branches were the only service channel available to the customer, but these were inefficient due to the lack of computerization.

To take advantage of the reforms being introduced, several dominant financial institutions such as UTI (India's largest mutual fund), HDFC (the biggest mortgage provider), the Industrial Development Bank of India, and ICICI (the two largest term lending institutions) set up banking subsidiaries. They and five other new private players were awarded banking licenses – a total of nine – by the RBI.

The advent of these new banks was a landmark in India's banking history. Middle-income and affluent Indians, especially in the major cities, finally got a taste of fast and efficient customer service and were presented with a wide choice of products and channels. They switched over to these new banks in droves. Between 1996 and 2001, the new players grew 54 percent a year. By the end of that period, they accounted for 6.2 percent of assets and 9.9 percent of profits.

Foreign banks were the other beneficiaries of the financial sector reforms. Until the mid-to-late 1990s, foreign banks faced significant restrictions in India: the number of branches they could open was restricted, they were not allowed to incorporate locally and had to operate as branches of their international parent, and they were not allowed to acquire over 20 percent equity in Indian banks. The regulatory environment has eased considerably in the last few years. Foreign banks now have the option of converting their Indian operations into local subsidiaries and thereby enjoying the advantage of lower taxation and the opportunity to build a much bigger branch network. The cap on foreign ownership of a local bank (except public sector banks) was raised in February 2003 to 74%.

Several foreign players have leveraged the relaxation of restrictions to establish a firm foothold in India. Dutch bank ING, which entered the market by acquiring a 10 percent stake in Vysya Bank in 1997, is a good example. ING took advantage of the gradual liberalization of foreign ownership to up its stake in Vysya to 20 percent in 1999 and again to 44 percent in 2002. It subsequently acquired management control. ING has formed several alliances with Vysya to enter the mutual fund, life insurance, and consumer finance businesses.

Citibank and HSBC, both of which have been in India for over 100 years, have also managed strong growth in the last five years. Citibank tripled its presence to 20 branches while HSBC's network expanded to 30, an increase of 10. Other foreign banks plan even more aggressive growth. Standard Chartered Bank aims to open 40 more branches by 2005 to bring its total to 100.

HDFC Bank: Creating value

If there is one bank in India that has consistently captured the investor's fancy ever since it was floated and managed to deliver superior returns, it is HDFC Bank. Its share price trades at three times price-to-book value, nearly five times the industry average and twice that of the next-best performing bank, ICICI. In 2002, *Forbes Global* magazine ranked it among the world's 200 best small companies (those with $1 billion or less in revenue) outside the United States.

One of the nine private-sector banks that set up shop in the mid-1990s, HDFC Bank has a pedigree that gives it a natural advantage over the competition. The bank's very name has been synonymous with trust and service in the Indian mortgage market. On top of this, the new bank strengthened its position by instilling a quality mindset among its staff. It hired only the best managers. A former Citibanker was brought in as CEO, while several executives from leading foreign banks filled senior positions in treasury, credit, operations, IT, and corporate banking. HDFC Bank was one of the first Indian banks to offer employees stock options, which proved a major attraction for top-notch talent.

The bank differentiated itself by focusing on specific niches where it has staked out the top position. HDFC Bank emerged as the leader in capital market services within five years of its establishment by capitalizing on the growth of electronic trading in India's stock exchanges and offering the entire gamut of services including clearing, depository services, and margin-lending for all participants. HDFC Bank has shot to the front in the retail business as well. In 2001, HDFC Bank was the largest issuer of debit cards and the third-largest cross-seller of mutual funds in the banking sector. It also saw a major opportunity in cash management services as large public-sector banks lacked the expertise and processing capacity despite their extensive branch networks. HDFC Bank leveraged its strength in technology and processing and its rapidly expanding presence to set up a robust cash management platform.

HDFC Bank's initiatives have been backed by robust credit skills and operational efficiency. The bank has managed to contain its non-performing assets to below 1 percent by putting in place a stringent credit-approval process and focusing on the top 300 companies in the country. The bank has made up for the low spread in this segment by strong cross-selling, as well as creating large corporate-centered supply-chain solutions. Sharp focus on costs has ensured a cost-to-income ratio of 36 percent, the lowest in its peer set.

HDFC Bank has proven itself to be a trendsetter in more ways than one. The bank heralded the consolidation era in Indian banking when it acquired Times Bank, a private-sector bank, in 2000. With $5 billion in assets, HDFC Bank's size is still relatively small compared to other banks such as the State Bank of India ($70 billion) and ICICI ($21 billion). Whatever path it takes to grow, HDFC Bank has already shown that a player with a global skill set and the ability to spot local opportunities can create significant value in the Indian financial sector.

The old guard strikes back

Even as the majority of public-sector banks have lost market share in recent years, a few such as the State Bank of India (SBI) and Life Insurance Corporation have begun to take some deliberate steps to reclaim their former dominance. These institutions are investing heavily in IT, re-engineering their business processes, and focusing on the previously ignored personal financial services segment. They are likely to play an industry-shaping role in the future.

After the banking sector opened to new entrants, SBI – the largest commercial bank with 9,000 branches and over 90 million customers – began losing market share. In 1999, SBI's share in retail deposits in the top 20 retail centers had declined to 15 percent. It only had a 2 percent share of the lucrative credit card business and 8 percent of the mortgages, though it controlled 24 percent of the overall banking market.

SBI then launched a concerted effort to increase its share in retail assets and drew up a blueprint to address the core reason for its loss of market share: its lagging operating capabilities. It earmarked $125 million for IT initiatives such as the implementation of a core banking platform, computerization and networking of its branches, and the launch of Internet and ATM channels over a span of three years. This was the largest technology investment announced by any Indian institution.

The results have already started to show. SBI now has 3,000 computerized branches, up from 1,211 in 1998, and 1,000 new ATMs. More than 150 high-potential branches offer Internet banking. The bank plans to have 80 percent of its business online by 2004. SBI's retail business too has grown. Its share in new mortgage disbursements increased to 15 percent in 2001. The following year, SBI accounted for 14 percent of credit cards, making it India's third-largest card issuer.

Life Insurance Corporation (LIC) is making similar large investments in IT and forming strategic alliances to counter competition from over 10 new private players. LIC has computerized all its 2,050 branches and introduced several technology-enabled initiatives such as online payments, information kiosks, and call centers for its urban customers. It acquired a large strategic stake in the Corporation Bank, the best performing public-sector bank, and sizable stakes in similar banks to form bancassurance alliances and expand its retail reach. Following the purchases, then chairman G.N. Bajpai declared that his vision was to transform LIC into a "financial super umbrella."

Between them, India's public-sector banks and government-owned insurance company have nearly 460 million customers. As these institutions invest significantly over the next few years to improve infrastructure and services, or get acquired by stronger and more customer-focused institutions, the corresponding impact on retail business growth will be huge.

Creeping consolidation

Financial reforms will continue to play out over the rest of this decade. As this happens, there is likely to be significant consolidation in the banking sector. The process has already started as small banks seek capital and high-performing banks seek scale. India's recent decision to permit a foreign strategic investor to own up to 74 percent of a local bank will further promote such transactions.

If consolidation works out to its logical end, the industry is likely to polarize into three distinct categories (see Exhibit 4.2):

Universal banks: With their international aspirations, two or three big players would have the potential to be leaders in Asia and industry-shapers. They would play across the spectrum of segments, products and geographies, and could account for 40–50 percent of the India market. SBI and ICICI are natural contenders.

Large domestic banks: The three or four such players of this type would have national scale but with a bigger presence in their home territory. Each would account for 5–7 percent of nationwide market share. The Bank of Baroda and Punjab National Bank are likely to fall into this category.

Small local banks: These players would use their entrepreneurial spirit, regional links, and product skills to identify and serve gaps in the financial sector. Included among them would be nearly 40 small foreign banks, which account for less than 5 percent of total bank capital. They could survive as niche players, using access to parent capital, technology, and management talent.

Exhibit 4.2 Likely evolution of India's banking sector after restructuring

Potential industry structure, 2005

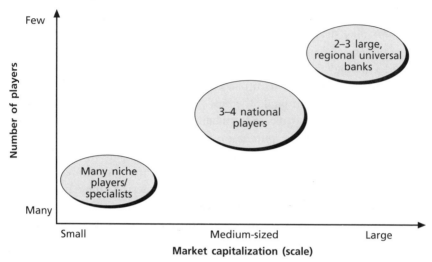

Source: McKinsey analysis

As several recent merger and acquisition (M&A) deals indicate, the universal banking aspirants will drive the consolidation process. Take HDFC Bank's acquisition of the Times Bank and LIC's purchase of a stake in the Corporation Bank. In 2001, ICICI Bank, the country's second-largest bank, acquired the Bank of Madura, an old private-sector bank, to boost its presence in southern India. It also has significant shares in the Federal Bank and the South Indian Bank, two other private-sector banks. Regulations mandate a minimum 51 percent state ownership in public-sector banks. The government is considering reducing this to 33 percent. Such a move would indicate a genuine commitment on Delhi's part to loosen its hold over these banks. The pace of consolidation would accelerate considerably.

AIMING FOR THE HIGH END

With the sharp rise in personal income levels among India's affluent and high-income households, not least because of the technology boom that has made many young entrepreneurs wealthy, this segment of the banking market has become a highly interesting opportunity. Rich Indians have traditionally been served by the veteran foreign banks such as Citibank and HSBC. But recently, others such as BNP Paribas and the new private-sector banks, including the HDFC Bank and the ICICI Bank, have launched targeted products aimed at the top-end customer. Leading brokerages such as Kotak Securities and DSP Merrill Lynch have created a niche in this market by providing strong research and execution capabilities in the equity markets to wealthy clients with a high appetite for risk.

The majority of the services offered by banks are bundled offerings, varying by convenience and the quality of advice given by relationship managers. These are not true private banking services. The lack of capital account convertibility and restrictions on the delivery of discretionary portfolio management prevent banks from offering customers a multi-currency global suite of products central to private banking.

Despite such regulatory constraints, wealth management services have shown significant growth. Banks that started providing them recently have had to raise the minimum deposit to be eligible two to three times to cope with the customer interest. HSBC, which started its wealth management service in 1999 with a minimum relationship size of $100,000, progressively raised it over three years to $300,000. Other banks such as ING, Deutsche, and BNP Paribas have taken similar steps.

The business is growing at an average rate of at least 30 percent a year, with Mumbai and Delhi accounting for 50–75 percent of the market. Revenue per customer, even for the lower end of the super-affluent segment, can run as high as $1,500 a year, suggesting that a relationship manager has the potential to generate $100,000 a year for his bank. By 2010, India will have about 900,000 households with an income greater than $100,000 a year (at 2002 prices), 50 percent more than in 2002. With such growth in prospect, the wealth management business is set to continue to expand just as robustly.

STRONG GROWTH IN MORTGAGES AND CARDS

Banks have also found attractive opportunities in retail banking. India has 52 million urban households. With nearly 60 percent of total income, this segment could be a very attractive one for banks to tap. The personal financial services market is dominated by deposit products, which account for more than 70 percent of the total income pool. This is not surprising considering India's high savings rate of 23.7 percent and the underdeveloped insurance and capital markets. While revenues from deposits and investment products are expected to grow an average 11–15 percent per year over the next few years in line with the overall growth of commercial banking, the fastest growing retail business will be credit products, including mortgages and credit cards (see Exhibit 4.3).

The mortgages market is growing strongly at 30 percent a year, driven by attractive tax benefits, lower interest rates, rising real incomes, and the availability of affordable real estate. Mortgage leader HDFC's market share of fresh disbursements has declined from 57 percent to 47 percent in the last three years, despite a healthy growth in its portfolio. The reason: Several

Exhibit 4.3 PFS revenue pool in India

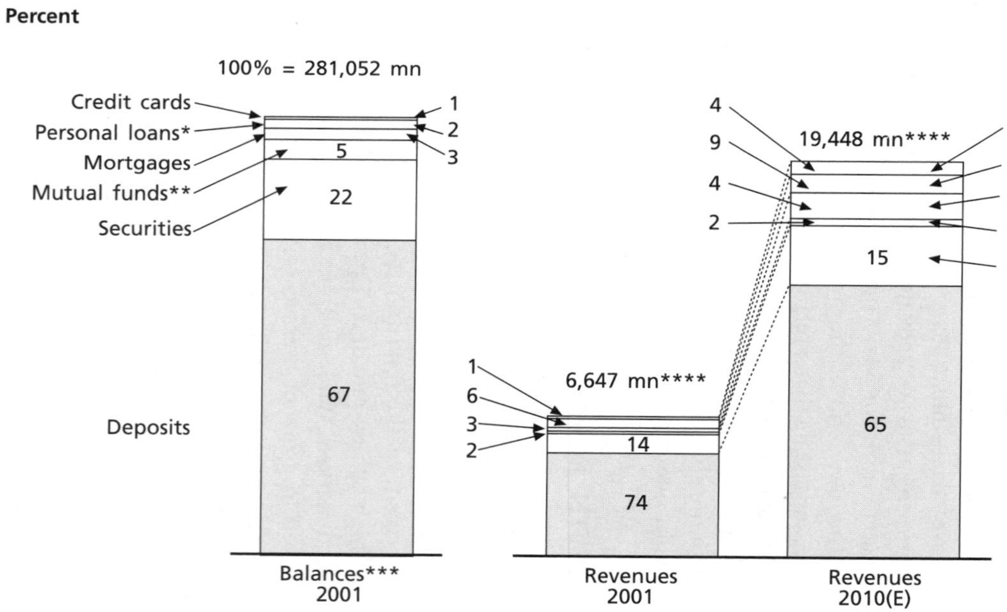

Percent

100% = 281,052 mn

	CAGR (00–10) balances	CAGR (00–10) revenue pool
Total	15	13
Credit cards	30	25
Personal loans*	22	17
Mortgages	24	20
Mutual funds**	20	15
Securities	13	14
Deposits	15	11

Balances*** 2001
- Credit cards 1
- Personal loans* 2
- Mortgages 3
- Mutual funds** 5
- Securities 22
- Deposits 67

Revenues 2001 — 6,647 mn****
- 1
- 6
- 3
- 2
- 14
- 74

Revenues 2010(E) — 19,448 mn****
- 4
- 9
- 4
- 2
- 15
- 65

* Includes secured (e.g., auto loans) and unsecured loans

** Includes only revenue accrued to distributors and not asset managers

*** Excludes life insurance ($32 billion) and long-term retirement products ($53 billion, including EPF and PPF)

**** Gross revenue; i.e., duration matched net interest revenue plus fees

Source: Reserve Bank of India (RBI); Lafferty; McKinsey analysis

foreign and new private and public-sector banks have entered into the fray to capture growth.

Until the early 1990s, the total mortgage market in India was only $1.6 billion or 0.5 percent of GDP. Average per capita income growth was less than 3 percent in real terms, making mortgages unaffordable for the typical retail customer. While HDFC was the dominant provider of mortgage loans, with a market share of nearly 60 percent, the other players were largely small finance companies. Banks had little or no presence.

But after economic liberalization was launched and the economy started growing rapidly, the mortgage market expanded, driven by a decline in interest rates and an increase in real incomes, especially in urban areas. In both 1995 and 1996, HDFC managed to push its mortgage disbursements up by over 35 percent. Recognizing the huge growth opportunity, leading banking institution such as SBI and ICICI made housing finance a priority. In 2001, SBI's mortgage loans more than doubled to $350 million, while ICICI's increased four-fold to reach $150 million. Foreign banks – including Citibank, HSBC, and Standard Chartered Bank – have also begun focusing on this market.

But despite strong growth in the last few years, the mortgage market is still small, with total assets of $8.2 billion in 2002 and penetration at just 1.7 percent of GDP, much lower than in Thailand (18 percent) or Malaysia (26 percent). Even if penetration were to double in the next five years, as it is widely expected to do, this would imply an annualized 30 percent growth rate over the next five years.

Still, the mortgage boom indicates the tremendous growth in personal financial services across India and the scramble by both foreign and domestic players to capture a share of the pie. Also holding great potential is the credit card market, which is so far highly underdeveloped. Despite a 30 percent compound annual growth rate in the number of cards issued over the last five years, there were still only 6.5 million cards in 2002 against a total pool of 250 million deposit holders. In 2000, only 1.5 percent of the total consumer expenditure of over $225 billion was transacted through cards and other electronic means – a proportion far lower than in other emerging economies.

The high growth of recent years is likely to continue, leading us to forecast that there will be over 35 million cards issued by 2010. Banks are aggressively moving into the market. The number of players has increased from less than five in the mid-1990s to over 30 players today. A 2001 McKinsey[1] survey revealed that nearly half of middle and upper income

---

[1] McKinsey Asia Personal Financial Services (PFS) Survey 2001.

consumers were open to taking out consumer loans, a sizable figure given the traditional aversion to credit. Meanwhile, the number of establishments accepting cards has been growing at an annual rate of over 30 percent to reach 100,000-plus merchants in 2002. The credit card base has been expanding fastest in the top eight metropolitan areas. Outside the top 50 urban areas, the opportunities are very thinly spread, leading players to hold back on investing in the marketing and technology infrastructure to cultivate franchises. Most players are likely to continue to focus on the biggest cities, which account for more than half of the most attractive consumer segments.

CAPTURING THE MASS MARKET

Beyond the high-end segments, the main retail opportunity is in the mass market. The new players, including foreign banks, which have typically maintained an up-market image, have been finding innovative ways to appeal to the low-end customer. Until a few years ago, most foreign banks required customers to maintain a minimum account balance of $2,000. Many catered mainly to executives at multinationals, wealthy non-resident Indians, and affluent businessmen. Both Citibank and Standard Chartered Bank are now offering credit or debit cards to those with an annual income of just $1,250.

In 1998, Citibank decided to expand its reach as part of its corporate mission to build a billion-strong global customer base by 2010. Bangalore, India's answer to Silicon Valley, became Citibank's testing ground for a mass-market campaign in India. While it kept to just one branch in the city, Citibank invested nearly $5 million in IT infrastructure and equipment, setting up 50 ATMs and 2,000 point-of-sale (POS) terminals across the city. It then launched a savings deposit product called Suvidha (meaning "convenience" in Hindi) for the mass market. Customers could open a deposit account with as little as $20 and maintain access through remote channels such as ATMs, POS terminals, e-banking, and call centers. Citibank discouraged face-to-face transactions in branches by charging a $2.50 fee each time a customer used a teller.

The scheme was a spectacular success. By early 2000, with still just a single branch, Citibank managed to build a franchise of nearly 100,000 customers and a deposit base of over $100 million in Bangalore. The customer per-branch ratio was nearly 20 times higher than the nationwide average. Inspired by its success, Citibank rolled out the same product in Mumbai and Delhi in 2001. Its Suvidha customer base swelled to 550,000. By mid-2002, about 8,000 new accounts were being opened each month. Suvidha clearly shows that, armed with the right products, a bank, including a foreign one not usually accustomed to catering to low-income customers, can create significant value in a large mass market.

LOOKING FOR NICHES

The strong competition in the Indian banking sector is forcing banks to look harder for new ways of generating revenue. There are two areas that have been gaining prominence: corporate banking and services for small and medium-sized enterprises (SMEs).

Corporate banking: The total corporate banking revenue pool in India is estimated to be $2.8 billion. Public-sector firms, with 26 percent of the revenues, form the largest segment, while multinationals, with 10 percent, make up the smallest. The corporate banking market is dominated by lending products that account for 59 percent of the total revenue, followed by cash management and deposits (12 percent), and foreign exchange (4 percent).

Competition is very high. Consequently, margins are thin: less than 100 basis points on working capital lending to high-credit-quality large corporate clients, 50 basis points for trade finance, and 2 basis points for cash management and foreign exchange (forex) services. These are likely to decline further. Over the rest of this decade, corporate banking revenue is estimated to increase by a modest 8 percent in contrast to growth of 30-plus percent expected in retail products such as cards and mortgages. However, players with strong risk management skills, innovative suite of fee-based products, and a solutions-centric mindset will continue to create value.

SMEs: The coming-of-age of the private-sector institutions and improved service standards in some public-sector banks over the last three years have sharply increased competition in the provision of corporate banking to large and very large companies. Having anticipated this, foreign banks started targeting small and medium-sized enterprises, which account for over 30 percent of India's GDP. This market had been traditionally served by public-sector banks, moneylenders, and small finance companies. SMEs had to contend with high borrowing costs, poor service, and inefficient transaction facilities. The three largest foreign banks in India – Citibank, Standard Chartered Bank, and HSBC – as well as the new private-sector domestic banks and niche players such as GE Capital, have filled these gaps and succeeded in capturing growth.

Citibank was among the first foreign players to recognize the value of catering to SMEs, launching its coverage through commercial vehicle financing. By 2001, it became the third-biggest provider of such loans. The bank tapped other emerging niches such as export financing. Citibank focused only on those sub-segments of the SME market that were attractive and where the bank could be dominant. The bank's SME revenues have doubled every year since 1999, and in 2001 it accounted for 15 percent of its entire wholesale business. Citibank has acknowledged that expansion of its reach in the SME market will power much of its future growth in India.

STRATEGIES TO WIN

Which players – foreign or domestic, privately owned or public – will come out ahead of the game in India? Simply put, the winners will be those that possess the following:

- Clear customer segmentation and a range of products and services that differentiates them from the rest of the pack;
- An unrelenting focus on cost efficiency and judicious outsourcing of products, services, or processes; and
- The entrepreneurial ability to face stiff competition.

For each type of player, there are specific priorities to pursue to stay in the game for the long haul.

Public-sector banks: The challenges for these banks are clear. None can claim to have fully computerized operations or networked branches. Overstaffing and inefficiency are widespread – average productivity is almost 4.5 times lower than that of their foreign counterparts. Almost all have failed to cultivate their retail franchise. Credit advances account for less than 17 percent of the portfolio at the most retail-focused bank. Retail exposure is only 4.5 percent of an average bank's credit book.

Despite these shortfalls, the old warhorses still have distinct strengths. They have unparalleled franchises and reach, accounting for 80 percent of assets and 95 percent of branches. They enjoy the explicit support of the central government, a significant confidence-booster for depositors. Finally, these banks are perceived to offer cheaper products and services than their private-sector rivals, a major selling point among mass-market and middle-class customers.

While these strengths may help public-sector banks recapture their former position, they will have to focus on three priorities.

First, these banks should radically reorganize operations. They are too centered on their branches, which are typically not computerized or networked. Staff and space are deployed mainly to provide services and to carry out back office work, with little time spent on acquiring new accounts. This leads to inefficiency, low sales, and customer dissatisfaction. Banks should invest heavily in technology and set up a core banking computer IT platform to boost efficiency, and offer convenient access and services to the consumer. This should be done in tandem with a radical redesign of branches to shift backroom functions out and into centralized data-processing factories. Branches can then be converted into a lean, electronically linked, sales-focused, and service-oriented channel to customers.

Second, banks should revisit their retail and corporate strategies to extract higher value out of their relationships. The average public-sector bank has a retail base of 7 million customers, almost all of them depositors. The cross-selling ratio for these customers is typically less than 1.1 products per account holder. As a first step, banks will have to defend this franchise against competition from private and foreign banks by offering customers conveniences such as telebanking, ATMs, and Internet banking – channels they can provide by investing in the right technology.

Finally, banks should aggressively put in place mechanisms to cross-sell investments, insurance, credit cards, mortgages, and other asset products that are growing at a far faster pace than deposits. Banks have two options. The first is to build the skills required to introduce the asset products from scratch. This would require building robust credit assessment skills, marketing savvy, strong technology-enabled processing capabilities, and a retail credit recovery system. Although this is likely to be time-consuming and tough, half the battle will be won if a bank can put in place regional or centralized processing factories. The alternative is to ally with global players who can provide the technology and expertise.

A revamp of operations and strategy has to be accompanied by radical restructuring and the implementation of performance management. Not all public-sector banks would be capable of taking such bold steps. Some are likely to face capital constraints that could keep them from making the requisite technology investments or pursuing the necessary organizational changes to make the transition into a more competitive player work. Still, a few such as SBI and Corporation Bank have started on the right path and are clearly positioned to win.

High-performance large private-sector and foreign banks: With the potential to become universal banks or large-scale national banks, the four banks in this category – ICICI Bank, HDFC Bank, Citibank, and Standard Chartered Bank – have been ahead of the pack in profitably capturing emerging opportunities in both retail and corporate banking. The challenge for them is to build large customer franchises in the face of constraints of their geographic reach. Consider the largest of the four, ICICI, which in 2002 had 500 branches. The average branch strength of the 27 public-sector banks was 1,715. For the four banks in this category to expand their network, the best strategy would be to pursue growth by acquisition.

Profitable regional and niche players: In this category are the rest of the 42 foreign banks in India and a select few of the 31 private-sector banks. While the majority of foreign banks operate in a limited capacity through a single branch that serves businesses from their home country, some such as BNP Paribas have expanded to introduce wealth management services. In contrast, the majority of private-sector banks focus on specific geographic areas, serving local communities. The challenge for these banks, especially the local private-sector ones, is to stay relevant amid the competitive onslaught from bigger rivals. A few of the better performing banks in this group would be ideal takeover targets for the four large high-performance institutions.

Foreign strategic investors: The leading foreign banks and new private-sector banks have shown that India's banking sector holds attractive potential for creating value. These banks have achieved average return on equity in the range of 19–24 percent over the last five years through a broad-based personal financial services and corporate play. Strategic investors from outside India wanting to get in on the act have three options: greenfield entry, acquisition, or a joint venture with an established domestic bank. Starting from scratch ensures greater management autonomy but could be difficult for a foreign entity. The central bank has not been as liberal in allowing foreign players to expand their branch networks as it has been with domestic banks.

Acquiring a strategic stake in an existing domestic bank offers several key advantages, including ready access to corporate and retail franchises and considerable freedom to expand branch operations. Overseas investors can also exercise more management control as the limit on foreign ownership of a domestic bank has been hiked from 20 percent to 74 percent.

Forming a product-specific joint venture with a local bank can create a win–win situation for both the foreign player and the domestic partner. The former brings the expertise and capital, while the latter provides access to its franchise and knowledge of the local market. There are several recent examples of such partnerships. In 1998, American financial services multinational GE Capital and SBI set up two joint ventures to market, issue, and service payment cards. The alliance has emerged as India's third-largest issuer of cards. Meanwhile, the venture bringing together British insurance group Prudential and ICICI Bank has become the biggest private-sector mutual fund in the country.

Several such opportunities will remain available through the rest of this decade, as almost all the large incumbents that have established a presence in high-growth areas want to source operational and product expertise from global players. Just like the players already in the game, an investor with an eye to riding India's rise will have to consider the nature of the market, particularly the segments where personal wealth is growing the fastest. A potential entrant will have to ask how big its aspirations are, which products and services it should focus on, and how much it can afford to spend. Get the answers right and the rewards could be enormous.

5

China: A Giant in a Delicate Balance

Macroeconomics

- GDP[1] ($bn) — 1,161
- GDP per capital ($) — 910
- PPP GDP per capita ($) — 5,117
- Exports ($bn/% of GDP) — 264/23
- Imports ($bn/% of GDP) — 232/20
- FDI inflow ($bn/% of GDP) — 44/4
- FDI outflow ($bn/% of GDP) — 1/0.09
- Foreign currency reserves ($bn/% of GDP) — 166/14
- External debt ($bn/% of GDP) — 141/12
- NPL of banks ($bn/% of total net loans) — 345/25
- National government borrowing ($bn/% of GDP/% external) — 124/11/23
- Top 3 trading partners — Japan, US, EU
- Number of corporates in Global Top 500[2] — 11

Socioeconomics

- Population (mn) — 1,276
- Number of households (mn) — 352
- Average urban household income ($) — 2,657
- Number of households earning >$100K p.a.[3] (mn) — 0.71
- Mobile phones/100 population — 11
- Internet subscribers/100 population — 3
- Urbanization (% of population) — 37
- % of population with university degrees — 3.6
- % of population above 65 years old in 2001 and 2021 — 7/13

Capital Markets

- Number of listed corporations   992
- Equity market capitalization ($bn/% of GDP)   517/45
- Trading volume ($bn/% of market cap)   598/116
- Debt market capitalization ($bn/% of GDP)   123/11
- Equity underwriting[4] ($bn/% of GDP)   12/1
- Debt underwriting[4] ($bn/% of GDP)   14/1
- M&A ($bn/% of GDP)   13/1.1
- Retail assets under management ($bn)   16
- Institutional assets under management ($bn)   77

Banking Markets

- Total loans of all financial institutions, including non-banks ($bn/% of GDP) 1,356/117
- Total deposits of all financial institutions, including
  non-banks ($bn/% of GDP)   1,870/161
- Mortgages ($bn/% of GDP)   68/6
- Personal loans ($bn/% of GDP)   12/1
- Credit card receivables ($bn/% of GDP)   0.06/0.005
- Credit cards per person above 15   N/A
- Credit card spend as % of household total spend   0.1
- Foreign ownership limit in 1997 and 2002[5] (%)   15/25
- Number of banks in Global Top 1,000 in 1997 and 2001   15/9
- Number of ATMs/1,000 urban population   0.07
- Number of branches/1,000 urban population   0.27
- Number of banking employees/1,000 urban population   3.55

---

[1] At 2001 prices
[2] The *Fortune Global 500*: July 22, 2002
[3] Rough estimates only
[4] Average from 1995–2001
[5] Foreign ownership limit in domestic banks is 25%, and one single foreign institution cannot hold
     more than 15% of the total shares

Note: All figures as of December 2001 unless otherwise indicated

China's Financial Landscape

Types	Number of institutions 1997	2002	Percent of total asset 2001	Top 3 players
State-owned commercial bank	4	4	61	• Industrial & Commercial Bank of China • Bank of China • China Construction Bank
State policy bank	3	3	8	• China Development Bank • Agriculture Development Bank • Export-Import Bank
Joint-stock commercial bank	12	11	11	• Bank of Communications • CITIC Industrial Bank • China Everbright Bank
City commercial bank*	61	108	4	• Bank of Shanghai • Bank of Beijing • Bank of Tianjin
Foreign bank	130	177	2	• HSBC • Citibank • Standard Chartered Bank
JV bank	12	13		• n/a
Trust and investment company	244	136	2	• CITIC
Finance company	71	71	2	• n/a
Leasing company	16	12	0	• n/a
Credit cooperative	114,963	39,202	10	• n/a
Total	**115,516**	**39,737**	**$2,589bn**	

* Urban credit cooperatives were consolidated into city commercial banks between 1997 and 2002

The Chinese acrobat balances on a tightrope high above the hushed spectators. A breeze blows gently at first, then swirls around her, setting the line swaying. Untethered and with no safety net below, the gritty trouper teeters forward but regains her composure. She is steady again – the show must go on.

Today, China's government is in the midst of its own thrilling high-wire act, delicately balancing the push for economic reform and the need to preserve social stability. Meanwhile, the rest of the world is holding its breath. If China keeps to its high-growth path and avoids the many pitfalls in its way, by the end of this decade it should emerge as an economic superpower to rival the United States. However, if the tightrope performance falls apart, what is supposed to be the greatest growth story ever told could turn into a tale of enormous potential unfulfilled.

In this chapter, after assessing China's tremendous potential and challenges, we look at where the attractive banking opportunities are and what foreign and local banks must do to be in a good position to exploit them.

TAKING MEASURE OF THE NEXT ECONOMIC SUPERPOWER

China is an emerging market that cannot be ignored. The drawing-card assumption reveals that the opportunity is simply too big to bypass. While the poor quality of available data makes precise projections practically impossible, there is no denying the enormity of the potential. At the end of 2001, China's GDP stood at only $1.2 trillion, compared to $4.2 trillion for Japan, a nation with one-tenth the population. However, by 2010, China will contribute more than 40 percent of Asia's GDP growth (see Exhibit 5.1). It is quickly becoming the economic engine of the region.

Foreign money has been pouring into China, turning the country into the workshop of the world. In 2002, China attracted $53 billion in foreign direct investment, more than 40 percent of all such capital flows to Asia. Already the dominant manufacturer of textiles, shoes, and toys, China is also a major maker of computer components, telecommunication devices, and other electronic goods that have been the growth-driving mainstays of many of East Asia's economies over the past two decades. A member of the World Trade Organization since 2001, China is one of the top 10 trading nations and has eclipsed the United States as the main trading partner of Taiwan and Japan. Leading up to 2010, China is expected to account for a quarter of Asia's export and import growth.

Yet this is a nation still in the early stages of its economic take-off. So far, growth has been concentrated in four economic spheres with about two

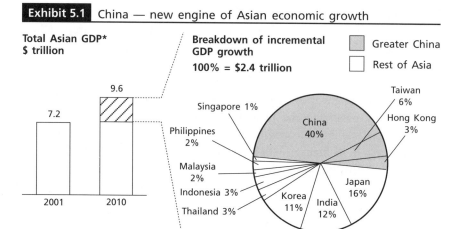

Exhibit 5.1 China — new engine of Asian economic growth

* At 2001 prices
Source: Global Insight; McKinsey analysis

dozen cities in the region running from the Beijing–Tianjin–Shanghai corridor and the Yangtze River Delta down through Fujian Province, which sits across the strait from Taiwan, to the Pearl River Delta that surrounds Hong Kong. While only about 10 percent of the total population live within this eastern swath of the country, the area contributes more than 30 percent of China's GDP and will continue to drive the development of the entire economy (see Exhibit 5.2).

In banking, the China market is still in its infancy. Wealth is very concentrated with less than 1 percent of the urban population controlling half of all retail deposits. Bank assets total $2.5 trillion, bigger than Switzerland's, but three times smaller than in the United States, which has only a fifth the number of people. Largely shaped by economic reforms since the early 1980s, the banking system is still evolving.

Under strict regulations similar to the Glass-Steagall Act in the United States, the banking, securities and insurance sectors are separate. The State Council oversees the People's Bank of China, the China Securities Regulatory Commission, and the China Insurance Regulatory Commission. The pace of regulatory change has picked up in recent years. Since January 2003, for example, banks and securities companies have been allowed to distribute insurance products. With the succession of new political leaders in late 2002 and early 2003, even more reforms of this nature are likely.

There are five main types of players in China's banking industry: the "Big Four" national state-owned banks; the 11 new regional and national "joint stock" commercial banks; about 110 city commercial banks; thousands of rural credit cooperatives; and about 180 foreign commercial banks. The Big Four dominate the industry and account for 60 percent of total bank assets,

84 percent of all branches, and more than two-thirds of bank employees. By international standards, the Big Four – Industrial and Commercial Bank of China (ICBC), Bank of China, Agricultural Bank of China, and China Construction Bank – are undeniably large institutions. ICBC, the biggest of the quartet, was the 23rd largest bank in the world by assets in 2001.

Exhibit 5.2 The four key economic spheres of China

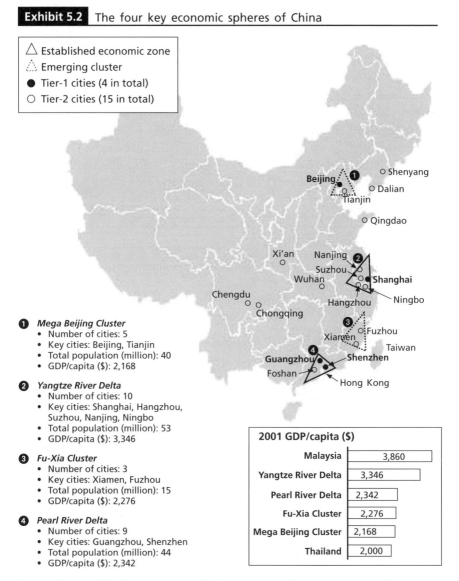

Source: National Statistical Bureau; City Statistical Yearbook and Statistical Yearbook of Provinces; McKinsey analysis

Profitability is another matter: The return on assets (ROAs) of the Big Four are all less than 0.4 percent, far below the international benchmark of 1.2 percent and even lower than those of the joint stock banks. Actual performance may be even worse, given that official numbers are much more optimistic than informed estimates based on international accounting standards (see Exhibit 5.3).

Owned jointly by the government and private shareholders, the 11 joint stock commercial banks, accounting for just over one-tenth of banking assets, sprang up in the last 15 years, a direct result of economic reforms. While these banks are much smaller in size than the Big Four, the more nimble and innovative of them pose a real threat to the dominant players. Emerging attackers such as China Merchants Bank, Shanghai Pudong Development Bank, and China Minsheng Bank are in a good position to "cherry pick" the best retail and corporate customers off the four large banks.

The 100-plus city commercial banks and tens of thousands of credit cooperatives are too small to have any real impact on banking in China over the rest of this decade. But a few city commercial banks – Bank of Shanghai, Bank of Beijing, and Bank of Tianjin, for example – are notable because they

Exhibit 5.3 Competitive positions of local banks

Profitability: ROA (Percent)
Reported ROAs are based on Chinese accounting standards (e.g., capping 1% of loan balances as bad debt provision); by international accounting standards, ROAs will be significantly lower.

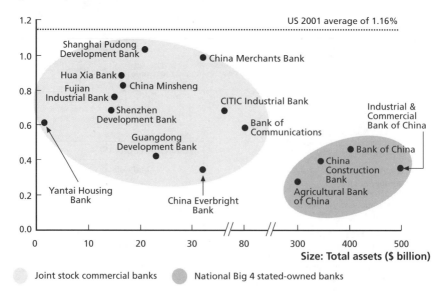

Source: Almanac of China's Finance and Banking; company reports; People's Bank of China (PBOC); Bankscope; McKinsey analysis

serve key economic and political power centers. In 2001, HSBC bought an 8 percent stake in the Bank of Shanghai, which may eventually serve as a vehicle for the global bank's China ambitions.

HSBC is just one of about 180 foreign banks that are already doing business in China on a limited basis. In the areas in which they are allowed to compete, some have been highly successful. For example, foreign players hold about a 40 percent combined market share of foreign-currency corporate loans and trade finance. Foreign banks, however, will not have full access to the quickly evolving domestic consumer market until 2007.

While both foreign and domestic players eagerly anticipate the myriad of opportunities that the gradual opening and development of China's banking markets will unleash, they must carefully shape sensible strategies based on a clear understanding of the tremendous challenges this giant faces – the delicate balancing acts that it has to perform.

FIVE BALANCING ACTS

There are really two Chinas – one that fights to preserve the old social order and one that yearns to be connected to the global economy; one that is state-owned and one that is privately held; one that is rich and one that is poor. For this nation to move forward, its leaders and people must find equilibrium between the two Chinas, between often-conflicting objectives.

Because of this, the Chinese government's actions are often perceived to be contradictory and arbitrary. The central administration in Beijing frequently seems to be "out of sync" with more progressive municipalities and provinces. But such is the nature of a giant's progress. Nothing goes smoothly, nothing is precise, nothing is problem-free. After all, the Chinese government is attempting five simultaneous balancing acts, a task made even more complicated because they are linked (see Exhibit 5.4). A slip in one could spell disaster in another.

To meet its economic and social goals while performing these balancing acts, the government will continue to employ regulation and direct intervention as its primary tools. This has two profound implications for banking. First, uncertainty will be high because regulations may change quickly as the government struggles to find the right balance between tolerance and control. While sweeping reforms are not likely, significant changes could happen swiftly, benefiting the opportunistic player who is well positioned. Second, regulations will continue distorting market behavior. Even after 2007, when the industry is to open fully to foreign competition, the government can be expected to protect domestic banks through regulations in areas not covered by its WTO commitments.

Let us look at each of the five balancing acts China has to perform:

Exhibit 5.4 The five balancing acts

One	Need to be ready for foreign competition	versus	Need to retain local control
Two	Need to resolve the non-performing loan problem	versus	Need to preserve the social contract
Three	Need to restructure state-owned enterprises (SOEs)	versus	Need to grow private enterprises
Four	Need to enrich the coastal cities	versus	Need to bring the western region along
Five	Need to fill the pension gap	versus	Need to prevent a securities market collapse

Implications on banking in China:

- Uncertainty will be huge; reforms will not be sweeping, but change can be rapid

- Market behavior is likely to be distorted and competition is likely to remain constrained

Source: McKinsey analysis

Balancing Act One – between the need to be ready for foreign competition and the need for local control: From the beginning of 2004 (for corporate banking) and 2007 (for retail banking), in line with China's WTO commitments, foreign banks will be allowed to compete with local counterparts on a more level playing field. Overseas institutions will be able to take deposits from and issue loans to local customers in renminbi, while restrictions on the geographies of branches foreign players can open will be lifted. The limit on foreign ownership – 15 percent officially, but up to 25 percent is permitted – may be raised. The government knows that Chinese banks are not strong enough and desperately need skills and training to compete. The most logical way for a Chinese bank to acquire them would be to forge an alliance with a foreign partner or shareholder.

But this could mean ceding management control to the foreign investor, something the government does not want to do for two reasons. First, in China, banks are regarded as more than mere commercial entities. They are expected to be socially responsible, too. If local banks are controlled by profit-driven foreigners, the government may not be able to mobilize them for social objectives, should the need arise. Second, nationalism is a factor. As in any country, the leadership would not want the domestic banking sector to be dominated by outsiders, no matter how valuable their participation. All the more so in China, where no political leader could bear the accusation of selling out to foreigners.

Overseas investors such as HSBC and Citibank have already begun acquiring minority stakes in Chinese banks. The government, for a while, appeared to be willing to let a private equity firm take management control of a local bank. In March 2003, Newbridge Capital was reported to have finalized the purchase of an 18 percent controlling stake in Shenzhen Development Bank. Such a deal would enable the government to boost the skills of the local player without ceding control to a foreign bank. In mid-May, however, the Shenzhen provincial government had second thoughts and refused to sell shares in the bank to Newbridge. Sometimes, the struggle of the balancing act blatantly rises to the surface.

While the competition from abroad post 2007 could act as a much-needed catalyst for banking reform, the government is right to worry about the ability of local players to compete. Should local depositors migrate too quickly to the new arrivals, the domestic financial system could be destabilized, given the fundamental weakness of Chinese banks as a result of their non-performing loans.

Balancing Act Two – between the need to resolve the non-performing loan problem and the need to preserve the social contract: In Asia, China's banks have racked up the largest amount of bad loans after Japan. Officially, non-performing loans (NPLs) are at about $345 billion, or 25 percent of total loans. Independent estimates put the real figure at twice that. This would imply that most banks are technically insolvent.

Yet a collapse of the banking system is unlikely because Chinese banks are highly liquid, with loans-to-deposits ratios typically around 70 percent. The stock of retail deposits – more than 80 percent of GDP in 2001 – has been growing by 18 percent a year since 1995. Moreover, the government implicitly guarantees bank deposits, giving customers a false sense of security. While there were sporadic bank runs in the late 1990s, all ended quietly.

Still, a liquidity crisis is possible. The flight of deposits to foreign institutions or to the capital markets could trigger such a scenario. It would take the migration of only a handful of sophisticated affluent customers to set off a major deposit drain since less than 1 percent of the urban population control 50 percent of all retail deposits. Even if the government could prevent this through regulatory intervention, should China's economic growth slow, the weaknesses of the banks would be exposed. Of course, the continuing flow of capital into China, plus the nation's more than $280 billion in foreign reserves – the second highest in the world – make this scenario unlikely. And because the economy is humming, the government feels less urgency to clean up the banks' balance sheets.

But the basis of future economic growth is a healthy financial sector that efficiently allocates capital to viable enterprises. The government is well aware of the risks of not cleaning up NPLs, as well as the rewards of dealing with them. Solving the problem will entail putting an end to the funding enjoyed by thousands of state-owned enterprises (SOEs). Starving SOEs of capital could lead to their bankruptcies, which would result in millions of lay-offs. State firms still provide a social safety net for their workers by providing them jobs, though this role has been gradually diminishing in other areas such as health care services. The legitimacy of the Chinese government rests on its ability to deliver on this social contract. For this reason, China has deliberately avoided a big-bang approach to the NPL problem.

To achieve the delicate balance between resolving the NPL problem and preserving the social contract, the government is betting on a gradual approach or "installment plan" to clean up NPLs. It has set up four bank-linked asset management companies (AMCs) – Huarong, Cinda, Orient, and Great Wall – to take over and dispose of bad debts. This approach avoids sudden dislocations and distributes write-off costs over time. By the end of 2002, less than 15 percent of the $170 billion in bad debts shifted to the AMCs had been disposed of. Global players such as Morgan Stanley and Goldman Sachs have shown some interest in bidding for distressed assets. Meanwhile, the mountain of NPLs on the banks' books keeps growing.

The installment plan carries a price in terms of foregone growth. It also signals forbearance, possibly encouraging banks to take greater risks. The approach may eventually cost taxpayers more than a head-on solution. And once the pain bites, the government could slow or halt the program. For now, Beijing appears unperturbed by the lack of progress. This equanimity is rooted in confidence that the economy can grow out of the problem. Assuming that the official NPL figure is accurate, that no more debts go bad, and that the increase in overall loans keeps pace with GDP, China would have to grow at least 20 percent a year for the rest of this decade if NPLs are to fall to a sustainable level of below 5 percent of total outstanding loans. An almost impossible feat – even if all new loans were efficiently allocated to the faster growing private enterprises that are becoming the growth engines across China. The NPL problem will clearly persist well into the next decade.

Balancing Act Three – between the need to restructure SOEs and the need to grow the private enterprises: As China's painful transformation into a market economy proceeds, the real challenge for the government is managing a hybrid economy. SOEs employ three-quarters of the working population but only generate about a third of GDP. Many are structurally unprofitable. Because of the need to maintain these de facto social security providers, state-owned banks are "advised" to offer them loans with capped interest rates. To be sure, banks have increasingly more freedom to decide to whom to lend. But banks often think they have no choice since particular SOEs already owe them so much, they believe that they must continue supporting these firms or risk never recovering a single *fen* should the companies go bankrupt. In reality, the banks are simply delaying the inevitable.

While more money is plowed into loss-making SOEs, private enterprises are starved for funds. China's controlled interest rate regime makes it impossible for banks to price loans to risk levels of smaller or newer private firms. Without a developed capital market and access to bank loans, private companies cannot grow fast enough to replace SOEs as the primary employers in the economy. A McKinsey study concluded that if funding were efficiently channeled to the private sector, China's GDP could be about 20 percent higher (see Exhibit 5.5).

With the government budget in deficit, state banks cannot keep funding SOEs at the expense of the private sector indefinitely. At some point, the balance will tip in the favor of the private sector. When it does, the size of China's wealthy elite will expand rapidly, raising the prospect of social tensions that must be carefully managed.

Balancing Act Four – between the need to enrich the coastal cities and the need to bring the western region along: China is not a single market of 1.2 billion consumers. For most players in the banking sector, the key target segment is the 50 million households earning more than $3,000 a year that are concentrated in the biggest cities in the eastern part of the country. The top

Exhibit 5.5 Inefficient allocation of capital

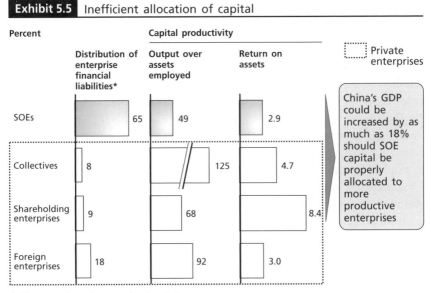

* Close statistical proxy for bank loans
Source: People's Bank of China (PBOC); McKinsey analysis

four of these municipalities – Shanghai, Beijing, Guangzhou, and Shenzhen – account for about 3 percent of the country's population, but generate 12 percent of the GDP. While income disparity is growing, it is critical that the development of the booming coastal region not slow down. The central government has launched a "Go West" campaign to encourage investment in the undeveloped western provinces, but results have been limited. If income distribution is uneven over the long term, social discontent could undermine political stability and trigger social unrest in poorer areas.

Balancing Act Five – between the need to fill the pension gap and the need to prevent a securities market collapse: The looming "pension gap" between savings and retirement needs could also exacerbate income disparities and raise social tensions. In 2002, only 7 percent of Chinese were above 65 years old. By 2030, this figure will rise to 16 percent. A rapidly aging population, combined with the successful one-child policy, is putting considerable pressure on the government to provide for its graying citizens. But China's pay-as-you-go pension system is on the brink of insolvency. The gap between savings and needs will amount to $110 billion by 2010. To finance this deficit, the government could sell shares in state-owned enterprises. But doing so would risk a collapse in stock prices, resulting in the loss of wealth and the erosion of government support among more affluent Chinese. If they come through, proposed pension reforms would result in the accumulation of pooled funds and strongly drive growth in the nascent primary and secondary securities markets.

No TURNING BACK

If China manages these balancing acts successfully, the economy should keep growing strongly, enhancing the prospects for preserving social and political stability. But should the country lose its footing on any of the five challenging tasks, much of its hard-earned progress could be undone.

There is no turning back. Unrelenting change is the likely course although timing will be unclear. During this difficult period of transition, local banks have a lot at stake. They have a shrinking window of opportunity in which to implement reforms to escape legacy problems. If China remains stable, foreign banks will benefit from a widening range of options in what will eventually become one of the largest banking markets in the world. They must be prepared, however, to ride out regulatory inconsistencies and other surprises as they target the most attractive opportunities.

OPPORTUNITIES FOR THE DECADE

The best way for local banks to prepare themselves to pursue new and potentially lucrative opportunities is to get the basics right and seriously tackle fundamental operational and risk management issues. An obvious priority would be to make corporate lending profitable. The traditional bias towards SOEs and the inability to price risk have meant that, for up to 80 percent of all new corporate loans, expected losses far exceed gross margins.

While the bad loans pile up, banks have been able to claim that their overall NPL ratios have declined. They can do so not because their ability to assess client risk has improved, but simply because of dilution from increases in retail loans, particularly mortgages, and the huge profits from this lending that allow higher write-offs on the corporate side. Since corporate lending accounts for nearly 90 percent of total loans, getting risk management under control will have a major impact on banks' bottom lines and is one of the most critical steps local banks can take to put their houses in order.

After all, over the rest of this decade, many exciting growth opportunities in wholesale and retail banking will be up for grabs. Local players already have the customers and the deposits. What they lack are the profit mindset and the fundamental skills crucial to success. Foreign competitors have all the skills but may have to watch from the sidelines for some time yet. Those few overseas banks with high aspirations and the appetite for risk must formulate business models that will allow them to cope with regulatory hurdles and eke out profits in an underdeveloped financial sector.

Wholesale banking: Corporate business can be profitable

Chinese corporations face three structural peculiarities of the banking sector. First, companies have no real alternative to deposit accounts for parking their cash and are unlikely to be offered any other options soon. Second, small and medium-sized enterprises are chronically starved of funding because banks are hesitant to extend loans to them. China's capital markets are as yet underdeveloped, with no second board for listing mid-sized corporations. Third, banks typically offer companies no other value-added services beyond lending. Given this situation, there are three key opportunities for banks to serve corporate clients.

An immediate opportunity exists in the competition for corporate deposits, which in 2001 stood at $530 billion in renminbi holdings and $46 billion in foreign currency. Banks earned about $6 billion in revenues from these deposits and could make more than $20 billion by 2010. At 1–1.5 percent, margins are attractive. Corporate balances are expected to grow by about 18 percent annually over the rest of this decade.

While the Big Four banks hold 70 percent of corporate deposits, local attackers and foreign banks need not be eclipsed. Under China's WTO commitments, by the end of 2003, foreign banks will be allowed to take renminbi deposits from local corporations. Because most companies are concentrated in the large cities and coastal provinces, local and foreign players with even a small branch network could target them effectively. By going for this business, banks can use the accumulated cash to fund other attractive opportunities such as SME lending and consumer finance, instead of raising money through the more expensive inter-bank market.

In the medium term, banks can hone their risk management skills so they can provide loans to poorly served small and medium-sized firms. Although they probably account for some 30–40 percent of national output, SMEs only get 10–15 percent of total commercial loans. Compare this to Korea, where the proportion is about 31 percent, and Taiwan, where it is around 36 percent, although SMEs in Taiwan only contribute 28 percent to national output. Chinese commercial banks cannot properly assess SMEs and so simply avoid lending to them. The banks use risk management systems that rule out financing any company with few assets. Existing credit bureaus do not provide meaningful data to help banks make decisions.

In addition, the capping of interest rates at 2–3 percent above the cost of funding prevents banks from pricing loans to SMEs to factor in potential losses and the higher operating costs associated with lending to these businesses. China is gradually removing these pricing restrictions. If banks are more responsive to the needs of SMEs, those with strong credit risk management systems could tap a market with more than $25 billion in revenue by 2010.

Also in the medium term, banks can develop fee-based products, which for now do not really exist, to offset corporate lending losses. This could result in as much as $8 billion to $13 billion in revenues by the end of the decade. In 2001, fee income accounted for only 5 percent of the total operating income of all Chinese banks combined. In more developed markets, such as the United States and Korea, non-interest income accounts for 10–20 percent of operating revenue. But in China, banks do not know what products to offer, how to package them, and what to charge. As in most markets, transaction fees could help banks substantially improve returns from corporate relationships.

Trade finance is an area of big potential that banks could develop. China's external trade, which totaled $500 billion in 2002, is set to expand to $1.5 trillion by 2010. The corporate banking trade finance revenue pool could grow to between $5 billion and $10 billion by the end of this decade. China's capital markets also offer sizable fee-revenue opportunities. They provide approximately 15 percent of private-sector financing. By 2010, this is expected to rise to 35 percent. Equity and debt underwriting is expected to grow at a compounded annual growth rate of 13 percent over the next several years to generate $2 billion in revenues by 2010. About half of this will come from small and mid-cap companies. Merger and acquisition

(M&A) activity is forecast to grow by 30 percent a year to hit up to $400 million in revenue by 2010.

Personal financial services: Going after the affluent

Chinese banks have never focused on the needs of their retail customers, even the wealthiest ones, viewing them merely as sources of deposits to fund lending to SOEs. This attitude and the lack of the skills needed to serve affluent clients have meant that banks have missed many potentially profitable opportunities in the past and risk continuing to do so in the future.

By 2010, China should overtake Korea to become the second-largest personal financial services (PFS) market in the region after Japan. The rapid growth of this business will be driven by five factors. First, strong economic growth is quickly expanding the middle class and enriching the wealthy. Second, the government is slowly withdrawing from the social welfare system, forcing individuals to save more. SOEs previously provided workers with free healthcare, housing, and education for children. Now, housing is only partly subsidized, while healthcare is arranged through a shared payment insurance scheme. Third, private ownership of housing is taking off. This is driving the demand for retail mortgage products. Fourth, the rapidly aging population will spur pension reforms and the development of mutual funds and life insurance. Finally, the government needs to replace government expenditure with private consumption as the driver of economic growth. The availability of consumer credit could spur individuals to spend.

The immediate battle in PFS will be for the deposits of the growing ranks of the affluent. Bank deposits accounted for about 80 percent of all personal financial services revenue in 2001 (see Exhibit 5.6). This dominance is likely to continue for some time, given the attractive spreads (about 200 basis points) and the lack of investment alternatives or retail banking products. Consumer finance – mortgages, auto finance, and credit cards – is only beginning in China. While less than 1 percent of the urban households hold more than half of bank deposits, the remaining portion is in the accounts of 19 million affluent urban households that earn more than $4,000 a year. By 2010, this segment will expand to about 90 million (see Exhibit 5.7). For banks aiming to maximize profits, attracting these customers will be critical.

Affluent account holders are increasingly dissatisfied with local banks, which offer them the same products and level of service as the poorest depositors. A McKinsey survey of 10 Asian markets showed that, after consumers in Hong Kong and Taiwan, affluent Chinese are the least satisfied with their current bank and the most likely to switch. In 2001, 27 percent of them opened a new account. One of the Big Four banks lost a fifth of its affluent customers over the period from 2000 to 2002.

Exhibit 5.6 China's personal financial services (PFS) revenue pools*

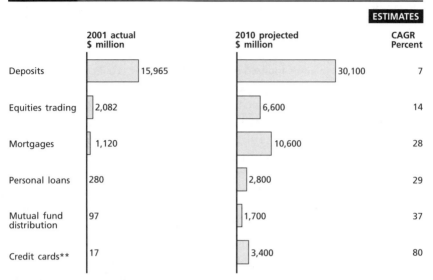

	2001 actual $ million	2010 projected $ million	ESTIMATES CAGR Percent
Deposits	15,965	30,100	7
Equities trading	2,082	6,600	14
Mortgages	1,120	10,600	28
Personal loans	280	2,800	29
Mutual fund distribution	97	1,700	37
Credit cards**	17	3,400	80

* Net interest revenue before losses (duration matched) and fee revenue
** Includes all fees from card issuing and merchant acquiring businesses
Source: People's Bank of China (PBOC); McKinsey analysis

In going for the affluent, much more is at stake than their deposits. With pension reforms, the development of the domestic capital markets, and eventual deregulation that would allow the flow of funds to markets outside China, a shift to more productive investment products is surely in the cards. Up to half of all new personal financial assets could flow to securities, mutual funds, and life insurance by 2010, generating about $9 billion in fee revenue.

Consumer finance is another emerging business that is highly attractive. By 2010, revenues generated by mortgages, auto finance, and credit cards in China will rank third in Asia behind Japan and Korea. Mortgages will be the biggest and most immediate opportunity, driven by high demand and supply encouraged by the State. They represent more than 80 percent of all retail lending, a dominant position that will continue for some time. We forecast that mortgages will bring in $10 billion in revenue by 2010. China started privatizing housing in 1986. Since 1995, total mortgage balances have grown at an annual compounded rate of over 100 percent.

The Big Four account for 97 percent of all mortgage balances. This superior position is due in part by their ability to capture the primary market through close ties with developers. With abundant deposits to fund mortgages, these giants have a clear advantage over smaller banks. But they face big risks too. Banks must finance an entire building project before the developer gives them the exclusive rights to offer mortgages to individuals.

Exhibit 5.7 Increasing affluence of China's urban population

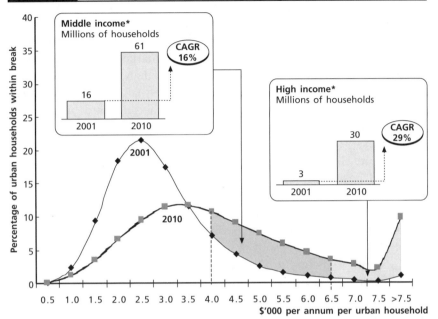

* Middle income defined as annual household income between $4K and 6.5K; high-income defined as annual household income above $6.5K.

Source: Asian Demographics; McKinsey analysis

In 2001, 65 percent of total property sales were in the primary market. In more developed cities such as Shanghai, secondary sales are beginning to outpace primary transactions. For well-equipped new entrants, this market is a major opportunity, not least because the Big Four are unable to provide the services and credit assessment needed to offer mortgages specifically for secondary buyers.

Auto loans are also increasing rapidly, almost doubling in 2002 alone. Revenues are expected to approach $3 billion by 2010. While vehicle ownership is still low, it is increasing sharply. There are 250 people per car in China, compared to 2.2 per car in the United States. With rising affluence, the Chinese automobile industry is expected to grow at more than 10 percent a year over the next decade. The number of households that can afford to buy a car stood at 7 million in 2002 and is expected to grow to more than 80 million in 2010. By then, China could become the world's third-largest automobile market after the United States and Japan.

Only 12 percent of all private car purchases in China are financed by loans, compared to the global average of 70 percent. China will reach that level by the end of this decade. One impediment to growth and profitability could be regulation. Auto financing usually carries a higher risk than collateralized lending, a factor that should be priced into a loan. China's fixed interest rate regime makes this tricky. The lack of a repossession law for creditors to recover a vehicle also means that loans are essentially unsecured.

The credit card market is the wild card that could prove the most interesting. Pent-up demand is high but the market has been severely constrained by a lack of supply. In 2001, more than 90 percent of cards circulating in China were debit cards. This will surely fall as innovative players such as China Merchants Bank begin to market real credit cards aggressively.

Other factors that may impede growth include restrictive regulations to curb access to unsecured credit, China's sub-standard payment infrastructure, limited acceptance among merchants, and the lack of an established positive credit bureau. Some of these deficiencies are being rectified. China UnionPay Company, a Shanghai-based national payment network set up in 2002 by more than 80 banks and a member of Visa International, aims to connect all payment systems in the country by 2005. In early 2003, over 80 percent of all point-of-sale terminals and 95 percent of all ATMs were connected to UnionPay's network.

Conventional wisdom is that the Chinese are traditionally frugal and prudent, unwilling to borrow money to finance regular purchases, as opposed to a house or car. This is a myth. According to a McKinsey study[1] conducted in 2001, Chinese people are no less willing to take out a loan than other Asians. Among the young, high-income[2] Chinese surveyed, 18 percent said they already had a credit card, compared to about 10 percent for the average affluent Chinese surveyed. These consumers reported that they made on average 7.4 transactions a month, compared to 4.3 for the average Chinese cardholder in the same survey.

If all the impediments to the development of China's credit card market are remedied, it could expand exponentially and by 2010 rival Taiwan's, the third largest credit card market in Asia. If growth were in line with the experience of other emerging markets, by the end of this decade China's credit card business would still be bigger than Hong Kong's and at least half the size of Taiwan's, with revenue exceeding $3 billion. Risk-adjusted margins hover around 900–1100 basis points for customers who avail of revolving credit facilities, much higher than the 300–800 basis points in developed markets such as the United States and United Kingdom.

---

[1] McKinsey Asia Personal Financial Services (PFS) Survey 2001.
[2] Chinese aged 20–45 with annual household income above $6,500 a year.

꙰

A small bank's big plays

One of the most innovative products China Merchants Bank offers its customers is a multi-purpose debit card. It integrates all cash withdrawal, point-of-sale and bill payment functions, and allows the user to access his or her accounts from anywhere in China. The first of its kind when it was introduced in Shenzhen in 1996 – other cards could only be used within the province in which they were issued – it quickly proved to be an attractive product among business travelers.

Despite its limited branch network, China Merchants has proven that innovation counts for something. It managed to achieve the highest customer-to-branch ratio of any Chinese bank: 44,000 account holders per branch, compared to 5,800 for most new regional and national commercial banks, and only 1,600 for the Big Four state banks. China Merchants also has the highest deposit balance per card, $670, compared to between $50 and $300 for the other major players.

This suggests that it has a much more affluent customer base, the perfect platform for launching new and innovative consumer finance products to keep its account holders satisfied. At the end of 2002, China Merchants launched its own credit card, with support from more than 40 former staff of Chinatrust Commercial Bank, Taiwan's top card issuer. The moral of the story: With the right mindset, a small player can make big profits in a large market.

꙰

LOCAL BANKS MUST SHED THEIR LEGACY MINDSET

Over the rest of this decade, China's emerging banking landscape will be an exciting battlefield. Each group of local banks has priorities to follow if they are to be ready to seize new opportunities and make profits.

With their network of more than 100,000 branches and 1.4 million employees, the four big state-owned banks are in a good position. Paradoxically, they are also under the most imminent threat from local and foreign attackers. While they will continue to dominate the local scene, protected by soft barriers and regulations, they also stand to lose their most attractive customers to more innovative players.

Although they are burdened by high costs, loan losses and the old command-economy mindset, we anticipate that up to two of the Big Four could make a serious attempt to deal with their legacy problems. Those that embark on a serious transformation process will likely capture the biggest share of future profits. But their commercial freedom may remain limited if the government continues to employ them as instruments of the state.

With China Merchants Bank, Shanghai Pudong Development Bank, and China Minsheng Bank the probable leaders among them, four or five joint stock commercial banks have the best chance of attracting the most profitable retail customers – the mass affluent and young borrowers. With the liberalization of interest rates, they will probably go after the SME lending business as well. These banks are a real threat to the Big Four and are set to grab a significant share of banking profits by 2010. After all, they have distinct advantages. They are more willing to shed old mindsets and are able to acquire skills faster than the Big Four. They have better market access than foreign players. Their main challenge is to avoid biting off more than they can chew, managing rapid expansion without taking on excessive financial and organizational risks.

As we have explained, local players have a shrinking window of opportunity in which to break free from their legacy banking problems before the full brunt of competition is unleashed. The key issue for any of the Big Four or joint stock commercial banks is operational, not strategic. Tremendous value can be unlocked by immediate performance improvement alone.

McKinsey analyzed one joint stock bank and found it had negative real value. A two-pronged approach to stop the bleeding in corporate banking and to grow its retail business could turn the bank around, with 88 percent of the value creation coming from improvements in corporate lending management and NPL recovery. Banks must address fundamental operational issues before they can exploit new growth opportunities.

The performance of most Chinese banks has been consistently poor. From the lack of debt recovery to the absence of cost control, from the inability to assess risk and measure profits, to inadequate management of assets and liabilities, local institutions are plagued by substantial problems that have led to bad decisions, mistakes, and losses. They make profits from deposit account spreads, only to lose much if not all of it in corporate lending.

The Achilles heel of China's banking system is poor credit risk practices. Reform credit risk management – and reap immediate rewards. If banks redesign credit systems, processes, and their organizations, expected annual loss rates on new loans could fall from 6–10 percent or higher to 2–3 percent. While this step alone would not make banks profitable since lending rates are capped, it could at least slow the flow of red ink, with any of the Big Four reducing losses by up to $4 billion. Banks would also do well to deal with existing non-performing loans. Working out bad debts and improving processes for dealing with NPLs could raise the sector-wide recovery rate from 15 percent (as estimated by Standard & Poor's) to over 50 percent.

With cost-to-income ratios typically close to or higher than 60 percent, banks urgently need to improve efficiency. Badly designed operating systems and overstaffing are the main problems. Rationalizing branch networks is critical to reducing costs. In China, there are only about 2,000 customers per branch, compared to 26,000 per branch in Singapore. The challenge for banks is to cope with the political pressure not to lay off workers.

Local banks must also understand the economics of their businesses and products. They often do not adequately incorporate the real cost of credit into loans and are unable to determine the true value of deposits due to the absence of fund transfer pricing. Building a comprehensive and reliable profit reporting system would allow a bank to identify clearly the areas where it is making and losing money. It could then focus on exactly where improvement is needed.

Those players that implement operational improvements will be prepared to pursue key growth opportunities. This will be a zero-sum game between nimble attackers and a defensive old guard. While some joint stock banks have already gotten their act together, especially in retail banking, none of the Big Four have adopted the profit mindset they need to stay competitive.

To make profits from lending to SMEs, a local bank would need to deliver standardized service at a low cost. It would need to upgrade risk management to enable it to identify and price risk appropriately, and to expand market share once the interest rate regime is liberalized. If any of the large banks focuses on better catering to the SME market, it could boost revenue by as much as $10 billion by 2010. For a bank to offset losses in large corporate lending, it must develop fee-based products and cross-sell them to clients. If a large bank makes the necessary effort, it could rake in an additional $2 billion in revenue by 2010.

On the retail side, the Big Four must move quickly to halt or at least slow the exodus of affluent customers. The key is to develop distinct services to meet the needs of these prized account holders. For any of the quartet to lose these customers would be disastrous – possibly up to $1 billion in annual profits forfeited by the end of this decade.

The next step would be to implement a consumer finance strategy. While the state-owned banks have embraced mortgage lending in support of government policy, they have failed to grasp the huge potential of other personal finance products, particularly credit cards. By 2010, non-mortgage consumer finance will account for up to 40 percent of total consumer credit revenue and could bring in $2 billion in profits.

In contrast to the Big Four, the innovative attackers among the joint stock banks are ahead of the curve. They are prepared to target the affluent segment aggressively. Some have already done so, acquiring a disproportionate share of high-income customers. About 20 percent of

China Merchants Bank's account holders have an annual income of more than $20,000, compared to only 2–4 percent for the typical local player. Many of the joint stock banks will forge alliances with foreign partners in a bid to outgun the Big Four.

If the priorities for local banks are clear, what is holding them back? The core problems are an antiquated mindset and a severe lack of skills. It is easy to trace the inefficiencies of the banking system to the vestiges of China's command economy. After all, banks are expected to be socially responsible, not commercially viable. Yet as the banking sector develops and opens up, local banks have only themselves to blame for their paralysis in the face of major problems.

Nothing better illustrates the legacy mindset than traditional lending practices. Most local banks are not averse to racking up losses by providing loans to insolvent SOEs. It is easy to blame state policy for unprofitable decisions. Local banks are in fact motivated by the fear that if they stop financing these firms, they will have to write off losses when those companies go bankrupt. In reality, they are merely delaying the inevitable.

Many of the banks are cautious about pursuing the high potential of credit cards because they perceive unsecured consumer lending to be too risky. Such fears are largely unfounded and easily offset by higher spreads and sound risk underwriting. But risk management skills are precisely what the local banks do not have. This deficiency fuels their insecurities. Instead of bold action, the local banks seek only to survive, unwilling to acquire the skills they need to be profitable. It is this status-quo mindset that banks must discard.

The unprofitable mindset

Bancassurance has generated a lot of interest in China. However, look beyond the hype and the key problem with banks becomes obvious: They are not motivated to be profitable. Instead of profit targets, branch managers must meet monthly quotas for accumulating deposits. Beyond the quotas, they are rewarded for selling bancassurance. Banks push insurance products to their customers. The customers buy policies using funds from their deposit accounts. The insurance companies take the money and promptly redeposit the cash into the banks.

What comes around goes around, but there are consequences. Banks pay retail depositors only 1.5 percent interest a year. The insurance firms have no other alternative but to put the payments they collect from policyholders back into the banks as corporate deposits earning 4 percent interest. Funds that had been in low-interest savings accounts now cost the bank more. For want of a bonus, profits are lost. This is the "unprofitable mindset" Chinese banks have to junk if they are to survive and prosper in the long term.

For foreign players, it pays to be prepared

As far as we are aware, few foreign commercial or retail banks have made any material profits in China's banking market. The possibility that this will change dramatically in the near future is not high. Even once the sector is fully open in 2007, foreign banks are likely still to have a tough time turning a profit. Several structural and regulatory barriers not covered under Beijing's commitments to the World Trade Organization stand in the way. For example, without a liquid inter-bank market or enough deposits to fund lending, foreign banks are constrained in what they can do by their small loan books. The other obstacles include the inconvertibility of the renminbi, the cap on interest rates, and limits on opening branches.

Eventually, China *will* become a profitable market for the foreign competitor. What overseas banks are buying into by setting up in this market now is an option, a claim to a chunk of what they all expect will be a very big pie. But why not wait until conditions are better? Many foreign firms, particularly listed ones, have to spin a China story, if only to satisfy shareholders and keep up appearances. When it comes to what will inevitably be one of the world's biggest banking markets, what bank would want to seem a laggard?

The most compelling reason for a foreign bank to establish a toehold in China during these formative years of its banking industry is that it pays to be prepared. Conditions and regulations can change anytime, offering immediate opportunities to serious foreign attackers poised to pounce. The learning curve in China is steep and operating in this market can be filled with surprises. It would be wise to come in early, get used to the environment, build up critical local management capacity, establish brand presence, and master the skills needed to succeed. Wait until the going is easier – and it may be too late.

Take credit cards. The market is small due to a lack of supply. Yet demand is high. Should the right conditions come together, there could be explosive growth. The question any foreign player must ask is whether it wants to be in a position to profit from this surge. The first mover could reap tremendous profits. But there is no telling when the right time to act will be. The foreign competitor can wade in now and tread through years of uncertainty, watching, and waiting. Or it can choose to postpone entering China until the market is more "normal," once the take-off phase is over. While holding back may mean that when a foreign bank does dive in, the waters are clear, or at least less murky, by then rivals that plunged in early will have staked out leading positions.

Whatever the timing of entry, foreign banks should be guided by three principles. First, the amount and scope of an investment must be appropriate and measured. While a bank should place bets that generate the cash flow needed to reach the break-even point in the medium term, it must be prepared to expand its platform quickly should an unexpected change in regulations suddenly throw up new opportunities. Second, investments should be diverse. The key is to make a series of well-considered bets and not commit too much to one pet project. Third, any investment should make commercial sense. The numbers, calculated over a time frame of three to five years, have to add up.

In an ever-changing market such as China, persistently pouring in cash to chase long-term hopes will only result in crushing disappointment. While *guanxi*, or networking, may be essential for business success in China, it is overrated. Forging alliances or cutting deals for the sake of winning friendship, favor, or preferences can lead to disaster. Any partnership must be founded on sound economics and business sense. If a local partner does not abandon its worst practices, the relationship is doomed. Dogged investment will yield frustration, not profits.

Before 2007, foreign banks can approach China in two ways: through organic growth in specific areas, or by taking minority stakes in local institutions. HSBC, Standard Chartered Bank, Bank of East Asia (BEA) and Citibank are the most prominent players with flagship branches in Shanghai and Shenzhen, focusing on niche foreign exchange-based products primarily for expatriates. The minimum asset base required of any foreign bank seeking to set up a branch is $20 billion. Entry is barred to those below that scale. While setting up a full branch in China signals a foreign player's long-term commitment, doing so rarely results in material benefits.

Regulations cap foreign ownership of local banks at 25 percent with an additional cap of 15 percent on a single investor. A minority stake gives the investor neither access nor influence, only a spectator's seat – not something many overseas banks really want. For this reason, foreign direct investment in financial institutions has remained tiny at only about 0.1 percent of all foreign direct investment (FDI) in China in 2001.

There are more creative options for exploring the Chinese market. A foreign player can gain access to retail distribution and business control in three ways: setting up a profit-sharing arrangement with a local branded partner to issue "white-label" products such as credit cards; providing back-office services to a local institution; or acquiring a minority stake in a medium-sized bank, while taking management control of specific product ventures. A good example of the third method is Citibank's $72 million purchase in early 2003 of a 5 percent minority stake in Shanghai Pudong Development Bank with an attractive option to increase the initial stake to 24.9 percent in 2008. The American multinational will have management control in the joint development of the Chinese bank's credit card business. The two will set up a card center in Shanghai and launch a separate venture once they obtain approval.

The key to success in China is creativity. Even though a minority stake may limit its influence and benefits, the foreign player can draw up a contract that includes a map of specific cooperative initiatives. Investments can be phased in, with additional tranches conditional on the fulfillment of agreed terms.

There is no question that global players such as Citibank possess the skills to capture the most attractive banking opportunities. The few foreign competitors that place the right bets will be in a good position. Over the rest of this decade, the biggest uncertainties will be regulation and access to customers and funding. The major strategic quandaries will revolve around when and where to invest, with whom to partner, and how to structure deals. It may not be until after 2010 that foreign players will reap the full rewards for their efforts and patience.

If its government carefully manages the balancing acts it must perform, China will offer enormous opportunities for both local and foreign players for a very long time. Consider Volkswagen, which entered China in the mid-1980s. By 2002, the German automaker had produced two million vehicles and enjoyed more than 40 percent market share. China was its second-largest market in the world and is expected to make up half of its future global growth. The lesson: Patience and perseverance are the ingredients of success.

For most global banks, a serious and measured approach to China is a bet worth placing. For local competitors the issue is will. The tools and conditions for making profits are there. What is needed are daring managers willing to pursue tough strategies and stay the course despite the pain. Without that crucial profit mindset, local banks stand to lose in a promising market that for now is theirs for the taking.

6

Taiwan: Capitalizing on Change

Capital Markets

- Number of listed corporations   586
- Equity market capitalization ($bn/% of GDP)   293/107
- Trading volume ($bn/% of market cap)   545/186
- Debt market capitalization ($bn/% of GDP)   37/14
- Equity underwriting[3] ($bn/% of GDP)   6/2
- Debt underwriting[3] ($bn/% of GDP)   19/7
- M&A ($bn/% of GDP)   9/3
- Retail assets under management ($bn)   24
- Institutional assets under management ($bn)   43

Banking Markets

- Total loans of all financial institutions, including non-banks ($bn/% of GDP)   446/163
- Total deposits of all financial institutions, including non-banks ($bn/% of GDP) 583/214
- Mortgages ($bn/% of GDP)   104/38
- Personal loans ($bn/% of GDP)   60/22
- Credit card receivables ($bn/% of GDP)   11/4
- Credit cards per person above 15   1.35
- Credit card spend as % of household total spend   20
- Foreign ownership limit in 1997 and 2002[4] (%)   15/100
- Number of banks in Global Top 1,000 in 1997 and 2001   17/22
- Number of ATMs/1,000 population   0.47
- Number of branches/1,000 population   0.13
- Number of banking employees/1,000 population   4.36

---

[1] At 2001 prices
[2] The *Fortune Global 500*: July 22, 2002
[3] Average from 1995–2001
[4] Ownership can be up to 100%, with approval from Taiwan government (Ministry of Finance) for
    ownership >25%

Note: All figures as of December 2001 unless otherwise indicated

Taiwan's Financial Landscape

Types	Number of institutions, 1997	Number of institutions, 2002	Percent of total assets 2001	Top 3 players
Government bank	15	15	57	• Bank of Taiwan • Taiwan Cooperative Bank • Land Bank of Taiwan
Local bank	32	37	29	• First Commercial Bank • Hua Nan Commercial Bank • Chang Hwa Commercial Bank
Foreign bank	46	38	5	• Citibank • ABN AMRO Bank • HSBC
Credit cooperative*	378	324	9	• n/a
Hybrid**	0	1	n/a	• Fubon and Citibank (Citigroup holds 15% of Fubon shares)
Total excluding hybrid	471	414	$747bn	

*   Credit cooperative includes credit cooperative associations; Credit Department of Farmers' Association and Credit
    Department of Fishermen's Association
** Fubon is also included in local bank category

F ew have summarized the challenges facing Taiwan's 52 commercial banks better than this CFO of a mid-sized high-tech company. "Local banks rarely understand my industry," he complained. "The bankers that come sometimes carry fancy titles, but let's face it, they are nothing more than loan officers with one product to sell – loans." He went on: "At any one time I have 15 banks offering me loans, but what I need are solutions. Eighty percent of my receivables are in US dollars, while my manufacturing costs are either in Taiwan dollars or mainland Chinese renminbi. Having excess funds from a recent IPO, I need to figure how to optimize my cash position and best plan for future investments in China. Ask a loan officer about hedging strategies and all you get is a blank stare. No one is providing the integrated services and real industry insights that I need to grow my business."

The frustrated executive's message: Taiwan's economy is undergoing a major transformation – and its financial sector has to change along with it. The relocation of local manufacturing to China and Southeast Asia, representing more than $100 billion in Taiwan investment between 1990 and 2001, is redefining the economy, banking customers' needs, and the risk profile of Taiwan's financial services industry. While Taiwan sidestepped the 1997 Asian financial crisis, the global technology downturn in 2001 and a subsequent doubling of non-performing loans (NPLs) were inescapable. In the late 1990s there was a fear that Taiwan's banks had become too resistant to change and would become a drag on the economy in much the same way that banks are pulling down Japan. The shift of investment to China and the bursting of the technology bubble, however, suggest that the bigger test for banks is to adjust their own operations and strategies to a permanently changed environment. This is a challenge that both banks and regulators can ignore at their peril.

Fortunately, regulators are responding. In 2001, new merger laws and the creation of financial holding companies gave license to Taiwan's strongest financial institutions to redefine the scope of their operations. The same year, regulatory changes gave foreign institutions the unprecedented opportunity to assume 100 percent ownership of existing banks in Taiwan – Asia's third-largest open-retail-banking market (see Exhibit 6.1).

Taiwan is attractive primarily for its large retail banking market of seven million households. Retail banking profits have been generated by a consumer-finance boom that began in the mid-1990s and has yet to lose steam despite the difficult economic environment. Consumer lending profits are expected to triple from 2002 to 2010. And while the economic elite is increasingly splitting its time between Taipei and Shanghai, the rising wealth of the top 10 percent of Taiwan households is an increasingly important source of profits for the island's banks. Many of these households, the mass affluent, derive their wealth from the small and medium-sized enterprises

| **Exhibit 6.1** | Taiwan is a "top 3" Asian retail banking market |

$ billion, 2001

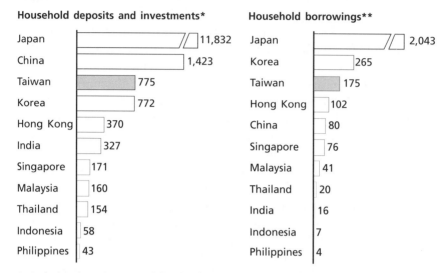

Household deposits and investments*

Japan	11,832
China	1,423
Taiwan	775
Korea	772
Hong Kong	370
India	327
Singapore	171
Malaysia	160
Thailand	154
Indonesia	58
Philippines	43

Household borrowings**

Japan	2,043
Korea	265
Taiwan	175
Hong Kong	102
China	80
Singapore	76
Malaysia	41
Thailand	20
India	16
Indonesia	7
Philippines	4

* Includes deposits, mutual funds, securities, life insurance, pensions, and other personal financial assets
** Includes mortgages, car loans, house repair loans, credit card receivables, cash advances and other personal loans
Source: Government statistics; Lafferty; McKinsey analysis

(SMEs) that they own. These nimble companies are also expected to become a growing profit center for Taiwan's innovative banks. Finally, the branch structures that cater to retail and SME needs are largely outmoded, and a concerted effort to increase their productivity could yield in excess of $1 billion in improved earnings market-wide.

Against this backdrop of opportunity is a banking system under siege. Rapidly rising write-offs from large corporate and real estate loans cut industry profits by more than half in 2001. Market fragmentation, combined with low single-digit returns on equity, is expected to fuel consolidation in the over-banked market by 2005. It is likely that, failing to recapitalize, up to a third of the 52 commercial banks will be absorbed by government banks. A few high-performing local banks, however, are likely to acquire larger networks and challenge Taiwan's historically dominant government-affiliated institutions. The battle for market leadership will intensify between the private and government sectors.

By 2005, a few private financial institutions from Taiwan such as Cathay, Chinatrust, and Fubon are expected to emerge from the domestic battle, ready to engage in a regional game. As a result of acquisitions, Taiwan's new market leaders may come to rival regional players such as Singapore's DBS and London-based Standard Chartered Bank in terms of market capitalization (see Exhibit 6.2).

When the PRC market opens more fully in 2007, a few local institutions will have the skills, operational scale, Mandarin-speaking management, and acquisition-ready currency to be viable competitors. Indeed, Taiwan may be one of the few markets in Asia – joined perhaps only by Singapore, Hong Kong, and South Korea – able to produce several financial institutions that can grow to become truly regional players. Of course, in tailing their successful Taiwan customers, local banks expanding abroad will find Greater China to be their natural hunting ground.

A future filled with customers moving across borders, new financial holding companies, domestic mergers, and international options makes for a much altered and potentially rich environment. Evidence suggests, however, that only a few banks in Taiwan will be able capitalize on the change to profitably take advantage of new growth opportunities. For the majority of banks, a back-to-basics approach centered on improving credit and enhancing operational efficiency will be critical for survival. This chapter explores the forces shaping Taiwan's dynamic environment, highlights market opportunities and challenges, and puts forth the imperatives for local and international banks with aspirations for Taiwan and Greater China.

DYNAMIC MARKET IN THE MAKING

In early 2001 Taiwan's Minister of Finance announced that it was the year for bank mergers. Most market observers agreed that with more than 50 commercial banks and several hundred poorly performing credit cooperatives serving a population of only 22 million, it was indeed time for some consolidation. By the end of that year, however, only one merger had occurred, while several high-profile ones announced by the government had fallen through. With this track record, will Taiwan be able to avoid Japan-style stagnation and see market change? In a word, yes. Here is why.

Regulatory building blocks in place

Following the 1997 Asian financial crisis, the South Korean government spelled out a new paradigm for financial services and led the transformation of the domestic market. No one in Taipei, however, has played as significant a role. Rather, as is often the case in Taiwan, important regulatory changes come piecemeal after negotiations among bureaucrats, political parties, and influential family groups. Yet Taiwan is slowly assembling the regulatory backbone to facilitate the creation of a dynamic marketplace.

Exhibit 6.2 Merged Taiwan institutions may achieve scale parities with regional leaders

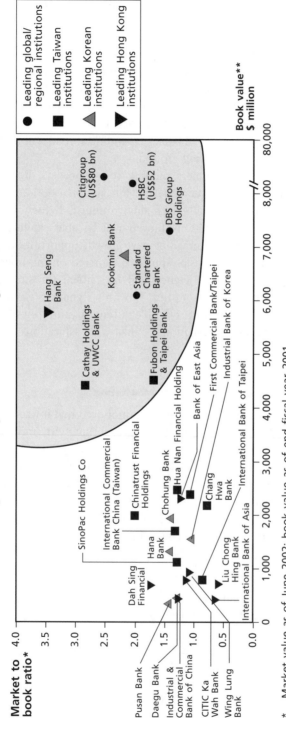

Strategic control map of Asian banks vs. global banks – 2002

*   Market value as of June 2002; book value as of end fiscal year 2001
** Based on common equity

Source: Bloomberg; McKinsey analysis

Financial holding companies (FHC), allowed from 2001, are at the core of key regulations changes. New FHC regulation allows a single entity to have controlling interests in companies engaged in banking, securities, property and casualty insurance, life insurance, and asset management. In short, it allows financial institutions in Taiwan to undertake a business scope similar to Europe's universal banks.

Critics would argue that creating such umbrella organizations sounds good in theory but, in fact, does little to change the market structure or improve performance. There are few cost synergies to be gained from combining the back-office operations of a securities firm and an insurer, for example. And even in Europe and the United States, cross-selling synergies among different financial services entities in the same company are often partially or completely hindered by clashing business cultures in the different units. Indeed, at least half of the financial holding companies formed in Taiwan (13 had been created by 2002) will probably do little more than add complexity and lessen accountability. By 2005, more likely than not, local media will be calling loudly for the unbundling of many of the FHCs because of poor performance.

What then is the real impact of the FHC Act? It is prompting leading financial entities to fundamentally rethink strategies. Many family and business groups that have long-held interests across financial business lines are now faced with an unprecedented opportunity to combine holdings. This new freedom is forcing many institutions to conduct detailed reviews of their businesses and ask fundamental questions. Which financial businesses really offer sustainable returns in Taiwan? Which customer groups are really worth targeting? Longer term, is it more attractive to distribute or manufacture financial products? In facing these questions, holding companies such as Chinatrust, Fubon, SinoPac, and Taishin appear to be developing a much sharper focus on where they will direct their energies and attention in the future.

Equally important, the FHC law is enabling family groups to cluster businesses under one shareholding, which is triggering market-transforming acquisitions. The Fubon purchase of government-controlled TaipeiBank in 2002 is a good example. Over several decades Fubon built up separate businesses in insurance, banking, securities, and asset management. Prior to the FHC law, banks could acquire other banks but unfortunately Fubon's bank, with less than 2 percent market share, was too small to make market-transforming acquisitions. A merger between Fubon and TaipeiBank would have put TaipeiBank's majority shareholders in control. But under the FHC, following the consolidation of Fubon's financial services businesses under Fubon FHC, the Fubon Group could subsume TaipeiBank into its holding company and maintain control as the majority shareholder through a share swap.

Much the same thing happened when the Cathay Group acquired United World Chinese Commercial Bank (UWCCB) in 2002. With these acquisitions, Cathay and Fubon jumped from owning smallish banks to controlling the largest privately owned banks on the island. The FHC Act is powerful because it is leading local institutions to consider new strategic choices and to undertake bolder acquisitions.

Liquidity-boosting measures: With non-performing loans (NPLs) spiking up to more than $30 billion, representing 15 percent of the banking industry's outstanding corporate loans in late 2001, asset restructuring and accompanying regulation are critical for a dynamic merger and acquisition (M&A) market to emerge. Without a clear plan to dispose of bad loans, market participants have determined that mergers and acquisitions are often too risky. Taiwan has responded by setting up asset management corporations (AMCs) that enable banks to amortize over five years the bad loans that are sold off. By mid-2002 the likes of Lone Star, Cerberus, and the global investment banks had purchased more than $3 billion of NPLs from local financial institutions for 25–35 cents on the dollar.

The government also responded by establishing a Resolution Trust Fund (RTF) in 2001, modeled after the American entity set up in the 1980s to clean up after the savings and loan debacle. Taiwan's RTF, which was to increase its capitalization to at least $17 billion in 2002, focuses on cleaning up the bottom end of the financial sector. That is where grassroots credit cooperatives are burdened with NPLs in excess of 40 percent of total loans outstanding. In 2002, laws were passed to enable banks to securitize loans and hence strengthen their capital adequacy ratios. The government announced that by the end of 2004, all banks had to bring NPLs down to below 5 percent and raise their capital adequacy ratios up to 8 percent.

Considering that at least a third of Taiwan's commercial banks lack the financial health to meet these requirements, the pressure to consolidate will surely build. And as the deadlines approach, the cost of waiting to act, especially for smaller players, will only increase. Government pressure is reaching all parts of the financial sector. Even the long-favored 10 government-affiliated banks, which together make up roughly half of Taiwan's banking market, are being ordered to shape up and find new partners, or have new partners forced on them. As a major shareholder in many of the larger institutions, the government's threat to sell its stakes and force market restructuring is legitimate. The banks' wiggle room is shrinking and the legal and liquidity mechanisms are increasingly in place to allow market forces to take charge of the banks that try to resist. While the consolidation of the Taiwan market is likely to occur in fits and starts, expect strong private players to lock in market leadership.

Underlying forces favor change and innovation

Mergers and acquisitions will clearly be a critical factor in Taiwan's market transformation. Equally important are the fundamental forces underpinning the dynamism of the market. These include the inescapable impact of the mainland on Taiwan, the continued fickleness of Taiwan consumers, the increasingly transparent operational weaknesses of local players, and the growing attractiveness of the island to foreign financial institutions. These fundamental forces are already exerting significant pressure on existing players and giving innovative businesses a unique opportunity to capture market share.

China creates new challenges and needs: The impact of the mainland on Taiwan and on bank customers' financial needs, specifically, should not be underestimated. Obviously, China will remain critical for Taiwan, both as a manufacturing base and as a large market for Taiwan goods. The fact that one-fourth of Taiwan's exports and two-thirds of its stock market capitalization at the end of 2001 were derived from the high-tech sector underpins China's importance to Taiwan. Because technology manufacturing is increasingly a global and commoditized industry, requiring competitors to capture ever-increasing efficiencies, Taiwan companies are naturally pushed to produce in markets that offer the best combination of skilled labor and lower costs. Not only does China offer these benefits, but it is also a technology market that is rapidly becoming one of the world's largest consumer of products that Taiwan produces; for example, mobile phones.

In 2002, China officially replaced the United States as Taiwan's largest trading partner. Equity analysts estimate that roughly 60,000 small and medium-sized enterprises in Taiwan have moved operations across the Strait. This represents more than one-third of the island's high-tech manufacturing capacity. McKinsey interviews with Taiwan companies (those with operations in Mainland China) suggest that about half of them aim to tap the Mainland China market. For Taiwan companies in traditional industries, such as packaged foods, the mainland market is beginning to account for the lion's share of revenues.

As of 2002, the number of Taiwan people living in China, primarily concentrated around Shanghai, ranged between 400,000 and 600,000. Put simply, as much as 3 percent of the island's population already lives on the mainland for much of the year. The Taiwan community has become so entrenched in its "second home" that some fancy footwork by healthcare providers makes it possible for someone from Taiwan to see a doctor in Shanghai and claim it on his national health insurance back home.

Restricted to opening only representative offices in China, Taiwan banks are poorly positioned to respond to this fundamental shift among their corporate and individual customers. The lament of the high-tech CFO quoted at the beginning of this chapter resonates widely among the Taiwan business community. Only a few Taiwan banks – First Commercial, Hua Nan and Chinatrust, among them – have been able to secure a branch license in Hong Kong to cater to the Taiwan companies that operate offshore entities there to serve mainland units. Several Taiwan financial institutions are in discussions with foreign banks to rent space on their international networks, so they can at least offer some services to their domestic corporate customers operating on the mainland. But these efforts could be too little too late. Increasingly, banks in mainland China such as the Bank of Shanghai are setting up "Taiwan desks" to provide renminbi services to Taiwan-based corporations and individuals.

To add insult to injury, Taiwan banks are often left holding the bad debt from closed plants and rising unemployment after companies relocate to the mainland. In fact, the shift to China has fundamentally increased the risks in southern Taiwan – the island's traditional manufacturing heartland. In 2002, when banks were forced to write off 4–5 percent of credit card debt island-wide, industry insiders believed that the write-offs in the south were two to three times bigger. The economic divide and risk differential between the north and south are expected to widen as the importance of China grows.

Many banks in Taiwan are pinning their long-term hopes for growth on the China market. To succeed, they will need strong earnings at home to fund expansion. Consolidation of the local market is required for banks to afford such investments in the mainland. And even then, entry into the China market will be possible only for the very few that are able to develop world-class skills and compete against foreign players eyeing the same prize.

Fickle consumers keep the market up for grabs: Since McKinsey began surveying several thousand middle and upper income households across Asia in 1998, Taiwan has consistently stood out for the high level of discontent among banking customers. It is perhaps not surprising that Taiwan consumers are among the most likely in Asia to switch service providers. Between 1998 and 2001, roughly 25 percent of consumers in Taiwan opened accounts with new financial institutions, more than in any other Asian market. While the banking sector is competitive and fragmented – about two-thirds of the banks have a market share of less than 2 percent each – the simple fact remains that many customer needs are going unmet. The market is very much up for grabs.

Consider the "George & Mary" card. George and Mary are cartoon characters developed to represent the freedom brought by the cash-advance card bearing their names. Cosmos Bank launched the card in Taiwan's crowded credit-card market in 2002. Within four months, it had issued roughly 400,000 of them, more cards than 60 percent of credit-card companies have typically issued after years in operation. Cosmo's success came from targeting lower income and generally younger customers with the product they need most: cash. Customers who produce a tax statement showing steady income and who pass credit checks are eligible for a credit line of roughly $5,000, readily available through ATMs. That line increases by $1,500 increments (up to $10,000) for every month of on-time payments. While packaged into a series of fees, the George & Mary card carries an average 18 percent interest rate, slightly below prevailing market rates. Cosmos demonstrated that by understanding customers' needs – and hopefully, the accompanying risks – it is possible to carve out a lucrative niche in Taiwan's largely me-too market place.

SinoPac demonstrated much the same ability with the success of its Money Management Account (MMA), launched in 2000. The MMA is an integrated investment and savings account that ties together securities and banking products to simplify transaction procedures and provide a quick, simple financial overview. By carefully targeting the MMA to higher income, actively trading customers, SinoPac is reported to have signed up more than 100,000 new mass-affluent account holders between 2000 and 2002. SinoPac's achievement is impressive, given that the main driver in selecting a bank is branch convenience. SinoPac was able to leverage the value-added nature of its services to overcome the fact that it has only about 50 branches, a fourth the size of government bank networks.

Local financial institutions are open to attack: Cosmos and SinoPac are successful, in part, because their banking counterparts do not know which customers they are losing or appreciate why they should be worried. The vast majority of financial institutions in Taiwan are not in a position to defend their customer bases. A quick scroll though a bank's deposit base often reveals, to the shock of management, that up to 30 percent of accounts are dormant. An attempt to conduct a telemarketing campaign often reveals that half of the telephone numbers are wrong. Such shortcomings often extend throughout the institutions and perhaps it is not a surprise that few banks have a clear understanding of the profitability of any given customer.

Lack of insight into customer profitability masks an even bigger problem. In most businesses, including banking, the "80/20 rule" applies: 20 percent of customers account for 80 percent of profits. In Taiwan's fragmented retail banking sector, customers' assets are dispersed across multiple institutions. As a result, often only 5–10 percent of customers, either those with large deposit balances or high margin loans, account for more than 100 percent of the net profits of any given bank.

In other words, the survivability of many banks in Taiwan hinges on a very small number of customers (see Exhibit 6.3). As a majority of financial

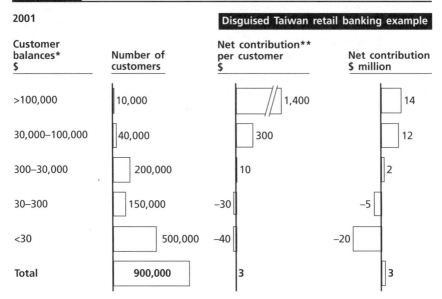

Exhibit 6.3 Taiwan retail banking profitability concentrated in few customers

* Balances include current deposits, saving deposits, time deposits, foreign currency, and mutual funds
** For liability products only; profitability estimates for retail customers only include mass market and mass affluent segments
Source: McKinsey analysis

institutions are unable to identify their customers that count most, they are in a poor position to defend themselves against competitors.

Needless to say, limited customer information is sure to frustrate new financial holding companies that expect to create value through cross-selling. Before anything else, they had better make sure another institution has not already stolen target customers. Obviously, the banks that can actually identify customers with huge profit potential and design services to meet their needs are likely to find exciting opportunities.

Growing foreign interest is raising the competitive bar: Significant regulatory change, a market in tremendous flux, unmet customer needs, and poor customer information are a formula for disaster in the domestic banks' fight to see off innovative competitors, particularly from overseas. Since the late 1990s, Taiwan has seen a substantial rise in the commitments made by foreign financial institutions. While the exit of foreign banks such as the Bank of Hawaii, the Bank of Boston, and the Royal Bank of Canada captured headlines, foreign players have in fact been deepening their presence through acquisitions and alliances. Citibank leads the pack with its $750 million investment in the Fubon Group in 2000. HSBC, ABN AMRO Bank, and

Investec all stepped in to purchase local asset management firms. Between 1998 and mid-2002, foreign financial institutions, including insurers, invested approximately $2 billion in strategic stakes in local financial institutions. Compare that to the period of 1993–1997, when foreign acquisitions in the local financial sector totaled less than $100 million.

Going forward, foreign financial institutions are likely to increase their role in Taiwan, albeit from a small base – 6 percent of assets in 2001. The introduction of the FHC law allows foreign entities to acquire up to 100 percent of local financial institutions. Taiwan's five million middle-class and affluent households – with a median income of $34,000 in 2001 – represent a substantial and immediate opportunity. In Asia, only Japan and Korea offer a larger retail market that is open to foreign competitors. The good news is that unlike in other markets, there are many local banks in Taiwan willing to sell to foreign entities.

Of course, meaningful shifts in market structure do not depend on acquisitions alone. By the end of 2001, foreign players held more than 30 percent of all credit card receivables in Taiwan. Between 1999 and 2001, new attackers such as AIG and Standard Chartered Bank deployed aggressive balance-transfer strategies, with temporarily low rates, to target the most attractive revolving customers. Quietly, AIG and Standard Chartered Bank captured 10 percent of card receivables. Both exploited the fact that as of 2001, Taiwan was the only market in Asia to have a well-established credit bureau that provided a full picture of an individual's lending exposure. AIG and Standard Chartered Bank leveraged this information to identify the good risks.

Only a few institutions in Taiwan have the skill to use credit-bureau information to defend and grow market share. This inability to manage critical information in credit cards will probably be laid bare with disastrous consequences if and when specialist global card companies such as MBNA, Household International, or Capital One enter Taiwan. In the United Kingdom, for example, foreign "mono-lines," as these international players are called, managed to capture 30 percent of new credit card receivables within five years of market entry in the late 1990s by employing superior risk management, segmentation, and marketing skills.

Growing foreign competition will accelerate change in Taiwan's banking market. By 2005 it is expected that the forces of market consolidation, coupled with the growing impact of China and changing customer needs, will redefine the competitive landscape. It may be debatable whether the expected change in market structure is an opportunity or a threat. What cannot be argued, however, is the need for defenders and attackers alike to deepen their customer knowledge, improve product innovation, and ready their M&A plans if they hope to compete profitably.

CORE OPPORTUNITIES AND CHALLENGES

The central issue for many banks in Taiwan is where to best focus their skill-building efforts to prepare for a changing marketplace. For a majority of them, core growth opportunities will be in personal financial services and in tailoring services for SMEs. The large corporate segment will likely continue to destroy value for local banks that are unable to compete in the global treasury and capital markets. To capture growth opportunities in personal financial services and SMEs, however, most banks must overcome significant internal challenges to compete effectively.

First, it is important to be clear that banking profits are increasingly elusive. Mervyn Davies, chief executive of Standard Chartered Bank, in a conversation once described Taiwan as "having the unique combination of OECD [or developed economy] pricing and emerging market risk." As one might expect with a market on the knife-edge of structural change, profitability is a critical issue. Indeed, in the financial sector, competitive pricing, increasing NPLs, and copycat services strategies have generally led to poor returns to shareholders (see Exhibit 6.4).

Even before the bursting of the global technology bubble, return on equity for the Taiwan banking industry was in steady decline, falling from 21 percent in 1991 to 12 percent in 1997. From 1998 to 2001, overall banking profits continued to deteriorate, contracting an average of 26 percent annually. At the end of 2001 industry return on equity reached 5 percent.

Of course, the fortunes of Taiwan's financial institutions are closely linked with the economy. Mirroring slides in Singapore and Hong Kong, exports contracted 17 percent in 2001, the largest annual drop in 47 years. With manufacturing moving to China, a natural question to ask is whether Taiwan still has attractive growth opportunities? It does, but the opportunities for financial institutions will be concentrated in personal financial services and in a limited number of corporate segments. While many domestic corporations at the forefront of the global high-tech sector will invest outside Taiwan, wealth will still funnel back. Additionally, Taiwan's traditional nimbleness suggests that it will be able to leverage its advantages in research and design to build new value-added businesses at home.

Looking ahead, there are four primary growth opportunities in financial services. Three lie in the broadly defined space of personal financial services and include opportunities in consumer finance, wealth management, and mass-market retail banking. The fourth opportunity lies in developing new services and networks to serve Taiwan's entrepreneurial SMEs. Leadership in each of these sectors, which would mean a market share of 5–10 percent, has the potential to generate at least $100 million in annual profits. The challenge for most banks in Taiwan, however, lies in building up the soft skills and

Exhibit 6.4 Taiwan financial institutions' returns have historically been poor

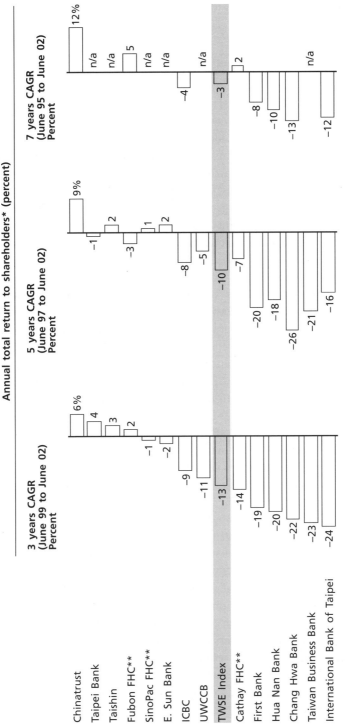

Annual total return to shareholders* (percent)

3 years CAGR (June 99 to June 02) Percent

5 years CAGR (June 97 to June 02) Percent

7 years CAGR (June 95 to June 02) Percent

	3 years	5 years	7 years
Chinatrust	6%	9%	12%
Taipei Bank	4	–1	n/a
Taishin	3	2	n/a
Fubon FHC**	2	–3	5
SinoPac FHC**	–1	1	n/a
E. Sun Bank	–2	2	n/a
ICBC	–9	–8	–4
UWCCB	–11	–5	n/a
TWSE Index	–13	–10	–3
Cathay FHC**	–14	–7	2
First Bank	–19	–20	–8
Hua Nan Bank	–20	–18	–10
Chang Hwa Bank	–22	–26	–13
Taiwan Business Bank	–23	–21	n/a
International Bank of Taipei	–24	–16	–12

* Total return to shareholders (TRS) includes dividends and capital gains
** "FHC" indicates financial holding company including the group's bank(s)
Source: Datastream

performance-oriented cultures that will enable institutions to take advantage of the opportunities.

Consumer finance boom: New models required

Between 1995 and 1997 the number of credit cards issued in Taiwan doubled. And between 1998 and 2001 the number of cards doubled again to 24 million. Card receivables grew by an annual compound rate of 27 percent in 1995–97 and 13 percent in 1998–2001, reaching a total $10.8 billion. There has also been an explosion in personal, unsecured lending that includes everything from general purpose loans to auto loans. Two of the local leaders in personal lending, Chinatrust and Taishin, expanded personal loans (not including credit cards or mortgages) annually by 46 percent and 131 percent, respectively, between 1998 and 2001. By the end of 2001 Chinatrust, the largest consumer finance player in Taiwan, had approximately $2.5 billion in outstanding balances from credit cards and personal loans, generating in excess of $100 million in estimated annual profits.

The growth opportunities are far from over. The average amount of unsecured debt per adult in Taiwan is equivalent to one month of income. In the United States, the average adult maintains unsecured debt levels equivalent to three months' income. The chance that Taiwan consumers will continue to increase their reliance on consumer credit is high and growing. Consumers are increasingly willing to use credit cards to make purchases. While spending on credit cards in 2001 represented 10 percent of total consumer expenditure, which is less than half of US levels, the proportion of card-based spending doubled in the five years leading up to 2001. Results from McKinsey's personal financial services survey indicate that people below age 45 are particularly willing to increase their borrowing to enhance lifestyle. McKinsey's analysis estimates that credit card revolving balances will triple between 2002 and 2010.

A new business model, however, will be required to extract profits. Despite all the growth in Taiwan, less than 10 of the roughly 50 credit card issuers make money. The problem is not write-offs, which run in the normal range of 4–5 percent. Interest rates are capped at 20 percent, certainly high enough to allow for attractive profits. Clearly, there are far too many for Taiwan's population of 22 million. An even bigger problem is that most credit card issuers are too focused on distributing plastic and not focused enough on earning profits. There appears to be an obsession among Taiwan banks for having their own credit card even when it is clear that the institution is unlikely to achieve requisite scale to make money. Many seem to view issuing credit cards as a necessary part of being a bank.

The obsession with plastic over profits extends to the top 10 players, many of which emphasize quantity of cards issued over the quality of the customers. Elaborate gifts are offered to sign up customers. Multiple alliances with retailers are created to tap active purchasers. The problem in Taiwan, like most markets in the world, is that people who carry out transactions only on their credit cards are not generally profit-generating customers. Those who use revolving credit facilities and are unlikely to default are. This suggests an opportunity for innovative players, foreign or local. Not only can they participate in the strong underlying growth in consumer finance in Taiwan, but they may also be able to steal significant market share through superior segmentation.

Mass-affluent banking: Battle for customers

In most developed markets, the mass-affluent segment (typically households with between $100,000 and $1 million in liquid savings) represents 40–50 percent of retail banking profits. In Taiwan, roughly 500,000 households, or 10 percent of the total, fall into this definition. Anecdotal evidence from local financial institutions suggests that such customers also represent roughly half of the profits in personal financial services. Local banks are now waking up to the fact that mass-affluent customers are an important source of current profits and future survival. The emergence of integrated financial services through holding companies is heating up the battle for this upper end of Taiwan's large middle class.

Unfortunately, the first response to this opportunity has typically been to build the infrastructure first and acquire the soft skills later. A tour of bank branches would reveal that at least a quarter of Taiwan banks have established some form of priority banking service. You can tell when a bank has such an offering – the amount of dark wood paneling and plush carpets increases substantially.

But what is really different? Scratch below the marble surfaces and you will find that the "financial advisors" are former tellers or bank clerks that have received limited training on financial products and services. A typical customer's product holdings remain largely in low-yielding time deposits, not in any of the much-advertised alternative investment products. And when you ask about the priority services they receive, account holders often remark that their young financial advisors seem to know less about the markets than they do.

The decorations for the affluent may be tasteful, but they are costly and a waste if not built upon with the right strategy. As of 2002, most of the affluent services had only succeeded in increasing the price of services. The right mass-affluent banking strategy can reap substantial rewards in Taiwan. Average financial service profits generated by mass-affluent customers are estimated to be in excess of $1,000 a year. This is substantial when one realizes that the non-affluent market segments generate, on average, less than $100 annually per customer. The largest portions of the profit pool for the mass affluent lie in mortgages and securities trading. Many of the units serving the mass affluent, however, pay relatively little attention to the borrowing and trading behavior of their clients, preferring to focus on deposit balances as the main indicator of whom should be given priority service.

Clearly, local banks will need to improve their service and product models to capture growth and profits from the mass affluent. The primary challenge lies in moving to a deeper understanding of customers to be able to execute needs-based selling. This is particularly true for the mass affluent. Roughly 30 percent of customers in this segment are extremely conservative and need a fair bit of personal advice to make investment decisions. Conversely, the wealthiest 20 percent of the mass affluent are extremely self-directed in their investments and are seeking financial institutions that provide the best market information and most efficient execution services. Understanding these differences is key to building successful mass-affluent services.

To step up to the challenge, local financial institutions will have to shift their focus away from building infrastructure to cultivating new soft skills. To do so, staff recruiting must shift to older individuals who can win the trust of clients. Training must be deepened in both products and customer needs. And management must form a deep understanding of where money is made in these segments, and how to differentiate their offerings and attract customers. The main battle for the affluent will most likely be played out among nimble operators such as Citibank, Chinatrust, Fubon, Taishin, and SinoPac, which will compete to attract money away from post-office savings accounts and the larger government-affiliated banks.

Retail mass market: Earnings improvement imperative

In the run-up to 2005, while the game for the mass affluent will be a land grab for customers, the remaining portion of the market – the 90 percent that makes up the retail mass market – will offer substantial opportunities for earnings improvement. Improving earnings in mass-market retail is critical as it often represents the largest share of a Taiwanese bank's cost base. Excellence in mass-market retail is often necessary for capturing post-merger synergies in banking markets poised for consolidation.

Branches are at the center of serving the mass market, and there is much work to be done regarding branches in Taiwan. Simply put, there are too many branches. Generally, they are too large, often in the wrong location, and largely focused on the wrong activities. These problems are rooted in history. Branches were set up by corporate bankers before true retail banking existed. Consequently, many are not ideally located. As the original objective of branches was to gather deposits, few of the tellers, officers, or branch managers hired in the last two decades ever expected to have to sell consumer products. Even in the 1990s, many of the branches set up were built around outdated processes inherited from the practices in the older government banks. Many, for instance, still host back-office processing activities in expensive retail branch space.

Hidden within this historic legacy is a substantial opportunity to improve profits. Back-office processes can be centralized and outsourced. Branches can be relocated to key retail zones at reduced size and cost. Part-time staff can be introduced to further reduce in-branch labor costs, while expensive transactions can be redirected. New recruiting, training, and incentive programs can be designed to stimulate sales. Many of these potential improvements are understood, in theory, by local banks, but few have taken the steps to implement them. In part, this is because the magnitude of the problem is not fully appreciated.

Other developed markets in Europe and the United States have faced the same conundrum as Taiwan in mass-market retail banking: so many customers, so few profits. Through systematic cost reduction and finding innovative ways to grow new fee-income streams, banks in the developed markets have been able to reduce cost-to-income ratios in the mass market from 80 percent-plus to approximately 50 percent. In Taiwan, with most local banks facing cost-to-income ratios well in excess of 85 percent in the mass market, similar profit improvement programs are critical. Based on McKinsey's experience, it should be possible for smaller banks to improve annual mass-market profits by at least $20 million, while the larger government banks could realize annual improvements in excess of $100 million for mass-market retail banking alone.

SMEs: Adopting a proactive approach

Taiwan's 900,000-plus SMEs (defined as having less than $3 million in sales) have historically fallen through the cracks of the financial services sector. In an environment that favored asset-based corporate lending, SMEs have not been on most banks' radar screens. This can be expected to change in the years leading up to 2005, as many banks come to realize that SMEs represent one of the few bright spots left in the largely unprofitable corporate banking sector.

SMEs account for 98 percent of the companies in Taiwan, 21 percent of the exports, and 70 percent of the island's labor force. Their needs are quite straightforward: reasonably easy access to credit, simple processing of foreign exchange and occasional letters of credit, and cost-effective remittance services linking Taiwan to Greater China and other international markets.

The problem for most SMEs is not so much that banks cannot perform these functions, but that few are interested in doing so. In fact, some small retail chain store owners, for example, resort to using personal credit cards to fund their monthly cash-flow requirements.

With the exception of government banks that are mandated by the authorities to meet at least some of the SMEs' needs, most banks ignore this segment for fear of its risks. But while doing business with SMEs entails real risks, the issue should be how to cater to them given the limited transparency of their performance and finances, not whether to serve them at all. Starting in the late 1990s, attacking banks such as SinoPac, Chinatrust, and TaChong began to look at the SME segment by financing the receivables of smaller companies due from large companies. This business, known as factoring, leverages the fact that many SMEs in Taiwan are part of larger, stable supply chains controlled by strong, blue-chip companies. Factoring allows banks to capture a price premium from financing SMEs, while accepting minimal risk. Factoring also provides another core advantage to banks, if they are smart enough to take advantage of this: By building a record of an SME's receivables flow, banks can gradually begin to piece together an outside-in picture of business volumes and cash flows that would allow rational pricing of potential risks.

The key strategic issue for building an SME client base is how to garner sufficient cash-flow indicators before taking on risk. Factoring is one innovative approach. Others include carefully sequencing payment and deposit products to build up customer information before granting loans. Alternatively, banks can package SME products with personal guarantees at the outset of relationships to minimize risks. This latter approach may be particularly interesting in Taiwan as many SME owners are affluent consumers, allowing banks to penetrate two interesting customer segments in one sweep.

To be successful in directly tapping the SME segments, financial institutions will have to avoid any tendencies to replicate the large corporate service model when serving SMEs. It is simply too costly with its more complex products, manual credit processes, and dedicated account officers. Rather, a new approach that leverages standard products, mobile sales forces, automated credit-scoring, and telephone-based centers for after-service will need to be developed.

FIVE CRITICAL OBSTACLES TO OVERCOME

The opportunities in consumer finance, wealth management, mass-market retail, and SMEs can be tapped by today's local leaders and laggards. The Taiwan market remains a dynamic setting where players that try to be innovative can take advantage of changing customer tastes and needs, as well as competitors' weaknesses to capture larger market shares. To do so, however, domestic financial institutions must overcome five obstacles that persistently undermine skill-building, degrade execution, and hinder momentum.

Failure to focus aspirations: Most senior management teams at financial institutions have high aspirations. The problem is that these goals are too broad. The arrival of the FHC law has exacerbated this problem by giving many people the feeling that they can be all things to all people. Institutions that choose to focus their market leadership on two or three of the growth opportunities outlined in this chapter will dramatically increase their chances for success.

Self-reliance to a fault: Perhaps as a by-product of Taiwan's entrepreneurial spirit, the first instinct of many bankers is to build their own capability, whether it be in IT, credit systems, or back-office processes. The desire of many banks to have their own credit card operations is a case in point. Financial institutions have tended to under-leverage outsourcing opportunities. Going forward, banks that choose to win in the fast-changing market will, in many cases, need to buy what they do not have and outsource processes that are not mission-critical. Institutions that are competing from a position of relative weakness today will need to forgo the natural urge for self-reliant developments. The market is simply moving too quickly.

Under-investment in soft skills: Even as they invest heavily in branches and ATMs, Taiwan financial institutions tend not to put as much money and effort in developing necessary soft skills. Most banks, for example, do not have real-time customer information to track exposures to even their largest corporate accounts. In most banks, no one is running analyses to understand the relative returns of large versus medium-sized companies. In many local banks, it is extremely difficult to find internal marketing people that develop products and design campaigns for specific customer segments. These gaps occur because banks have traditionally focused on their infrastructure investment, rather than on building customer-driven insights. Going forward, the winning banks will balance their outlays for hardware with investments in people and the soft skills that are critical to better serving customers. It may be uncomfortable for many banks to hire such people as their market salaries often top those of incumbent managers.

Embracing change half way: Many banks in Taiwan have every intention of changing to capture new opportunities. At one government-affiliated institution, management decided it should strengthen the bank's position in consumer finance. It hired a promising manager from outside to drive the business. An audit some 18 months later revealed that pay scales had been converted to a commission structure and lead sales were making more money than many of the senior managers in the bank. This was unacceptable to senior management, though these are quite common practices in the market. The new business manager hired only 18 months earlier with great hopes had his decision rights rescinded. Many of Taiwan's financial institutions want to change but find it extremely difficult to break their hierarchical structures and adopt new practices that might be threatening to incumbent employees.

Not fully implementing performance management: Not all employees are necessarily interested in being part of a leading institution. If an institution, however, wants to capture a leading position in serving the mass affluent, for example, the support of all staff is needed.

The only way to surmount such a challenge is to introduce rigorous performance management built on a clear set of strategic and financial goals. Individuals who contribute to those goals need to be rewarded. Those who do not must be asked to consider other careers. Many banks in Taiwan have begun to experiment with key performance indicators (KPIs) and have put much more stringent performance review mechanisms in place. The problem is that most banks are good at rewarding the high performers but not at effectively dealing with low performers.

The simple fact is that banks in Taiwan have been uncomfortable firing people who do not contribute. Even in the private banks, low-performing staff are shuffled from branch to branch, rather than shown the door. True performance management, with clear positive and negative consequences, will need to be instituted for banks to make their way into a winner's circle with increasingly tough admission standards.

To overcome the five hurdles outlined above requires a fundamental shift in the mindset of top management. Aspirations will have to be linked to a clear understanding of profitability, investments will have to be reprioritized from hardware to soft skills, and longstanding personal relationships will have to be put aside to ensure organizational effectiveness and the creation of true high-performance cultures.

The irony in all this is that managers who are willing to surmount the hurdles will be better positioned to provide long-term opportunities for a majority of their employees. And those who resist change in favor of a kinder, gentler culture will put the long-term interests of the very people they wish to protect at risk.

CONFRONTING A CHANGING MARKET

In 1997, when McKinsey began writing its first edition of *Banking in Asia*, we saw the need for future winners in Taiwan to increase their focus on key products and customers. In a sense, this has happened. The top-performing five local private institutions (Fubon, Chinatrust, SinoPac, Taishin, and

E. Sun) and four foreign banks (Citibank, HSBC, Standard Chartered Bank, and ABN AMRO) have made a significant push in the most attractive retail and corporate segments. As a consequence, the share of banking profits controlled by these nine banks has grown from 18 percent in 1997 to 48 percent by the end of 2001. These same nine players controlled only 15 percent of the lending assets at the end of 2001.

Clearly, these figures point to market changes already well underway. While it is true that the best performing banks have seen their share of profits increase in part because they escaped the worst corporate NPLs, the rise nonetheless does mark a shift in power. The high-performing banks now have stronger earning power to invest in marketing, skill-building, or acquisitions. Equally, Taiwan's larger government and government-affiliated banks are on the defensive. If they do not undertake radical improvements in their risk controls, business mix, and operations, they will find themselves increasingly at risk of being taken over.

In fact, the risk to the larger and lower performing banks is increasing. For much of the 1990s, the smaller, high-performing local and foreign banks built their earnings on new products such as credit cards, unsecured personal loans, and sales of investment products. This enlarged the size of the overall banking market. In the years leading up to 2007, the picture will change. While credit cards and unsecured personal loans will continue to offer strong growth, successful attackers are likely to make decisive moves in the mass-affluent and SME sectors. Such moves stand to rapidly erode the profit margins of the large government and government-affiliated banks that have long dominated SME services and deposits in general. The years leading up to 2007 will see much stronger direct competition between Taiwan's newer high-performing players and the larger incumbents that will increasingly be fighting for survival.

Do the small, high-performing banks have it made? Not necessarily. With most having less than a 5 percent market share and under 100 branches each, these top performers must consolidate their leadership position and diversify earnings. To ensure that they remain at the forefront of personal financial services, the high performers must succeed in significantly expanding the size of their branch networks. Branch convenience is a critical element for the mass affluent. Fubon and Cathay's acquisition of TaipeiBank and UWCCB, respectively, provide these players with a head start among top performers looking to transform their branch distribution.

Clearly, the small, local, high-performing banks will need to pursue domestic bank acquisitions to secure their rights to long-term market leadership. Equally, it makes sense for the smaller, high-performing banks to consider strategic alliances with foreign partners. A foreign bank partnership can bring the necessary skills to help local banks defend their leadership in

Taiwan's retail markets, as well as possibly provide the capital and clout to help make bold moves in the China market once it opens.

But how do the larger, domestic incumbent banks such as Taiwan Cooperative, Chang Hwa, and the International Bank of Taipei get back in the game? The medium-sized and large incumbent banks have a narrowing window of opportunity to respond to the rapid changes in the market. If they are to survive and be meaningful players in a decade, they will have to take decisive action in the years leading up to 2005.

First, action must focus on banking and avoid the distractions of getting involved in other financial businesses under the auspices of financial holding companies. Deep customer information, established sales cultures, and a willingness to actively manage performance are the key success factors for multi-business financial holding companies. Banks that lack these will be better served by first strengthening their core businesses. This will be easier to do rather than straying into life insurance, for example, which has its own significant challenges. Second, incumbents must take steps to clean up their balance sheets. Without a clean book, their ability to generate stronger earnings and attract new capital will be severely hampered. Third, they must improve their earnings by realizing substantial productivity gains in their branches and back-office operations. While this will involve tough human resource reductions, there are literally hundreds of millions of dollars in earnings improvement waiting to be captured. Changing the business mix in favor of retail is the fourth critical step that incumbent banks in Taiwan, large or small, must undertake.

Incumbents should also consider alliances with foreign partners as they undertake their decisive turnarounds. While the high-performing local banks have done a great job of achieving leadership in the most attractive retail products, these markets are by no means locked up. A partnership with a foreign bank may provide risk-based pricing skills, for example, which could help an incumbent make a real play for the fast-growing consumer finance market. Equally, alliances with a foreign player could help large incumbents, in particular, to develop the superior service model, in SME for example, to help defend their traditional market share. While a foreign alliance can certainly help incumbents to strengthen their hand as competition intensifies, they are not a replacement for the four critical steps outlined above.

Should foreign banks such as Citibank, Standard Chartered Bank, and HSBC enter the acquisition fray? As of 2001, foreign banks can take majority control of local banks through offshore financial holding companies. At the end of 2002, none had done so. Concerns over transaction pricing, risk in the corporate book, and potential problems with reducing headcount have kept foreign buyers on the sidelines. Until the government is ready to provide assurances on the possibility of making headcount reductions, foreign institutions really cannot take the risk of acquiring one of Taiwan's larger banks outright. Such moves are unlikely to happen before 2005.

Foreign players have two realistic options in Taiwan over the medium term. The first is to pursue organic growth, which a number of foreign banks such as Standard Chartered Bank and Citibank have done successfully. In fact, Citibank, which has a long history in Taiwan, is believed to generate the highest economic profit (adjusted for capital and risk costs) of any bank on the island based on its organic business. In the current competitive market structure, an organic play is suited primarily to mono-line companies such as consumer finance or bancassurance players that embody true skill-based advantages.

The second real option available to foreign banks is to take a minority stake in one of the leading local financial holding companies. Such a stake can be used to cement a series of product joint ventures between the local financial holding company and a foreign partner. This is an attractive option for foreign players looking to build a potential long-term partnership to tap the Greater China market. In effect, this is the path that Citibank has taken in part with its $750 million investment in the Fubon Group (initially securing Citibank a 15 percent stake). Both Fubon and Citibank have been reported in the press to be committed to jointly developing the China market when it opens, although as of 2002, there was no visible cooperation between the two in China. Looking beyond to 2010, at a minimum, a strong presence in Taiwan – specifically, Taipei and its environs – would provide access to one of Greater China's wealthier areas. But an investment in a Taiwan-based FHC must be justified by aspirations for Taiwan alone. The China angle should be assessed as an additional value option, given the uncertainty of the relationship between Taiwan and the mainland.

While it is easy to step back and paint a panoramic view that places Taiwan financial institutions at the center of the Greater China market, it is also easy to create false allure. The China market will eventually be an equally competitive and challenging venue for all foreign players. Taiwan's banks come with certain cultural and linguistic advantages, but it is only when these are combined with true world-class product skills and sufficient capital backing that a real advantage is created. The period until 2007, when the China market opens, will be a crucial period for Taiwan's leading banks to build dominance at home so that a few may earn the right to venture across the Strait and become a Greater China player. Local banks that capitalize on the changing forces of the Taiwan market and overcome traditional internal barriers to change will be best positioned to earn this right.

7

Hong Kong: Bridging a Painful Transition

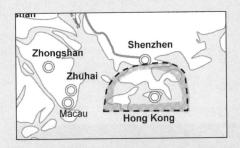

Macroeconomics

- GDP[1] ($bn)   164
- GDP per capital ($)   24,385
- PPP GDP per capita ($)   29,999
- Exports ($bn/% of GDP)   191/116
- Imports ($bn/% of GDP)   199/121
- FDI inflow ($bn/% of GDP)   23/14
- FDI outflow ($bn/% of GDP)   9/5
- Foreign currency reserves ($bn/% of GDP)   111/68
- External debt ($bn/% of GDP)   46/28
- NPL of banks ($bn/% of total net loans)   11/4
- National government borrowing
  ($bn/% of GDP/% external)   0/0/0
- Top 3 trading partners   China, US, Japan
- Number of corporates in Global Top 500[2]   0

Socioeconomics

- Population (mn)   7
- Number of households (mn)   2
- Average household income ($)   46,010
- Number of households earning >$100K p.a. (mn)   0.19
- Mobile phones/100 population   85
- Internet subscribers/100 population   43
- Urbanization (% of population)   94
- % of population with university degrees   19.1
- % of population above 65 years old in 2001
  and 2021   11/19

Capital Markets

- Number of listed corporations — 867
- Equity market capitalization ($bn/% of GDP) — 506/309
- Trading volume ($bn/% of market cap) — 241/48
- Debt market capitalization ($bn/% of GDP) — 63/38
- Equity underwriting[3] ($bn/% of GDP) — 11/7
- Debt underwriting[3] ($bn/% of GDP)2 — 33/20
- M&A ($bn/% of GDP) — 15/9
- Retail assets under management ($bn) — 24
- Institutional assets under management ($bn) — 143

Banking Markets

- Total loans of all financial institutions, including non-banks ($bn/% of GDP) — 281/171
- Total deposits of all financial institutions, including non-banks ($bn/% of GDP) — 432/263
- Mortgages ($bn/% of GDP) — 83/51
- Personal loans ($bn/% of GDP) — 11/6
- Credit card receivables ($bn%/% of GDP) — 7/4
- Credit cards per person above 15 — 2.16
- Credit card spend as % of household total spend — 29
- Foreign ownership limit in 1997 and 2002 — 100/100
- Number of banks in Global Top 1,000 in 1997 and 2001 — 12/14
- Number of ATMs/1,000 population — 0.38
- Number of branches/1,000 population — 0.19
- Number of banking employees/1,000 population — 11.08

---

[1] At 2001 prices
[2] *The Fortune Global 500*: July 22, 2002
[3] Average from 1995–2001

Note: All figures as of December 2001 unless otherwise indicated

Hong Kong's Financial Landscape

Types	Number of institutions, 1997	Number of institutions, 2002	Percent of total assets 2001	Top 3 players
Local incorporated full license bank	31	27	66	• HSBC • Hang Seng Bank • Bank of East Asia
Foreign incorporated full license bank	149	120	29	• Bank of China (BOC) Group • Standard Chartered Bank • Citibank
Restricted license bank	66	49	4	• Hang Seng Finance • JP Morgan Securities
Deposit taking company	115	54	1	• Hang Seng Credit • Inchroy Credit • Dao Heng Finance
Money lender	n/a	>800	n/a	• Aeon Credit Services
Hybrid*	n/a	2	n/a	• DBS Kwong On** • DBS Dao Heng**
Total excluding money lender and hybrid	**361**	**250**	**$790bn**	

* Also included in local bank category
** Known as DBS Bank (Hong Kong) from July 2003

Fireworks sparkled in the sky above Victoria Harbor on the evening of July 1, 2002. Hong Kong was celebrating the fifth anniversary of its return to China. But despite the revelry, the mood was bleak. Unemployment stood at 7.8 percent, the highest for 40 years. With the economy in a deflationary spiral, consumer confidence was flagging. Real estate values had fallen 54 percent from their peak in 1997, leaving roughly 30 percent of owners holding negative equity. The Hang Seng stock market index had dropped 33 percent from its high in 1999. By the end of 2002, personal bankruptcies had rocketed to over 25,000 cases, one out of every 100 households. Hopes that recovery was on the way were cruelly dashed in March 2003 when a highly infectious respiratory disease spread to Hong Kong from southern China, resulting in hundreds of deaths and a World Health Organization advisory against travel to the city.

Indeed, the crushing effect of the Severe Acute Respiratory Syndrome, or SARS, outbreak underscored how living next to booming China is not always a blessing. In some ways, it may even be a curse. With the economic giant at its doorstep, Hong Kong's traditional role as a gateway to the mainland is under serious threat. Perhaps Hong Kong was simply thriving on borrowed time during the period when China closed its doors to the world in 1949 to the handover. Can Hong Kong retain or even bolster its status as a leading financial and services hub – or does it face decades of gradual economic decline?

The future is uncertain, not least because Hong Kong is facing major structural shifts brought on by the rapid development of China. The key to survival is for Hong Kong to become more deeply embedded in the southern Pearl River Delta (PRD) where throughout the 1990s the economy has grown at roughly 15–20 percent a year, about twice the rate of the nation as a whole. Hong Kong's logistics expertise, global trading networks, legal infrastructure, and world-class financing skills are critical to the continued development of the PRD. University of Hong Kong Professor Michael Enright estimates that in 2002 Hong Kong companies employed about 10 million people or a quarter of all workers in this part of southern China. As cross-border travel becomes easier, and as highways under construction in the area are completed, Hong Kong is in the center of one of the fastest growing regions in the world.

The macroeconomic opportunities available to Hong Kong do not automatically mean smooth sailing for local and international banks with substantial operations in the special administrative region (SAR) of China. While many businesses can pursue plans in China immediately, banks in Hong Kong will not be able to make a full play for the market until 2007. Institutions with wholesale banking operations in the mainland will be allowed to provide renminbi financing from 2004, but must wait three more years before China allows foreign banks to enter the retail banking market under its World Trade Organization commitments.

This represents a serious challenge for most Hong Kong banks for two reasons. First, a majority of their growth and profitability in the past has come from retail products. These businesses are now bringing in significantly lower returns on the back of slower growth, tighter margins, and increased provisioning for consumer finance write-offs. Second, the make-up of the Hong Kong retail market is undergoing dramatic change. The rich are becoming richer on the back of their ventures in China, while the middle and lower classes face growing unemployment, reduced salaries, and limited prospects for improving their economic position in the medium term. Prior to 1997, a fresh graduate of the University of Hong Kong could expect a starting salary of roughly $18,000 a year. By 2003, after four years of deflation, the figure had dropped to $12,000.

Banks in Hong Kong must react to these structural changes to survive. Inevitably, this means a clear shift in business models, a radical restructuring of distribution networks, and a consolidation of the many small banks that continue to operate. The winners will be those players that distinguish their services to the growing ranks of affluent customers from both Hong Kong and the mainland, design creative ways to cater to small and mid-sized corporations expanding into the PRD, and reduced their cost base to serve the shrinking retail mass market profitably.

By 2010, we expect the banking landscape to look much different from that of the 1980s and 1990s. While the market will continue to be dominated by major players such as HSBC, Hang Seng, the Bank of China group, Standard Chartered Bank, and DBS, overall competition will increase as these incumbents and large Chinese banks from the mainland consolidate their position in Hong Kong through the acquisition of the 30-odd smaller banks. By the turn of the decade, the structure of the Hong Kong market will resemble Singapore's today, dominated by a few large players. The difference will be that few will be truly local institutions.

Some would doubt that Hong Kong will remain the leading metropolis within the prosperous PRD. If the Hong Kong government moves quickly to build closer economic links across the region, Hong Kong can strengthen and substantially deepen its role as the "Chicago of the PRD," acting as a regional financial and services hub for the manufacturing and commodity businesses that surround it. This is a substantial opportunity for Hong Kong and its citizens. It will be much tougher for Hong Kong to lay sole claim to the mantle of the "New York of Greater China" – the main financial intermediary between China and the world. Boosted by Beijing's favor, ambitious Shanghai has already shown that it will put up a stiff challenge for this coveted role.

Whatever Hong Kong's future position, its days as a stand-alone banking market are numbered. In this chapter, we analyze the structural changes that are reshaping Hong Kong and pinpoint the opportunities that will help banks to bridge the difficult transition to 2007 when organic growth across the PRD should become a reality.

AT CHINA'S DOORSTEP, UNPRECEDENTED CHALLENGES

The "gentlemen's club" of Hong Kong banking has finally come under pressure to break up. Traditionally dominated by the three note-issuing banks – HSBC, Standard Chartered Bank, and the Bank of China group – Hong Kong's banking landscape has long been characterized as a cartel. With their market power, the leaders created a pricing umbrella under which more than 30 local banks thrived, enjoying high margins despite each having less than a 2 percent share of banking assets. Since 1997, the cozy club has been transformed into a raging battlefield as margins have plummeted, risks have risen, and transaction volumes declined.

Undeniably, cyclical forces are partly responsible for Hong Kong's woes. The financial crisis of 1997 and the subsequent global slowdown weigh heavily. But these problems are further complicated by the structural shifts triggered by the rapid growth of China, with its low-cost economy that is luring away jobs and opportunities not just from Hong Kong, but from many other markets around the world. On top of this, the liberalization and shake-up of the banking sector have further heightened the challenges Hong Kong's banks face.

A more porous border with a China determined to turn itself into a global manufacturing power on the back of its abundance of cheap and driven workers has resulted in a significant relocation of factories from Hong Kong to the mainland, mainly to the PRD. These two factors have resulted in a significant flow of investment from Hong Kong to the mainland, as well as the relocation of factories and workshops, mainly to the PRD. Since 1992, manufacturing as a percentage of Hong Kong's GDP has slipped from 18 percent to 5 percent and is expected to continue to decline. But perhaps more troubling for Hong Kong is that service-sector jobs – now the backbone of SAR's economy – will also surely shift to China. The wage differential of approximately 4:1 is too high for Hong Kong companies to resist moving middle-level management and administrative roles to the mainland, where talent is increasingly available.

Hong Kong's role as the middleman for Greater China has also come under threat as some Taiwanese business that once flowed through the city is going direct. In 2003, the number of Taiwanese people living in China was estimated to be three times higher than those from Hong Kong. Taiwan investors are gaining the means to navigate the China market without the support of Hong Kong. Once direct air and sea links are allowed between the mainland and Taiwan, Hong Kong's role as intermediary will be diminished further.

The permanent shifts in Hong Kong's underlying economy and the cyclical effects of the global slowdown led to an all-time high unemployment rate of 7.8 percent in 2002. Even when the global economy recovers and the effects of SARS and the war in Iraq play out, the fact is that many of the lost jobs will never again be available and salaries are not likely to return to previous levels soon.

Naturally, capital and talent are moving across the border in pursuit of new opportunities. In 2001, nearly a quarter of a million Hong Kong people were working and living in China. By the end of that year, about 100,000 had bought property in the mainland – 60 percent of them in Shenzhen, the special economic zone adjacent to Hong Kong; 30 percent in the rest of the PRD; and 10 percent in Shanghai. These investors have contributed to a real-estate market boom in several Chinese cities since the late 1990s. According to a 2003 report in the newspaper *China Securities*, one survey forecast that 370,000 Hong Kong people will buy property in Shenzhen by 2005. Property market analysts predicted that in the next 10 years up to a million Hong Kong residents, or 14 percent of the SAR's current population, would move to Shenzhen.

The combined effect of rising domestic unemployment, declining income, and the flight of capital and talent is reducing demand for real estate, a traditional source of wealth creation for the economy and individuals. Before 1997, Hong Kong had one of the most expensive property markets in the world. By 2002, values had collapsed by more than 50 percent. To be sure, the plunge in demand was partly triggered by the financial crisis in 1997, but it was also exacerbated by a change in policy. In the past, real estate was artificially overvalued because the government restricted the supply of land. Speculators took advantage, confident that prices would keep rising.

In 1997, Chief Executive Tung Chee-hwa announced that Hong Kong would increase the supply of land, adding 85,000 new apartment units every year in a bid to increase home ownership among the 60 percent of the population living in rented accommodation. In addition, the government would sell 250,000 public rental flats to tenants over 10 years. Though Tung abandoned his housing policy three years later, it contributed to the collapse of prices and the drop in wealth levels. Real estate values are unlikely to recover in the medium term because of the structural changes in the Hong Kong economy.

Unprecedented unemployment and declining income levels have led to soaring personal bankruptcies. In 2002, some 25,000 individuals filed for bankruptcy, a 28-fold increase over 1998. The average bankrupt carried unsecured debt in excess of $64,000, indicating that desperate individuals were borrowing from several banks to keep afloat before eventually running out of options. Bankruptcies were spread across all income segments, in line with the overall income distribution of the population, demonstrating the deep impact of Hong Kong's economic transition.

The fortunes of Hong Kong's banks, long among the most profitable in Asia, have been dealt a blow by these changes in market fundamentals. Further heightening the challenges ahead for them are the liberalization of the banking sector and the emergence of greater competition.

RESPONDING TO LIBERALIZATION AND COMPETITION

For any bank to set future strategy, it is important to understand how competitive the banking market in Hong Kong has become since 1997. In July 2000, Hong Kong finally deregulated deposit interest rates. This came at a time when banks were already in the midst of an aggressive mortgage war to maintain business volumes in a flattening market. Anticipation of the break-up of the interest-rate cartel put further pressure on margins and drove banks to push aggressively to develop unsecured personal lending businesses that offered higher returns, but led in part to the sharp rise in bankruptcies.

The mortgage price war would have been unthinkable in the old days of clubby rivalry. Spreads shrunk by 300 basis points between 1998 and 2001. In the late 1990s, incumbents and an invigorated Bank of China began to consolidate their positions through aggressive pricing. The price war extended to the corporate lending market on the back of declining business volumes that stemmed in part from migration of companies to the PRD.

Thinning margins and diminishing transactions forced banks to seek new growth engines. The credit card market became a popular target. Borrowing balances shot up 19 percent each year between 1995 and 2001. Costs skyrocketed as banks relied on promotional giveaways including televisions, radios, mobile phones, and other goodies to attract customers. The unsecured lending market grew quickly, building up huge underlying risks. Hong Kong did not have a positive credit bureau. Some 50,000 to 75,000 cardholders took on enormous levels of personal debt. While banks thought they were making prudent credit decisions based on the information they had, the high level of competition in the market, combined with poor information and the lack of transparency, led to charge-offs in personal unsecured lending at almost 13 percent of total balances in 2002. This was one of the highest rates ever anywhere in the world.

This story of banks rapidly pouring resources into developing new product lines only to find disappointment is becoming commonplace in Hong Kong. In the late 1990s, the government instituted a defined-contribution pension plan to help Hong Kong's aging population prepare for retirement. The new scheme was handled through the banks. Several signed up to offer products and hired dedicated sales forces. Leading up to the launch, Citibank decided that far too many players were in the race and withdrew. In late 2002, Citibank did it again, announcing it would exit from the home financing business in Hong Kong, and sell its mortgage portfolio due to unacceptably low returns and rising delinquency.

Liberalization and the breaking up of the banking cartel have increased market volatility. There are simply too many banks competing for diminishing profits. Mortgage volumes are unlikely to rise until prices recover enough for a significant number of property owners holding negative equity to find relief. Unsecured personal borrowing margins, among the highest in Asia prior to the bankruptcy crisis, will come under pressure, even as a positive credit bureau is launched in 2003 and banks adopt risk-based pricing strategies. Corporate loans, which exceeded $330 billion in 1998 but dropped to $179 million in 2001, will grow only marginally until Hong Kong banks are comfortable lending in China.

The picture in Hong Kong in the run-up to 2007, when China fully opens to foreign banks, is one of slow growth and growing competition. The large banks will consolidate their positions through mergers to maintain volumes and lower costs. The small banks will have to combine with each other if they are to reach the $20 billion in assets that China has set as the requirement to play in its market. We believe that this transition period will be a difficult one for Hong Kong, as banks are forced to restructure their business models to cope with the new realities.

NEW BUSINESS MODELS NEEDED

With the dramatic shifts in the real economy and the banking sector, old business models are no longer sustainable. Hong Kong presents banks with unique opportunities. The three most compelling are in retail banking, in consumer finance, and in capturing cross-border capital flows in and out of China. With the competition intense, only a few institutions will win.

Retail banking: Better service, lower costs

In 2001, retail banking revenues in Hong Kong stood at more than $6 billion, the sixth-highest in Asia. By 2010, this is forecast to grow to almost $10 billion. The sources of this revenue will change as the income gap widens. Both foreign and local banks must decide whether to go after the affluent market – households with more than $100,000 in liquid assets – and how to revise their cost structures to serve the mass market profitably.

China's strong growth has resulted in an interesting phenomenon in Hong Kong. The SAR's managerial and entrepreneurial talent has benefited from the mainland's economic boom – and will continue to do so. According to Asian Demographics forecasts, the number of households earning more than $100,000 will double over the coming decade. While the city's affluent do much of their business in China, most keep their families in Hong Kong because of better schooling and health services. Wealthy mainlanders are also parking their money in Hong Kong. And Chinese are now the top-spending tourists, with each visitor shelling out an average of $663, edging out the typical American who drops $650. During the 2003 Chinese New Year holidays, a tourist from Shanghai bought $14,000 worth of jewelry, while another picked up a $15,000 diamond. Once Hong Kong opens up its labor market to talent from the mainland to help drive growth in the finance and services sectors, highly skilled and educated mainlanders will swell the ranks of the SAR's affluent.

Meanwhile, the migration of low-end manufacturing and business activities across the border is reducing the earning opportunities of the majority of Hong Kong people. This is further exacerbated by the trickling in of low-cost skilled Chinese labor, eager to emulate those who came before them and build a better life in the city. The lower income segments, the bottom half of the social ladder, are seeing their income decline. This will continue for some time – at least until Hong Kong snaps out of its deflationary spiral or the wage and cost differential with the mainland is severely reduced.

Because of this polarization (see Exhibit 7.1), banks in Hong Kong must revise their service model. Many realize that they must differentiate services for affluent customers or risk losing them. A number have set up VIP centers with such trappings as a special roped-off area in branches and a dedicated teller window. "Red carpet retail banking" has been effective in making prized clients feel privileged, but it misses the point.

The hardware may be there but the software is not. What is needed badly is a business model that truly adds value. Nearly two-thirds of Hong Kong consumers are concerned about having enough money for retirement and are seeking higher grade services such as investment advice. In 2000, Credit Suisse, through its Winterthur insurance subsidiary, got together with several local banks to offer premier financial planning services that provide investment and protection products. Backed by Winterthur's direct sales force, this effort led to growth in assets under management that exceeded projections.

Exhibit 7.1 Income polarization in Hong Kong

Annual household income ($ '000)		% of Hong Kong households in segment	% of total income controlled by segment
> 100		9	38
90–100	Tax-paying*	1.7	4
80–89		2.2	4
70–79		3	5
60–69		4.1	6
50–59	Non-tax-paying*	5.9	7
40–49		8.5	8
30–39		12.6	9
20–29		18	10
10–19		21.7	7
<10		13.2	2

* Based on media reports that less than 40% of Hong Kong's population pay taxes
Source: Asian Demographics; McKinsey analysis

For the retail mass market, the main issue is more efficiency than growth. Walk along Queen's Road in Hong Kong's Central business district and you pass at least three bank branches every 100 meters. There are only about 8,000–10,000 customers per branch in Hong Kong, compared to about 26,000 per branch in Singapore. Given the high rental costs in Hong Kong, maintaining a branch network is expensive.

The key is to rationalize distribution costs, in part by changing customer behavior. Mass market accounts must become profitable again, as has happened in Europe. Small depositors could be given ATM-only access. Those customers that insist on teller service would have to pay for it. In other developed markets, such measures have brought cost-to-income ratios for mass-market segments down from over 100 percent to 60 percent. While Hong Kong banks have had limited incentive to experiment with such approaches, the removal of the pricing cartel now leaves them little choice.

As each bank develops its business model, many will naturally want to serve all segments. They must resist this urge. In other developed markets, typically only a handful of banks succeed in building a sizable and expandable position in the affluent segment. Most Hong Kong banks will have to redesign their distribution networks and processes to eke out attractive enough returns. But the investment required to reshape a bank's cost base will be too high for many of the smaller players. For this reason, mergers with similar institutions will be the only option.

Consumer finance: The key is insight

Even though banks in 2002 saw negative returns from consumer finance, mainly due to the rise in personal bankruptcies, and are set to do so again in 2003, the long-term prospects for this business remain interesting. Indeed, the market will look more and more like those in mature economies in North America and Europe, with a few leading players racking up decent profits through superior risk-based pricing. Average industry interest rates will drop from 20 percent plus to 12–15 percent, enough for leading players to pull in attractive ROEs. The launch of a positive credit bureau and the increased transparency this will bring mean that only the strongest players with the best skills will survive. Small players will be forced to exit the credit card and unsecured personal loan markets, which have typically been fragmented.

In 2001, personal borrowing through credit cards and personal loans amounted to 11 percent of GDP, compared to 23 percent in the United States. On average, most people in Hong Kong carry unsecured balances equivalent to one or two months' income, about half the US level. This suggests further capacity for growth. But credit distribution is an issue, as demonstrated by the recent rash of bankruptcies when a small number of consumers built up enormous debts of up to 42 months' income (see Exhibit 7.2). The new credit bureau will make it possible for banks to lend to individuals at levels they can afford. This increased transparency will mean that lending will expand more evenly across the population. But the number of players that will make profits in this expanded market will shrink.

Hong Kong's credit bureau will turn consumer finance into a much more sophisticated game. Armed with information they did not have before, banks will be able to target customers with products and pricing better fitted to their needs and relative degree of risk. Banks in the United States and several European markets have been doing this for the past decade. To win, players must have the skills to employ a host of demographic and consumer behavior data to segment their target market carefully. Real insight into customer needs and risks will allow them to discard business models based on acquisitions and promotions. But few banks in Hong Kong are prepared to play the new game. Most lack the basic customer data such as income levels, up-to-date job information, and purchasing patterns to craft highly differentiated offerings.

The situation will not change overnight. From June 2003, banks will be allowed to tap the bureau for information only on new customers or existing customers applying for new credit. Those limits will be lifted two years later. Hong Kong chose to roll out its credit bureau in phases to avoid having every bank review their personal loans at the same time. This could have led to a credit crunch, a destructive pricing war, or both. But laggards among Hong

| Exhibit 7.2 | High indebtedness of bankrupts across all income segments |

Monthly income HK$ '000	% of adult population* Percent	% of bankrupt population** Percent	Total unsecured debt to monthly income Times
>30	8	6	1.4 · 33
16–30	25	30	1.1 · 38
10–15	23	25	1.6 · 50
<10	34	29	2.2 · 175
No income	10	10	N/A · Sample average 42 times

☐ Average product owner*   ■ Bankrupt mean**

* Based on Asia Market Intelligence survey of 909 respondents in 2000
** Based on Official Receiver's Office sample of 563 bankrupt customers in 2000
Source: Asia Market Intelligence; Official Receiver's Office; McKinsey analysis

Kong's banks would do well not to wait until 2005 before honing their risk management skills and customer insight. Should a new attacker such as a US mono-line player enter the market, it could move quickly and gain an advantage as all its customers and business would be new.

Consumer finance will be a rich prize for the handful of competitors who adopt the right business model. It will be a more complex game than in the past, owing both to the arrival of a positive credit bureau and the new risks associated with the increase of cross-border travel and migration between Hong Kong and the mainland. Only banks that can afford to invest in new technologies and skills will survive the transition.

Cross-border flows: Carving out a role

Historically, Hong Kong has been the primary gateway for financial flows in and out of China. Indeed, the Stock Exchange of Hong Kong has long striven to solidify its status as the "New York of Greater China." Some doubt the SAR's ability to do so. There is a growing belief that the PRD region will eventually replace Hong Kong as the logistics hub for imports and exports, and that Shanghai will someday surpass Hong Kong as China's premier financial center.

In reality, Hong Kong is well placed to put a lock on its position as the regional financial and services hub for southern China, a role similar to that which Chicago plays for the US Midwest. And the plain truth is that for most of the coming decade, Hong Kong will serve as Greater China's New York even as Shanghai, favored by the central government in Beijing, lays claim to that title. This means that Hong Kong banks, its largest in particular, will have many opportunities to profit from the cross-border flows of capital, trade, commerce, and people.

For Hong Kong to achieve its ambitions, increased integration with the PRD region is critical. The PRD consists of nine major Chinese cities, with a total of more than 40 million people. It represents only 3.5 percent of the national population but generates about 9 percent of China's GDP (see Exhibit 7.3). Over the rest of this decade, the PRD will remain a key manufacturing center and be home to a growing number of local SMEs and other similar companies from Hong Kong and Taiwan.

The PRD will require substantial capital and a wide range of financial services to develop its manufacturing muscle. None of the Chinese cities in the region except Hong Kong will be able to provide the sophisticated skills, international networks, and legal systems needed. The SAR offers much more. Although roads, ports, airports, and other infrastructure have been built in the PRD, Hong Kong's well-planned facilities are a cut above the rest. No other city possesses the knowledge and management expertise to cope with region's growing trade flows.

While the Hong Kong government will have to build closer links with key cities in the PRD, banks in the SAR can play a critical role in bolstering the city's "Chicago" role. From 2004, foreign banks in China, including those from Hong Kong, will be able to offer a full range of services to Chinese corporations. The growing needs of Hong Kong and mainland Chinese small and medium-sized companies represent significant revenue opportunities in traditional banking businesses such as lending, factoring, trade finance, and cash management.

Hong Kong banks can build on established relationships with local and global companies to make significant inroads into the PRD. As they boost their knowledge of the manufacturing supply chains throughout the area, these players will be well positioned to take calculated risks with a growing breed of professionally managed Chinese companies. This is not to say that Hong Kong banks will be without competition from Chinese counterparts. Yet players from the SAR have a window of opportunity to use their better skills and capabilities to lock in long-term corporate relationships before mainland banks are able to match their service offerings.

Exhibit 7.3　Profile of the Pearl River Delta (PRD)

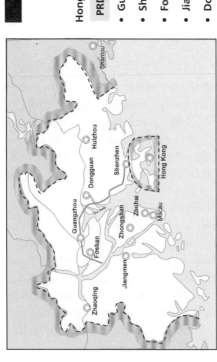

PRD in aggregate		PRD relative to whole of China
Population	44 mn	3.5% of national population
GDP	$103 b	8.9% of national GDP
GDP growth	13 percent	About twice national GDP growth rate
GDP per capita	$2,342	Almost 3 times national average

Key statistics of Hong Kong and cities in the PRD

	Population '01 (million)	Nominal GDP '01 ($ billion)	Annual GDP growth '98–'01 (percent)	GDP per capita '01 ($)
Hong Kong	6.7	164.0	1	24,385
PRD cities:				
● Guangzhou	10.1	32.4	13	3,210
● Shenzhen	7.3	23.6	15	3,316
● Foshan	6.3	12.9	11	2,160
● Jiangmen	3.8	7.4	9	1,941
● Dongguan	6.5	7.0	18	1,072
● Huizhou	3.3	5.8	11	1,774
● Zhaoqing	3.4	5.0	4	1,448
● Zhuhai	1.3	4.4	11	3,435
● Zhongshan	2.4	4.4	14	1,849

Source: National Statistical Bureau; People's Republic of China (PBOC); Hong Kong government

Hong Kong's strong position in the global financial markets will continue to provide its banks with major advantages in traditional banking services. With their extensive experience in China trade, the SAR's large financial institutions have seen substantial growth in their clearing and settlement businesses. Between 1995 and 2000, total settlement and clearing through Hong Kong's financial system increased from $8.5 trillion to $13.8 trillion. In 2001, foreign exchange trading volume hovered around $17 trillion. Although this was a drop of about 15 percent from 1998, Singapore's forex trading volume plummeted about 35 percent over the same period.

The SAR's play to secure its role as the dominant player in the PRD is a bet it must win if it is to benefit from the fast growth of this dynamic region. The key for Hong Kong banks is to deepen their presence in the PRD. They must work closely with logistics and service companies to leverage the SAR's strengths fully. This will strengthen Hong Kong's role as the region's Chicago. But this opportunity will only be available to large banks with the $20 billion in assets that China has set as the requirement to enter its market. These players must also have the international trade networks and financial resources to pursue cross-border opportunities.

While the drive to be the Chicago of the PRD offers significant opportunities for Hong Kong's commercial banks, the battle to be the preeminent financial center of Greater China over the long term is a matter for the world's "bulge bracket" investment banks that dominate underwriting and institutional trading. While Hong Kong aspires to confirm its position, this claim is likely to be challenged. The key question is how long Hong Kong's capital markets can provide better financing options and liquidity than their Chinese counterparts. The SAR's skills, legal infrastructure, and market openness are major advantages that will take some time for Shanghai or any other Chinese city to match (see sidebar).

Today, of course, Hong Kong's capital markets are the key intermediates of global capital flows to China. From 1995 to 2001, the market capitalization of Hong Kong-listed "red chips" and H-shares increased by 41 percent a year, while the overall capitalization of the Hong Kong market rose just 9 percent. Chinese companies' share of the Hong Kong market's capitalization expanded from 5 percent to 26 percent. China's capital markets lack the deep institutional investor base needed to place and trade large blocks of shares. In addition, China's exchanges still place restrictions on the flow of foreign capital.

For most of the rest of this decade, Hong Kong will continue to be the favored market for large Chinese companies seeking to raise capital from investors in the West. The more that Hong Kong can do to attract top mainland financial services talent to the SAR, the better the chances are that the city will retain its regional role in the world's capital markets.

Shanghai: Hong Kong's heir apparent?

If there is any city in China regarded as the heir apparent to Hong Kong as a regional financial hub, it is Shanghai. While this sprawling metropolis may one day usurp its rival, it has some way to go. Though the somnolent skyscrapers in the Lujiazhui financial district of Pudong, across the Huangpu River from the famous Bund, may suggest otherwise, Shanghai is today more of a manufacturing center. At the end of 2002, financial services contributed only 10 percent to its GDP, while manufacturing accounted for more than 45 percent.

To be sure, Shanghai has surged forward at astonishing speed, building impressive infrastructure, the hardware of development, including a stylish airport, a web of elevated highways, and a cutting-edge maglev rail line. Yet for all these accomplishments, China's second city cannot quickly duplicate the unique "software" that Hong Kong has in abundance. The former British colony, for one thing, has the legal environment necessary for financial stability and investor confidence. The rule of law is not built in a day. It will take at least one or two decades before Shanghai acquires the capabilities to match Hong Kong's.

Beyond 2010, political will and ambitious Shanghai's get-up-and-go drive will surely lead to a material shift of financial flows away from Hong Kong. By then, the space-age towers in Pudong may actually be fully occupied and bustling. And Shanghai's stock market may be as respected as Hong Kong's is today. Few doubt that Beijing is determined to bestow on Shanghai the title of "New York of Greater China," even if this means relegating Hong Kong to a position beside or even below the throne. Still, it will take many years before the crown prince is ready, or able, to become king.

PREPARING FOR THE NEW MARKET STRUCTURE

In 2002 and early 2003, we met with a number of key banking executives in Hong Kong. While many felt battered by the bankruptcy crisis, most were calm, even sanguine, about the future. Much will change in the years leading up to 2007, but the majority were waiting to get a better read on the markets, instead of formulating plans of action. We believe that, with major structural shifts playing out, the time for Hong Kong banks to ponder their next move is quickly running out.

Chinese banks: New attackers

With their strong customer base in their home market, Chinese banks in Hong Kong will inevitably be tempted to lay claim to a share of the global flows in and out of China. The Bank of China has already built a substantial position in SAR and its recent listing on the Hong Kong stock market gives it greater freedom to pursue an aggressive strategy. Several of the large and mid-sized Chinese banks will secure a beachhead in Hong Kong by buying one or more of the small local banks. As Chinese banks have traditionally been less concerned with generating hefty shareholder returns in the short term, their arrival will further increase the competitive dynamics of Hong Kong's increasingly volatile banking sector.

Hong Kong banks: Merge to survive

Many of Hong Kong's small banks are in for a difficult time. Only a few players with the size and skills to compete will win in the race to pursue the opportunities spelled out in this chapter. The rest are in an awkward position: They face the possible entry of big competitors in their home market and are not large enough to qualify to do business in the mainland after 2007. While they may not be ready to accept it, many will have to dress themselves up for sale.

Most of Hong Kong's small banks are not in financial distress. They hold adequate reserves against moderate levels of NPLs and are generally well capitalized. The main issue is the lack of growth in a maturing market with increasingly tough competition. As of March 2003, only two domestic banks – Hang Seng Bank, a subsidiary of HSBC, and the Bank of East Asia – had assets in excess of the $20 billion needed to qualify for full participation in the China market once foreign banks are allowed in. Shanghai Commercial Bank, the next biggest, held just $9 billion in assets.

To grow, a small bank must either become a niche player in Hong Kong or merge with others to build sufficient scale to compete more broadly at home and possibly in Southern China. While consolidation may happen, many small banks are owned by families typically reluctant to sell out to rival clans. As a result, many would opt for a takeover by a global bank or a Chinese institution wanting to enter the market. Whatever course they take, these small banks cannot afford to wait, given their limited growth options. If they dither long, their value will only fall, diminishing their chances of finding a buyer willing to pay a good price.

Global banks: Focusing on the PRD

For global banks in Hong Kong, the priority is to strengthen their game and plot strategies to capture cross-border flows. Consolidation in the market that will come in waves leading up to 2007 could offer interesting merger and alliance opportunities. Time is largely on the side of the multinational banks, although they could be preempted by aggressive Chinese banks seeking to use Hong Kong as an international window to the world.

Global players need to sharpen their focus and skills on the growing mass affluent, and restructure their cost base to maintain profits from the mass market. They are already well positioned to ride the growing cross-border flow of trade, commerce, and investment. In the run-up to 1997, global banks should consider dropping low-margin businesses in Hong Kong, as Citibank had done with mortgages, and refocus efforts on high-growth opportunities in the PRD.

The key question for foreign banks not already in Hong Kong is whether to set up a presence in the SAR at all. Even though there are attractive slivers of opportunity in consumer finance and wealth management, the potential revenues that could be generated in Hong Kong alone would have no significant impact on the global bottom line of a major multinational player.

Nonetheless, several foreign players have in recent years increased their presence in Hong Kong. Notable examples include DBS Bank of Singapore, GE Capital from the United States, and Melbourne-based ANZ. The main strategic rationale for foreign banks to enter Hong Kong now is to place a long-term bet on the SAR solidifying its role as the Chicago of the PRD. Indeed, if Hong Kong strengthens and confirms its position as the leading city in southern China, a regional network headquartered in the city could well become an important part of a multinational bank's global business over the rest of this decade.

※ ※ ※

At the July 1, 2002, swearing-in ceremony for his second term as Hong Kong's chief executive, Tung Chee-hwa acknowledged the challenges facing the SAR, but struck a typically upbeat note: "In the past, at each turning point, Hong Kong people, seasoned in turning adversity into opportunity, have always prevailed ... The path ahead is one of hope, though laden with many challenges."

Indeed, over five decades of tumultuous change, Hong Kong has created a vibrant economy by sheer will, amazing resilience, and entrepreneurial wits. This magnetic metropolis is not about to crumble, nor will its bright lights fade. But with the competitive dynamics in Asia changing swiftly and dramatically as the Chinese giant emerges, Hong Kong will have to reassess and reinforce its roles in Greater China and in the burgeoning PRD. For its banks, the key issue is to eke out growth and profits to bridge the period before the China market opens fully in 2007. Waiting until then without responding to the structural shifts shaking the banking landscape is simply not a viable option.

8

Singapore: Club Rules Broken

Macroeconomics

- GDP[1] ($bn) — 86
- GDP per capital ($) — 20,980
- PPP GDP per capita ($) — 27,120
- Exports ($bn/% of GDP) — 122/142
- Imports ($bn/% of GDP) — 110/128
- FDI inflow ($bn/% of GDP) — 5.5/6
- FDI outflow ($bn/% of GDP) — 8.3/10
- Foreign currency reserves ($bn/% of GDP) — 80/93
- External debt ($bn/% of GDP) — 10/12
- NPL of banks ($bn/% of total net loans) — 8/6
- National government borrowing
  ($bn/% of GDP/% external) — 77/90/0
- Top 3 trading partners — Malaysia, US, Japan
- Number of corporates in Global Top 500[2] — 1

Socioeconomics

- Population (mn) — 4
- Number of households (mn) — 0.95
- Average household income ($) — 35,547
- Number of households earning >$100K p.a. (mn) — 0.04
- Mobile phones/100 population — 68
- Internet subscribers/100 population — 71
- Urbanization (% of population) — 100
- % of population with university degrees — 16.9
- % of population above 65 years old in 2001
  and 2021 — 7/15

Capital Markets

- Number of listed corporations — 511
- Equity market capitalization ($bn/% of GDP) — 117/136
- Trading volume ($bn/% of market cap) — 71/61
- Debt market capitalization ($bn/% of GDP) — 41/48
- Equity underwriting[3] ($bn/% of GDP) — 3/3
- Debt underwriting[3] ($bn/% of GDP) — 10/12
- M&A ($bn/% of GDP) — 16/19
- Retail assets under management ($bn) — 6
- Institutional assets under management ($bn) — 171

Banking Markets

- Total loans of all financial institutions, including non-banks ($bn/% of GDP) — 144/168
- Total deposits of all financial institutions, including non-banks ($bn/% of GDP) — 144/167
- Mortgages ($bn/% of GDP) — 58/68
- Personal loans ($bn/% of GDP) — 17/19
- Credit card receivables ($bn/% of GDP) — 2/2
- Credit cards per person above 15 — 1.03
- Credit card spend as % of household total spend — 23
- Foreign ownership limit in 1997 and 2002 (%) — 40/100
- Number of banks in Global Top 1,000 in 1997 and 2001 — 8/4
- Number of ATMs/1,000 population[2] — 0.44
- Number of branches/1,000 population — 0.12
- Number of banking employees/1,000 population — N/A

---

[1] At 2001 prices
[2] *The Fortune Global 500*: July 22, 2002
[3] Total NPL of Singapore incorporated banks

Note: All figures as of December 2001 unless otherwise indicated

Singapore's Financial Landscape

Types	Number of institutions, 1997	Number of institutions, 2002	Percent of total assets 2001	Top 3 players
Government owned bank	1*	0	n/a	n/a
Local commercial bank	6*	3**	58	• DBS Bank • United Overseas Bank (UOB) • Oversea-Chinese Banking Corp. (OCBC)
Foreign full license commercial bank	22	22	} 36	• Citibank • ABN AMRO Bank • BNP Paribas
Foreign wholesale license commercial bank	13	33		• Deutsche Bank • UBS AG • Rabobank Nederland
Foreign offshore commercial bank	105	59		• Landesbank Baden–Wurttemberg • Norinchukin Bank • Toronto–Dominion Bank
Merchant bank	80	55	2	• National Australia Merchant • Credit Suisse First Boston • Merrill Lynch
Finance company	19	7	4	• Hong Leong Finance • OCBC Finance • Singapore Investments & Finance
Representative office	64	55	n/a	• n/a
Total excluding representative offices	**247**	**179**	**$227bn**	

* Besides the seven major banks, there are six other banks which are subsidiaries of UOB, OCBC, and OUB with separate banking licenses.
** Besides the three major banks, there are three other banks which are subsidiaries of UOB and OCBC with separate banking licenses.

Until 1999, Singapore's banking sector seemed to be like an exclusive gentlemen's club where every member knew the rules and scrupulously observed them. No rushed moves, no cutthroat tactics. The financial crisis that erupted in 1997 appeared to do little to upset the calm. The Singapore economy was relatively unaffected and the five major local banks – confident that the Monetary Authority of Singapore (MAS) would continue to shield them from foreign competitors – remained comfortably cocooned in a cozy oligopoly.

However, the peace was broken. In 1999, the MAS announced a five-year plan to liberalize the banking sector and remove regulatory barriers such as restrictions on opening branches that had constrained foreign institutions from competing on an even playing field with local players. At about the same time, two of Singapore's smaller banks, Overseas Union Bank (OUB) and Keppel TatLee, started what would develop into an aggressive mortgage price war rarely seen in Asia. By 2001, all banks were selling mortgages with first-year rates below cost.

The stuffy club room turned into banking's equivalent of a cantina full of dueling duelers. Keppel TatLee, itself the product of a merger, was taken over by Oversea-Chinese Banking Corp. (OCBC). Meanwhile, United Overseas Bank (UOB) acquired OUB, leaving rival bidder DBS Bank short. In the middle of the takeover battle for OUB, the chairman of state-controlled DBS, S. Dhanabalan, was forced to issue an unprecedented public apology after the bank's advisors alleged during a roadshow presentation that UOB's offer made no economic sense and instead was "designed to keep family control intact without regard for shareholder value."[1] The club had not tossed all standards of decorum out the window.

All this drama set rumors flowing as fast as the beer from the Boat Quay bar taps. Was another takeover in the cards? And what would happen once Citibank is allowed to open branches wherever it wants? Inquiring bankers wanted to know.

Far from being dull, Singapore has turned out to be an exciting and unpredictable banking market, as competitive forces and liberalization have fueled consolidation. The island republic's banks are emerging as potential international players. And Singapore is deepening its role as the financial center for Southeast Asia and bolstering its claim to becoming a banking hub for Asia. Singapore is a promising market that still contains attractive opportunities for banks operating domestically, particularly in the areas of

---

1 "DBS says sorry to UOB and OUB," *Straits Times*, (*August 1, 2001*), quoting a document – "Preliminary Analysis of the UOB Bid" – prepared by an overseas office of DBS' financial advisor and distributed during a roadshow in Europe.

wealth management, mass-market consumer banking, and small and medium-sized commercial banking. Singapore is also an increasingly powerful hub for regional businesses such as private banking and asset management.

THE SHIFTING LANDSCAPE

Situated at the southern tip of the Malay Peninsula, the city-state of Singapore is home to 4 million people and boasts a GDP per capita of $20,980. Despite its small population, many banks have prospered on the back of the Lion City's enormous wealth. Revenues are healthy. For example, total revenue from the consumer banking business reached $2.8 billion in 2001.

This is one of Asia's most liberal banking markets. Competing against the three local universal banks – DBS, UOB, and OCBC – are many foreign players. They can operate freely in commercial, corporate, and investment banking. The MAS, Singapore's financial regulator and de facto central bank, is gradually deregulating consumer banking. The largest foreign players – Citibank, HSBC, and Standard Chartered Bank – have captured about 27 percent of the total $144 billion in deposits despite MAS-imposed limits such as a cap on branch numbers.

By the end of 2002, the MAS had issued Qualifying Full Banking (QFB) licenses to six foreign banks – ABN AMRO Bank, BNP Paribas, Citibank, HSBC, Standard Chartered Bank, HSBC and Maybank. (Another 16 foreign banks have regular full banking licenses that carry some limitations, such as on the number of branches and ATMs, and 33 have restricted licensing arrangements.) QFB licenses allow foreign operators to compete against local banks, with few restrictions. Foreign banks, for example, cannot use the shared domestic ATM networks, but with the QFB licence, they can set up one of their own. They also cannot open more than 15 branches. The MAS is expected to lift the remaining regulatory barriers over the next few years, and it is still unclear what impact the Singapore–US free trade agreement concluded in 2003 will have on further liberalization of the industry.

Compared to other Asian markets, Singapore weathered the 1997 crisis well due to prudent government policies and its robust economy. Banks were well capitalized before the crisis – and still are. The capital-adequacy ratio remained at around 19 percent from 1995 to 2002. At the end of that period, non-performing loans (NPLs) stood at 5.6 percent of $144 billion total banking loans in 2001, down from a peak of 8.5 percent in 1999.

Lion City trio: Singapore's banks in profile

DBS
Assets (2002): $83 billion
Pre-tax profits (2002): $808 million
Ownership: Government investment company Temasek Holdings
   (12.64 percent) and MND Holdings (Private) Limited (13.89 percent)
Employees: 13,536 for the group, and 6,466 for Singapore bank only
Branches: 270 worldwide, 107 in Singapore
Presence in Hong Kong and Thailand through acquisitions
Acquired Singapore government-owned POSBank in 1998

UOB
Assets (2002): $60 billion
Pre-tax profits (2002): $801 million
Ownership: Wee family
Employees: 12,142 for the group, and 3,125 for Singapore bank only
Branches: 263 worldwide, 87 in Singapore
Presence in Malaysia and Thailand
Acquired Singapore's OUB in 2001

OCBC
Assets (2002): $47 billion
Pre-tax profits (2002): $506 million
Ownership: Lee family
Employees: 8,567 for the group, and 3,198 for Singapore bank only
Branches: 115 worldwide, 67 in Singapore
Presence in Malaysia
Acquired Singapore government-linked Keppel TatLee in 2001

Driven by the MAS, which consistently applied pressure on bank owners to merge, the consolidation of the banking sector is largely complete. So too is the consolidation of finance companies. With assets of $3 billion, Hong Leong Finance remains the only independent firm of any significance. The MAS may soon turn its attention to rationalizing the insurance sector, in which more than 60 companies fight over a thin slice of just $4 billion in premiums.

The recent flurry of takeovers in the banking sector has naturally led many industry watchers to conclude that the Singapore market is saturated. This may be the case in consumer finance. Total consumer loans are equivalent to 89 percent of GDP in 2001, higher than in the United States or any other Asian market. However, due to the high price of real estate, mortgages represent about 76 percent of these borrowings – one of the highest percentages in Asia.

While waiting for economic growth to resume, Singapore banks are trying to optimize their business models at the micro level. A credit bureau has been launched to share information among banks and help them make faster and more accurate credit assessments. Following the bank mergers, several branches were closed and a few hundred employees laid off. Costs remain a major concern: Even with cost-to-income ratios in the high 30s to mid-40s, banks in Singapore remain significantly over-staffed and inefficient. The cost-to-income ratios are more a reflection of attractive spreads than they are of strong operating efficiencies. For example, the three local banks employ 13,000 people to handle $190 billion in assets in 2002. Simulations show that if they were competing in Europe with higher labor costs and lower spreads, they would probably not make any money.

SEARCHING FOR GROWTH

Banks looking for growth opportunities may have a hard time finding a rich vein to tap. Credit cards could offer some opportunities as penetration rates, at one card per adult, are still below many other developed economies with two to four cards per adult. But transaction volumes are already in line with other markets, suggesting that consumer spending habits are not likely to drive up demand for cards. Besides, the MAS restricts the issuance of cards only to individuals earning more than S$30,000, or $16,666 a year, about 65 percent of the adult population.

So where are the pockets of growth? Here are three segments that we think offer the most interesting opportunities in the Singapore market.

Wealth management: Catering to the mass affluent

At only 7 percent of GDP (versus 32 percent for the United States), the mutual funds market will resume strong growth as soon as the economy and the stock markets recover. One indication of consumer interest is that capital-guaranteed products have been launched successfully during a bear market.

Bancassurance may be another growth area. Banks already distribute 30 percent of life premiums. Singapore institutions are following the trend set by their French, Spanish, and Italian counterparts a decade ago. OCBC led the charge in 2000 by distributing the life products of sister company Great Eastern Holdings. In 2001, DBS followed suit when it was finally able to divest the small Insurance Corporation of Singapore and enter a landmark agreement with UK-based Aviva.

Growth in life insurance and mutual funds should be fueled by the progressive shift of retirement assets from management by the Central

Provident Fund (CPF), Singapore's mandatory defined-contribution scheme. In 2000, the government largely allowed contributors to select freely their asset manager, but because of the bear market, most consumers preferred to remain with the CPF. About $35 billion in retirement savings could flow to the private sector when consumers become more bullish about investments in general.

These product categories – mutual funds, bancassurance, and pensions – are just three examples of a bigger need: wealth management. As Singaporeans become wealthier and the "mass-affluent" class swells, banks offering quality advice and an open-product architecture will benefit if they are able to build stronger relationships and improve cross-selling. They should also aim to take advantage of asset consolidation. Most mass-affluent households have accounts with all local banks and at least one foreign bank.

We estimate that the mass-affluent consumer segment – households earning more than $100,000 a year – generate in excess of $750 million in annual banking revenues. Consumer research shows that despite some resistance to taking advice, let alone paying for it, Singaporeans are recognizing that they need help. Interest in managed products is growing. Because they know Singaporean consumers and are trusted by them, banks are likely to do much better in this business than financial advisers who are perceived as glorified insurance agents.

But local banks have been struggling to develop credible offerings, both on the advisory front end and at the product back end. Foreign banks dominate the market for investments by focusing on the most affluent households and serving them with professional relationship managers. They have also pioneered alternative products such as hedge funds or Equity-Linked Notes (ELNs) for the most sophisticated investors. In Europe, these products are offered to many mass-affluent investors. With markets likely to remain volatile for some time to come, Singapore banks should consider broadening their product range, introducing alternative investments, and deepening the skills of their sales force.

Mass-market banking: Riches in the heartland

With so much hype about serving affluent customers, banks have largely forgotten about the Singapore mass market. After all, the conventional wisdom is that in Asia, the high-end segment is where the money is. This is not true in Singapore simply because wealth distribution is a lot flatter than in developing markets. The average Singaporean living in a public housing estate is many times wealthier than his or her Malaysian counterpart. The mass-market segment, generates about half of total consumer banking revenues, or $1.4 billion a year.

Competition is a lot less intense than in the affluent segment. Our research shows that customers in this segment are much less price sensitive and much more easier to satisfy than their affluent counterparts. So far, DBS has dominated the mass-market segment through its POSBank brand, but no bank is currently capturing its full potential, particularly in the growth areas of retirement savings and consumer finance.

Small and medium-sized enterprises (SMEs): In need of service

SMEs may be another growth area in the Singapore market. Dismissed by corporate bankers and misunderstood by retail bankers, small and mid-sized businesses have not been well served. There are 100,000 SMEs in Singapore, of which probably 20,000 or so have acceptable credit prospects. Banks are now realizing that this market segment is less competitive and less price-sensitive than the corporate market, and often more resilient during economic downturns. Several banks, notably DBS, have revamped their distribution, risk assessment, and product offering to seduce SMEs.

Difficulties remain. We believe that banks have not yet cracked the code to success in serving this segment, particularly the lower end. First, the cost structures are too high. Second, good risk assessment is not systematic, with large and growing NPLs giving banks second thoughts. Finally, developing services for SMEs seems to be a low priority for Singapore banks, which appear to be preoccupied with post-merger integration and regional expansion. This may be good news for those who specialize in this market, such as tiny but successful finance company Hong Leong Finance, which seems to have found the right combination of a competent sales force, prudent risk management, and low operating costs.

BANKS IN SEARCH OF A FUTURE

While we do not have a crystal ball that allows us to predict the future of financial markets, we can pinpoint trends that help better anticipate what lies ahead for Singapore banking.

Hub ambitions

For Singapore to survive, the city-state must define its unique qualities and enhance them. As a small country surrounded by larger markets that are aiming to catch up, Singapore risks being marginalized and over the years losing its relevance on the international scene. The domestic banking market is still the largest in Southeast Asia but this cannot last. Singapore must identify slivers in which it can compete regionally if not globally.

In late 2001, the government launched a major effort to reinvent Singapore's economy, assembling representatives of all sectors in an

Economic Review Committee. Among other things, the panel sought to determine how Singapore could compete against financial hubs such as Hong Kong, London, and Zurich, as well as offshore centers such as Bermuda for reinsurance, or Luxemburg and Dublin for asset management. It concluded that Singapore should focus on becoming a hub for wealth management, global processing, and risk management.

The island republic is already an important private banking center, with $120 billion in assets booked by the many private banks with operations in the city. Its chief competitor in Asia is Hong Kong, which used to be the offshore center of choice for money from China, Taiwan, and the Philippines. However, Hong Kong's attractiveness as a neutral and confidential haven, particularly for wealthy overseas Chinese and Taiwanese demanding discretion, has eroded since the 1997 handover by Britain to China of sovereignty over the territory. As a consequence, money is increasingly flowing to Singapore, which has long been the preferred parking space for wealth from Indonesia, Malaysia, and Thailand.

Singapore has further strengthened its position over Hong Kong by luring money from Europeans looking for an alternative to Switzerland, the premier private banking center that has come under pressure from European Union countries to reduce secrecy and provide greater assistance in tracking down tax-evaders. In the future, Hong Kong and Singapore are likely to vie for money flowing out of Japan in search of higher returns. Japanese private wealth far exceeds that of any other Asian market. The city that captures the lion's share of these funds will be able to claim leadership in the private banking business in Asia.

Singapore is also an increasingly attractive asset management hub, rivaling Hong Kong in terms of assets under management and number of managers. In 2001, excluding institutional funds not available for private management, about $177 billion in assets were managed by institutions in Singapore. By 2010, that figure is expected to grow to $350 billion. Hong Kong-based institutions managed $166 billion in 2001 and are expected to have at least $410 billion in assets under management by 2010.

Regulations governing asset management in Singapore are very flexible and allow for easy registration, feeder funds, and alternative investments. Singapore could become even more attractive if some money currently managed by government institutions such as the CPF, MAS, and state holding companies Temasek and the Government of Singapore Investment Corporation or GIC, is channeled to institutional investors.

Transforming Singapore into a hub for regional processing is in our view an extremely ambitious if not unrealistic challenge, given the high labor costs compared to competitors such as India. Singapore offers excellent infrastructure, and some banks have used it as a base for back-office activities as Citibank has done with credit cards. However, this remains unusual mainly because of difficulties banks have faced in even consolidating some operations between Singapore and Malaysia. The intense rivalry between Singapore and Malaysia has often prevented such initiatives from receiving regulatory approval from both sides.

For Singapore to become a hub for risk management would be an intriguing challenge that would probably entail setting up an alternative risk exchange. But it is not immediately clear that successful business models can be developed for those risks that are not currently traded. And for risks already traded, adding capacity in Singapore may not appeal to market players dealing in London and Bermuda.

In conclusion, Singapore represents a tremendous platform for financial institutions operating in Asia. Its unique combination of good government, business-favorable regulations, access to surrounding markets, and talent are only matched by Hong Kong, which is struggling to define its role now that it is part of China. Singapore has the potential to be a relevant financial center in Asia, at least for certain slivers of business. New entrants should understand that the local market is small and largely controlled by existing players. They should regard Singapore as a base camp for a foray into Asia, rather than a market in which they can become a major force.

Expanding in the region

Singapore banks are aiming to grow by expanding into other markets. This is not an easy strategy and previous attempts have been only marginally successful so far. Both DBS and UOB made aggressive moves in Thailand in 1998, buying Thai Danu and Radanasin, respectively, only to discover that NPLs of their new acquisitions were increasing much faster than they had anticipated. DBS then acquired Dao Heng Bank, one of Hong Kong's best banks, in 2001 but had to pay a very high price for it at 3.3 times its book value.

Rumors often swirl that one of the three big banks is poised to make a purchase in China, even though it is not clear whether any foreign banker could generate meaningful returns there in the short term. To expand internationally, Singapore banks should first prove that they could create value by leveraging scale or skills that they might have at home or nearby. Malaysia would be the easiest and most logical showcase. Both OCBC and UOB have reasonably successful operations there that are run independently with little back-office or technology processing in common with their Singapore bases.

Malaysia can also be a major growth opportunity for Singapore banks. Consumers and corporates alike are underserved by the local banks. Culture and geographic proximity mean that management coordination would be easy. Processing consolidation and scale building should be negotiated with MAS and its counterpart Bank Negara Malaysia. The two sides could agree on a division of functions. For example, technology may be based in Singapore, while Malaysia would host call centers.

After Malaysia, Indonesia or the Philippines might be the next targets for Singapore banks. Geographic proximity increases the chances of a successful deal. But banks would have to consider the higher political risk in these two markets. Finally, if Singapore banks need to make an acquisition to gain a foothold in North Asia, other markets such as Korea or Taiwan might be more attractive targets than China, as they offer tangible growth potential and greater transparency in the medium term.

Singapore banks can also consider alliances as an alternative path to going internationally alone. Western or Australian banks may be interested in joining forces, bringing products or technologies and combining them with the Asian expertise that Singapore banks bring.

DBS, for example, having now built a regional footprint, has recently refocused its efforts on strengthening its capabilities, integrating what it has acquired and enhancing the profitability of its core businesses. Until recently, DBS' mantra was about building a regional franchise. With CEO Jack Tai recently at the helm, the bank's new catchphrases are "execution" and "focus on deliverying shareholder value", while clearly turning more cautious on acquisition opportunities, be they in China or Indonesia. This is also the strategy adopted by rival OCBC, where new CEO David Conner is following a strategy of building skills and capabilities, consolidating the bank's presence in Singapore and Malaysia, and cautiously expanding into a third country within 3 years.

To achieve this, both CEOs continue to supplement their banks' skill base by recruiting experienced bankers and executives with international banking backgrounds, harmonizing platforms and reducing costs aggressively. DBS is even testing large-scale outsourcing options. If Tai succeeds in realizing the synergies from DBS' capabilities and turning its mass-market and SME franchises into highly profitable operations before its main regional rivals do, he may well be able to prove DBS' detractors wrong and position the bank for a second wave of regional condolidation.

Growth at all costs is hardly a sustainable strategy anymore. The international expansion of Singapore banks is still at an early stage and the winner of this battle will be the player that first demonstrates that it can add value to an international acquisition or alliance by, at the very least, leveraging back-office, systems and support services across borders. Larger maneuvers should be reserved for when adequate experience has been built.

9

Southeast Asia: What does not Glitter may yet be Gold

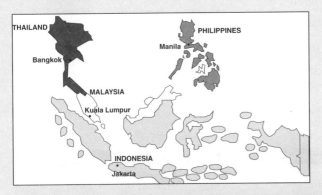

Macroeconomics

	Indonesia	Malaysia	Philippines	Thailand
• GDP[1] ($bn)	145	88	71	115
• GDP per capital ($)	680	3,700	927	1,837
• PPP GDP per capita ($)	4,099	8,614	2,960	7,692
• Exports ($bn/% of GDP)	58/40	90/102	31/44	63/55
• Imports ($bn/% of GDP)	35/24	72/82	28/39	69/60
• FDI inflow ($bn/% of GDP)	−3.2/−2.2[2]	2.5/3	1.8/2.5	2.8/2.4
• FDI outflow ($bn/% of GDP)	0.18/0.1	1.5/2	0.2/0.3	0.13/0.1
• Foreign currency reserves ($bn/% of GDP)	28/19	29/33	13/18	32/28
• External debt ($bn/% of GDP)	145/100	52/59	51/72	82/71
• NPL of banks ($bn/% of total net loans)	4/12	14/11	6/17	9/11
• National government borrowing ($bn/% of GDP/% external)	71/49/100	38/43/16	15/21/59	62/54/58
• Top 3 trading partners	Japan/ US/ Singapore	US/ Singapore/ Netherlands	US/ EU, NIEs[3]	Japan/ US/ Singapore
• Number of corporates in Global Top 500[4]	0	0	0	0

Socioeconomics

	Indonesia	Malaysia	Philippines	Thailand
• Population (mn)	214	24	77	62
• Number of households (mn)	52	5	16	17
• Average household income ($)	683	8,901	2,881	3,207
• Number of households earning >US$100K p.a. (mn)[5]	0.12	0.03	0.04	0.04
• Mobile phones/100 population	3	32	13	13
• Internet subscribers/100 population	1	22	4	10
• Urbanization (% of population)	40	63	59	23
• % of population with university degrees	5.1	14.5	23	11.5
• % of population above 65 years old in 2001 and 2021	5/9	4/8	4/7	6/13

Capital Markets

	Indonesia	Malaysia	Philippines	Thailand
• Number of listed corporations	315	807	232	385
• Equity market capitalization ($bn/% of GDP)	23/16	119/135	21/30	36/31
• Trading volume ($bn/% of market cap)	10/43	21/18	3/14	31/86
• Debt market capitalization ($bn/% of GDP)	10/7	63/72	9/13	15/13
• Equity underwriting[6] ($bn/% of GDP)	4/3	2/2	1/1	2/2
• Debt underwriting[6] ($bn/% of GDP)	13/9	11/13	7/10	12/10
• M&A ($bn/% of GDP)	6/4	9/10	4/6	2/2
• Retail assets under management ($bn)	0.5	11	0	4
• Institutional assets under management ($bn)	0.7	2	1	6

Banking Markets

	Indonesia	Malaysia	Philippines	Thailand
• Total loans[7] ($bn/% of GDP)	30/21	124/141	40/56	107/93
• Total deposits[7] ($bn/% of GDP)	79/54	99/113	41/58	148/129
• Mortgages ($bn/% of GDP)	2/1	23/26	1/2	21/18
• Personal loans (US$bn/% of GDP)	4/3	18/21	2/2	13/11
• Credit card receivables ($bn/% of GDP)	0.8/1	2/2	1/1	0.7/1
• Credit cards per person above 15	0.05	0.26	0.07	0.12
• Credit card spend as % of household total spend	9	18	4	19
• Foreign ownership limit in 1997 and 2002 (%)	85/99	30/30	40/100	25/100
• Number of banks in Global Top 1,000 in 1997 and 2001	6/3	8/11	2/2	2/8
• Number of ATMs/1,000 population	0.04	0.17	0.05	0.1
• Number of branches/1,000 population	0.03	0.11	0.05	0.06
• Number of banking employees/ 1,000 population	0.74	4.39	1.93	1.47

---

[1] At 2001 prices.
[2] At least one of the three components of FDI (equity capital, reinvested earnings or intra-company loans) is negative, and not offset by positive amounts of the remaining components. These are instances of reverse investment or disinvestment.
[3] NIEs include Hong Kong, South Korea, Singapore, and Taiwan.
[4] The *Fortune Global 500*: July 22, 2002
[5] Rough estimates only
[6] Average 1995–2001
[7] Of all financial institutions, including non-banks

Note: All figures as of December 2001 unless otherwise indicated

When Bank Central Asia (BCA) came up for sale in 2002, Standard Chartered Bank (SCB) quickly emerged as the favorite to buy it. One of Indonesia's largest and most successful banks, BCA was the crown jewel in the portfolio of the Indonesian Banking Restructuring Agency (IBRA), and London-based SCB aimed to gain a strong foothold in Indonesia at a reasonable price. IBRA had taken over BCA in 1998 after it ran into trouble when its owners, the ethnic Chinese Salim family, failed to repay loans they had drawn from the bank, and riots in Jakarta spurred a run by small depositors. IBRA stabilized the bank, transferring its non-performing loans (NPLs) to its asset management unit, recapitalizing the bank for roughly 60 trillion rupiah (roughly $6 billion, based on average exchange rate in 1998) and installing a new management team.

With nearly $10 billion in assets and an estimated 60 percent penetration of Jakarta's mass affluent, BCA became by far the best retail banking franchise in the 220 million-strong Indonesian market. In 2002, the State decided to sell a 51 percent stake. The government appeared to favor a strategic investor such as SCB. But IBRA surprised the banking community when it announced that a consortium led by Farallon Capital Management, a US private equity fund, and local cigarette-maker Djarum had won control. Even more surprising was the acquisition price of $531 million, arguably low at a price-to-book ratio of less than 1.0.

The twists in the BCA saga highlight the complexity and unpredictability of banking in Southeast Asia. Things are often not as they appear; the unexpected can happen. To the casual observer, the region seems burdened with uncertainty, offering little potential for financial institutions. Many investors have even gone so far as to write off the region, at least temporarily, preferring to focus on the bigger economies of North Asia or India.

Yet deeper analysis reveals that Southeast Asia may in fact present relatively attractive opportunities in the near-to-medium term. These markets are marked by healthy margins and a low level of competition, meaning that players with the right skills and reasonable scale can make good profits in the short term. This chapter reflects on the myths and realities of this perplexing region and offers a perspective on where the opportunities will be for the next few years.

For a foreign player, Southeast Asia offers a marketplace that is relatively inviting to foreign ownership. After all, attractive consumer segments are largely untapped, English is widely spoken, and local institutions would benefit from the exportable skills of a foreign entrant. For local players, this is a marketplace with significant room to consolidate positions in order to achieve synergies. Competition is not yet intense, and local context, networks, and distribution are critical to win. Attractive product margins should attract foreigners, and thus the local incumbent banks need to ensure they build a robust franchise to win in the coming decade.

Our focus in this chapter is limited to Indonesia, Malaysia, the Philippines, and Thailand. We covered Singapore, a much more advanced market, in Chapter 8.

COLLATERAL DAMAGE

In 1997 and 1998, Southeast Asia's economies were in meltdown. Thailand's currency, the baht, collapsed first, followed by the Indonesian rupiah. Malaysia and the Philippines were less affected by the financial crisis, but their economies ground to a halt. While these countries have bounced back into growth, recovery has been modest and fragile. The damage done to the image of what were once the dynamic darlings of investors has been harder to repair. Most international bankers dismiss these markets as having little near-term potential.

Adding to the perception problem is the widespread view that, when compared to Korea for example, Southeast Asian countries have not done much to restructure their economies and clean up their banking sectors. They are also widely regarded as somewhat inhospitable to foreigners, an impression fueled by the difficulties some foreign entrants have had. Standard Chartered Bank, for example, has failed in two attempts to acquire one of Indonesia's nationalized banks. Besides the obvious concerns that these economies remain weak, there are fears that NPLs are worse than they appear and could grow again to prohibitive levels. The endemic corruption plaguing the region is considered a major impediment to establishing a level marketplace in which locals and foreigners alike can compete. Finally, security concerns and the fear of terrorism have only added to investor worries.

We believe that some of these views are at least partially wrong and that banking in Southeast Asia may be an interesting bet. We will show in particular that the region, while limited in size, contains an attractive collection of short-term opportunities that can be captured by skilled institutions.

SIZING UP THE REGION

To get a handle on the opportunities that Southeast Asia offers, an understanding of the diversity and magnitude of the market is required (see Exhibit 9.1).

While Southeast Asia is generally open to overseas players, many investors consider it a small market, particularly when set against the large economies of China, Japan, and Korea. But the numbers support a different view. Total banking assets in 2001 exceeded $450 billion, which is roughly 150 percent

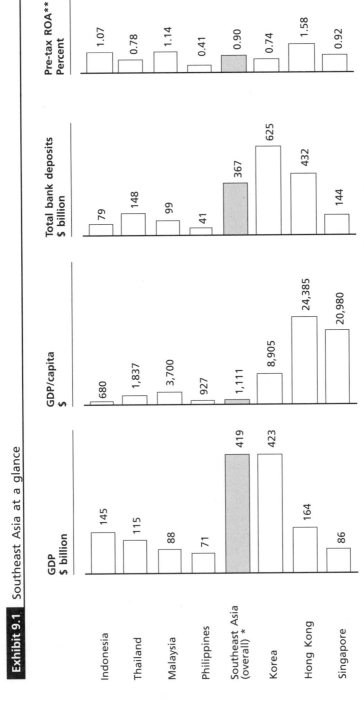

Exhibit 9.1 Southeast Asia at a glance

* Arithmetic sum for GDP and bank deposits, weighted average for GDP/capita and pre-tax ROA
** Top 10 commercial banks except Malaysia (Top 5) and Singapore (Top 3)

Source: Central banks; Global Insight; McKinsey analysis

the size of India's asset base. There are already 24 Southeast Asian institutions among the top 1,000 banks in the world, ranked by assets.[1] Players such as Maybank in Malaysia, Bangkok Bank in Thailand, and Bank Mandiri in Indonesia are large market leaders in their own right. A hypothetical bank with a presence in the four countries and an average return on assets (ROA) of 2 percent (HSBC and Citibank often achieve that or better in each market) could make $100 million in profits with only a 1.25 percent market share. As competition in these markets is not as fierce as elsewhere, foreign entrants can build a meaningful position, easily attaining the necessary threshold with just a single acquisition in each country and only a few branches.

This supports our view that Southeast Asia is a much more attractive opportunity than most realize. It is a region where strong players can realistically achieve success in the medium term. At the very least, the region may provide an elegant way to generate profits while waiting for the long-term China potential to materialize.

Southeast Asia, of course, is made up of several countries, some very small – there are 10 members in the Association of Southeast Asian Nations, or ASEAN. This means that while it is possible to regard the region as one market, important hurdles must be addressed. A regional approach could be adopted, with some functions such as IT, operations, and English-language call centers based in Singapore, Malaysia, or the Philippines. Management talent, a scarce resource, can be deployed to cover several countries. But banking remains a local business. Products and customer services must be customized to meet specific market expectations and regulations. As a result, a play in Southeast Asia must be a 'multi-local' strategy that is adjusted appropriately according to the needs and tastes of each market.

MIXED PROGRESS

The extent to which Southeast Asian governments have restructured their banking systems and economies since the crisis varies widely. Malaysia and Indonesia have made meaningful progress, while little has happened in Thailand, and even less in the Philippines.

Consolidation has been considerable in the faster moving pair: Malaysia forced 58 domestic institutions (commercial banks, merchant banks and finance companies) in 1999 into 10 groups by 2001; Indonesia closed more than 80 institutions since the crisis in 1997. Both countries created asset management companies, or AMCs, to take over bad loans from the banks,

---

1 *The Banker's* Top 1000 World Banks lists five banks in Indonesia, 13 in Malaysia, 13 in the Philippines, and eight in Thailand.

restructure them, and sell them off. Banks were recapitalized when necessary. The bank recapitalization program cost the Indonesian government and its foreign lenders about $40 billion.

While Indonesia sold three of its best private-sector banks (Bank Central Asia, Bank Danamon, and Bank Niaga) to foreign buyers, Malaysia has been reticent about selling controlling stakes to overseas players. It is the only Southeast Asian country to maintain a limit of 30 percent on foreign ownership. However, Kuala Lumpur is pushing domestic banks to benchmark themselves against the foreign competition to prepare for the complete opening of its financial sector, expected in the next three to four years.

In both Indonesia and Malaysia, the larger institutions, most of them state-run, have brought in professional management. For example, Indonesia's Bank Mandiri, under the initial leadership of Robby Djohan, replaced many former managers with new blood from the private sector, including a few foreigners.

Meanwhile, in the Philippines and Thailand, many of the larger institutions such as Metrobank and Bangkok Bank are still family-run, with little incentive to sell controlling stakes to foreigners, challenge the existing oligopoly, or start a merger and acquisition (M&A) war. Consolidation has been limited. In 2002, the Philippines had 42 commercial banks, down from 55 some five years earlier, while Thailand went from 15 commercial banks to 13 over the same period.

Few foreign investors have entered the banking sector in Thailand and the Philippines. Most of those who have done so acquired small institutions and lost a lot of money in the course of cleaning up the balance sheets. Banks in the two countries are still burdened with NPLs, with little improvement in sight. The Philippines, where the NPL ratio in 2001 was 17 percent of total loans, has been debating the creation of an AMC, but given the lack of government funding, the private sector must come up with its own solution. The chances of that are slim. In Thailand, the NPL ratio was reported to be 11 percent in 2001, although this figure is widely believed to be far below the real number. By the end of 2002, the Thailand Asset Management Company, which had been set up the year before, had not made much progress and regulations do not force banks to recognize the true level of their bad loans.

The difference in restructuring progress shows. Average total annual returns to shareholders in the five years preceding December 2001 were –31 percent in Thailand and –18 percent in the Philippines, compared to –16 percent in Indonesia and –5 percent in Malaysia. In 2002, the ROA for Malaysia's top banks was 1.1 percent, while it was 0.9 percent for Indonesia's banks. Returns were poorer in the other two banking sectors. Meanwhile, the largest institutions in the Philippines had an ROA of 0.7 percent, while in Thailand it was about 0.1 percent.

The diversity of Southeast Asia suggests that each market requires a different strategy for success. Typical turnaround skills such as cost reduction and NPL workout are necessary across the board, but are particularly crucial in Thailand and in the Philippines. Growth strategies and business-building skills such as enhancing consumer banking offerings and implementing alliances with specialists, including bancassurance providers, are the keys in Malaysia and in Indonesia.

Even though they have both significantly restructured their banking sectors, Malaysia and Indonesia present major challenges for investors, particularly foreign players. Malaysian regulations, while evolving fast, are still very conservative and protective of domestic institutions. Political and social risks remain high in Indonesia. On Transparency International's Corruption Perceptions Index for 2002, it ranked 96th out of 102 countries surveyed, at the same level as Kenya, and slightly worse than Uganda and Vietnam.

NEIGHBORHOOD ATTRACTIONS

Southeast Asia's bad reputation may be a blessing in disguise. This period of weak investor interest offers a window of opportunity for local institutions and regulators to get in gear and initiate or finalize the necessary restructuring while the hungry and aggressive multinationals are busy exploring the China option. It also creates a significant opportunity for players with a different risk appetite to seize major assets at bargain prices, as in the case of Farallon's purchase of BCA.

For several reasons, we believe that Southeast Asia has the potential to be an attractive hunting ground for strategic and financial investors looking for targeted market opportunities. For the local incumbent that confirms its position as a domestic leader, the marketplace offers significant profit potential, given the attractive product margins and growing sophistication of the customer base.

Markets are open to foreign institutions: With the exception of Malaysia, there are no foreign ownership limits in Southeast Asia. (In contrast, the cap is 74 percent in India and 25 percent in China.) While a local partner may not be legally necessary, foreign investors may find one useful, as Farallon did in Indonesia.

Consumer markets are largely under-penetrated: Given their levels of GDP per capita, consumer products have not penetrated the markets as much as one would expect. In McKinsey's personal financial services (PFS) surveys, consumers say they are ready to use new products, such as life insurance, credit cards, mortgages, and mutual funds. There are 10 times fewer credit cards per adult in Malaysia than in Korea. Correcting for the difference in GDP per capita, there are still 50 percent more consumer loans in Korea than in Malaysia. Southeast Asian consumers are also increasingly concerned about financial security after retirement and are looking for advice and products to address these worries.

Competition is not intense: To a large extent, local institutions have not been exposed yet to the level of competition already found in Korea or Taiwan. Bankers have maintained cozy oligopolies and avoided aggressive moves to undercut competitors' prices. In this club-like environment, it is considered improper to steal talent from another bank. The one exception to that rule has been Citibank. The global giant has served as something of an incubator for Southeast Asian management talent, training generations of highly skilled bankers who eventually went on to become top executives at local institutions.

GE Capital: Bringing in the skills

Active in Asia since 1992, GE Capital has been a leading global provider of consumer finance, equipment leasing and financing, and insurance services. Its strategy is to drive toward integrated financial services. GE Capital expects to grow its assets in Asia by 40 percent a year mainly through acquisitions and partnerships.

In Thailand, GE Capital has focused on consumer finance and distressed debt restructuring. It set up a partnership with Bank of Ayudhya to distribute credit cards. With Goldman Sachs, it acquired distressed commercial and consumer assets during the crisis.

GE Capital is also in Indonesia, where it has a consumer credit joint venture with the Astra Group. We estimate that in Thailand and Indonesia together, GE Capital manages more than one million credit cards. Although this number may seem small, it represents more than 8 percent of the combined card market in these two countries.

Spreads are still attractive: In 2001, mortgage spreads in Malaysia, the Philippines, and Thailand were on average about twice as high as those in Korea, Hong Kong, and Taiwan, while spreads on mutual funds distribution were 150 basis points higher.

Economic activity is concentrated in a few highly populated cities: This means that distribution and access to customers are much easier than in other regions. For example, Metro Manila, capital of the Philippines, represents 13 percent of the country's population, while Jakarta, Surabaya, and Bandung account for 11.6 percent of Indonesia's population. In contrast, only 5.8 percent of China's people live in the mainland's 13 biggest cities, while 7.6 percent of India's citizens reside in its top 12 urban areas.

English is widely spoken: It is an official language in the Philippines and Malaysia, and is well understood and spoken by educated managers in Indonesia and Thailand. This again contrasts with Korea, Taiwan, and China, and should contribute to making Southeast Asia an investor favorite once again.

REWARDS FOR THE INNOVATIVE

Across Southeast Asia there is significant untapped demand that will materialize with the appropriate supply of new products. According to our projections, consumer markets are expected to grow between 7 and 16 percent every year until 2010. This will be driven by three businesses: consumer finance, banking and asset management for the affluent, and services catering to the needs of small and medium-sized enterprises.

Consumer finance: Spending spree

Traditional Asian values encourage people to save. Western-style marketing tries to get them to spend. In Southeast Asia, the urge to splurge is winning. There were more than three times more credit cards circulating in the region in 2001 than in India and China combined.

The trend is set to continue as credit bureaus are set up and restrictions on the minimum monthly salary to qualify for a card are lifted. Card penetration is still low – there are only 0.26 cards per adult in Malaysia. Foreign institutions such as GE Capital have brought their marketing, credit analysis skills, and processing prowess to partnerships with local institutions. In addition, spreads in most consumer finance products are still very attractive: between 1,500 and 3,200 basis points in credit cards, between 400 and 650 basis points in other unsecured lending, and between 300 and 500 basis points for mortgages.

To win in the consumer finance game will require specific skills. Risk management, while complex, is key and must be implemented along with vigorous collection skills. This is particularly important because credit bureaus are not yet fully operational, banks are venturing progressively down-market towards sub-prime lending, and slower economic growth increases the risks of bankruptcies.

Marketing is critical to beating the competition in acquiring customers. Citibank excels at this and has built large cards and mortgage sales forces across the region. Customer relationship management (CRM) and analytical marketing are equally important to understanding customer behavior and tailoring and testing products before any large-scale launch. Multinational financial institutions that can combine operations across many countries and manage them from one base, as Citibank does in Singapore with its credit card processing, would have significant structural advantages.

Most winners in consumer finance have been foreign players. They account for 63 percent of credit card receivables in Thailand, 50 percent in the Philippines, 48 percent in Malaysia, and 47 percent in Indonesia. Citibank is among the top five in each of the four markets; Standard Chartered Bank ranks third in Malaysia, fifth in Thailand and Indonesia, and seventh in the Philippines. HSBC and GE Capital are close behind. These institutions bring marketing and sales skills, credit scoring techniques, and operating scale beyond anything except what only a few local players could achieve.

Affluent banking and wealth management: Retirement plans

In Asia, wealthy individuals and families are increasingly demanding advice and a wide range of investments to protect and grow their assets. This trend is further fueled by aging demographics and the realization that government-sponsored retirement systems will not meet the majority of their needs. In Thailand, the Philippines, and Indonesia, state pension schemes provide little coverage. This is driving the affluent to accelerate the planning and saving for their needs during their golden years. There are also concerns that children may not be willing or able to take care of their parents as previous generations have done. According to surveys, three-quarters of affluent Thais and Filipinos believe that they will have to rely on their own savings after they retire.

We estimate the latent demand for better retirement solutions at between $100 billion and $200 billion. Much of this will require the conversion of savings currently invested in low-yield deposits. The winners in wealth management have so far been foreign players, as local banks have not yet managed to develop the required capabilities for a number of reasons.

First, there are few long-term investment products in local currencies. In particular, capital guaranteed funds have not yet reached their potential. Second, consumers are neither well informed about the need to plan, nor convinced that they need professional advice; although recent stock market crashes have helped open many eyes. Finally, banks do not have the qualified workforces that can be trusted to provide financial advice, or the training programs in place to develop them. One simple way local banks have gotten started is by offering insurance through partnerships. Success depends on how well the branches have been trained and motivated to sell these new products. Examples of recent partnerships include Maybank and Fortis in Malaysia, Metrobank and AXA in the Philippines, and Lippo Bank and AIG in Indonesia.

To succeed, banks will need to master several skills. It is important to have well-educated and well-paid sales forces supported by financial planning tools. Also essential is a wide product range combining bancassurance, equity and bond mutual funds, guaranteed funds, and increasingly, as in Europe, alternative investments such as hedge funds and private equity. This will most likely be realized through an open-platform architecture rather than by stubbornly creating expensive proprietary products that often perform poorly. A good reputation, which sometimes can be boosted by an alliance with a private bank or foreign securities firm, is also important. Finally, since most wealthy individuals are also business owners, banks should be able to link their SME services with their wealth management offerings.

Competition in this area will come from many corners: insurance agents scrambling to turn themselves into financial planners, stockbrokers, and independent financial advisers. We believe that banks, because of the stability they promise and their access to customers, are likely to win this race.

SME banking: Untapped opportunities

Corporate banking is likely to remain marginal for local institutions that do not have the products and services, such as cash management, that generate fee income. Poor underwriting and low spreads seem endemic to the region. Most local institutions, even the largest ones, have destroyed enormous amounts of value through corporate banking in the last five years. We see no sign of improvement. Indeed, with many banks scrambling to place their excess liquidity with the very few healthy large corporations, net interest margins have collapsed and NPLs are on the rise again in several countries.

Serving large corporations is often regarded as essential when it comes to being a banking leader. Unfortunately, few institutions are yet capable of accurately calculating risk-adjusted returns on capital and are therefore falsely comforted by the illusion that they are making good money in the corporate segment. Wishful thinking triumphs over experience.

Meanwhile, small and medium-sized enterprises (SMEs) are being largely ignored and served through retail-banking channels. In many traditional local banks, SMEs are served by branch managers, who in many cases do everything from marketing and loan analysis to credit approval and recovery! This model has worked well for some niche banks with deep links to certain communities, as Bank NISP and Bank Buana have with ethnic Chinese traders, manufacturers, and retailers in Indonesia.

Still, the SME market is largely untapped, an opportunity waiting to be exploited. Niche banks are too small to serve the whole market, and bigger banks have little appetite to launch an attack, preferring to chase after the more glamorous large corporate loan business. However, the SME market can be as attractive as the mass affluent segment. Banks that develop the right distribution, credit, and recovery skills stand to make significant profits. The winners will be those players that combine elements of service with low-cost distribution, who know how to make good credit and pricing decisions with incomplete or unreliable financial information, and who can deal with their NPLs. Given the difficulty in delivering these capabilities consistently across the various markets of Southeast Asia, we expect local competition to stay somewhat shielded from foreign banks, and spreads to remain comfortable.

While we see opportunities across Southeast Asia, it is up to individual players to decide which to go after and how to manage the risks. For many, doing nothing means stagnation, heavy losses, or even failure. In the rest of this chapter, we take a closer look at the four markets in the region, and the special challenges and opportunities they offer.

MALAYSIA: CONSOLIDATION LEADER

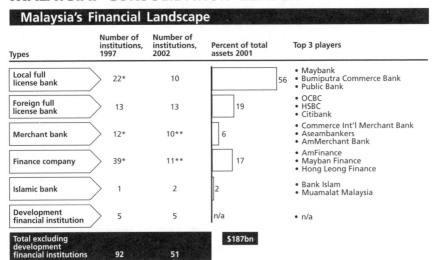

Malaysia's Financial Landscape

Types	Number of institutions, 1997	Number of institutions, 2002	Percent of total assets 2001	Top 3 players
Local full license bank	22*	10	56	• Maybank • Bumiputra Commerce Bank • Public Bank
Foreign full license bank	13	13	19	• OCBC • HSBC • Citibank
Merchant bank	12*	10**	6	• Commerce Int'l Merchant Bank • Aseambankers • AmMerchant Bank
Finance company	39*	11**	17	• AmFinance • Mayban Finance • Hong Leong Finance
Islamic bank	1	2	2	• Bank Islam • Muamalat Malaysia
Development financial institution	5	5	n/a	• n/a
Total excluding development financial institutions	92	51	$187bn	

* By 1999, there were only 58 institutions, which were eventually merged into 10 banking groups by 2001.

** Except for one finance company, the 10 merchant banks and 10 finance companies are part of the 10 banking groups with the 10 commercial banks as "anchor" institutions.

Source: Central bank; annual reports

Without doubt, Malaysia is the country in Southeast Asia that has made the most progress in restructuring its banking sector after the crisis. In 1999, the government implemented a restructuring plan to clean up bank balance sheets, grouping NPLs into the state agency Danaharta. Over the next two years, the 58 domestic institutions (commercial banks, merchant banks and finance companies) were forced to consolidate into 10 groups built around designated "anchor" institutions, the country's largest and most robust. Originally, there were only to be six anchor banks, but a number of small yet profitable ethnic Chinese-owned institutions successfully lobbied the government to include them. Foreign-owned banks, most of them in much better shape than their local counterparts, were not affected by this process.

Ambitious as it was, the forced consolidation has largely been completed. While some banks still need to work through post-merger integration, customers have just 10 local groups from which to choose. Malaysia's banks are certainly larger than they were pre-crisis, but as with most banks in Southeast Asia, they are not as profitable as they potentially could be – and certainly not to the level of their foreign rivals.

In April 2001, Bank Negara Malaysia, the central bank, released a master plan for the financial sector, outlining strategic priorities for further restructuring. Malaysian banks have been shielded from international competition by protective regulations. They must now shape up if they are to have a reasonable chance of long-term survival once the government lifts constraints on foreign ownership and the operations of overseas banks. In a speech at the Malaysian Banking and Financial Services Summit in May 2002, Dr Zeti Akhtar Aziz, Governor of the central bank, made the point explicitly: "Foreign banks have generally been better able to identify and react to changes in the market much faster than most domestic banking institutions." In short, the overseas institutions provide the benchmark for ROA, technology, customer service, productivity, skills and governance. Domestic institutions that do not shape up will disappear.

With the central bank so determined, Malaysia should emerge from the crisis and the global economic downturn with Southeast Asia's second strongest financial system behind Singapore's. Some storm clouds are still threatening and important challenges remain. First, employee-friendly regulations and unions have prevented banks from capturing the efficiency gains that should have resulted from consolidation. Despite cheap labor and excellent cost-to-income ratios of between 30 to 40 percent, most Malaysian banks are grossly overstaffed – and do not appear to be doing much about it. We estimate that if staffing were streamlined, banks could improve their cost-to-income ratios by 5–10 points.

Second, another wave of consolidation is inevitable. Even after significant sector rationalization, Malaysian banks are still too small. Only Maybank has assets in excess of $30 billion. Most players will find it difficult to gain the financial muscle to improve their skills to compete domestically and expand regionally. The first consolidation was a complex process, and the next one, expected by 2005, is likely to be even more challenging as 10 groups would vie for no more than six spots.

Third, the Malaysian corporate sector – once marked by cronyism – is recovering but remains weak. This is depriving banks of attractive asset-building opportunities. Malaysia may well be one of the few countries where lending to large corporations is more risky than lending to middle-market customers, a situation not reflected in the spreads. Banks are subsidizing large borrowers at the expense of smaller ones. This is untenable in the long term as foreign institutions with better risk management and pricing systems will jump on the arbitrage.

Malaysia offers a number of interesting opportunities for banks to capture in the coming years. One may be Islamic banking, the provision of financial services consistent with Muslim practices and principles. Banks, for example, charge fees in lieu of interest. This niche could help Malaysia expand its international influence throughout Asia, particularly in Indonesia and the Middle East. According to the central bank chief, Islamic banking has captured more than 8 percent of the assets in the Malaysian banking system in 2002 and should account for 20 percent by 2010.

We believe that the jury is still out on the long-term potential of the Islamic banking play, considering that the market today does not provide adequate hedge instruments to protect what is essentially a fixed-rate lending system. The majority of so-called Islamic products are also bought by non-Muslim investors looking for interest-rate diversification. Unless Islamic banking is the only form of banking authorized, as it is in some Middle East countries, it will not be widely accepted and growth will level off. Still, we see potential in banks offering a diversified product portfolio that includes Islamic banking services to meet investors' and borrowers' needs.

INDONESIA: SIGNIFICANT PROGRESS AFTER A SLOW START

Indonesia's Financial Landscape

Types	Number of institutions, 1997	Number of institutions, 2002	Percent of total assets 2001	Top 3 players
Government bank	34	31	50	• Bank Mandiri • Bank Negara Indonesia • Bank Rakyat Indonesia
Local commercial bank	144	80	35	• Bank Central Asia (BCA) • Bank Danamon Indonesia • Bank Internasional Indonesia
Foreign bank	44	34	12	• Citibank • HSBC • ABN AMRO Bank
State-owned pawnshop	1	1	0.2	• Pegadaian
Rural credit bank/ cooperative	9,008	8,690	n/a	• n/a
Finance company	248	246	3	• n/a
Hybrid*	34	24	n/a	• Sumitomo Indonesia • Mizuho Indonesia • UFJ Indonesia
Total excluding hybrid	9,479	9,082	$107bn	

* Also included in foreign bank category

Source: Central bank; annual reports

Indonesian banking has a positive future. While the country and the banking sector are fraught with problems, there are two clear positive indicators. First, the economics remain attractive. There are not many other countries that will offer better spreads over the rest of this decade. Moreover, even moderate growth in GDP per capita should have a significant impact on the demand for basic banking products, such as consumer credit.

Since the administration of President Megawati Sukarnoputri came into office in 2001, the government has moved with real determination to fix the banking sector. IBRA has been effective in privatizing the nationalized banks – often selling to foreign players that are able to add value to the assets. These sales should upgrade the banking sector slowly but surely over the coming decade. Moreover, Jakarta has indicated that further consolidation is in the cards.

Since 1997, Indonesia has become synonymous with volatility and high political and economic risk. No country of similar economic importance is weighed down by such a bad reputation. The list of worries is long: no properly functioning legal system, endemic corruption at all levels of society, and unethical business practices by most government-owned companies and many family-owned conglomerates. And as if all this were not enough, there is now a widespread sense that Indonesia's social fabric is unraveling and that the country could break apart.

Is banking in Indonesia too risky? It may be, as the misfortunes of Standard Chartered Bank illustrate. But it is also profitable. In 2001, the country's five largest banks, all ranked in the world's top 1,000, had a combined ROA of 1.14 percent. To understand how this could be possible, it is important to examine events since the financial meltdown of 1997.

After the crisis, the Indonesian economy and banking system were in turmoil. In 1998, GDP contracted by more than 13 percent. The JSX stock market index plummeted from 721 to 276. In the following year, external debt reached $150 billion, NPLs rose to 48 percent of total loans, and foreign direct investment shrunk to a fourth of what it had been in 1995. Many banks wantonly violated the regulations of the central bank (in particular, rules governing related-party lending), which was unable to ensure proper supervision. This led to a vicious circle – a lack of liquidity, negative spreads, falling asset values, currency exposure mismatch, and eventually bank runs that hit the small, private institutions.

The central government was initially slow to react, but eventually took more decisive steps. By the end of 2000, 89 banks had been closed, with their assets frozen, or were forced to merge into larger, more robust institutions. Four banks were taken over by IBRA. Another seven were jointly recapitalized by the government and their original owners. The cost of the recapitalization program exceeded $40 billion, one of the most spectacular banking initiatives ever.

In 2002, the top four banks in the country had been recapitalized, with most of their loan assets transferred to IBRA. Consequently, these banks had capital-adequacy ratios between 13 percent and 32 percent, and superlative ROAs largely created by the generous yield offered by a mix of fixed-rate and variable-rate government bonds.

Spreads remain high, in part because of high interest rates and a relative absence of aggressive competition among banks. With valuations driven to rock bottom levels by investor mistrust, acquiring a bank is not only feasible – many banks are for sale – but cheap. This can be one way to get a foothold in one of Asia's largest consumer markets. But while specialized private equity funds may have shown interest, the mainstream international banks have generally avoided the country altogether, scared off not just by the high risks, but also by the complexities of pulling off a successful acquisition. As a result, the banking industry remains largely the playing field of domestic banks.

The outlook for the sector depends mainly on the pace of the economy's recovery. We are likely to see sustained growth in the mass affluent and affluent classes, which will generate most of the profitability in the banking sector over the next three to five years.

There are still about 111 local banks operating, most of them small with limited skills, reach, and capital. The central bank may accelerate the consolidation process by raising capital-adequacy requirements or through Malaysia-style coercion. The government has to face the difficult task of consolidating and selling off the banks it owns, including Bank Negara Indonesia (BNI), once the country's flagship financial institution, but much reduced in size after its balance sheet was cleaned up. For its part, IBRA must complete the disposal of the banks it holds into the private sector.

But perhaps Indonesia's biggest challenge is to assert the rule of law. Banks cannot start lending again if they have no support from the legal system to act on non-performing assets. This is obviously an issue that goes beyond the banking industry, and one that could take decades before serious progress is achieved.

Recent Indonesian history suggests that decisive moves are rarely easy. "Indonesia never misses an opportunity to miss an opportunity," a senior official at a multilateral institution once observed. Yet this unfortunate country has never failed to prove the doomsayers wrong; it seems to possess the necessary resources to pull itself out of the most desperate situations.

THAILAND: LITTLE PROGRESS AFTER A FAST START

Thailand's Financial Landscape

Types	Number of institutions, 1997	Number of institutions, 2002	Percent of total assets 2001	Top 3 players
Government bank	1	3	21	• Krung Thai Bank • Siam City Bank • BankThai
Local full license bank	14	10	48	• Bangkok Bank • Thai Farmers Bank • Siam Commercial Bank
Foreign full license bank	20	18	9	• Sumitomo-Mitsui • Citibank • Dai-Ichi Kangyo
Government specific-purposes*	6	6	19	• Government Savings Bank • Bank for Agriculture and Agricultural Cooperatives • Government Housing Bank
Finance company	35	21	3	• National Finance • Tisco • Kiatnakino
Credit foncier	12	9	0.1	• Thanapat • Land and Houses • Unico Housing
Money lender	0	4	n/a	• GE Capital • Aeon • Cetelem
Hybrid**	0	4	n/a	• Bank of Asia (ABN AMRO Bank) • DBS Thai Danu • Standard Chartered Nakornthon
Total excluding money lender and hybrid	88	67	$185bn	

* Exclude Asset Management Corporation, Thai Asset Management Company and Secondary Mortgage Corporation
** Also included in local bank category

Source: Central bank; annual reports

While it was one of the first to consolidate under-performing players, set up an AMC, and publicly assert its intentions to reform, Thailand has not fulfilled its initial promise. Since the end of the crisis, little real improvement has taken place and the banking sector has stagnated. For this reason, banking is likely to polarize in the coming decade. The winners will include players that rapidly mobilize to upgrade capabilities, bring in top domestic and foreign talent, continue to clean up balance sheets, institutionalize new shareholding structures and corporate governance, and forge value-added strategic alliances. Only a handful will make it. Frontrunners include local institutions such as Kasikorn Bank, Bangkok Bank, and Siam Commercial Bank. Other winners will be foreign mono-line players in consumer finance. The rest will fall into the other category: the losers.

To understand why, let's review recent developments. The Thai banking sector once included some of the largest financial institutions in Southeast Asia. Before the financial crisis, Bangkok Bank, owned by the Sophonpanich family, was the best capitalized bank in the region, excluding Singapore, and the 202nd in the world. By 2001, it had slipped to 415th in the world and second in the region, excluding Singapore.

The first economy to go into turmoil when the baht collapsed on July 2, 1997, Thailand seemed poised for a rapid rebound. The Bank of Thailand moved swiftly to close bankrupt finance companies. The central bank lifted restrictions on foreign ownership and pushed four small institutions into the hands of foreign buyers. The move was a wake-up call for the large conservative Thai banks that had enjoyed comfortable returns without offering a high level of service and convenience to customers. Two bankrupt institutions, First Bangkok City Bank and the Bangkok Bank of Commerce, were merged into the state-owned Krung Thai Bank. By 1999, the country's banking system seemed to be moving in the right direction. Only the growing NPL problem needed to be addressed.

But the restructuring of the banking sector ground to a halt. At the start of 2003, the NPL problem had still not been resolved, with non-performing loans at 34 percent of total loans, based on non-official industry estimates. Unlike in Indonesia where there was a forced review of the banking system and a systematic transparency imposed, banks in Thailand were allowed to hide their bad debts. Returns dropped, with most banks reporting losses in 2001. Only a few asset sales took place (a joint venture between GE Capital and investment bank Goldman Sachs played a key role in buying up distressed assets). There may be some light at the end of the tunnel: The Thailand Asset Management Company, set up by Prime Minister Thaksin Shinawatra, has begun to operate, albeit slowly.

Considerable challenges certainly remain. The country's economic recovery is still sluggish. While there has been some excitement in consumer finance recently, banks have few other opportunities to resume lending. Foreign investors have not come back yet. To compound this problem, Thailand's legal system still heavily favors debtors. The return to profitability depends largely on the cleaning up of bank balance sheets.

Another problem is that, with 13 banks still operating, the banking system is crowded. There has been little consolidation. In 2002, the top three banks' shares of total deposits were lower than they were seven years before. The Government owns several banks including Krung Thai, BankThai and Siam City, and will have to decide how to restructure or divest. Many of these banks have overlapping business models or lack distinctiveness and long-term prospects. It is not clear either how consolidation would happen in the private sector. Only Bank of Ayudhya and Thai Military Bank, consistent under-performers valued at less than $300 million by the market in September 2002, seem bound to shape up or disappear.

Finally, bank efficiency is poor. A 2002 McKinsey study of Thai competitiveness revealed that the productivity of local banks was about half that of their American counterparts due to a number of factors ranging from lack of automation to antiquated management practices. Government ownership has also been a negative factor.

Despite these problems, Thailand offers some opportunities, particularly in consumer banking. Driven by foreign institutions such as France's Cetelem, consumer finance is growing, though not robustly enough to restore bank profitability. The number of credit cards in circulation has risen sharply to about 5.5 million in 2002, 38 percent more than what it was four years earlier. Consumers at all income levels are eager to pay with plastic. GE Capital has built a strong consumer lending business by financing automobiles, issuing private label cards such as PowerBuy, and offering personal loans. Wealth management is also an area poised for growth over the rest of the decade. While the demand for asset management, life insurance, and investment advice is still small, it is ramping up among the growing middle class.

THE PHILIPPINES: STUCK IN A MIRE OF BAD DEBT

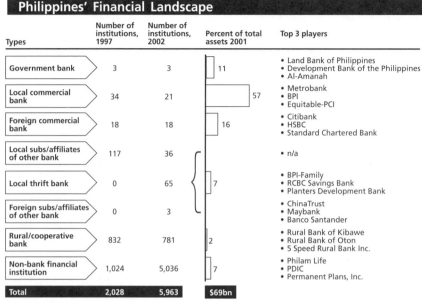

Philippines' Financial Landscape

Types	Number of institutions, 1997	Number of institutions, 2002	Percent of total assets 2001	Top 3 players
Government bank	3	3	11	• Land Bank of Philippines • Development Bank of the Philippines • Al-Amanah
Local commercial bank	34	21	57	• Metrobank • BPI • Equitable-PCI
Foreign commercial bank	18	18	16	• Citibank • HSBC • Standard Chartered Bank
Local subs/affiliates of other bank	117	36		• n/a
Local thrift bank	0	65	7	• BPI-Family • RCBC Savings Bank • Planters Development Bank
Foreign subs/affiliates of other bank	0	3		• ChinaTrust • Maybank • Banco Santander
Rural/cooperative bank	832	781	2	• Rural Bank of Kibawe • Rural Bank of Oton • 5 Speed Rural Bank Inc.
Non-bank financial institution	1,024	5,036	7	• Philam Life • PDIC • Permanent Plans, Inc.
Total	**2,028**	**5,963**	**$69bn**	

Source: Central bank; annual reports

Little has happened in the Philippines banking sector since the Asian crisis. While the country was not badly affected by the regional meltdown, its economy slowed significantly and has still not recovered. The ousting of former actor and veteran politician Joseph "Erap" Estrada from the presidency and his replacement by economist Gloria Macapagal-Arroyo in early 2001 improved the economic outlook, but overall indicators have remained weak. Even with its population of over 70 million, one of the largest in Southeast Asia, the Philippines is drifting below the radar reach of most investors and analysts. It will remain there so long as the banking sector is fundamentally unsound.

Of grave concern is the level of bad debts. NPLs are at about 17 percent of total loans, one of the highest levels in Asia. The government has been debating whether to create an asset management company as others have done, but little progress has been made. Private alternatives have been mooted. As a result of the inaction, lending is weak and banks are struggling to generate enough income to cover costs.

Market forces triggered a flurry of takeovers in 1999, with Metrobank and Bank of the Philippine Islands (BPI) consolidating their leadership positions by acquiring smaller, weaker banks. Equitable Banking Corp. took over PCI Bank to create the country's third-largest domestic player. However, the banking system remains fragmented, with about 42 commercial banks in operation. The largest, Metrobank, does not even reach $10 billion in assets – it is ranked no. 356 in the world by tier-one capital. Not much effort has been made by the central bank to accelerate the consolidation process, though officials recognize that it must happen eventually. One way to do this would be to impose stricter prudential regulations and require more accurate reporting of bad loans.

As in Thailand, Philippine banks are inefficient. High cost-to-income ratios can be partially explained by poor revenue. Another reason is that the country's stringent social protection laws and powerful unions have prevented banks from aggressively downsizing their workforces to meet slower demand. Banks are also dedicating too much money and labor hours to chasing too few good corporate clients. While spreads on corporate lending are still high – 100 to 200 basis points – the risks are even greater and many banks are still failing to earn enough to cover the cost of capital. We expect sluggish returns for many domestic players over the next few years.

There may be a bright side. the Philippines is one of the countries that will benefit most from the increasing focus on consumer banking. While aggregate customer numbers in such businesses as credit cards, mortgages, asset management, or life insurance are small even by Asian standards, the lack of new products has arguably been a major contributor to weak demand. People do not want what they do not know about. Yet Philippine consumers are hungry for innovation, as shown by the widespread use of mobile phones and text-messaging by the middle class. A bank would certainly attract customers by providing new products and friendly, efficient services to a standard higher than anything already on offer. The player that figures out how to seduce the consumer will win big.

Some banks are aiming to do just that. BPI, owned by the Zobel family that controls the Ayala Corp. conglomerate, has started modernizing its image and delivery channels. Metrobank is distributing the life-insurance products of France's AXA group. Foreign banks are also in the hunt, presenting a formidable threat to the weaker domestic banks. Citibank is the third-biggest lender in the country, sharing that ranking with Equitable PCI. Both are only just behind market leaders, Metrobank and BPI. However, the ROE of Citibank's Philippine operations is above 27 percent, while BPI's is 10 percent, and Metrobank's 6 percent. The undeniable conclusion: Philippine players have a long way to go before they have the skills necessary to reap the bulk of the profits in the fast-expanding consumer banking market.

Meeting the Challenges

Southeast Asia offers opportunities for both local and foreign institutions. Today's winners – mostly large state-owned banks or family-owned ones –

may not be tomorrow's, as new and largely untapped opportunities continue to bubble to the surface. Building the necessary skills – particularly in the areas of distribution, products, operations, and risk management – should be a critical component of each CEO's agenda. In addition, mergers, acquisitions, and alliances will remain major tools with which to restructure the industry, acquire capabilities, eliminate weaker players, and build scale.

Significant risk factors exist, in particular the weak economic and business environments. Southeast Asian economies are highly dependent on the United States, Japan, and, to a lesser extent, Europe. With these markets in a slump, Southeast Asia's economic growth will be far short of the levels reached in the boom years between 1995 and 1997.

There are other concerns. In the Philippines and Thailand, the banking industry is largely not earning its cost of capital. In Indonesia, rampant corruption and the absence of law enforcement could undermine market forces. In Malaysia, no timetable has been set for the removal of certain protectionist measures that are hindering the restructuring of key industries. And in all markets, deficient state-owned institutions are still protected, even though doing so has already wasted billions of dollars.

Not surprisingly, many private domestic banks are struggling to build a winning platform for the next decade. The opportunities that we have highlighted above may escape them and end up being captured by foreign institutions or protected state banks. For a local bank to stay on the leading edge, we propose that a CEO implement the following measures:

- To selectively inject new management talent with the right mindset and capabilities needed to make a clean break with the past.
- To revamp credit risk processes. In particular, centralize credit decisions, automate consumer scoring, overhaul collections, and make accurate provisions.
- To protect depositors, tightly control the treasury function to monitor liquidity, improve yields without undue risks, and limit open positions.
- To manage NPLs aggressively to minimize restructuring costs.
- To downsize. Most banks are overstaffed at all levels. While labor costs are not as high as in developed markets, overstaffing creates systemic inefficiencies, and encourages poor attitudes among employees.
- To reduce purchasing costs and eliminate corruption that occurs at the interface between the bank and its suppliers and customers.
- To identify the markets where the bank will dominate, and stop pretending to be everything to everyone. A bank does not have a strategy unless it is capable of articulating which markets it does not want to serve.

- To focus relentlessly on the bottom line and shareholder value. To do this, define a turnaround strategy early, set goals that can be measured frequently and accurately, and convince investors that the bank has a plan of action.
- To win in the consolidation game and inject new capital as soon as a credible turnaround story is in place. This capital may come from the market or from a foreign partner that brings skills, products, and technologies that can generate a competitive advantage.

A domestic bank, regardless of the market, should consider this to-do list a recipe for survival. In the words of management icon Jack Welch, the former GE boss: "Face reality as it is, not as it was or as you wish it to be."[2]

2 *Jack, Straight from the Gut*, Jack Welch with John A. Byrne, Warner Books, 2001, pp. 103 and 450.

PART 2

BUSINESS LINES:

PROFIT PRIORITIES

10

Personal Financial Services: Many Aspire, Few Attain

Providing financial services to individuals in Asia can be both lucrative and challenging. Across the region, leading global players and aggressive local banks are pursuing exciting growth opportunities. In this vigorous environment, however, most banks are struggling to make sustainable profits. With only a few exceptions, multinational institutions have created only small retail market positions, which have yet to contribute significant profits to their global parents. Most local retail banks have concentrated their investments in building distribution "hardware." As a result, in many markets, the number of branches and ATMs per capita approach, or even exceed, levels found in mature markets in North America and Europe. Still, profits have come under pressure. There is a growing realization that "soft" skills – marketing, customer segmentation, credit underwriting, and performance management, among others – are now more important than hardware and networks. Developing these capabilities is the core of the retail banking challenge.

Asia has already gotten a taste of the incredible potential of personal financial services (PFS) – providing individuals with both credit products such as mortgages and credit cards, and savings products including deposits, mutual funds, and securities. In recent years, certain PFS markets have gone through surprising growth spurts. For example, from 1995 to 2001, outstanding credit balances in Korea grew to 353 trillion won, an almost twofold increase in local currency terms. This expansion was triggered in part by government policies that encouraged the introduction of credit cards to capture more economic activity within the national tax system. In less developed markets such as India and China, individual bank deposits have risen 11 percent and 18 percent a year respectively since 1995, as incomes have gone up sharply.

Over the rest of this decade, PFS represents arguably the biggest set of banking opportunities across Asia. We estimate that by 2010, the total revenue pool for the region could almost double from its size in 2001 to exceed $390 billion. PFS also has good profit potential, with gross product margins that are often up to twice those found in the leading developed markets in North America and Europe. As a result, the potential of PFS far outstrips that of corporate banking, which will remain plagued by a large amount of non-performing loans (NPLs), razor-thin margins, and gradual disintermediation by the capital markets. For local and foreign banks with high aspirations in Asia, capturing value in PFS will be absolutely essential.

The impressive growth of this business is being driven by a unique combination of converging trends. First and foremost, per capita income and wealth across the region are continuing to increase. In the years leading up to 2010, average household income will rise by more than 3 percent annually. This will result in even more robust growth in PFS revenues, which are expected to increase at a rate of over 7 percent a year.

Much of Asia consists of poor households on the verge of reaching the wealth levels at which consumers start to accumulate disposable income and use PFS products. The financial assets of individuals – largely held as bank deposits in Asia's case – increase dramatically when an economy attains an average income above what is required to meet basic needs (see Exhibit 10.1). Once this inflection point is reached, the propensity of Asians to save accelerates asset accumulation. As income levels grow over the rest of the decade, we expect that close to 300 million people in Asia's emerging economies will open their first savings account, driving rapid financial asset growth in these markets.

The second trend driving PFS growth is changing attitudes toward credit. Although consumer credit levels are still modest in lower income countries across the region, borrowing money is becoming more acceptable. Younger people, in particular, are willing to use credit and are doing so when their incomes and market conditions allow.

The third trend is the growing demand for more sophisticated and varied financial products, particularly for savings and investment. In most markets, banks usually offered little beyond deposit accounts. Now, asset and wealth management products and services are being introduced across the region. As customers become more sophisticated in their understanding of these

Exhibit 10.1 Personal financial assets S-curve 2001

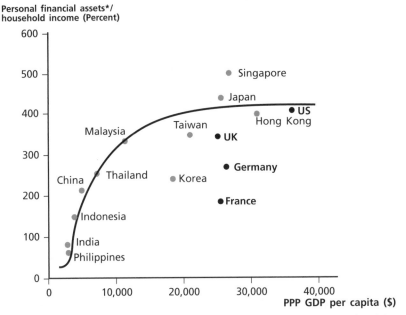

Personal financial assets*/
household income (Percent)

* Include deposits, mutual funds, life insurance, pensions and securities (equities and fixed income products)

Source: Asian Demographics; Global Insight; central banks; World Federation of Exchange (FIBV); McKinsey analysis

investments, and as the underlying securities markets deepen, asset volumes will grow strongly.

Finally, deregulation is creating a richer environment. As recently as the late 1990s, most countries in Asia restricted banks to traditional deposit-taking, payment services, and lending. Today, mutual funds, insurance, securities, and a variety of financial products can all be bought from the same institution or through the same channel. Restrictions on foreign players entering markets and allying with local players are also being lifted. In Japan, Korea, Taiwan, and much of Southeast Asia, local banks and insurers are moving to set up "financial holding companies" with broad suites of businesses.

Taken together, these trends are fueling one of the biggest revenue growth opportunities in banking globally. Yet why do most banks and other players providing financial services to individuals fail to make sizable profits? Bankers have yet to jettison their old ways and acquire the soft skills needed to build profitable retail businesses. Customers are viewed as a cheap source of funds for corporate lending. Branches are low-service, high-cost outlets where customers endure long waits to conduct simple transactions. Targeted marketing, cross-selling skills and effective sales cultures are lacking. In many markets, bank employees and managers are so highly paid that retail operations are uneconomic. Operational processes and IT systems were designed to prevent errors and process corporate loans, not to handle massive flows of consumer transactions at the lowest possible cost.

All of these factors mean high costs and undifferentiated service that cut into the profits of what should be a very attractive business. To acquire and instill a profit mindset, bankers must fundamentally transform the core elements of their retail businesses. They must start with a clean slate and design PFS businesses that provide high value for customers, delivered with the efficiency of a leading retailer.

THE MONEY AND THE MARKETS

The PFS market offers a collection of distinct, yet linked opportunities. This is one of the key challenges. Although in theory many products and services can be sold by every local bank to most of its customers through a shared set of channels, in practice, cost-effective cross-selling is hard to achieve. As competition intensifies and customers become more sophisticated, products and channels have to be specialized and tailored to the conditions of the local market. This is especially true for competitors targeting the largest PFS growth and profit opportunities. We expect these opportunities to be concentrated in three areas:

Consumer finance: This is an immediate opportunity in the high-growth markets across the region. In emerging markets such as China, India, and the Philippines, where there are large numbers of households earning just enough income to raise them above basic subsistence levels, secured credit will be the fastest growing need. In more mature markets, unsecured credit products such as credit cards will provide more significant growth and scale.

Mass affluent banking: Emerging mass affluent customers – households with more than $100,000 in income or liquid assets – will richly reward players that capture their deposits in the short term and truly add value to their wealth through the right service model in the medium to long term. This will be a scale opportunity in the more mature markets such as Korea, Taiwan, Hong Kong, Singapore, and Japan, as well as in urban pockets in China and India.

Mass-market banking: Cost-effective delivery of products and services to the person in the street is arguably one of the greatest challenges for any bank. For local banks with legacy retail banking businesses, it should be the top priority. The opportunity to generate profits by significantly improving mass-market banking efficiency is as compelling in Japan as it is in India.

All of these opportunities are present in each of the markets in Asia, though scale, growth rates, and market drivers vary dramatically. The region's economies fall into three broad categories, based on the levels of personal wealth and product needs. Grouping the markets based on these fundamental characteristics is a helpful way to understand how PFS opportunities are evolving and the factors that affect their timing and attractiveness.

Emerging markets: These markets include China, India, Indonesia, Malaysia, the Philippines, and Thailand – countries that have lower average incomes than the rest of Asia, but are growing quickly. Demand for core banking products, such as deposits and secured loans, will outpace economic growth rates. This group of markets will be the engine of growth in the region, contributing more than half of net PFS revenue increases by 2010 (see Exhibit 10.2). This growth will not be uniformly distributed. In these economies, the top 5 percent of the population typically accounts for 20–40 percent of all income and will be the most attractive PFS customers. Across these countries, there will be only about 20–30 cities that will represent the lion's share of PFS growth. As a result, targeted opportunities in mass affluent banking will gain momentum in the second half of this decade.

Margins are usually high in emerging markets and, due to high growth in demand, are likely to remain at reasonable levels even with increasing competition. So, while volumes are still comparatively low for many PFS products, the absolute revenue pools cannot be ignored. Even though local players are positioned right in the midst of these revenue pools, they are often hampered by a lack of skills or antiquated mindsets that reduce their ability to create profits. Foreign players, on the other hand, have to contend with regulatory barriers in some markets such as China.

Maturing markets: These include Hong Kong, Korea, Singapore, and Taiwan – economies that have slightly slower growth rates than the emerging markets, but have higher wealth levels and more complex product needs. Accounting for less than 10 percent of Asia's population, these markets will continue to contribute over 20 percent of the total Asian PFS revenue over the rest of this decade. On the personal asset side, mass affluent customers will likely shift deposits to higher margin investment products as regulatory and market reforms play out. On the credit side, the demand for unsecured lending products such as credit cards will grow, although there will likely be some near-term contraction as several markets deal with bad debts accumulated during the credit growth spurts in the late 1990s and beginning of this decade.

Hong Kong and Singapore are small, relatively saturated markets with limited growth potential. As the considerably bigger and less mature markets of Korea and Taiwan open up, they will become more critical battlefields for

Exhibit 10.2 Total personal financial services (PFS) revenue pools*

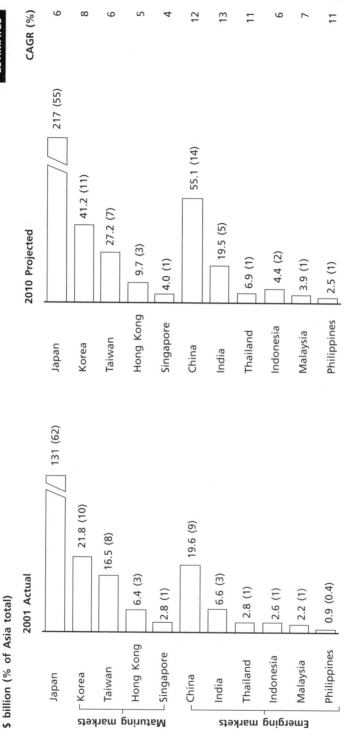

$ billion (% of Asia total)

ESTIMATES

2001 Actual

Japan	131 (62)
Korea	21.8 (10)
Taiwan	16.5 (8)
Hong Kong	6.4 (3)
Singapore	2.8 (1)
China	19.6 (9)
India	6.6 (3)
Thailand	2.8 (1)
Indonesia	2.6 (1)
Malaysia	2.2 (1)
Philippines	0.9 (0.4)

2010 Projected

		CAGR (%)
Japan	217 (55)	6
Korea	41.2 (11)	8
Taiwan	27.2 (7)	6
Hong Kong	9.7 (3)	5
Singapore	4.0 (1)	4
China	55.1 (14)	12
India	19.5 (5)	13
Thailand	6.9 (1)	11
Indonesia	4.4 (2)	6
Malaysia	3.9 (1)	7
Philippines	2.5 (1)	11

Maturing markets

Emerging markets

* Include revenue from mortgages, personal loans, credit cards, deposits, equities trading, and mutual fund distribution
Source: Central banks; Lafferty; McKinsey analysis

both local and foreign players. Players in these markets must move from old-style retail banking to a more sophisticated approach that requires skilful targeting of the limited pool of high-value customers, such as mass affluent investors or borrowers with good risk profiles.

Japan: This is Asia's biggest PFS market, accounting for almost two-thirds of all revenues in 2001. By 2010, due to more rapid growth in other markets and its own economic woes, this will probably drop to slightly above 50 percent. Even then, there are major opportunities for players to make profits. Personal financial assets are still locked mainly in deposits. Some of these funds will move to higher yield investments once Japan tackles the problems with its financial system and market conditions improve. There is a large pent-up demand among the rapidly aging population for better performing investment products and wealth management services. Retail credit growth is likely to be modest. One exception is unsecured personal loans. This market has been driven not by banks, but by consumer finance companies with innovative lending techniques. We expect this $80 billion asset market to continue growing, in part due to more focused competition by banks expanding into new customer segments.

In Japan, a major PFS opportunity lies in improving the profitability of existing retail banking operations. Most banks have antiquated branch structures and processes aimed at serving the corporate market and huge numbers of unprofitable retail accounts. Costs need to be cut, branch networks restructured, core operations redesigned, and pricing improved. Given the size of the market, we estimate that the banking system could generate up to $100 billion in much-needed retail profits by 2010.

For banks across Asia, the argument for going after the PFS opportunity is strong, especially when compared to corporate banking. What is less clear to most players is that developing sustainable and profitable businesses requires a high level of skills. By the end of this decade, there will be only a handful of winners and a trail of losers. Many aspire, few attain. In the rest of this chapter, we examine the nature and scale of each of the PFS opportunities, the challenges banks face, and the steps that both local and regional players need to take to increase their odds of succeeding.

Consumer Finance: Managing the Risks

"Neither a borrower nor a lender be." That was the mantra of Asians a generation ago. Unlike their grandparents, young people today are ready to embrace easy credit to realize their material dreams. A McKinsey survey in 2001 showed that about 60 percent of Asian consumers between the ages of 20 and 30 are willing to borrow money on an unsecured basis – a credit card cash advance, for example – to meet daily needs.

Banks and finance companies have latched onto this attitude change and shifted to focus on consumer lending: mortgages, personal loans, and credit cards. Across the 11 Asian markets, consumer loans grew an average 23 percent a year in local currency terms from 1995 to 2001. The figure for corporate loans was only 4 percent.

Robust growth in consumer credit will continue through the decade, making this a huge opportunity. Unlike wealth management, which is further off on the horizon, many consumers are ready to borrow now. As Exhibit 10.3 shows, when average household income reaches about $5,000, people are able to borrow money (because they have debt repayment ability) and consumer credit balances grow. Several countries in Asia have crossed this point. There is also immense potential in lower income markets with high economic growth rates. All this translates into a substantial near-term opportunity that could have a major impact on banks' bottom lines.

To realize these profits, banks will need new marketing and credit management skills. In response to growing default rates in markets such as Hong Kong, positive credit bureaus are being set up. Beyond blacklisting deadbeat borrowers, these agencies are sharing credit histories and payment

Exhibit 10.3   Consumer leverage S-curve 2001

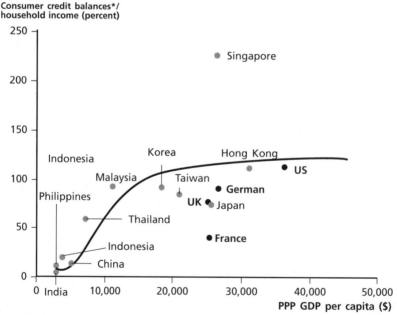

* Include mortgages, secured and unsecured personal loans, and credit card receivables

Source: Asian Demographics; Global Insight; central banks; Lafferty; McKinsey analysis

records with banks, boosting their ability to design, market and underwrite credit products. Players that excel at these soft skills will have a leg up over rivals in the battle for profits.

Specific product capabilities can also make a difference. While mortgages and credit cards are available in all the markets, penetration and profits vary widely. In Japan, for example, over 100 million credit cards have been issued. But the vast majority of unsecured credit profits come from cash advances and specialized consumer finance loans, not revolving credit card balances. The winners to date have been mono-line consumer finance players providing short-term unsecured loans. Another pattern may emerge in China, where the number of debit cards is growing rapidly.

What does this mean for the competitive landscape? In advanced consumer credit markets, mono-line players dominate the business. For example, six of the top 10 card issuers in the United States are dedicated card companies. The main mortgage providers are specialists with national franchises such as Countrywide Credit. While mono-lines are unlikely to be as strong a force in Asia, they will be a major factor in shaping the nature of competition. Foreign card specialists already dominate the smaller markets in Southeast Asia. Elsewhere, global players will raise competitive market standards with their credit and marketing skills. Local banks may be left behind unless they make a quantum leap in product quality and service levels.

In many countries, leading local banks are forging alliances with global players to jump-start their businesses and learn credit scoring and marketing skills. But transplanting skills across different cultures and markets is not an easy task. Take the case of the Taiwan credit card provider that was purchased by a large American bank. The buyer immediately put in place its "best-in-class" credit scoring model. The initial results were shocking: Default rates increased dramatically. An investigation revealed that most of the bad debtors belonged to professions that were previously screened out by the bank's old vetting system. The new process had no data on those types of customers and therefore failed to identify them as high risks.

Local conditions are a factor in determining credit risk. Straight-out transplantation of even the most sophisticated models from developed markets will not go smoothly. Adjustments need to be made. It takes time for scoring systems to accumulate the data necessary to develop strong predictive powers. The credit markets in Asia present challenges for local and foreign players alike. The winners will be those who possess real insight into consumer behavior and implement the rigorous business models that will allow them to meet customer credit needs profitably.

Emerging markets, Secured lending offers attractive growth

Consumer finance in the emerging markets – China, India, Indonesia, Malaysia, the Philippines, and Thailand – is still at a low base. Consumer credit revenue in these six markets combined is less than Taiwan's. But credit growth rates are rising. Expansion will be led by robust growth in secured lending products. China's mortgage and auto credit markets are set to grow strongly, driving overall consumer credit balances up an estimated 32 percent a year through the end of the decade. By 2010, we estimate that total annual revenues from consumer credit products in China alone will reach over $17 billion (see Exhibit 10.4).

With the exception of Malaysia, consumer lending is fairly new in the emerging markets of Asia. As consumers get wealthier, they naturally aspire to own property and cars, and need financing for these purchases. Across the emerging markets, mortgage balances will grow at an annually compounded rate of 22 percent through to 2010, when they will represent about three-quarters of all consumer loans. Personal loans and credit card balances will grow respectively at about 17 percent and 23 percent annually. By the end of the decade, these unsecured products will still account for less than 30 percent of all consumer loans in the emerging markets.

Local players with large distribution networks and deep deposit bases are well positioned to capture the volume-driven mortgage and auto finance businesses. In India, where consumer finance has taken off, local institutions HDFC Bank and ICICI Bank already dominate the mortgage market. The risk management and customer segmentation skills required for secured lending are considerably lower than those for unsecured lending, making it easier for local banks to compete with international banks.

Even China's state-owned banks have gone into the mortgage loan business with gusto because doing so is in step with state policy. They have captured more than 70 percent of the primary mortgage market. Foreign players, in contrast, are ill positioned to capture this opportunity due to their lack of access to physical distribution channels and local currency funding.

In China and elsewhere, having a large distribution network through branches is critical for mortgages because customers usually require face-to-face interaction before taking up such big loans. Big local banks often have entrenched partnerships with property developers and agents that push their products. Since mortgages do not differ much, customers usually settle for these convenient offerings. Low funding costs are another important factor. Big local banks will continue to dominate because they fund the business with cheap deposits accumulated through their large branch networks.

Exhibit 10.4 Consumer credit revenue pools*

$ billion (% of Asia total)

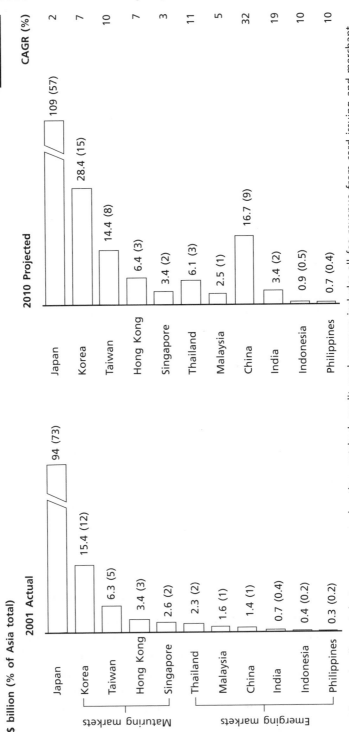

	2001 Actual	2010 Projected	ESTIMATES CAGR (%)
Japan	94 (73)	109 (57)	2
Korea	15.4 (12)	28.4 (15)	7
Taiwan	6.3 (5)	14.4 (8)	10
Hong Kong	3.4 (3)	6.4 (3)	7
Singapore	2.6 (2)	3.4 (2)	3
Thailand	2.3 (2)	6.1 (3)	11
Malaysia	1.6 (1)	2.5 (1)	5
China	1.4 (1)	16.7 (9)	32
India	0.7 (0.4)	3.4 (2)	19
Indonesia	0.4 (0.2)	0.9 (0.5)	10
Philippines	0.3 (0.2)	0.7 (0.4)	10

Maturing markets: Japan, Korea, Taiwan, Hong Kong, Singapore

Emerging markets: Thailand, Malaysia, China, India, Indonesia, Philippines

* All term lending product revenues are duration matched; credit card revenue includes all fee revenue from card issuing and merchant acquiring businesses

Source: Central banks; Lafferty; McKinsey analysis

While entrenched local players are in a strong position to continue to dominate secured lending, in the nascent but profitable business of unsecured consumer finance, the incumbents are missing out. This is particularly true in the large, more restricted markets where retail-focused domestic attackers are routing the large legacy banks. In China, for example, nimble and innovative players have already made waves. Despite its small branch network, China Merchants Bank has managed to achieve the highest customer-to-branch ratio in the market – 44,000 customers per branch, compared to 1,600 customers per branch for the "Big Four" state-owned giants. At the start of 2003, the upstart had $670 in deposits per debit card in contrast to the $50–$300 in balances per card at other major banks. This indicates that China Merchants has a much more affluent customer base – the perfect platform for launching a credit card.

In the smaller but more open emerging markets, foreign players have expanded aggressively and significantly raised the bar for local banks. With their marketing smarts, financial prowess and risk management skills, the overseas banks have a clear edge. In 2001, Citibank had more than a million credit cardholders in Thailand, nearly a fifth of the total. That same year, foreign banks accounted for more than 40 percent of total credit cards balances in the seven Asian emerging markets.

Most local banks in the emerging markets have clung to their antiquated ways, not bothering to remedy their severe lack of skills. In China, for example, the big state banks still focus on corporate loans and limit their forays into unsecured lending, because they perceived the risks to be higher. They regard personal loans as small deals that do not warrant the effort. Instead, they persist on racking up heavy losses from corporate lending. This is not all that surprising. After all, these institutions are simply not prepared to launch a meaningful consumer lending effort, given their inadequate credit underwriting skills, inefficient systems, and other problems that would prevent them from mass-manufacturing consumer loans at low cost and manageable risk.

Maturing markets, the action is in unsecured loans

In the four maturing markets, the mortgage business is saturated. In fact, competition in Singapore and Hong Kong has driven margins down so much that many banks are probably losing money on housing loans. Meanwhile, other types of consumer lending will continue to drive growth. Net interest and fee revenue from personal loans and credit cards in Korea, Taiwan, Hong Kong, and Singapore is expected to jump from $22 billion in 2001 to $44 billion by 2010.

Winning in unsecured credit is all about gaining superior skills, particularly customer segmentation, credit underwriting, and low-cost processing. In relatively high-growth markets such as Asia, positions can change as nimble local attackers or skilled foreign players make their moves and quickly outflank the incumbent banks.

The challenge for the legacy players is to develop effective segmentation strategies that first identify, then acquire and retain their most profitable customers. In credit cards, for example, the customers who roll over their balances – referred to as "revolvers" – normally account for less than 30 percent of the customer base, but generate more than 90 percent of revenues. A leading credit card player in Hong Kong realized that profits could be increased by one-third, simply by consolidating the remaining balances of its high-value revolvers from competitors. It further discovered that at least 15–17 percent of customers that did not use their revolving credit facilities were actually "hidden revolvers," borrowing on another bank's card. These insights prompted the card issuer to track both the needs and total value of its customers, allowing it to better target its marketing.

Credit underwriting is another challenge for incumbents. In most of Asia, growth in unsecured lending has preceded the development of risk management infrastructure such as credit bureaus. Hong Kong's and Korea's recent experiences are valuable case studies. Individual bankruptcies in Hong Kong went from fewer than 1,000 cases in 1998 to over 25,000 in 2002. This comes out to a rate of five bankruptcies for every thousand adults, compared to seven per thousand in the United States. However, in Hong Kong, the amount of debt per bankruptcy is a shocking 42 times monthly income, twice the level in the United States (see Exhibit 10.5). In Korea the 2002 figure was equally shocking at 40 times monthly income. Credit card loan-loss ratios have hit double digits in Hong Kong and are expected to hit double digits in Korea, unprecedented for a developed market.

The problem is the lack of shared credit information. Banks unknowingly provide additional credit to people already overextended. This problem went out of control in Hong Kong from 1999 to 2002. To compound the problem, customers could draw funds on their unsecured cards to make mortgage payments. The banks had no way of detecting defaults early. According to one leading card issuer in Hong Kong, a third of those declaring bankruptcy are up to date on payments one month before filing, while one-third continue to pay off their debt right up until they go bankrupt.

With increasing transparency, players that are able to leverage better customer credit information to identify customers with good risk profiles and price them appropriately will be in a position to lure away these accounts from those who continue to charge the same standard rate to everybody. In this way, skilled and aggressive attackers can make real inroads in high-growth markets.

Exhibit 10.5 Lack of positive credit data-sharing results in extreme personal indebtedness

Average unsecured debt to monthly income multiple

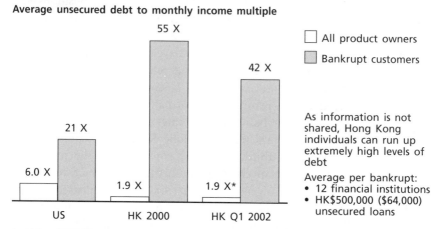

□ All product owners

▨ Bankrupt customers

55 X

42 X

21 X

6.0 X

1.9 X

1.9 X*

US

HK 2000

HK Q1 2002

As information is not shared, Hong Kong individuals can run up extremely high levels of debt

Average per bankrupt:
• 12 financial institutions
• HK$500,000 ($64,000) unsecured loans

* Using 2000 figures

Source: Asia Market Intelligence; Official Receiver's Office; Federal Reserve; Federal Financial Institutions Examination Council; McKinsey analysis

Japan: Slivers of growth in personal loans and card-cashing

Japan is a market of paradoxes. Since 2000, while its major credit markets have been in the doldrums, somehow the mortgage market has gone against the trend, expanding at record levels. In 2001, mortgage balances grew by over 5 percent as banks competed against each other, offering loans at 1 percent interest. Meanwhile, total corporate lending shrunk by 4 percent. Banks were trying to mitigate their corporate losses from poor underwriting decisions of decades past.

But was the retail mortgage bet a good strategy, or the genesis of a future problem? Most likely the latter. Even with long-term deposit interest rates near zero, a 1 percent mortgage did not make money. The short-term spurt in the mortgage market was driven by the fall in interest rates and desperate attempts by banks with excess deposits to find creditworthy assets in which to invest. And the medium to long-term outlook for the mortgage business is not promising, given the rapid aging of Japan's population.

Although relatively mature, the other credit markets in Japan offer more opportunities. Total unsecured credit is around 13 percent of GDP, compared to 23 percent in the United States. Japan, however, is unlikely to follow America's growth pattern. For example, while credit card penetration is high, revolving ratios are low – about 15 percent of total outstanding card receivables, compared with more than 80 percent in the United States.

Historically, the most profitable segment of Japan's consumer finance market has been unsecured short-term loans drawn for general spending purposes. Consumer finance companies including the four market leaders – Takefuji, Acom, Promise, and Aiful – have driven the growth of the market. It was not until these firms arrived that the personal credit business really took off. Unlike banks, they are aggressive and manage risk better, sharing credit information amongst themselves. Their data are of higher quality than the credit card companies. This allows them to grant credit to low-income customers, a very profitable segment that both banks and card firms avoid. The consumer finance players also employ innovative techniques such as handling credit applications through unmanned ATM-like kiosks, effectively addressing the need for privacy among Japanese borrowers.

While the total consumer credit market is expected to be practically flat through the rest of the decade, there will be growth in some segments. Credit card cashing is expanding among the middle class. Also on the rise: sub-prime unsecured consumer finance for less creditworthy customers willing to pay higher interest rates. Given the continuing economic problems of Japan, this means that razor-sharp underwriting skills will increasingly become a key competitive advantage. In a mature market where consumers are already bombarded with innovative marketing campaigns, the challenge for both local and foreign competitors will be to compete with and steal market share from the established players.

Targeting the "Starbucks generation"

Starbucks, the ubiquitous coffee and cafe company, is one of the fastest growing global brands ever. In 1987, it had just 17 outlets, mainly in the northwestern US city of Seattle. By early 2003, the familiar green logo was hanging at nearly 6,500 locations around the world, from Detroit to Dubai, from Beirut to Beijing. Starbucks arrived in Asia only in 1996 when it opened stores in Japan and Singapore. In short order, the chain that is now something of an icon of the globalization age became a fixture in the region's major cities.

What is stunning about the Starbucks story is that the brand holds tremendous appeal among young people that transcends culture and language. Step into a Starbucks in Paris, Pattaya, or Pittsburgh in mid-morning, and you will see tables filled with java junkies idly sipping lattes or a snappily dressed suit stopping at the counter to pick up a "tall cap". Truly admirable is Starbucks' ability to penetrate markets in Asia, previously thought to be diehard tea territory, impervious to the coffee culture. But innovative marketing and brand name strength have turned tea devotees into coffee nuts.

Credit card players in Asia can learn from Starbucks. The hip consumer wants a card that meets both his or her "image" requirements and financial needs. There is a segment of middle to high-income consumers aged 20 to 40 that accords as much importance to brand as to utility. The convergence of taste, fashion, and necessity creates a unique opportunity for a regional player to focus on card-carrying members of the "Starbucks generation" with a product that offers prestige, recognition, and the chance to have fun and be cool. An innovative competitor – perhaps a Japanese consumer finance firm or a bank in Hong Kong or Taiwan with the ability to venture beyond home base – could target these affluent consumers across markets, particularly in North Asia. Like the first morning cup of joe, this is an immediate opportunity not to be missed.

Mass Affluent Banking: Services for Asia's New Rich

Across Asia, offshore private banks have been actively working to bring in deposits from well-to-do individuals. While a few multinational banks have done very well, the offshore volume is still relatively small compared to the total money available. The difficulties are rooted in customer inertia and regulatory barriers. In 2002, the top 10 private banks control less than 5 percent of the wealth in the region, most of which is dispersed among many different local banks that offer all their customers the same generic, old-fashioned services.

In 2001, total personal financial assets in Asia added up to $16.4 trillion of which $2.7 trillion is held by so-called mass affluent customers, each with assets between $100,000 and $1 million, while $5.3 trillion belongs to "high net worth individuals" with assets above a million dollars each (see Exhibit 10.6). Serving the high net worth segment is a specialized game dominated by a few European and US private banks. For most global, regional and local banks, winning in Asian wealth management means successfully targeting the onshore wealth of the mass affluent, which represents around 1.2 percent of the region's households. Based on the income metric, the elite segment of households making more than $100,000 per year will grow to more than nine million households by 2010, up from six million in 2001 (see Exhibit 10.7).

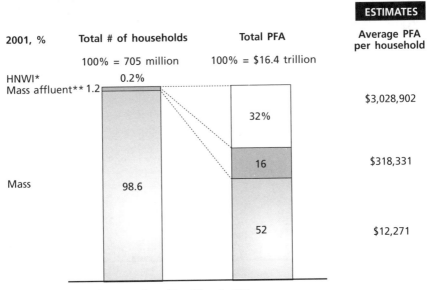

Exhibit 10.6 Less than 1.5% of Asia's households control close to 50% of all personal financial asssets (PFA)

2001, %	Total # of households	Total PFA	ESTIMATES Average PFA per household
	100% = 705 million	100% = $16.4 trillion	
HNWI*	0.2%		$3,028,902
Mass affluent**	1.2	32%	
		16	$318,331
Mass	98.6	52	$12,271

* Households with more than $1 million in PFA
** Households with more than $100,000, but less than US$1 million in PFA
Source: Analyst reports; Datamonitor; McKinsey analysis

However, these projections should be regarded with some caution. Over half of this wealth remains locked in simple bank accounts. (In the United States, less than 20 percent of personal financial assets are in deposits.) Structural factors that would enable a shift from deposits to more productive products are absent in Asia. More to the point, there are few "more productive" alternatives in reality, thanks to unattractive securities markets. Across the region, with the exception of Hong Kong, equities consistently under-performed both real estate and time-deposit investments during the period from 1991 to 2001 (see Exhibit 10.8). Despite changes in the regulatory environment and the proliferation of new products and services, the underlying factors have not materially improved.

Without real reform of the capital markets, it will be a tough sell to persuade mass affluent customers to pull their money out of deposits to invest in stocks. But forces are at work that could profoundly transform the landscape in the next decade. Until these changes take place, however, real wealth management will remain a modest opportunity for most banks. In the immediate term, competitors will engage in a fierce battle for the deposits of the mass affluent. Banks will have to work hard to keep their customers. Meanwhile, they need to begin working out an effective wealth management

Exhibit 10.7 Mass affluent households with annual income >$100,000

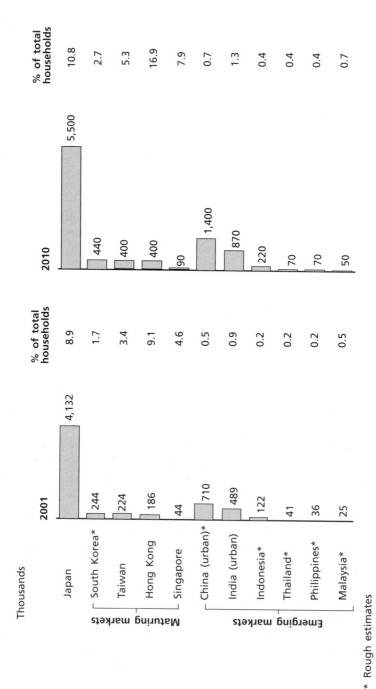

Thousands

	2001	% of total households	2010	% of total households
Maturing markets				
Japan	4,132	8.9	5,500	10.8
South Korea*	244	1.7	440	2.7
Taiwan	224	3.4	400	5.3
Hong Kong	186	9.1	400	16.9
Singapore	44	4.6	90	7.9
Emerging markets				
China (urban)*	710	0.5	1,400	0.7
India (urban)	489	0.9	870	1.3
Indonesia*	122	0.2	220	0.4
Thailand*	41	0.2	70	0.4
Philippines*	36	0.2	70	0.4
Malaysia*	25	0.5	50	0.7

* Rough estimates

Source: Asian Demographics; National Council of Applied Economic Research (India); McKinsey analysis

Exhibit 10.8 Financial returns across asset classes in Asian markets and the US: 1991–2001

	Annualized returns %			Asset class performance	
	Equities	Residential real estate	Time deposits	Best performing	Worst performing
Japan	-7.5	-2.7	1.6	Time deposits	Equities
Singapore	3.0	5.8	3.4	Real estate	Equities
Hong Kong	10.3	1.5	5.7	Equities	Real estate
Taiwan	1.6	-1.8	6.7	Time deposits	Real estate
Korea**	1.3	-1.7	9.6	Time deposits	Equities
Indonesia***	4.1	4.5	17.5	Time deposits	Equities
Thailand***	-11.3	2.9	7.8	Time deposits	Equities
Malaysia	2.2	4.8	6.6	Time deposits	Equities
India	5.3	n/a	10.4	Time deposits	Equities
Philippines****	-12.0	n/a	10.3	Time deposits	Equities
United States	12.2	10.6	5.1	Equities	Time deposits

*   Returns represent price returns of major indices not including dividends
**   Real estate is represented by general property prices and not only residential real estate values
***   1992–2001
**** 1993–2001

Source: Datastream, Bank of Japan, Japan Real Estate Institute, Monetary Authority of Singapore, Urban Redevelopment Authority, Info Winner Database, Sinyi Realty, Bank of Korea, Korea Land Corporation, Bank Indonesia, Bank of Thailand, Bank Negara Malaysia, Valuation Department (Malaysia), National Council of Real Estate Investment Fiduciaries (US)

model now because when the big asset shift finally happens, it could be rapid, as was the case in the United States and Europe.

To be sure, affluent customers already account for a critical share of the retail profits of most Asian banks. The key to capturing and retaining funds is to build superior soft skills. The widely different needs of each customer segment must be identified and understood. New sales and service processes have to be created to support offerings for the affluent. On the other hand, only a handful of banks will be able to make catering to wealthy customers truly profitable as most will simply add costs without deepening relationships. The state-owned banks with large networks have the most to lose since they have traditionally captured the biggest share of deposits thanks to their large branch networks. Attackers that distinguish themselves, build specialized skills in new-format branches, and bring together more valuable customer propositions will win over the most attractive customers.

Emerging markets: Focus on transactions and lending

Typically, the distribution of wealth is skewed in the emerging markets. Only about 5 percent of the population controls 20–40 percent of the income pool and resides in 20–30 cities in the country. In India and China, while the absolute size of the mass affluent segment is big, with a combined total of about 1–2 million households, they represent less than 1 percent of the total population. As the local investment markets are in an early stage of development, there are few real alternatives to deposits, which still account for two-thirds of personal financial assets. In some cases, capital controls restrict wealth from legally flowing out of the country, further limiting investment opportunities.

To attract deposits, players in these markets should focus on getting transaction services right. For example, more valuable customers should be given priority access. To make the relationship profitable, this must be augmented with a robust range of lending products, including mortgages, credit cards, and personal loans. If investment products are available and margins attractive, a bank can earn additional fee revenue by selling mutual funds or life insurance.

Maturing markets: Wealth management is still developing

In the maturing markets of South Korea, Taiwan, Hong Kong, and Singapore, on average about 5 percent of the population makes more than $100,000 a year. The most sophisticated bank customers provide interesting immediate opportunities. More than 55 percent of personal financial assets are already in investment and savings products other than deposits, a higher proportion than in the emerging markets or Japan.

Investment markets in the maturing economies have been developing fast and consumers have reacted positively to the first affluent banking business models of frontrunners such as Citibank, HSBC, and innovative local players. In Korea, for example, Citibank attracted $250 million in one year, after opening a branch in a swank Seoul neighborhood. To head off a deposit drain, local banks blocked off and redecorated areas of their branches to serve wealthy customers, marking these cozy corners with grandiose brand names such as VIP-lounge, Royal Plaza, and Honors Club.

Banks that execute such attempts at "red carpet" retail banking typically make only cosmetic changes in their hardware, without making the effort to acquire the necessary software, such as new products and services, or financial planning know-how. That affluent customers are flattered by the privileged treatment is beside the point. In fact, with this approach, banks deploy expensive employees to take care of low value-added transactions, which are difficult to be redirected back into automated channels.

Early difficulties notwithstanding, the maturing markets may overtake Japan in developing real wealth management within this decade. Players should keep an eye on the bigger markets such as Korea and Taiwan, and position their resources to pursue emerging opportunities.

Japan: Waiting and waiting for the funds to flow

Japan is naturally in a league of its own. With 75 percent of Asia's wealth, it is the region's biggest market – and an enigma for foreign wealth managers. The Japanese are struggling to find interesting domestic investment alternatives. The stock market was hitting 20-year lows in early 2003, real estate values remain depressed, and interest rates hover near zero. With personal assets mainly in cash, tax planning is one of the very few value-added services that a wealth manager can provide. Domestic trust banks with large distribution networks have longstanding relationships with their customers and know-how to cater to their needs. Because of this, competitors with new offerings can have a tough time luring business away.

Unless the yen tumbles and allocating assets to a well-diversified global portfolio becomes the preferred way for Japanese customers to invest their long-term savings, foreign players have limited value to offer. With Japan in its second decade of economic stagnation, this scenario may well become a reality before 2010. Interviews we have had with experts confirm that a growing group of wealthy and progressive Japanese is starting to look for better returns than yen-based fixed-income products provide. For the first time since the heady days of the Japanese "economic miracle", affluent individuals are beginning to reallocate significant portions of their wealth to dollar- and euro-based investments. The unpleasant truth is that this trickle could turn into a flood if a sudden loss of confidence in the yen drives more assets overseas. While this might be a boon to some global bankers, it would significantly reduce the wealth of millions of Japanese households.

Offshore private banking: Enticing the elite

High net worth individuals have long sought to place their money in safe havens under the management of private bankers. Offshore private banking has become a targeted but attractive business opportunity since this elite group of customers, who make up less than 1 percent of Asia's population, control a third of all personal financial assets in the region – close to $5 trillion (see Exhibit 10.9).

However, this is a game for only a few select global players with the brand, reach, and expertise. Private banking clients are not easily impressed by single-digit investment performance. Financial planning and asset allocation can be challenging since a majority of clients are entrepreneurs who may need funds on short notice to make major investments. Other customers include senior executives at large

Exhibit 10.9 Banking patterns of affluent and wealthy customers

Wealth of high-net-worth individuals (HNWI) by region – 2001   Estimates

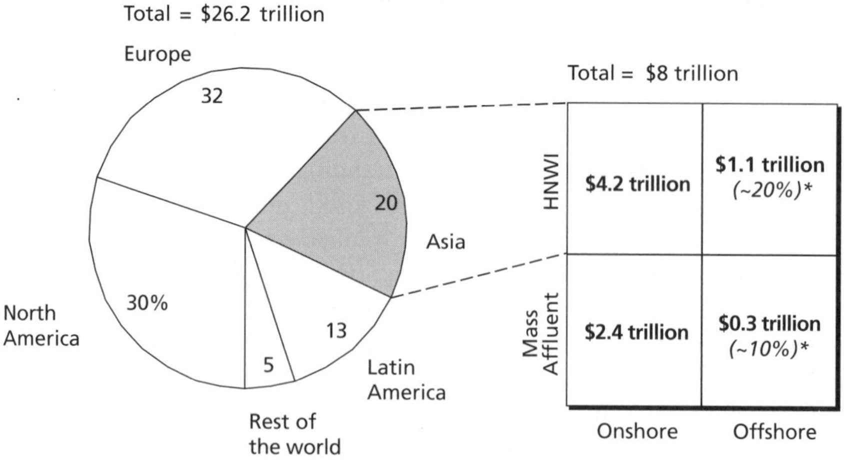

*   Based on expert interviews and analyst reports
Source: Merrill Lynch World Wealth Report 2002; Citibank; BCG Global *Wealth 2002*

multinationals who require a full suite of financial, tax, and estate planning, as well as a broad range of investment vehicles.

Despite the financial crisis, offshore private banking has been growing at 20–30 percent annually. There are several reasons for this: the lack of products and services domestically; the high skill level of international players; the low level of trust in the domestic financial markets and governments; and tax considerations.

Although offshore private banks handle only a fifth of the wealth of Asia's rich, this ratio is likely to increase. The regional financial turmoil and continued political uncertainties in some countries are prompting high net worth Asians to be more discriminating about where to place their money. Markets are opening up and limits on the flow of capital across borders are disappearing. Because of persistent political and economic uncertainties, the rich are stashing at least part of their assets in safe havens in and out of the region. Wealthy individuals in Southeast Asia who are worried about stability at home have kept steady the flow of funds into Singapore, a key private banking hub. Hong Kong, meanwhile, has emerged as the primary offshore center for North Asia, catering to clients in Japan, Korea, Taiwan, and China.

While the private banking market is fragmented with the top five players controlling less than 20 percent of all private banking assets under management in the region (see Exhibit 10.10), leaders are beginning to emerge. UBS and Citibank are sitting atop the league table at the end of 2002, each with around $50 billion under each management, followed by HSBC and Credit Suisse with assets of $35 billion and $25 billion, respectively.

This is still a tough game in which margins are thin. Many players lack the critical mass of assets and are struggling to make money. Building an offshore private banking infrastructure is costly due to the high level of skills required. Convincing customers to move assets abroad can take some doing. Regulatory barriers slow, if not block, capital flight. Currency conversion restrictions or cumbersome transaction notification requirements have also hampered the flow of funds.

Customers tend to prefer large fixed-income products, limiting revenue potential. Although this has improved with the advent of structured products and alternative assets, the global stock market downturn has hurt everybody, particularly the private banks applying a brokerage model, due to reduced trading volumes and the shrinking asset base.

Going forward to 2010, Asian and global banks should consider gearing up their efforts, particularly with the prospect of substantial funds in Japan flowing offshore. Economic stagnation has increased the likelihood of eventual yen devaluation, which is raising concerns among high net worth Japanese. Many are considering non-yen instruments, particularly with yen interest rates so low. This could be a golden opportunity for offshore specialists. If only 1–2 percent of Japan's high net worth individuals decide to shift their assets abroad, this could trigger an immediate flow of between $25 billion and $50 billion out of the country.

Mass Market Banking: Getting the Economics Right

For most customers, banking means long queues at the branch, regular stops for cash from an ATM, and the monthly statement in the mail. Many account holders may not even have an ATM card. The reality is that fewer than half of a typical local bank's customers do more than deposit and withdraw cash from their accounts. Wealth management applies to only a thin sliver of the market, which is why it is only a medium-term play in most places. For the most part, 80 percent of a bank's customer base are "mass market" accounts that account for a large share of costs but contribute little to profits.

In consumer banking in Asia, the benchmark "80/20 rule" where 20 percent of customers generate 80 percent of profits does not apply. Instead, only 5–10 percent of the customers account for over 100 percent of net profits, while the others are either break-even or loss making. Unprofitable customers are heavily subsidized by the profitable ones – the mass affluent customers and borrowers. This puts the typical bank in a precarious position, with its profitability at great risk if knowledgeable attackers swoop in to "cherry pick" the most attractive customers. Cracking the mass market could arguably be the top priority for local banks if they hope to protect their most profitable customers, while taking on the sprightly competition, especially mono-line players, in such battlefields as consumer finance and wealth management.

Two factors drive the challenging economics of the banking mass market: the low productivity of retail banks that results in a high cost base; and the burden of numerous, unprofitable micro-deposit accounts. A study by the McKinsey Global Institute shows that overall productivity of Asian retail banks lags behind that of banks in the United States and Europe. A typical Thai or Korean bank is only about half as productive as an American bank, while an Indian bank can be as little as one-tenth as productive.

Exhibit 10.10	Global players emerge as leaders in Asian offshore private banking

			Rough estimates	
Bank	**Asian private banking assets – 2002** $ billions		**Asian-based relationship managers** Numbers	**Estimated market share**** Percent
• UBS	~50		~200	~5.0
• Citibank	~50		~175	~5.0
• HSBC	~35		~130	~3.3
• Credit Suisse	~25		~80	~2.5
• JP Morgan Chase	~25		~75	~2.5
• Merrill Lynch*	~15		~200	~1.5
• Goldman Sachs	~15		~40	~1.5
• BNP	~10		~60	~1.0
• Morgan Stanley	~10		~50	~1.0
• ABN AMRO	~9		~60	~0.9
				Total <25

* Including business handled by financial consultants
** Assets managed by bank/total assets managed by all private banks
Source: McKinsey interviews

This is partly explained by the "sticky" preference of Asian consumers for cash-based transactions. For example, 40 percent of all payment transactions at Thai banks are cash based, compared to only 3 percent in the United States. In addition, more than half of consumers still want to do their banking in branches. The typical Asian bank operates on an outmoded labor-intensive service model. Most Asian banks continue to locate back-office facilities in branches, with only a few of the most advanced institutions outsourcing or centralizing these operations. Peel back corporate banking and other retail businesses such as credit cards, and it becomes clear that the mass market economics at most Asian banks are badly off kilter.

Besides the inability to manage costs, local banks seldom understand the economics on the liabilities side of their balance sheets. Banks often fail to attract the best customers with high balances whom they need to justify the cost of running the branches. Many deposit accounts "bleed" money: They cost more to service than they are worth. The more such accounts are acquired, the more money the bank bleeds! It accepts the losses in the false hope that one day these accounts will turn profitable – perhaps if the customers increase their balances or use more products. Banks never turn away a customer.

FOR LOCAL BANKS, NEW SKILLS AND NEW MINDSETS

The good news is that it is not too late for local banks to strengthen their hand. But those who aspire to high performance will need a fresh mindset. Developing new skills – either from scratch or through alliances – is the central challenge for Asian banks. The days of simply investing in hardware and building networks are over. For those who can upgrade their capabilities and focus on how to make profits, there are few markets that offer the long-term growth opportunities of Asia.

Local banks have to get core business processes right. This is critical not only to protect their consumer finance, and wealth management businesses, but also to make mass-market operations sustainable. Banks need to extract more profits from their networks and enhance their abilities to acquire attractive customers. The key is to create true sales networks and cultures, become more savvy on pricing, introduce real performance management, centralize operations, and redesign service operations to enhance speed, quality, and cost effectiveness.

All of this goes against the traditional mindset. A new approach is needed in the way that banking is conducted and how the roles of branch networks are defined. The biggest challenge for a big local player is to change behavior across a large, dispersed organization where people have the processing skills, but lack customer understanding and are resistant to employing critical new tools.

Performance management: Foundation of success

Many Asian banks started out as small enterprises, often owned by families, with shareholders limited to only a few individuals who serve on the boards or in senior management roles. Shareholder value and performance have typically not been on the list of these banks' priorities. The profit mindset has been absent.

Not that banks lack the desire to do well. They simply do not have the culture and skills needed to achieve a high level of performance. Aspirations at the top are not shared by every employee. Traditional management approaches based on senior managers having intimate knowledge of every function are no longer feasible as banks consolidate and organizations become increasingly large and complex. The problem is that these banks do not have the proper processes to cope with large-scale operations.

As a result, systematic performance management is missing in most Asian banks. Incomplete information leads to vague target-setting at every level of the organization, which means that consequence management is neither justified nor enforceable. Profit growth is limited.

There are a few leading-edge exceptions. Korea's Housing & Commercial Bank (H&CB) is one of the best examples. In 1998, the bank publicly announced it would focus on profit and shareholder value creation. In the same year, it introduced the first stock-option-based compensation program in the country. It also designed a sophisticated managerial accounting and costing system, and developed a mechanism to measure and reward performance. By 2001, H&CB was the biggest bank in Korea, thanks to its merger with Kookmin Bank. As a testament to its performance aspirations, its share price rose by more than 40 percent a year from 1997 to 2001.

Marketing and sales: From volume to profits

Traditionally, the focus of retail banking operations has been on generating customer volume, rather than customer quality and profit potential. As a result, many Asian banks today have extremely concentrated customer profitability. It is not surprising that banks looking to improve earnings following the 1997–98 financial crisis have focused on cross-selling to retail customers.

For many banks, expanding the product range and generating higher profits per customer is a challenge. From the more developed markets such as Taiwan to emerging markets such as Thailand, bank CEOs are beginning to ask why their investments in technology and customer relationship management (CRM) capabilities are not paying off.

There are three principal hurdles that Asian financial institutions need to overcome in moving to state-of-the-art marketing and sales practices. At the top of the list is the lack of accurate customer information. In Taiwan and Hong Kong, for example, it is not unusual for banks to have the wrong phone numbers or addresses for up to 40 percent of their customers. In less-developed markets like Thailand or Malaysia, this figure might be as high as 70 percent. In some markets such as China, information may have been altered to avoid tax liabilities or questions about the origin of funds.

The second hurdle is finding ways to inject selling skills into the bank. This problem is particularly acute in China and India, where in 2001 the largest player in each market had 44,000 and 9,000 branches, respectively. In smaller markets, such as Malaysia or Taiwan, the high degree of branch autonomy is the issue. Managers resist directives from head office on how to sell to customers and ignore lists prepared for them that note the propensity of each customer to buy a certain product. As few banks have successfully centralized control of sales, the headquarters is often at the mercy of hundreds of autonomous branch managers, many of whom are steeped in corporate banking but know little, if anything, about retail banking. Instead of forcing the issue, the senior management team resorts to designing the perfect IT or CRM solution. The intention is to devise the best customer segmentation approach and use it to convince branch managers to change their ways. But after months of investment, the plan usually unravels.

This leads to the third hurdle Asian banks must overcome in adopting marketing best practices. Too often, the focus is on investing in new hardware, while not enough time is spent on testing ideas and working out effective end-to-end processes. Banks must adopt a much more aggressive test-and-learn approach. But if this is to be effective, internal divisions between headquarters and branches will have to be dismantled so that staff work together to determine what really will succeed.

Distribution: Reconfiguring branch networks

Hurl a brick out a window in Taipei and you will hit a banker on the head. So claims a senior executive at a local bank who contends that Taiwan is "over-banked" and "over-branched." It is not the only place. In many other markets, banks have too many branches and ATMs. Cost-to-income ratios in the mass retail business of Asian banks often exceed 90 percent. Most players should look long and hard at their distribution channels.

The first priority would be to review branch locations. Cities have changed substantially over the last 20 years, but banks have generally kept their outlet positions unchanged. Although some branches in supermarkets, malls, and new office blocks have been added to the network, old branches are rarely ever closed. But banks are now able to access data that would indicate to them the best sites. Leading banks such as Standard Chartered Bank in Hong Kong have begun to reconfigure their network based on a better understanding of customer location and needs. Such players, however, are the exception rather than the rule.

Branches are often in expensive retail locations in cities. To save money, banks can reduce branch sizes by centralizing back-office operations. Further cost-cutting can be achieved by engaging part-time employees. Most branches are fully staffed despite the fact that customer volumes vary by approximately 30 percent from month to month, and even more so during the course of any given day of operation.

Ultimately, the size of many banks' branch networks will have to shrink for them to generate attractive returns from the mass market. This will occur partly through consolidation, but banks also have to increase customer usage of alternative channels to reduce reliance on branches. Both consumers and branch managers must be educated about phone banking and ATM services. The ubiquitous passbook savings account should be phased out to force changes in channel behavior and ease branch traffic.

Restructuring distribution will not be an easy task. At the heart of the challenge lie new skills and insights to locate branches more smartly and direct flows across channels more efficiently. Fortunately, except in Japan, Asia's fast-growing urban populations are disproportionately young. These customers are more likely to adjust their behavior and accept new channels.

IT and systems processing: A chance to leapfrog

As a result of low labor costs, the lack of customer sophistication, and limited competition from foreign financial services providers, Asian banks have to date made only modest investments in processing technology to achieve greater centralization and automation. As a result, productivity and customer service significantly lag when it comes to best practice.

Faced with a more competitive environment, most realize that new technologies will ultimately change the traditional banking business models. Some banks have started to act, focusing attention on customer interface, with services such as online and mobile-phone banking. But technological advances in the middle and back office have been limited. Unless addressed, this may pose a major threat to competitiveness in the long run.

Leading foreign banks such as Citibank have been using technology for some time to lower costs by centralizing and automating processes, allowing them to achieve economies of scale and productivity gains. In the past, these banks consolidated such operations in each market. Many have now set up regional or even global hubs in low-cost locations such as India, China, Malaysia, and the Philippines to handle large-scale transaction processing.

Domestic Asian banks lack the scale to make significant investments in technology to pay off. This is prompting even the largest ones to outsource IT and other business processes. Malaysia's Bumiputra-Commerce Bank set up an outsourcing agreement with Electronic Data Systems Corp., known as EDS, which has taken over a significant part of BCB's back-office operations and is to provide IT services to other banks at a later stage. There are many other types of outsourcing arrangements. Asian banks could create some of the most cost-efficient banking platforms in the world by combining their low labor costs with the best international systems available through outsourcing.

Credit: Skills have to be strengthened

Most Asian banks have weak credit skills. Credit sales and approvals are generally not strictly separated, with approvals usually based mainly on the credit officer's subjective judgment and not on statistically validated scoring models. Rating models that are in place are not discriminating enough. Too often, there is very little connection between rating and pricing. And banks often have no specialized collection and workout procedures.

To cover the risks resulting from these deficiencies, banks demand very high collateral, which limits business opportunities, especially in sub-prime and unsecured lending. A major reason for this weak credit culture is the absence until recently of competition from abroad. Local banks traditionally have had a huge advantage, thanks to well-established corporate banking networks and their dense branch network.

Foreign banks, however, have been strengthening their position in consumer finance and are expected to do the same in commercial lending. In a growing number of Asian markets, foreign players dominate the credit card market, with a market share sometimes exceeding 40 percent. In addition to their superior marketing and distribution skills, their success comes from sophisticated scoring models that make it easier to overcome doubts about the reliability of information and to screen risks more carefully.

With the setting up of credit bureaus across Asia, the playing field is leveling, allowing international players to fill information gaps and bring their established credit underwriting skills and processes to bear. Faced with increased competition, as well as regulatory requirements for capital adequacy to be implemented with the New Basel Capital Accord (known as Basel II), some leading Asian banks have started to respond. They are strengthening their credit skills considerably by separating marketing and credit functions, investing in credit scoring systems, and setting up separate bad debt workout units.

REGIONAL PLAYERS MUST GAIN ACCESS

Regional players who aspire to make profits in personal financial services need to be strongly committed. This will be a tougher game than corporate banking or asset management. Having a global skill set or dominance in one's home market is not enough to qualify a bank to expand across Asia – and make profits. Mono-line players, such as credit specialists, need to invest in adapting skills and models to local behavior patterns and risk factors. Broader affluent or mass-market players need to be ready to make significant acquisitions to establish distribution footprints, or alternatively, to develop business models to tap targeted segments.

For leading regional players, the question is how to keep up or accelerate growth across the region. As local players upgrade their capabilities, the gap between them and the regional stars is closing slowly but steadily. While Citibank is probably already large enough to continue its organic growth strategy – it has roughly 175 branches across Asia – the others need to explore alternative ways to achieve growth without costs going out of control.

For example, even multinational Standard Chartered Bank decided that it was too expensive to have so many branches in Taipei. Instead, it set up a flagship center at one of the city's main intersections. The bank purchased a traditional London taxi to fetch customers, a novel way to offer convenience without investing too much in distribution. Time will tell whether this is the right strategy.

Regional players need to develop skills for entering and expanding in new markets. One option is creative alliances, such as the venture between France's Cetelem and Thai Farmers Bank. Cetelem is trading its skills and products for access to the Thai market. In China, foreign players will not be able to compete head-on with local banks until 2007. But a competitor from overseas can gain distribution and keep business control either by developing "white-label" products sold through a partner's channels, or acquiring a minority stake in a medium-sized bank and taking over the management of product-specific ventures. One example is Citibank's purchase of a 5 percent stake in Shanghai Pudong Development Bank. Citibank is to set up and operate the Chinese bank's credit card services. ABN AMRO Bank has followed suit, taking a 33 percent stake in Shanghai-based Xiangcai Hefeng Fund Management, putting it on course to become the first foreign firm to conduct business in China's $500 billion A-share market.

Finally, in some markets it is possible to acquire and turn around a small local bank. This strategy will lead to faster growth, but can only work if the buyer injects the necessary people, skills, and technology to ensure consistent quality in each country and branch location. Newbridge Capital accomplished this in Korea after it bought a controlling stake in Korea First Bank after the financial crisis. Given that capital players like Newbridge will eventually look to exit their investments, these types of moves also present potential opportunities for strategic investors wanting to enter a market.

Once a player has established positions in several markets, there is a further opportunity to tap operational scale synergies, a privilege local players do not get. Several regional banks have already consolidated back-office activities in single locations to serve their regional operations. Citibank, for example, processes all its credit card transactions outside the United States in Singapore to save costs. China and India have emerged as popular places in which to set up, largely due to the cheap labor. But this is not the only factor in deciding on a base. Productivity, skill level, infrastructure, and even language, have to be considered as well.

THE PFS CHALLENGE

Across Asia, the personal financial services markets hold some of the most lucrative opportunities in banking. Consumer finance will certainly grow as income levels rise and more individuals demand credit. Rising wealth will motivate large numbers of more affluent individuals to search for higher returns on investments and better ways to manage their financial affairs. If incumbents restructure their processes and organizations, mass-market banking has the potential to contribute significant profits to players in a good position to capture the flow of households entering the banking system.

In many ways, this is a game that plays to the inherent strengths of local banks with existing distribution networks, customer bases, and brands. The challenge – and it is substantial – is to overcome traditional mindsets and organizational structures that were designed for a past era. No longer can serving the corporate customer be a bank's primary focus. New skills – especially the soft skills of marketing, sales, product design, and risk management – are essential.

Making profits is even more difficult. Banks must pull simultaneously on all the levers that control the business – and with the right force. Operations have to be standardized to reduce costs, yet service levels need to match the demands of increasingly picky customers. Prices have to reflect the value delivered, without providing an opening for competitors to steal away customers. For bankers used to the face-to-face service levels of the corporate world, designing finely tuned, low-cost retail operations is a novel challenge.

Global and regional banks operating across Asia have to overcome different hurdles to build a profitable PFS business. Some may decide to leverage global products and skills to compete. This alone can generate profits, often with limited incremental investments. But in most cases, the long-term scale of the business captured will be limited. If this strategy is pursued in too many small markets, it could lead to the thin deployment of scarce management talent, excess infrastructure costs, and low net profits.

The bigger question facing most regional players is whether to build or acquire direct distribution capability. In some businesses, such as private banking, this can be done with targeted organic building efforts. In most PFS businesses, however, this requires buying a major distribution network. While this can be done, it almost always requires significant investment and effort to improve the acquired operations. In more mature markets such as Japan and Korea, it is often not practical to build distribution to cover a large share of the total market or to buy a major network. In these situations, alliances with strong local players should be given serious consideration.

For both local and regional players in Asia, personal financial services should prove irresistible to senior bankers facing slow growth and tremendous structural problems in other businesses. Turning the many opportunities that are available into real profits is a goal worthy of capable contenders who are up to the challenge. As in the quest for the proverbial Holy Grail, many will aspire but few will truly attain.

11

Asset Management: Turning Savers into Investors

Asia will offer asset managers some of the biggest opportunities in the world over the next decade. A huge pool of assets in Japan – second in size only to those in the United States – sits locked mainly in low-yielding deposits and fixed-income pension accounts. Favorable demographics and rising incomes are driving the rapid accumulation of large pools of new assets in many of the region's other markets. Governments are loosening regulations. Banks and other players with customer bases and distribution channels are hungry for attractive products to sell. Although the distributors are likely to take more than their "fair" share, local and global asset managers alike need to give serious consideration to joining the fight for the revenues that will come from managing these assets. The challenge will be to generate commensurate profits – an elusive goal for most already in the game.

Across the region, total retail and institutional assets, estimated at $6.8 trillion in 2001, will increase to almost $11 trillion by the end of the decade (see Exhibit 11.1). While wealthy Japan will still account for 60 percent of assets under management, the rest of Asia will grow more quickly as the level of affluence continues to increase. Retail funds will rise rapidly, but it is the institutional assets – funds held by pensions, insurers, and corporations – that will continue to make up the bulk of the market. An increasing amount of these assets

Exhibit 11.1 Projected growth of Asia's asset management fund pools

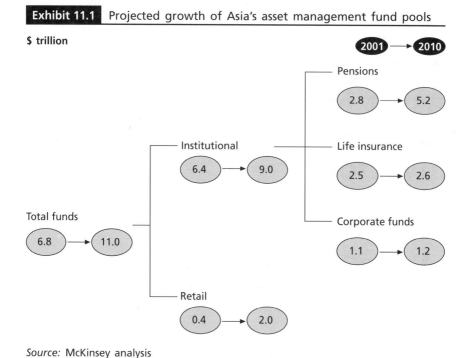

$ trillion

Source: McKinsey analysis

will be managed by outside parties. We estimate that $3.8 trillion in institutional assets will be available for external managers by the end of 2010, 160 percent the level in 2001.

For banks in Asia's markets, the stakes are high: Retail asset management alone (excluding distribution) could generate net revenue equivalent to about 50 percent of what the credit card business (on a risk-adjusted basis) is expected to bring in by 2010, but with a much higher return on equity. In 2001, we estimate that regional distribution fees revenue was $10 billion and revenue from managing assets, often referred to as "manufacturing," was $12 billion. By 2010, regional distribution fees could reach $37 billion and revenues from "manufacturing," could hit $27 billion a year.

While the prospects are enticing, many product manufacturers – both local and international – are likely to be disappointed. The dual challenges of accessing captive distribution networks, mostly through alliances, and building the skills and track records to appeal to customers will be tough to meet. Only the best prepared will generate adequate profits. A small number of international players will capture enough share and scale to impact their global bottom line and a few domestic players will build the required skills, in part by learning how to access international talent.

DRIVERS OF GROWTH

Reminiscent of Europe and the United States in the 1980s and 1990s, demographic, behavioral and regulatory trends are likely to combine to drive impressive financial asset accumulation in Asia for the rest of this decade and beyond.

Aging populations: The populations in Asia, particularly in the larger economies of North Asia, are aging rapidly. The number of people over 60 years old is expected to double in two decades. During this period, the average age of the population in Japan – the country in Asia with the highest proportion of elderly citizens – will rise from 41 years of age to 47. In Asia today, an average of 10 workers support a single retiree. In 50 years, this ratio will drop to three workers per retiree. Japan will see the most dramatic change: In 2001, four Japanese workers support every retiree. By 2021, this will drop to two working adults per retiree and by 2051, to just one.

Changing behavior of retail investors: With the graying of Asian societies, people are becoming more concerned about their retirement and savings. Heightening these worries are the recent economic crisis, which badly hit the value of property and stock portfolios, and the changing structure of families. Traditional support networks are breaking down and parents are having fewer children. There also is a growing awareness of ongoing pension reforms. In a McKinsey survey conducted in 2001, 77 percent of respondents in Korea said they were concerned about having enough money for retirement, with only 43 percent reckoning that their savings and investments would provide for their needs.[1] Anxiety about the future will inspire Asians to shift their investments away from low-yielding deposits and real estate toward securities and managed products.

Improved supply of funds: Banks are increasingly focusing on fee-based products, a push that will lead to their growing clientele base becoming better educated about investments and asset management. As in mature markets in the 1980s and 1990s, the future growth of mutual funds will be driven in part by the more efficient supply of a greater number of products.

Pension reform: Regulatory changes across the region in response to aging populations are fueling the growth of pension markets (see Exhibit 11.2). Governments are trying to influence how much people save and how they invest. Singapore is one of the few Asian nations to have mandated retirement savings for its citizens. Other Asian public pension programs are not as developed as those in Singapore, Malaysia, and Hong Kong, but many are considering reforms to better secure their citizens' future. The extent of

---

[1] McKinsey Asia Personal Financial Services (PFS) Survey 2001.

Exhibit 11.2   Pension reforms across Asia

	Pension asset size ($bn)	Pension form	Reforms implemented/planned
Japan	2,450	DB/DC*	Defined-contribution plans introduced recently (401k type).
Korea	125	DB/Limited DC	No expected regulatory reforms in the near future.
Hong Kong	25	DC	Newly constituted Mandatory Provident Fund (MPF) to expand pension benefits and offer opportunities to external managers.
Taiwan	12	Limited DC	Draft pension reform bill focuses on three options to set up retirement benefit funds.
China	5	Limited DB	National Social Security Fund (NSSF) created recently to solve the potential liability gap under current pay-as-you-go system.
Singapore	52	DC	Steps to increase allocation of Central Provident Fund (CPF) and non-pension funds to professional fund managers. Supplementary retirement scheme introduced in 2001.
Malaysia	46	DC	No major reform expected.
Thailand	8	Limited DB	No major reform expected.
Indonesia	3	Limited DB	No major reform expected.
Philippines	5	–	–
India	36	Limited DB/DC	No major reform expected.

* DC – Defined Contribution; DB – Defined Benefit

Source: Press releases; interviews

these changes will determine how fast pension markets grow and how large they may become.

Changing behavior of institutional investors: An increasing number of corporations and institutional investors are choosing to outsource fund management. As assets grow and the demand for higher returns increase, investors are turning to external managers with more sophisticated products, track records that promise superior performance over time, and the scale necessary to invest across a diversified range of asset classes.

WHERE THE MONEY IS

The asset management tidal wave will not affect all markets equally. Japan, with a total of $2 trillion externally managed, currently represents a staggering 74 percent of all assets available to managers in Asia and just under 60 percent of the total management revenue. Four markets in North Asia – Korea, Hong Kong, China, and Taiwan – account for 18 percent of assets. In Southeast Asia, only Singapore stands out, with about 6 percent of available assets, thanks to its very large pool of institutional funds. Other Southeast Asian markets are small and will remain so, even though they are all expected to grow very fast. Though it has accumulated a significant amount of pension savings, Malaysia will be relatively unattractive for asset managers unless it starts to outsource assets much more aggressively.

The existing market hierarchy will not fundamentally change during this decade. Japan will see a natural erosion of its dominance but should still represent about two-thirds of assets by the end of 2010. Only China will double its relative share of assets, propelling it to third position behind Japan and Korea.

Although this growth picture will apply to both segments of the asset management business, the institutional market – currently six times larger than the mutual fund market across Asia – will not grow as fast. At the same time, growth in retail assets under management is hard to predict, given the need to change individual investor behavior across a large number of conservative markets. We estimate that retail funds under management could increase more than fourfold to reach $2 trillion in Asia by 2010. These funds could generate $49 billion in combined management and distribution revenues, or more than three times the revenue from institutional assets.

The growth and potential revenue from asset management should be enticing to most financial institutions. The hard part is to generate profits. Several factors have been impeding most players from doing so. First, fast growth and high margins have made it a competitive game. Second, the costs of setting up shop as an asset manager – the license, the staff, and the marketing force – are high and need to be replicated in each market. Third, most Asian markets are still relatively small. Finally, the bargaining power of asset managers is low when pitted against the large concentrated distributors.

So far, these factors have somewhat diminished the attractiveness of Asian markets. Among retail players in Japan, for example, only the captive asset management subsidiaries of the top three domestic brokers make significant profits. Over two-thirds of total retail asset management revenues in Japan go to distributors, while marketing costs have been high and sales growth inconsistent.

So what are the prospects for global asset managers trying to build a stake in Asia? Until now, few foreign asset managers have generated sizable profits in the region, especially on the retail side. Some have made profits in niche markets, such as sub-advisory institutional mandates or the distribution of international funds to more sophisticated consumers. But the past 10 years have been a disappointment for the Asian operations of most global asset managers. We estimate that they currently capture less than 5 percent of the total revenue generated by retail services and certainly no more than 15 percent of all asset management revenue.

What went wrong? First, Japan – the focus of many initiatives – has disappointed because growth has been slower than expected and channels, particularly in retail, have proven harder to penetrate than expected. Second, with few exceptions, the fragmentation of the rest of Asia and the small size of these markets have made it very difficult to design strategies that could have any impact. That is not to say that profits have not been possible in some smaller markets such as the Philippines and Indonesia, where margins are high and where the affluent population is easily targeted with a limited branch and sales force network. But these gains have not contributed significant profits to global players. Third, channels have proven less productive than anticipated across Asia.

Creating a franchise that generates material profits for a global operation would require building significant positions in Japan and several other markets: "Japan is a must; North Asia a plus," the saying goes. Of course, some will ask if it is worth the effort and the risk. After all, to generate any material impact on shareholder value would require that Asia accounts for at least 5 percent of worldwide assets under management by the end of the decade. The top 20 global asset managers each have more than $350 billion in assets under management globally and should have 50–100 percent more by 2010. This means that for an Asian operation to have material value it would need to manage $25 billion to $50 billion in assets. Given the nature of these markets, this would only be possible with sustained commitment and investment.

So who would benefit? The most likely winners would be the strong local banks. While many may not have the best asset management skills, they already "own" the customers. This gives them a strong negotiating position to enable them to capture a large share of distribution fees and a growing share of management revenues, even if they do not actually engage in fund management themselves. They could capture up to $37 billion in total revenue – more than half the total available – by the end of the decade. For skilled players who choose to do so, local banks are well positioned to "incubate" their fund management businesses behind proprietary and captive networks. They have better brands than brokers; better networks than insurers. And they have the deposits and critical information to serve their clients. This is a game for them to lose!

Asset management also represents an attractive opportunity for the very few global banks and fund managers with access to multiple local retail distribution networks. While the distribution networks of these players may be smaller than those of local institutions, they are often focused on more attractive, wealthier clients. At the same time, they benefit from having the large scale, name recognition, and reputation to attract and retain the required talent to build the skills and track records essential to sustaining performance.

RETAIL ASSET MANAGEMENT: TIMING IS EVERYTHING

Hong Kong provides a good illustration of the forces driving the emergence of retail funds across Asia. Between 1996 – prior to the onset of the financial crisis – and 2001, the retail mutual funds market grew from $8 billion to $24 billion. This significant expansion was driven by fundamental changes in supply and demand. Retail customers, increasingly worried about retirement and wealth preservation, became more aware of the benefits of pooled savings and investment diversification. In search of attractive fees to replace the meager spreads on deposits, banks broadened their mutual funds and life insurance offerings, and invested heavily in training their sales forces. The launch of the Mandatory Provident Fund made those efforts even more important. Products more suited to customer needs were launched. In 2001, 43 percent of the funds sold in Hong Kong either had principal guarantees or included some form of wealth preservation.

The forces driving growth in Hong Kong are also at work in many other markets, although in different forms. Exhibit 11.3 shows the expected growth in the retail asset management business in Asia over the rest of this decade. The total market in the region should grow very fast from $400 billion in 2001 to close to $2 trillion in 2010. Japan should represent the single biggest opportunity, but other markets will also expand quickly, with China, Korea, and Taiwan way ahead.

Exhibit 11.3 Retail assets under management (AuM) in Asia: 2001 and 2010   Estimates

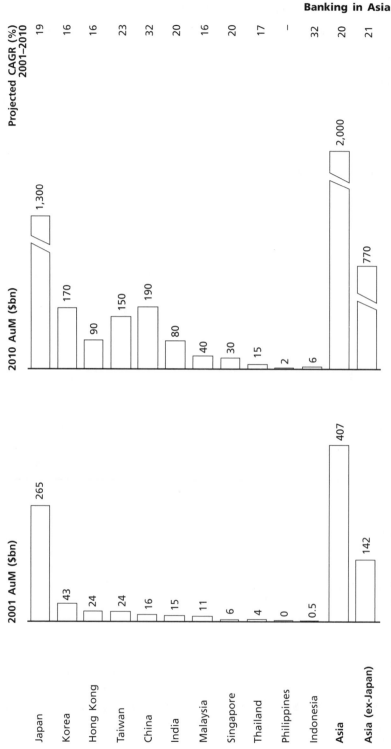

Source: Bank of Japan; Bank of Korea; The Securities and Futures Commission of Hong Kong (SFC) Survey 2001; Association of Mutual Funds in India (AMFI); Monetary Authority of Singapore (MAS); The Office of the Securities & Exchange Commission (SEC) Thailand; Datamonitor; central banks; McKinsey analysis

Asian markets are evolving in similar ways and exhibit shared customer behavior patterns. As a result, there is a common set of principles necessary to compete in these otherwise disparate countries.

Local products and risk-limiting products are necessary: Tailoring a product portfolio to domestic needs is key in most markets. After the 1997–1999 crisis, the focus of retail investors has been shifting to wealth preservation, going beyond the previous over-arching emphasis on wealth creation and speculation. This means retail investors are looking more and more for products that limit risk, such as those with guarantees on the principal or other assurances. This caution is less an indication of inherent investor conservatism than it is a reaction to the disappointments investors across Asia have had over the past 10 years (see Exhibit 11.4). Whereas US equities consistently outperform more conservative fixed-income investments such as time deposits, in all Asian markets except Hong Kong, the reverse has been true. And even in Hong Kong, retail investors have come to understand the need for more conservative investments. Residential property values there plummeted by more than 54 percent after hitting a speculative peak in 1997, while domestic stocks fell sharply after 1999.

Despite the dismal performance of Asia's stock markets, local investors keep over 80 percent of their invested money in domestic securities. In the decade leading up to 2010, deregulation will free capital flows in many markets, and international diversification will no doubt grow. But don't hold your breath: Limits on foreign holdings will likely remain. Even in developed markets, where capital flows are entirely open, foreign holdings in mutual funds rarely exceed 25 percent. For international funds, asset managers usually need to set up local structures. This requires a market-by-market approach that can be costly if a broad global product range is to be "replicated" domestically.

Access and control of retail channels are critical to educate and serve retail investors: In the early stages of market development, retail funds are sold not bought. A former head of Standard Chartered Bank's retail asset management operation once estimated that it takes about 25 minutes to market a mutual fund to a first-time consumer in Asia. At Sumitomo Mitsui Bank in Japan, the effort is expected to take 45 minutes, spread out over two or three customer visits. The client must learn how a fund works, determine what risks he or she is prepared to take, and then select a fund with an attractive performance record. The salesperson must be knowledgeable enough to answer questions and build customer confidence.

More often than not, the initial selling pitch has to be made face to face. In a survey conducted across more than 10 countries in Asia, 57 percent of affluent respondents preferred in-person interactions. Most of the experiments to sell advice and funds remotely to Asian customers have failed

Exhibit 11.4 Financial returns across asset classes in Asian markets and the US: 1991–2001

	Annualized returns %			Asset class performance	
	Equities*	Residential real estate	Time deposits	Best performing	Worst performing
Japan	-7.5	-2.7	1.6	Time deposits	Equities
Singapore	3.0	5.8	3.4	Real estate	Equities
Hong Kong	10.3	1.5	5.7	Equities	Real estate
Taiwan	1.6	-1.8	6.7	Time deposits	Real estate
Korea**	1.3	-1.7	9.6	Time deposits	Equities
Indonesia***	4.1	4.5	17.5	Time deposits	Equities
Thailand***	-11.3	2.9	7.8	Time deposits	Equities
Malaysia	2.2	4.8	6.6	Time deposits	Equities
India	5.3	n/a	10.4	Time deposits	Equities
Philippines****	-12.0	n/a	10.3	Time deposits	Equities
United States	12.2	10.6	5.1	Equities	Time deposits

*   Returns represent price returns of major indices not including dividends
**   Real estate is represented by general property prices and not only residential real estate
***   1992–2001
**** 1993–2001

Source: Datastream; Bank of Japan; Japan Real Estate Institute; Monetary Authority of Singapore; Urban Redevelopment Authority; Info Winner Database; Sinyi Realty; Bank of Korea; Korea Land Corporation; Bank Indonesia; Bank of Thailand; Bank Negara Malaysia; Valuation Department (Malaysia); National Council of Real Estate Investment Fiduciaries (US)

miserably. Banks that have existing face-to-face channels supported by existing products have an advantage as distributors. In most markets, regulations tend to favor local banks, while their brands enjoy consumer trust. The largest banks are the best positioned. Across all markets, the top five domestic banks on average have 50 percent of the branches and 60 percent of total deposits.

Revenue and profits are mainly captured by distributors: Given the likely hegemony of the banks over distribution, one of the main challenges for fund manufacturers will surely be to prevent distributors from capturing the lion's share of the profits. This may be in vain. In most Asian markets, distributors keep most of the high load fees. And they are starting to take a large share of the management fees as well. In Hong Kong, large banks demand 30–50 percent of the management fees from fund manufacturers. In Japan, even foreign managers with distinctive products typically give up 50 percent of management fees to the network. In markets such as Taiwan, where leading manufacturers usually kept all of the management fee, smaller entrants are now ceding up to half to the banks, setting the stage for a deterioration of manufacturers' economics over the long term. Distributors captured 82 percent of the overall retail asset management revenues in Japan in 2001 and more than half in the rest of Asia.

Beyond these common themes, the markets vary widely. By the end of the decade, the two largest – Japan and China – will require radically different approaches and strategies from those appropriate for the rest of Asia.

Japan: Ever the hard nut to crack

Five-year projections for Japan's retail asset management market are astonishing for their repetitiveness. They can be reissued without change every three to five years! The gap in retirement resources to maintain average lifestyles is expected to reach $200 billion annually by 2020. This is finally waking the Japanese up to the urgency of increasing the returns on their savings and investments. No doubt, the market will benefit from two recent changes: first, the pension reforms that have already been implemented, and second, the increased supply and access now that banks are allowed to distribute funds through their networks.

While the impact of these reforms will materialize in the long term, there remain major uncertainties in a market that has been flat for a decade. Several hard-to-predict factors have kept individuals from shifting savings to managed funds as expected. These include the stagnant economy and retail investors' enduring trust in the banking system. Also an issue: the continued poor performance of the local stock market. In early 2003, the Nikkei index was hovering around 8,500, down from its 1991 high of 39,000.

Our projections for the next decade assume that mutual funds will reach 50 percent of current penetration levels in the United States. If the Japanese move just 8 percent of their liquid assets, excluding real estate, into mutual funds, the market will roughly quadruple to $1.3 trillion by 2010. As conditions improve in Japan, this is not difficult to imagine. In 1990, before a long bull run in the United States and a long bear slump in Japan, mutual funds reached nearly equivalent penetration levels in these two markets. This demonstrates that nothing fundamental in Japan is preventing mutual funds from finally taking off. Only the timing is hard to predict.

Japan, however, is not an easy market for asset managers that do not have proprietary channels. The three largest domestic brokers – Nomura Securities, Daiwa Securities, and Nikko Cordial Securities – wield considerable power and are the ubiquitous behemoths of the market, with a combined share of more than 60 percent of funds distribution. Independent asset managers that dare to sell through this channel face considerable challenges.

The experience of Goldman Sachs illustrates what can happen. To attract local customers, the American investment firm built a well-designed suite of products based on international bond funds swapped back into Japanese yen. The launch was a success. Marketing through the major domestic brokers and advertising, including slots on TV, Goldman gathered around $10 billion in new retail assets in less than three years. But as the Japanese stock market turned up in the late 1990s, Goldman was hit by heavy redemptions. The brokers began pushing equities hard to their clients, churning them out of Goldman's fixed-income products. The result: Goldman's total retail assets under management dropped by roughly a half.

Their marketing power does not mean that the position of domestic securities brokers is secure. As long-term retail investors enter the market, they will be looking for distributors that provide them with better value – high-quality products and more useful information and wealth management advice. This trend will play to the strengths of the banks, which will almost certainly win a bigger share of fund distribution – fast. Since they were allowed to sell funds through branches in 1997, banks had already captured 21 percent of the distribution of new funds in 2001 and 30 percent in 2002. Sumitomo Mitsui Bank has been the most effective distributor to date. It succeeded by selectively hiring experienced sales staff from brokerage firms and systematically marketing funds to the customers with the highest profit potential, identifying them using leading-edge database analysis techniques.

China: High growth, high risk

While the mutual fund market in China is still in its infancy, the regulatory, demographic and behavioral ingredients are already in place for it to take off.

We forecast that by 2010 this will be the largest market in Asia after Japan, with $189 billion in assets under management, and combined management and distribution revenues of almost $3 billion. But how the market will develop and how fast it will grow remain uncertain.

Regulatory changes are transforming the structure of the industry and opening it to new foreign and domestic players. Until 2001, the only choice for retail investors was a limited number of closed-end funds. This raised two challenges. First, because of the way they are priced and traded – most often at a discount to the aggregate value of assets held – closed-end funds are difficult to understand and hence not widely accepted by retail investors. Second, manipulation of the market has made investors wary and distrustful.

The launch of open-end funds was intended to address these two issues at once. Licenses had been awarded to 17 such funds by 2002. Mutual fund companies are more tightly regulated than closed-end funds and have been encouraged to find foreign partners to implement best management and investment practices. By the end of 2003, up to 10 joint ventures should be operating in China.

With these foundations in place, China's mutual funds have great potential for growth. At the start of 2003, consumers had accumulated a whopping $972 billion in retail deposits, but allocated only 1 percent to mutual funds. Because of reforms that are aimed at dismantling traditional social safety nets, many Chinese are rightly worried about their retirement savings and are likely to shift some of their deposits into the more attractive investment products now available. By 2010, if the penetration level of mutual funds reaches just 4 percent of personal assets – a quarter of where it is today in the United States – this will mean $189 billion under management, a larger pool than the total for all of Asia excluding Japan in 2001!

Despite this tremendous potential, two main hurdles will have to be surmounted. First, fundamental questions remain about what products can be sold and which ones are sellable. The domestic equity market – A-shares accessible only by local investors – is notoriously volatile and over-valued. Professionally managing equity funds in China is a tricky if not impossible task. Money market and bond funds are likely to become the linchpin of growth in the short to medium term. Supply will be plentiful as they allow the government to meet spending needs through bond issuance. The first such fund was launched by brokerage firm Nanfang Securities in August 2002.

Second, effective sales forces will need to be built to sell these products. Currently, most brokers do not even have a dedicated sales staff, while retail traders have very little interaction with salespeople. Most Chinese banks are saddled with large, but generally ineffective branch networks that have poor sales performance and provide no incentives to motivate tellers and relationship managers.

In theory, banks are in a good position as they own large networks and have access to the very deposits to be disintermediated. Having been authorized to sell open-end mutual funds ahead of brokers and funds management firms, they account for 60 percent of fund sales. Yet China may turn out to be one of the few markets where "mono-line" wealth management players such as Fidelity, Schwab, or a domestic equivalent, could build a dominant position before the banks have the time to get their act together. Already, some of the bigger brokers have access to a large base of affluent clients and are becoming more customer-focused.

The rest of Asia: Limited opportunities

Beyond Japan and China, the region's small and medium-sized markets offer some attractive niche opportunities for asset managers and local distributors. Taiwan, Korea, and, to a lesser extent, Hong Kong and India will be the largest markets in the rest of Asia by 2010. Taiwan and Korea should grow to about $152 billion and $166 billion in assets, respectively, while Hong Kong and India should each reach about $88 billion and $76 billion, respectively – enough to interest domestic and international players alike.

With 10 percent market share in the mutual funds distribution market, a leading Taiwanese bank would be able to collect $60 million in distribution fees, which by 2010 should be about five to 10 percent of the profit of one of the leading financial holding companies. Coupled with bancassurance and the additional deposits captured from wealth management customers, the boost to the bank's fee-based revenues should be substantial.

Taiwan, Hong Kong, Korea, and India may also prove attractive to global players, although none are likely to be huge markets. A typical asset manager without a proprietary network but with a 5 percent market share could capture $30 million to $50 million in revenues on a base of $5 billion to $7 billion in assets, sufficient to create a reasonably profitable business.

Over this decade, the remaining markets in the region – those in Southeast Asia in particular – should grow to have about $20 billion in assets under management each, small even by Asian standards. While few global players will find attractive growth in these markets, skilled locals should be able to generate healthy enough fee revenues.

Priorities for the players

While they have critical advantages over local brokers and foreign aspirants, local banks will likely evolve into "open platforms" that carry a range of products, thus providing opportunities for other manufacturers. Still, in the three largest markets outside Japan, banks are set to continue dominating the retail asset management business. In Hong Kong, the largest banking networks – HSBC, Standard Chartered Bank, Citibank, Hang Seng Bank, and Bank of China – capture more than 80 percent of the market. Japan is different: The three largest distributors there are brokers. Banks have only recently been allowed to sell funds, but they may yet capture the bulk of the distribution market over time.

Local banks need the skills to win

In Asia's markets, the battle for long-term dominance is still to be fought. Local banks must address two key challenges if they are to solidify leading positions. The first and most important is to create effective sales forces. Few people at the branch level understand asset management products any better than the individuals to whom they are selling the products. Training tellers to sell is a difficult proposition. They are unaccustomed to pushing products, much less educating customers on investing. In addition, teller turnover is typically high – 40 percent a year in Hong Kong branches prior to the 1997–98 financial crisis.

For local banks wanting to gain the full benefit of their asset management businesses, there is no alternative to tackling the challenge of building effective sales forces. This requires fundamental changes in various areas from the types of individuals hired to the incentive systems. Attention must be paid to organizational design, with enough of the right talent deployed appropriately. For example, basing a group of financial advisors in selected branches may be more effective than posting a single one in every branch.

Some manufacturers are trying to prompt partners to make the necessary changes. This is the approach that most life insurers are taking for annuities and the sales of unit-linked products. Insurers often desire to strike agreements that are practically exclusive. Given the lack of direct control over the channel, this can be difficult for the manufacturing partner. Out of frustration or by design, some have set up their own sales channels to supplement their partners'. For example, in Hong Kong, Credit Suisse set up service centers to cater to the customers of the medium-sized banks with which it has alliances.

The second challenge for local banks is to develop fund manufacturing capabilities or excellent product-sourcing skills. In many cases, it makes sense not to manufacture funds directly. Top-quality management resources are scarce at most Asian banks. Are the revenues from asset management manufacturing worth it when consumer finance, mortgages and wealth management customer businesses are the main priorities? Unless they believe that they can expand the business outside their networks over time, the additional revenue stream from manufacturing may not be sufficient for many Asian banks to reallocate resources.

Even if a bank decides to manufacture funds, customers will want to choose from a wide range of products. This is necessary to give customers the sense that their bank is an impartial advisor with no hidden agenda. Leading banks such as Standard Chartered Bank have decided that building large internal retail asset management capabilities does not make sense and that an open platform is more appealing. Adopting this model makes structuring winning alliances all the more important. This means that many banks will need the capability to manage links with several providers.

Asset management subsidiaries need outside channels

For brokers, banks, and insurers who want to construct their own asset management divisions or have already done so, one question has to be answered: How will these subsidiaries break out of their proprietary channels and distribute funds through other outlets? In mature markets such as Japan, they have had the luxury of a captive market. Going forward, they will need to possess the fund performance records and marketing abilities that will allow them to build up a solid share of the business. In particular, they need to strengthen their core investment skills.

This is a difficult task. Acquisitions may be a short cut, but Asian firms have had mixed results with takeovers so far. In Japan, the top management spots in acquired subsidiaries or the joint ventures of asset management subsidiaries have typically been filled by bankers, not asset managers. The banks are not willing to pay top fund managers truly competitive compensation. All this has meant that cultivating the professional environment essential to high performance has been impossible. Over the long term, some independent asset managers will solve some of these problems and become meaningful competitors in the market. But in the short term, only a few will succeed in developing the high-performing businesses with the skills and results needed to penetrate other financial institutions' networks.

Few foreign players will be profitable

By 2001, global players managed to capture only 5 percent of the combined retail fund distribution and management revenues in Asia. Their core challenge has been accessing retail customers and gaining at least some control over effective distribution networks. In a few limited markets with concentrated pools of affluent investors such as Hong Kong, it is possible to build a small proprietary network. But in the major retail markets of Japan, Korea, Taiwan, and eventually China, access to a large existing distribution network is needed.

Because there are too few synergies for asset managers among the markets in Asia, local infrastructures have to be developed one territory at a time. Leveraging product offerings across markets is difficult, given the differences in the nature of demand and regulations. Alliances must be negotiated bank by bank, market by market. Licenses for product manufacturing and distribution are needed in every jurisdiction. To have an impact, a player has to build critical mass in each market. In Japan, where only a small portion of fees goes to manufacturers, break-even scale is around $10 billion in retail assets under management. In other markets such as India, where manufacturers have lower costs and earn higher fees, break-even is closer to $1 billion. Placing too many modest bets in too many markets results in an unwieldy regional network of sub-scale operations.

Jardine Fleming, now part of JP Morgan Fleming Asset Management, is a successful example of a firm that built a network of proprietary advice centers to reach out to retail investors. Highly successful in Hong Kong, the strategy propelled Jardine to a leading position among asset managers in Asia. Direct control of its distribution channels ensured that Jardine's funds were aggressively marketed. By often being both distributor and manufacturer, Jardine earned attractive up-front commissions and reasonably steady annual fees. In the future, should Jardine choose to sell other financial services, it is well positioned to identify suitable clients and market directly to them.

Such an integrated approach, however, is not without risks. A network built from scratch entails high fixed costs, especially in a volatile environment such as Asia. In addition, because the extent of direct distribution may be limited, building these channels to market mainly one product is likely to prove expensive, especially once up-front fees start falling.

For most foreign players, the better option would be to arrange distribution contracts or alliances. Two models have been used: leveraging fund manufacturing across a wide range of channels through a series of non-exclusive distribution contracts, or developing a deep relationship with a powerful domestic institution willing to set up a more comprehensive alliance.

American fund management giant Fidelity Investments' venture in Japan is an example of the first strategy. Fidelity is a rare breed in this market, by virtue of having built a significant and sustainable mutual fund business. While Merrill Lynch met serious difficulties in reaching scale through its own larger network and Schwab never got off the ground in an alliance with Tokio Marine, the largest non-life insurer in Japan, Fidelity, succeeded. Its value proposition to Japanese savers of bottom-up research-driven fund management has held up well, as returns have been better than for most others. Meanwhile, its distribution strategy – leveraged access to more than

100 brokerages, banks and life insurance companies, combined with strong brand recognition – has allowed Fidelity to reach out to customers without investing too heavily on a large and expensive face-to-face network.

Fidelity is just scratching the surface of what is undoubtedly a very large market. Future success depends on three factors. First, Fidelity must continue to control its many alliances. Second, extraordinary returns are likely only if it is able to leverage its initial success to capture retail deposit assets shifting to mutual funds and the opportunities opened by reforms in pension regulations. Finally, Fidelity needs to convince its customers to stick with them even as new products emerge and preferences change. Japanese retail investors currently allocate only 10 percent of their mutual fund investments into equity funds, the business in which Fidelity stands out among its domestic competitors.

For an example of the second model, the "core platform" partnership, consider the alliance of German financial services group Allianz with Hana Bank of Korea. In 2000, Allianz bought an 11 percent stake in Hana, taking a seat on the bank's board of directors. While the scope of this alliance spans a series of products including life insurance, it provides Allianz with sustainable access to one of the largest and most dynamic retail networks in Korea. In exchange, Allianz provides capital that Hana needs for expansion and enhances Hana's operations by training the sales force and introducing new approaches to lowering risk. While it is still too soon to assess how successful this venture has been, it is worth noting that in early 2002, the alliance was broadened beyond its original focus on asset management to include life insurance.

INSTITUTIONAL ASSET MANAGEMENT: PERFORMANCE PAYS OFF

While retail asset management will expand significantly in most markets, the development of Asia's economies will also drive double-digit increases in institutional assets everywhere except Japan. Pension reforms are creating large pools of assets, life insurance is growing robustly, and corporations are looking to invest and manage their liquid assets and pension funds. Institutional and pension assets across Asia are set to grow from about $6.4 trillion in 2001 to about $9 trillion by 2010. Despite slow growth, Japan will stay the biggest market. With $5 trillion in assets, it now accounts for more than 80 percent of the region's total.

As institutional sponsors become more sophisticated, they will put more assets out to external management. In Japan, about 34 percent of institutional assets were outsourced in 2001. This will likely increase slightly over the next 5–10 years. In the rest of Asia, half of institutional assets were given to outside managers in 2001. This will inch up to an estimated 54 percent by 2010 (see Exhibit 11.5). As a result, overall assets available for external management should grow from $2.4 trillion in 2001 to $3.8 trillion in 2010, with Japan accounting for 60 percent of the total.

Asia's institutional asset management markets are at varied stages of development. Japan is unique. It is by far the largest market in terms of revenue even if margins on most products are already razor thin at just 10–20 basis points. Hong Kong and Singapore, with $142 billion and $171 billion in externally managed institutional assets, respectively, are the next largest markets and offer attractive opportunities. But they are already highly competitive. Korea, with $116 billion in assets and likely to grow to $350 billion by 2010, will become more interesting over the long term, while China will grow very quickly, particularly if current reforms are successful. It should reach more than $322 billion in assets by the end of the decade. Other markets, such as Taiwan, may present fewer lucrative opportunities but could become much more exciting once pension system reforms are implemented.

Japan: All about building scale

Given Japan's special position and size, asset managers are naturally attracted to this market. But achieving profitability is a challenge. The institutional market for external managers – $1.8 trillion in assets under management in 2001 – is growing at about 2 percent a year and is expected to reach $2.2 trillion by 2010. Margins are slim but likely to improve slightly as more assets are put into equities and more specialized investment strategies. Management revenues are expected to grow at 4 percent a year. They stood at $4.5 billion in 2001 and should rise to $6.8 billion in 2010.

There are opportunities to tap. Consider the following key factors driving the market:

Favorable pension reforms are being implemented after years of uncertainty: A 401(k)-style defined-contribution pension plan was approved in early 2001. Current tax rules make defined contribution plans only modestly attractive, but it is likely that tax-deferred contribution limits will eventually be raised. Once this happens, individuals will begin making their own investment decisions over a large share of their retirement assets.

Clients want asset managers that have proven they can deliver: While institutional investors are sensitive to price, they are also increasingly aware of performance standards. As a result, they are turning to asset managers with established track records and operations. More and more corporate and public pension funds are being allocated to foreign managers that provide better returns.

Exhibit 11.5 Institutional assets in Asia: 2001 and 2010 Estimates

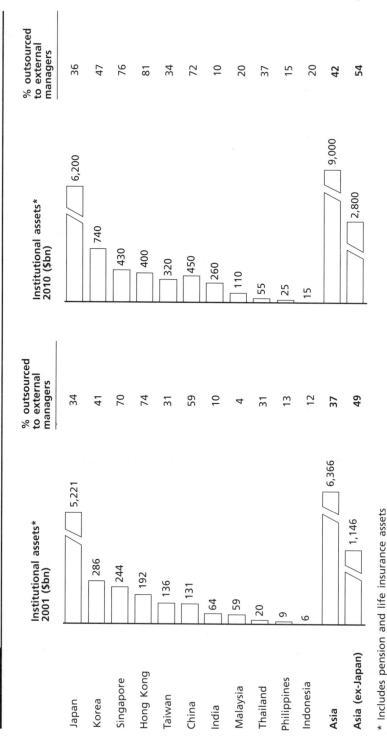

	Institutional assets* 2001 ($bn)	% outsourced to external managers	Institutional assets* 2010 ($bn)	% outsourced to external managers
Japan	5,221	34	6,200	36
Korea	286	41	740	47
Singapore	244	70	430	76
Hong Kong	192	74	400	81
Taiwan	136	31	320	34
China	131	59	450	72
India	64	10	260	10
Malaysia	59	4	110	20
Thailand	20	31	55	37
Philippines	9	13	25	15
Indonesia	6	12	15	20
Asia	**6,366**	**37**	**9,000**	**42**
Asia (ex-Japan)	**1,146**	**49**	**2,800**	**54**

* Includes pension and life insurance assets

Source: Bank of Japan; Bank of Korea; The Securities and Futures Commission of Hong Kong (SFC) Survey 2001; Association of Mutual Funds in India (AMFI); Monetary Authority of Singapore (MAS); The Office of the Securities & Exchange Commission (SEC) Thailand; Datamonitor; central banks; McKinsey analysis

This heightened demand for performance is creating new opportunities for managers. Whereas previous mandates from pension funds tended to be "balanced," or bundled, across many asset classes, sponsors are gradually turning to specialists. There are also opportunities to set up comprehensive sub-management alliances in which a foreign institutional manager is allocated all of a Japanese institution's funds in a given class. For example, Putnam Investments, a subsidiary of Marsh & McLennan Companies, established a joint venture with Nippon Life to manage the Japanese group's US assets. By 2002, the joint venture (JV) was managing a pool of well over $10 billion in institutional assets.

In challenging economic times, players with critical mass have the edge: With the competition intense, the Japan market has been marked by low margins. Average management fees range between 10 and 20 basis points, especially for bonds and money market instruments, which are still the bulk of the business. Some players have been able to consistently charge fees at the higher end by differentiating themselves through service and performance. Still, fees in Japan compare poorly with the 50 basis points or more, attainable in other Asian markets. Thin margins make scale essential for those who want to build a significant domestic presence and do not want to rely solely on their international capabilities. Minimum scale in Japan's institutional market is more than $10 billion in assets under management. This can be achieved only by those with the skills and performance to beat out legacy players such as trust banks for attractive mandates.

To succeed, all players must have both a solid track record and the necessary skills: Contrary to what happened in the mutual fund market, leading foreign players have already reached minimum economic scale and captured a significant market share. Indeed, foreign asset managers (including JVs) have around 21 percent of the market for funds managed by independents. The need to develop track records and distinctive management skills has led some large Japanese asset managers to link up with global partners.

France's Société Générale (SG) offers an interesting example of how a foreigner stepped up its position in Japan. It acquired Yamaichi Asset Management in 1998, after the famous brokerage went bankrupt. SG then formed partnerships with several banks and insurance companies to sell both defined-benefit and 401(k)-style pension funds to corporations. Concentrating on product development, SG Yamaichi launched funds focused on Japanese and international equities, as well as bond funds and global balanced funds.

Arguably the most successful example of a strong Japanese player hooking up with a global player to create a distinctive institutional asset management business is Nikko Securities, now known as the Cordial Group. In the 1980s, Nikko Asset Management formed a joint venture with Wells Fargo Bank of

California to build an index asset management business. Wells Fargo sold its half of the business to Barclays Bank in 1996. The resulting joint venture, Nikko Barclays Global Investors, leveraged Nikko's relationships to acquire institutional customers. The JV offered a range of index-oriented funds with good track records. In 2001, the company was no. 2 in the Japan market, with a 2.3 percent share and $46 billion in assets under management.

Hong Kong, Singapore, and Korea: Established markets

In the rest of Asia, institutional markets will remain fragmented but three already established markets stand out. With a combined $429 billion in externally managed institutional assets, Hong Kong, Singapore, and Korea represent 75 percent of the available opportunity in Asia outside Japan.

Although already highly competitive, Hong Kong and Singapore are both relatively large markets that will further benefit from increased fund allocation to external asset managers. Winners will be players able to compete on products and performance rather than distribution capabilities. Institutional asset managers should grow their distribution operations organically to serve both pension funds and non-pension asset holders.

Let us review each market in turn.

In Hong Kong, the launch of the Mandatory Provident Fund (MPF) in 2000 was the major breakthrough that institutional asset managers had been waiting for. Fully outsourced to external managers, it is likely to grow into a $45 billion market by 2010.

HSBC, AIA-Jardine Fleming, and AXA are the leading players, each with more than 1,000 agents distributing their products to enterprises.

New entrants will have difficulty making profits. Employers select MPF service providers. This means that commercial banks and institutions with established access to companies have a strong advantage. If the pension market is likely to be difficult for new players, there may be other opportunities they can pursue such as corporate assets outsourced to external managers. These funds are expected to more than double to almost $250 billion by the end of the decade. Again, performance will be the deciding factor in winning clients.

In Singapore, outsourced institutional funds are likely to grow from $171 billion in 2002 to $330 billion by 2010. The market is dominated by funds from the government or state-linked entities. Due to their relatively conservative approach, these public institutions look for external managers with a solid track record, a broad and innovative product range, and strong local presence, in part to learn skills from them.

With the market at an early stage of development, no players have emerged as clear winners. Large managers with a strong performance record are expected to gain scale and compete effectively to manage government funds.

The Central Provident Fund (CPF), Singapore's mandatory pension system, is expected to grow at a slightly faster rate than other institutional funds – around 8 percent a year over the next five years – while increasingly popular corporate pension funds will grow at 25–30 percent a year.

In contrast to Hong Kong, Singapore's pension market will reward players with direct or indirect access to retail clients. The pensioner, not the employer, chooses the asset allocation and fund manager. This difference between Hong Kong and Singapore illustrates how critical a deep understanding of regulatory trends across markets is.

Korea is the third-largest market in Asia outside Japan and is likely to become the biggest by the end of the decade. It will grow from $116 billion in assets available for external managers in 2002 to $350 billion in 2010, thanks to the growth of pension and corporate funds. Asset managers must have direct relationships with companies, given that the investment trust management companies, or ITMCs, which dominate the retail market, also lead the institutional and pension sector.

Another peculiarity of the Korean market is that 41 percent of institutional assets are in guaranteed saving vehicles such as beneficiary certificates. This places a constraint on those vying with the established ITMCs. Performance, the main driver of competition in all other markets, is for now only one of many success factors. For this reason, many foreign entrants are looking to forge partnerships with ITMCs. Eventually, we expect more institutional assets to go into higher performance products as corporations regain financial health after the 1998 crisis and demand better returns.

China: New industry rising

With $77 billion in assets under management, the Chinese institutional asset management market is the fourth largest in Asia outside Japan, running behind Korea, Hong Kong, and Singapore. In revenue terms, it is already comparable to these markets, with annual fees paid ranging from $500 million to $1 billion. Pension reforms and increased use of external managers by non-financial corporations will drive further growth. By 2010, the market should become comparable to its three larger rivals, with more than $322 billion under management and $2 billion in fees.

But big changes have to happen first. The industry's present foundations are likely to crumble to make way for a more professional and regulated structure. Thanks to aggressive measures taken by the public pensions and larger listed corporations, this transformation should be well under way by the end of the decade. Ultimately, the China market will be no different from other institutional markets: Performance will talk and marginal players operating in "gray" and "black" areas will disappear over time. While the corporate pension market will remain small, public pension reform will be the linchpin for change, shaping the development of a large market in which competent managers with good track records will succeed.

The pay-as-you-go system introduced in China in 1995 lacked funding and suffered from poor collection. The pension liability gap that built up could have reached up to $100 billion by 2010. The National Social Security Fund (NSSF) was created to bridge this shortfall. New funds accumulated by NSSF are expected to grow to about $70 billion before 2010 and will be fully outsourced to external managers. Potential fees could range between $140 million and $210 million a year.

This may seem small. But the NSSF is setting standards that will shape future industry practices. The NSSF Council is developing rules and procedures for allocating funds to external managers. It hired the Canadian Pension Plan to set up a process for selecting investment managers and is working with Boston-based investment management group State Street to develop portfolio and risk management. The NSSF will be an opportunity for asset managers able to deliver best-in-class operational performance and invest in the necessary IT systems, risk controls, and administration.

Corporate funds represent another major opportunity that will be hard to capture. Chinese non-financial corporations currently hold $660 billion in liquid assets and are allowed to invest with relatively few restrictions. They regularly outsource these funds to asset managers mainly because banks do not provide sophisticated cash management services. In 2002, $74 billion was available for external management. This pool is likely to grow to around $140 billion by the end of the decade, generating $800 million in revenue.

Attractive as this sounds, taking full advantage of this opportunity will not be easy for two reasons. First, most corporations insist on profit-sharing schemes and guarantees rather than fee-based arrangements. The largest and more sophisticated companies will pay fees but they represent a minority. Second, this is still a very fragmented market where the top 100 corporations account for $14 billion in cash but represent a paltry 2 percent of the market.

While China's insurance companies will have $150 billion available for investment by 2010, they are unlikely to represent a significant opportunity for institutional managers. The amount of assets to be outsourced is likely to be small. And for now, regulations require these firms to buy mutual funds.

Thousands of unregulated private funds manage the majority of assets of China's private companies. They provide guarantees and earn performance-based fees from their corporate clients. In a highly volatile market, they take risks that larger discretionary asset managers, affiliates of the biggest and best known brokers, would be unwilling to take. By the end of the decade, market forces will reshape the industry. Skilled, professional firms will dominate because they alone will have access to the largest mandates from major corporations and pension funds. As in all Asia's other markets, performance will win over time.

But to succeed in China, players will also have to possess the right strategy. The challenges of investing in China are significant. The volatile and overvalued A-share market has proven a tough arena for managers to achieve consistent performance. Equities are not the only interesting option. Managers are able to invest in a diverse set of assets, including government bonds. This is the case for most funds bought for short-term cash management. Venture capital and principal investment funds have reaped healthy returns by investing in private companies. With thousands of such firms waiting to be allowed to tap the A-share market, this will continue to be a major opportunity for institutional asset managers and their clients. Some firms are building attractive businesses based on this model.

The domestic affiliates of the largest brokers will be the first to benefit from market growth. They already hold discretionary or "segregated" asset management licenses and will be able to access the funds thanks to deep and well-established corporate relationships. To maintain their edge, they will need to invest significantly in beefing up their processes and monitoring, possibly by forging alliances with foreign players.

For foreign players, creating alliances will be essential to access the required licenses and relationships. The current regulatory regime allows joint ventures with mutual fund companies. It however only allows technical agreements with firms holding segregated asset management licenses, which are needed to serve institutional businesses and, in particular, corporate funds.

In the short term, some will find it more feasible to focus on the NSSF opportunity by setting up mutual fund joint ventures. Some may want to wait for the corporate funds market to develop more acceptable fee arrangements. This is the less risky option. But first movers will have the key advantage of selecting the best partners from among the leading comprehensive securities firms with the right connections. As it so often happens in China, those daring enough to push the limits by building new types of agreements that test the tolerance of regulators and policymakers could end up with a strong lead.

※ ※ ※

Indeed, in the battle for market share not just in China but in all the Asian markets, the winners will be the innovative risk-takers – be they local banks, foreign institutions, or joint ventures – that are able to hone their product design and marketing skills to the high level needed to tap successfully the growing retail and institutional client bases. While the demand for asset management services will expand significantly as Asia's savers turn into increasingly savvy investors, only a few players – the best performers and the ones that time their moves right – are bound to be profitable in what is and will remain a highly competitive business.

12

Corporate Banking: It's the Model, Not the Business

C orporate bankers are under siege. Long the earnings mainstay of banks in Asia, corporate business is generating weak returns on its core credit product. Non-performing loans (NPLs) are way up, with provisions for bad debts taxing the entire loan book. And a large proportion of customers are simply value-destroying. At the same time, the lucrative, and faster growing areas of corporate banking – small business banking and fee-based services – have proved hard to crack, requiring new skills and capabilities in areas where Asian banks have not excelled in the past, such as risk management, efficient delivery, and product development.

In general, most banks are destroying value in this business, although they may not be aware of it. This is tough news, given that the corporate banking accounts for 60–70 percent of the asset base of most banks in Asia. Customers will not make it any easier in the future. Under pressure themselves to better manage finances, inventories, and cash flow, corporate customers are more demanding of their banks to provide better solutions. Overall, generating competitive returns on shareholder equity in corporate banking is a rough business, and the Bank for International Settlements' new "Basel II" capital adequacy standards, which require more capital for higher risk loans, will make the job all the more difficult.

All this raises a fundamental question for the CEO: Is the corporate bank in a slow decline, displaced by lower cost, non-bank sources of finance and services? Or is the poor performance a result of an outdated strategy and operating model?

In our view, it is the latter. The vast majority of commercial borrowers will remain dependent on banks for financial capital and for highly valued transactional and risk-management services. This becomes obvious when considering that alternative sources of debt-financing have been slow to develop and only the top corporates have access to them. In other words, banks have a clear and unique value-adding role in the market and thus should be able to command market rates of return on the capital they deploy in their business.

We also believe, however, that corporate business needs to be scaled down and refocused on profitable segments and customers. Little has been done to ensure that the corporate bank delivers market rates of return customer by customer. Few are delivering on the promise of cross-selling fee-based products to compensate for the credit "loss-leader." The issue, therefore, is not whether banks can compete and earn their cost of capital – we believe they can – but what changes in strategy and core operations are necessary to do so. It is the business model, not the business.

A PROGRAM FOR CHANGE

Restoring the value of the core corporate banking franchise involves a two-step change program driven by the CEO. The first step is to shift from the credit-centric model to a multi-product offering and to make it work, even shedding the credit where possible. This is crucial because in many cases it will be difficult for the bank to win market-level returns on the credit alone. This must be done in tandem with a move to a segment-based model, essentially shifting from "horizontal" coverage and a product model serving all segments, to a series of "vertical" models tailored to the needs of individual segments. The bank must also realistically determine in which segments it can compete, and where it is profitable to do so. Where it cannot, the CEO must be prepared to exit or downsize.

The second step requires the achievement of operational excellence in fundamental aspects of the business. This includes underwriting and pricing, account and customer profitability management, performance management, and enabling systems, including coverage models, organization, and management information systems (MIS).

The combination of these two steps – shifting from a credit-centric to a multi-product offering and achieving operational excellence in core aspects of the business – will result in a smaller but higher performing corporate bank, operating only in select segments and offering a broader range of services.

While the path forward is clear, the transition will be enormously difficult. Internally, many banks will have trouble abandoning a deep-seated, legacy mindset rooted in relationship-based lending and volume growth, and the performance system that promotes it. The challenge will be to focus instead on profitability. Customer by customer, banks will need to ferret out "value-destroyers" and restructure or sever these relationships, even if they are longstanding ones. Organizationally, banks must introduce coverage models that vary by segment, and transform branches from "mini-banks" into high-performing distribution channels. In addition, banks must acquire new talent, skills, and capabilities.

There are also external challenges to change. In the near term, fixing the business model will run counter to many accepted market practices, and breaching them will have its costs. For example, adopting a fundamentally rational pricing approach by pricing credit relative to risk and capital deployed in an irrational market means sacrificing market share to competitors willing to under-price. If a bank does not make the mindset shift away from volume and toward profits, this will be hard to accept. In addition, the loss of market share can hurt a listed institution's stock price in the short term, as top-line growth diminishes even if earnings quality improves. There will also be resistance in the public sector as the culture of directed lending runs deep in many Asian markets.

The good news is that some banks have already successfully made, or are making, the transition. Chinatrust Commercial Bank – a Taiwan bank that consistently outperforms its local rivals – has successfully shifted its focus away from large corporate clients. UnionBank of the Philippines has introduced a winning cash management product that is creating a pricing umbrella on credit and helping it make inroads into small businesses. A bank in India redirected its strategy to focus on its top 200 corporate customers with emphasis on fee-based products, setting as its targets, return on equity (ROEs) of around 20 percent. These banks are not only restoring profitability to their corporate book by moving into the lucrative segments before their competitors. They are also beating their competitors to the exit on questionable accounts that would otherwise impair earnings downstream.

In this chapter, we address four central questions facing the CEO: what the real story is behind corporate bank performance and the sources of value destruction; whether this value-destruction is inherent to the business or the business model; what changes in the business model – both in strategy and operations – are needed over time to restore and sustain profitability; and how tough it will be to implement these changes and what must be done to manage the transition. The answers will define the CEO's corporate banking agenda for the next five years, determining the future shape and size of the business.

TRACKING DOWN THE VALUE DESTROYERS

Corporate banking has become a fickle business. In years past, the corporate bank has been the earnings anchor for many local institutions. Protected through restricted entry and limits on branch network expansion, local banks were able to hold a competitive advantage over foreign players and earn handsome returns in the corporate lending market. Much of this has changed, however, as markets have opened up. New entrants and slower growth have led to much more intense price competition. Local banks, keen on protecting market share, have under-priced the credit product.

The rationale for most banks is clear: Credit is used as a loss leader, an entry point for cross-selling other fee-based services, and an instrument to gain privileged information about the borrower and deal flow in the market. To succeed with this tactical approach, it is imperative that banks win sufficient non-credit business and keep credit quality at a high level. But the corporate bank is failing at this. Credit is under-priced relative to the capital costs, fee-based services cannot make up the difference, and NPLs are soaring.

As Exhibit 12.1 shows, margins in most Asian markets are typically set too low to deliver market rates of return on required equity. In none of the 11 markets covered in this book is credit priced at a margin sufficient to earn

Exhibit 12.1 Persistent under-pricing on credit

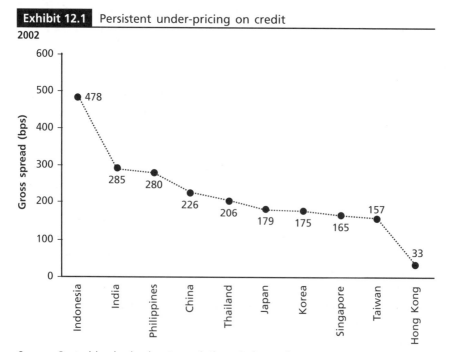

Source: Central banks; bankers' associations; industry data

ROEs in the neighborhood of the capital costs. For example, in the Philippines, ROE is less than 8 percent on average, even lower once proper allocations are made for provisioning and risk.

At present, banks show little desire to restore discipline to their pricing policy. A "volume mindset" typically prevails in the industry, and there is great pressure on the front line – even in the credit-underwriting group – to deliver this volume. Because other competitors take a similar approach, banks avoid imposing more rational pricing on their borrowers. Unless the CEO is prepared to focus on the profitability of accounts, as opposed to volume, irrational pricing will be hard to correct.

The credit business can be used to generate ancillary, fee-based business, which can bring ROEs up to respectable levels. This is the intended model. However, for many banks, this is not being achieved. For example, in a sample of 30 of the largest loans from a bank in North Asia, barely half – only 40 percent of the capital allocated – earned return on assets (ROAs) in the territory of 1.3 percent, which translates to about 15 percent ROE assuming 8 percent capital (see Exhibit 12.2). Bringing the lagging loans up to the market rate of return would have added another 6 percent ROE to the bank's total bottom line. This pattern is repeated across Asia's markets.

In general, fee-based business is not well developed. In Japan and Korea, for example, it accounts for only 37 percent and 20 percent, respectively, of interest earnings. In Taiwan, fee income often makes up less than 10 percent

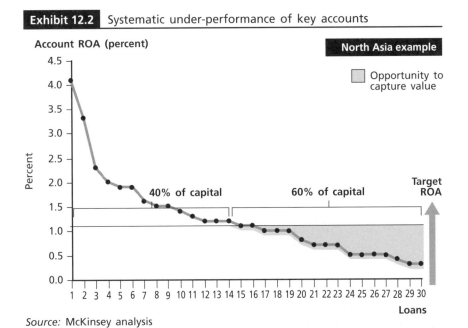

Exhibit 12.2 Systematic under-performance of key accounts

Source: McKinsey analysis

of earnings. By comparison, the percentage at leading banks in the United States is 75 percent. As a consequence, the fee business only fills part of the gap created by the under-pricing of credit.

NPLs are a huge drag on the earnings performance of the corporate bank, putting even more pressure on the performing portion of the loan book. In the years 1998–2001, bad loan provisions ate up 60 percent of all operating earnings on average across Asia, the equivalent to $180 billion in lost earnings (see Exhibit 12.3). Most banks have taken few active steps to deal with this problem.

What drives value destruction

The persistent question on the minds of CEOs is whether the performance of the corporate bank reflects a fundamentally weakened competitive position for banks in the corporate sector relative to foreign banks and emerging capital markets, or if the poor performance is simply revealing weaknesses in the strategic and operating model of the corporate bank. As we have already stated, we believe it is the latter.

Exhibit 12.3　NPLs cut deeply into bank profitability

Annual average, 1998–2001

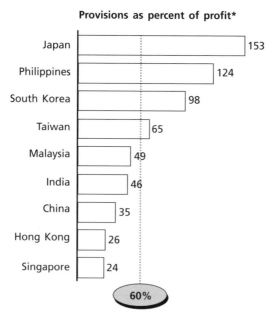

Provisions as percent of profit*

Japan	153
Philippines	124
South Korea	98
Taiwan	65
Malaysia	49
India	46
China	35
Hong Kong	26
Singapore	24

60%

* Pre-provision operating profit
Source: Bankscope; McKinsey analysis

This is apparent in three ways. First, debt financing remains the province of only the largest, highest quality borrowers, leaving most commercial enterprises dependent on banks for credit, as well as other financial services. Second, banks continue to follow a "horizontal" model in the corporate bank, serving the large and mid-market corporations with a similar model. Third, banks continue to under-perform in numerous operational disciplines, resulting in poor earnings and low credit quality.

A clear role for banks in the commercial sector

Without question, banks play a critical role in intermediating capital between commercial borrowers and savers. They will continue to do so. This is especially true in Asia, where size and the lack of information complicate the assessment of creditworthiness. Resolving those problems is exactly the business of banking. Direct debt financing, especially in international markets, is typically open only to multinationals, and the largest and highest quality local corporations, leaving a vast majority of big and small commercial borrowers reliant on banks for their credit needs.

The limits on access to alternative sources of funding are apparent in a review of debt issues by leading Asian companies. Of the 295 issuances of debt to the market – domestic and international – that took place in six Asian markets in 2002, more than 70 percent were by the top 100 companies in those markets, and another 15 percent was by corporations in the next 400. That leaves the vast majority of commercial customers of all sizes dependent on banks for credit and high-value transactional and risk-management services.

The role of banks is also apparent in the structure of corporate financial liabilities. In spite of the 1997 financial crisis and the awareness it created of the hazards of relying on banks for lending, banks still played as important a role in raising capital in 2001, as they had in any of the previous five years. The percent of total capital intermediated through banks in Asia has fallen to 88 percent, a drop of only about two percentage points since 1995 (see Exhibit 12.4). This is true whether or not Japan is included in the calculation.

These realities help explain why corporate banking represents the lion's share of assets and revenues in banking in every market in Asia. Corporate loans amounted to $11 trillion in 2001, nearly four times the value of retail loans. Corporate deposits totaled $4.5 trillion, representing 35 percent of all deposits generated across the 11 major markets. Total revenues from corporate banking, when treasury and cash management are factored in, were nearly $200 billion.

The issue is not whether banks have a value-adding role to play and can earn their cost of capital. It is whether the banks themselves can abandon

| Exhibit 12.4 | Corporates remain heavily bank-dependent for credit |

%, $billion

* Domestic debt securities issued by corporate issuers
** Total domestic loans outstanding, including loans to consumers, corporates, financial institutions, governments and others
Source: Central banks; Bank for International Settlements (BIS)

practices that have led to persistent economic losses. Certainly the business cycle and the Asian financial crisis have played their parts, but a good number of the wounds banks suffer in corporate banking are self-inflicted.

Persisting with the "horizontal" model

There are increasingly divergent corporate client segments emerging with distinct needs and buying behavior. The profitability of corporate client relationships also tends to vary considerably. In an internal McKinsey survey of the buying patterns of corporate customers, only multinational corporations (MNCs) and the largest of the big corporations put price as the priority in selecting a provider for banking services. For many large and mid-sized companies, knowledge of customer needs was the important consideration, while the quality of the relationship manager was the primary factor among small businesses.

The offerings desired also vary by segment. In Hong Kong and Taiwan, for example, large corporations have diverse product needs and want solutions tailored to their needs, but also favor disaggregation of financial providers. Mid-sized companies also have diverse needs but due to the relative lack of resources and expertise, tend to favor bundled offerings from one or a few providers. Small businesses are similar. They increasingly want products and services packaged, and do not want to wade through a host of choices.

While some banks are trying to incorporate better market intelligence and knowledge of segments into their approaches, they largely persist with a "horizontal" coverage and product model. Basically, the large corporate and mid-market segments are served with variations of the same relationship-based model. For smaller credits, this can prove expensive. Full relationship teams or relationship managers (RMs) coverage is costly. Furthermore, the incarnations of this model have not effectively incorporated product specialists. In many banks, there is in fact no specialized unit focusing on developing new products. It is typically managed by the front-line people, or dreamed up by the group head, but with little follow-through within the organization. Without products or product specialists, fee-based services cannot be fully exploited.

A litany of operational hazards

Strategic challenges notwithstanding, value destruction in corporate banking has its roots in the operating platform. Too many Asian banks are fundamentally weak in just about every critical area of operations. These weaknesses have been covered up in the past by wide margins, a rapidly growing loan book, and a protected market, but they have been laid bare by the Asian crisis and the opening up of domestic markets to foreign competition.

There are four fundamental and mutually reinforcing operational problems banks must address: mis-pricing of credit relative to risk and the capital deployed; weak credit underwriting and risk management systems, which are exacerbated by a mindset focused on credit volume rather than on overall relationship profits; a lack of transparency on actual customer and portfolio performance; and the lack of systematic management of NPLs.

Pricing at a loss: As we have already discussed, pricing is a major issue. Even where initial margins on individual credits are adequate, the adjustments for risk costs render the credit uneconomic. Some banks do try to do some sort of risk-based pricing, placing loans into "risk buckets" and setting pricing boundaries on those loans. But relationships often overwhelm these schemes, creating a slew of exceptions. In one bank, the exception rate on loan pricing – the proportion of loans that were not priced in line with internal standards – was 75 percent. Every single one of those loans was under-priced relative to the bank's guidelines, and certainly under-priced relative to true risk costs. At another institution, there was a similar story on the deposit side: Book rates on deposits were systematically raised for incremental placements.

Part of this mis-pricing is a response to foreign competition. Large Japanese banks have been notorious for entering markets elsewhere in Asia and undercutting local banks on credit prices to capture volume. Local institutions have often had to defend market position against these competitors at the expense of profitability. Banks are not solely to blame for this mis-pricing, which can also be traced to the directed credit culture of many Asian markets. This imposes a huge subsidy cost on the lending banks. In South Korea, for example, without much regard to the economic burden imposed, the government has compelled banks to provide large loans for industrial restructuring to certain borrowers at preferential rates, often several percentage points below commercial levels.

Relationship-based underwriting and risk management: Underwriting presents enormous problems. Standards are not uniform in most institutions, automated systems are not tested or relied on, and there is insufficient industry specialization in-house, which makes it difficult to detect risks within a business or to tell if a particular client is in a precarious market position. Many credit officers are not equipped to do a cash flow study or incisive financial analysis. Instead, most rely more on their inside knowledge of customers to make a judgment call. While the business cycle certainly creates unexpected outcomes that even the best credit officers cannot anticipate, the high levels of NPLs across the region demonstrate that no matter what the economic conditions, there is a systematic problem in the underwriting model.

Risk management is also a problem. Once a credit is initially made, it becomes nearly impossible subsequently to lower the exposure, even if conditions change. Credits can be easily rolled over based on the word of the relationship manager. Controls put in place to manage risk are also frequently breached or are one-sided. One bank allowed for a regular review of credits, but gave the relationship manager veto power over any recommendations to re-price or strengthen the lending terms. A review of internal credit ratings of one Asian client showed that credit officers typically gave a stronger rating to loans they reviewed than that assigned by an automated rating system. The credit officers rarely rated a loan "below normal." Consequently, loans were not declared to be at risk, even though the automated system was systematically downgrading the credit over time.

Such exceptions are frequently made because of volume incentives built into performance systems. When relationship managers are rewarded for volume, they naturally are willing to give in on price to get the business. And when NPLs or provisions are not factored into the relationship manager's performance in any material way, there is no mechanism to hold them accountable for the negative consequences of their decisions. Credit departments lend a hand here. Many of them also receive incentives based on volume and are thus sympathetic to arguments by front-line officers that there are exceptional circumstances that justify a credit.

Little transparency on profitability and weak account planning: There is a marked lack of transparency in relationship profitability, preventing banks from capturing market-level returns even on the performing portion of their portfolios. Typically, CEOs and the corporate business units do not know the total relationship value of any given credit. One bank in Southeast Asia insisted that the total relationship value of large corporate customers was enough to justify the below-cost pricing of bill payment and payroll services. It took three months to gather the information to assess the major accounts, which revealed ongoing losses. The services were ultimately re-priced, and the accounts upgraded.

To raise the level of cross-selling requires systematic planning account by account, including evaluation of each customer's industry, market position, overall performance, and, of course, total value to the bank. Such a review can reveal each borrower's needs and the bank's own share of wallet (or how much banking business the corporate is doing, and what this bank's particular share is of that business). We examined credits for a major bank in Southeast Asia and the contribution to total value of each bit of business. Once everything was added up – credit, cash management, advisory fees – the account in question was still destroying value relative to the cost of capital involved in providing the services. Few banks have such transparency on an account-by-account basis. But without it, banks remain unaware of how their pricing decisions affect their profitability and whether their fee-based business is making up the difference.

Passive management of NPLs: Despite the magnitude of the NPL problem across Asia, many institutions have not been aggressive in attempting to deal with it. Many banks still do not have dedicated workout units, and those that do often do not deploy the best talent to them. In many cases, the full magnitude of the problem has not been addressed. Many borrowers in trouble are allowed to roll over credit to avoid having a loan declared to be in default, adding to the bank's bad-debt burden. Workout units are usually not adequately staffed and do not have clear performance targets or proper incentives. This puts at risk enormous value. In the aggregate across Asia, a 1 percent increase in recovery value against principal is worth nearly $9 billion.

There is also a prevailing mindset among managers and shareholders in many Asian markets that they can "grow out of the problem." This is especially true in Japan. Banks there are hoping that economic recovery will put enough good loans on the books to drive NPL ratios to normal levels and generate the earnings needed for provisions. Similarly, managers are banking on property-sector recovery to raise the liquidation value of collateral.

THE CHANGE CHALLENGE

To address these issues, banks must make strategic and operational changes to their business model. The strategic changes should be on two levels: first, evolving from lender to "solutions provider," and second, adopting a segment-by-segment plan based on profitability and capabilities.

From lender to solutions provider

Most of the corporate banking revenues at Asian banks accrue from lending. This is largely due to the longstanding focus on size of the asset base and revenues instead of return on capital. But this is unlikely to be profitable. To generate sustainable profits, banks will need to shed much of their low-margin lending to top-tier corporations, initiate steps to make loans less capital-intensive, and upgrade their product capabilities in fee-based products such as cash management, trade finance, treasury and risk management, and financial advisory services.

Shrink lending exposure, especially to top-tier corporates: Lending to top corporations usually offers low returns on capital since margins are inadequate relative to the high regulatory capital requirements. In many of these firms, risk is relatively lower, alternative sources of capital abound, and capital required by regulators exceeds that required by the market. Added pressure on margins arises from a willingness of competitors to under-price in an effort to win volume. Thus a typical investment-grade corporation in Asia generates an ROE of only about 5 percent. Boosting this through fee income may be difficult, given that top-name borrowers often choose different providers for other services. The good news is that as banks disaggregate their credit and non-credit decisions, it is easier for new banks to capture a share of business around a particular product. Owning the credit relationship becomes less necessary.

Initiate steps for less capital-intensive lending: The increasing focus on shareholder value and the steadily deteriorating economics are prodding banks around the world to shift away from traditional "originate-to-hold" lending. Banks are securitizing credit, selling loans, and using credit derivatives to improve the economics of their lending operations. Shedding credit risk has clear benefits, one of which is regulatory capital relief. Because the Basel I requirements do not differentiate credit risk at the corporate level, banks are left holding more capital than they should for their best credits. Selling off such loans to entities that are not governed by Basel standards eases that burden.

Securitization and loan sales also have benefits beyond regulatory arbitrage. They allow banks that are particularly good at pricing and deal-structuring to leverage those skills and the fund-raising skills of others. Also, securitization or outright loan sales allow banks to diversify away from the names, sectors, and regions in which they are concentrated, and sell credit protection (by buying loans from other banks) in areas where they are underweight.

Markets for securitization products are beginning to grow in Asia, with deals taking place in India, South Korea, and Taiwan. Hong Kong, Singapore, and some others are making efforts to promote their development. Taking advantage of these markets requires specific capabilities, especially in assessing credit risk. These include risk-based pricing, portfolio analysis, and performance management measurement. In addition, banks need to develop trading skills and networks in the secondary credit markets, and make organizational decisions on the role and powers of the credit portfolio management unit. Banks also can engage in collaborative market-building measures to help the market increase and deepen. These would include gaining agreement with other banks on standardizing and simplifying loan documentation to meet the needs of potential investors, and lobbying regulators to ease legal roadblocks such as high stamp duties.

Upgrade capabilities in fee-based products: Unlike lending, fee-based products typically incur minimal or no charge on capital. This means that returns on capital are far more attractive. The key areas here are transaction products such as cash management and trade finance, treasury and risk management, merger and acquisition (M&A), and other financial advisory services.

Many Asian banks need to upgrade their products and internal capabilities to gain and maintain a share within the fee-based business. Selling fee-based services and products requires a specific set of skills, a particular coverage model, and strong product capabilities. For example, to sell risk management and treasury products, the sales force needs analytical tools to assess its client's asset-liability risks. It will want to take these tools to the point of sale. The coverage model must also evolve. A differentiated coverage approach may be appropriate – proactive senior sales executives to handle sophisticated clients and a reactive "call center" team for the regular transaction needs of smaller customers.

The toughest challenge for many banks will be to acquire the products that clients need. In some cases, these can be manufactured. In other cases, a distributor model – the bank offers its distribution network to a product provider – would be more appropriate. Organizing the product specialists and the front line will also be difficult.

Segment by segment

Customer needs and the ability of banks to compete vary significantly by segment. Hence, the profitability of the corporate banking business varies by both customer type and market. Banks will need to focus their growth plans on segments with the highest profitability and the best growth prospects, and those where they have the capabilities to compete. This requires a thorough assessment of buying behavior, product needs, and competition faced in each segment. For most local banks, such an analysis will pose questions about serving value-destroying accounts and may well lead to a redirection of focus to second-tier corporations, mid-sized, or small businesses.

MNCs and top-tier corporations: This segment is likely to be profitable only for banks that have or can build "best-in-class" product capabilities. Most companies in this segment have access to capital market funding. The fee-based transaction and advisory services they require are relatively complex. Overall, this is a segment that will require strong product-structuring skills, multi-currency and multi-location capabilities, and cutting-edge IT systems. Consequently, this segment is likely to be best suited to "bulge-bracket" investment banks or international universal banks such as Citibank and HSBC, and the handful of leading banks in each market that may be well positioned to cater to the financing and transactions needs of these companies.

To compete in this segment, Asian banks will need very strong local currency funding and transaction capabilities compared to foreign banks. To enhance profitability, banks should consider "originating to sell" their credit exposure, or coursing the financing through the capital markets from the beginning. Otherwise, the bank has to price against non-bank alternatives with fewer capital costs. Overall, success in this top segment will require a strong branch network, a large local client base, and IT systems that meet the flexibility and information needs of big clients.

Second-tier corporates and middle market: Companies in this segment have less ability to unbundle purchases of banking products than the top-tier corporations and MNCs. In addition, local banks have some competitive advantages over the foreign banks, given their lower cost delivery models, stronger domestic presence, and existing lending relationships. The hurdle of product capabilities is also lower than that for top-tier corporations. Cash management or risk management needs, for example, are going to be less complex and thus easier for many local players to meet. This could be an extremely profitable segment for most Asian banks if they were to improve their credit risk assessment capabilities, price credit to reflect risk exposure and capital consumption, and enhance cross-selling of fee-based products.

Investment banking services in this segment will also be attractive for a few local players. Second-tier and mid-market corporations have a range of capital market needs that local banks can dominate. This includes acting as advisor to mid-sized companies that are undergoing a change of ownership, providing the investment banking products and services for growth and expansion that are traditionally reserved for large customers, and offering wealth management services for owners.

Small business: In emerging markets, small business banking is potentially attractive. Many small enterprise owners also present a good cross-selling opportunity for the retail bank. Profits from small and medium-sized enterprises (SMEs) banking come from credit products, where margins are still substantial, and cash management. While this niche may be highly attractive, success has been elusive, in spite of the clear advantage local players have over foreign banks thanks to their extensive branch networks, local market knowledge, and relationships. In part, this is because the typical approach to this segment has often been a simple adaptation of the higher cost corporate banking coverage model, and because the necessary risk underwriting systems have been lacking.

To succeed in this segment requires low-cost operations, particularly in terms of the coverage model and underwriting process; strong risk management to minimize losses; and attractive but not necessarily distinctive products. In terms of coverage models, banks have tended to oscillate between using a costly corporate bank coverage model or designating SMEs as one segment for the branch sales people to handle along with retail business. Neither approach is effective. While there are several solutions, we have seen dedicated SME relationship managers and dedicated service centers at the branch level work well. Banks can also set up high-impact, low-cost channels aimed at SMEs, such as a special call-in number, web sites, branch space, or even designated branches.

SMEs do not require sophisticated product support, but they also do not have a great deal of time to sift through a variety of product offerings and they do not need tailored solutions. Banks will find that "packaged options" or "product packs" appeal to small businesses. For instance, packaging together foreign exchange risk management and cash management services with specific features is easier for SMEs to digest. While such an offering may not be custom tailored, it does speak to their specific needs. This also keeps production costs low and requires less expertise from the sales force.

Now for the Hard Part

Where corporate banking should be going is clear. Implementing the changes needed is the problem. Few banks will manage the transformation well. It will require a departure from deep-seated practices – a fundamental mindset shift. Asian banks must abandon the old ways that led to value destruction. This is where the true battle lies. Specifically, success requires five key operational and organizational initiatives, as shown (see Exhibit 12.5). Some of these will pay off quickly; others will take time to affect the bottom line.

Exhibit 12.5 It is all about "how"

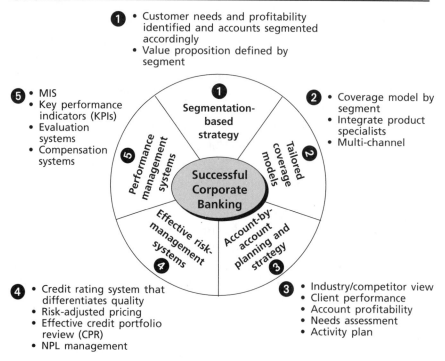

① • Customer needs and profitability identified and accounts segmented accordingly
• Value proposition defined by segment

⑤ • MIS
• Key performance indicators (KPIs)
• Evaluation systems
• Compensation systems

② • Coverage model by segment
• Integrate product specialists
• Multi-channel

④ • Credit rating system that differentiates quality
• Risk-adjusted pricing
• Effective credit portfolio review (CPR)
• NPL management

③ • Industry/competitor view
• Client performance
• Account profitability
• Needs assessment
• Activity plan

Source: McKinsey analysis

All of them will require a strong talent pool to implement. Below, we discuss each initiative separately and in some detail. But as will be apparent, they are linked and mutually reinforcing.

1 Define customer segments and test for competitiveness

Corporate client relationships tend to vary widely in terms of profitability. It is important for banks to prioritize different customer groups based on a segmentation of their customer base. Segments are typically defined by customer revenue or asset size. In some size segments, subdivision by industry is also important. The level of detail in these size segments depends on the use of the segmentation process. A high-level segmentation is sufficient for the purposes of setting strategic direction. A more detailed segmentation – defining specific product or service needs against sub-segments of an industry – is needed for developing sales propositions and designing specific products.

Choosing which industry segments to focus on depends on evaluating a number of additional factors. Chief among them is the profitability of the segment. Growth prospects and competitive intensity are also important considerations.

Serving the individual segments of course requires well-defined value propositions. These can be developed and tested with market research, and then piloted. Pilots are exceptionally powerful as they provide the product development team with information on the value of various features and key buying attributes before making a full commitment.

Defining the segments and the value proposition for each one is not a static exercise. Views on segments and what it takes to succeed evolve over time as trends and competitor behavior shift. Keeping abreast of the developments in a segment is no easy task. It requires a deep knowledge of an industry, its value creation points, moves by competitors in an industry and their relative position, and changes in technology and other innovations. One way to stay on top of every development is to appoint industry segment champions. These individuals accumulate industry experience and information, and work closely with relationship or account managers (RMs or AMs).

2 Tailor coverage and organizational models to each segment

To ensure effective and efficient customer service, banks need to tailor their coverage model for each customer segment based on client needs and economics. In addition, they may need to consider alignment of relationship and product units along industry sectors.

Coverage models will be dictated by both client needs and economics. Each client requires some combination of relationship manager and product specialist support. Larger, more sophisticated customers will want access to dedicated product specialists and demand coordinated service from the bank. Smaller clients will need relatively simpler products and are unlikely to require much time or advice from specialists. Banks will also have to assess the most cost-efficient means of serving their clients. Coverage ratios, or number of clients per banker, will depend on the profit potential of clients.

A team-based approach is best suited for high-priority clients with multi-product needs. Best practice banks often form "Client Service Teams" (CSTs) for their most sophisticated customers. CSTs are usually coordinated by a relationship manager and include relevant product specialists. Banks can only afford to align their most experienced and high-cost resources behind clients that generate enough profits (calculated after deducting the cost of capital).

Somewhat smaller corporate clients who use the banks mainly for one product could be served by a dedicated specialist from the relevant product group. This type of coverage model might be applicable, for instance, to a hedge fund that primarily uses treasury products. A low-cost "lending-led" coverage model could be used for most other clients. This would require a dedicated relationship manager who understands credit products, supported by a pool of product specialists on an as-needed basis. There is usually no dedicated product support for such clients.

Besides selecting the appropriate coverage models for their clients, banks must also determine how to organize and integrate their front-line teams and product specialists. While relationship managers will typically be organized geographically, product specialists can be organized by geography, industry, or product. Each system has its own advantages. The right organizational model depends on the target segment, the dispersion of the client network and the distinctiveness of products.

3 Adopt rigorous account planning and customer strategies

A critical step to ensuring that the segment and coverage strategy delivers bottom-line impact is the account-planning process. Account planning should be conducted for each account that has been identified as a priority, with high value or potential for the bank. Typically, the process should be led by the relationship manager handling the account. The relationship manager may have an assistant who helps with the data collection and organization. An account plan should be reviewed at least once a year, and should be updated every time there is a change involving the customer in question such as new personnel or deals.

A smart account-planning process has four basic components. First, the bank must have a clear view of the client's situation and risks. This includes all the standard financial analyses, but beyond that it requires developing a deep understanding of the borrower's industry, its competitive position in that business, and the risks that may arise. The latter two factors are the "forward-looking" aspects of the evaluation and are often left out.

The second key element is preparing – and regularly updating – a detailed view of *total* account profitability. It is astonishing how few banks truly understand the extent of the profitability, or the absence of it, of their key accounts. In one bank in Southeast Asia, it took six weeks to determine whether or not the top 10 accounts were delivering sufficient profits to cover the cost of capital. This transparency is critical if a bank is to know how to price credit and to understand how much ancillary business is needed to make the account economic. Without this transparency, the notion of cross-selling is simply wishful thinking, and value is routinely given away in negotiations without understanding what is secured in return. In developing a view on profitability, banks must also be careful to fully allocate costs.

Typically, this is not done, and thus profitability, when it is measured at all, is overstated.

Armed with a clear view of the client's competitive position and profitability, the CST can assess needs and measure potential "size of wallet." This means thinking like the company's "shadow Chief Financial Officer" to assess core needs in financing and transaction services. The bank's potential share of that business then needs to be determined. Is there, for example, an opportunity to shift short-term credit into longer term base-load facilities, easing the client's risks and the bank's? Are there factoring opportunities? Is there an opportunity to reach into the borrower's supply chain and provide payables financing, and in the process develop new relationships with the client's network of SMEs? Are there risks the client is taking unduly, which affect the company's profitability and the bank's credit risk such as on input prices? For example, the review of several industrial corporations led one bank to recommend and broker hedging instruments against the cost of fuel. This overall process should take place with the full team, including product specialists. It can lead to entirely new insights and ideas on business development opportunities.

The final step is to prepare an activity plan with specific targets and timelines. How will the bank approach the customer, with what offer, and with what targets in terms of business volume and profitability? How is regular contact maintained? How does the bank communicate profitability thresholds to the borrower and link the need for other business with the provision of credit? From this strategy should come clear goals and targets for evaluating the performance of the RMs and the product managers. This would include sales targets for individual products.

Based on McKinsey clients' experiences, account planning can indeed lead to significant upside from improved sales performance. A mid-sized bank in Taiwan experienced 25 percent higher sales roughly six months after its relationship managers started using account planning. It was not easy to implement, though. At the early stage, complaints were common: "There's too much work," "We lack information to make projections," and "We have known these companies for 10–20 years – no tools are needed!"

To facilitate the adoption process, several factors are critical. There must be senior management buy-in. RMs need to feel that account planning is something management values and expects from them. Early on, there should be a mechanism in place to audit the account plans being completed and to reward relationship managers accordingly. Product specialists must be integrated into the effort and rewarded. Although relationship managers are the ones responsible for completing the account plans, the participation of product specialists is critical to ensure that the goals set are aligned with those of product units, and adequate product support is provided.

4 Revamp risk management

While corporate lending has been a core businesses of Asian banks, underwriting and risk management skills have remained underdeveloped. Going forward, banks will need to make significant changes across the entire credit process from credit appraisal and rating systems to portfolio and NPL management.

Credit underwriting – ratings and appraisals: Asian banks will need to shift from evaluating credit based on relationships to assessing cash flows and repayment capacity. This of course might require local banks to sever many longstanding lending relationships. In the past, many banks lacked rating systems that could distinguish the different degrees of credit risk. Rating systems were primarily used to classify past payment performance, usually according to regulatory guidelines. After the Asian crisis, however, banks started realizing the value of differentiating credit risks at the time of origination. Some have already begun instituting internal rating systems as a tool to assist in approval, pricing, monitoring, and portfolio management. Banks will need to develop different types of rating systems for large and mid-sized corporations and SMEs, and set pricing accordingly.

Larger credits need to be individually assessed by experienced officers. Here the key challenge will be to standardize risk assessment parameters and guidelines across the bank, while attracting and retaining high-quality talent to handle credit assessment. In addition to factors such as country and industry risk, credit officers will need to evaluate companies based on other details, including competitive position, quality of management, feasibility of future strategic plans, and soundness of financial management (hedging practices, for example). Such a thorough qualitative assessment should help an officer determine a client's expected cash flow and ability to cover interest payments, and hence, the risk of default. In addition, banks will need to build and maintain databases that track and assess the probability of default, and place credits into different risk categories.

For small business, the size of the exposure will usually not justify individual assessment of all credits. Here the need for more accurate evaluation has to be balanced against the need for efficiency. In this segment, Asian banks are rapidly moving toward a combined financial scoring and credit officer assessment system. A financial scoring model is typically used first to classify loans into "white–gray–black" bands. "White" loans carry little risk and are priced at lower spreads, while "black" loans are rejected since they are deemed too risky. "Gray" loans are reviewed by credit officers based on a highly standardized set of quantitative and qualitative parameters, each with predetermined weightings.

One key error that local banks often make is to import generic scoring models from other markets. These typically do not have reliable predictive power when it comes to small Asian credits. Given the large number of small business credits in a typical bank's portfolio, significant improvements in predictive power can usually be attained by developing customized scoring systems based on local data. In addition, automating the entire process is very important for ensuring cost-effective credit assessment.

In addition to differentiating the risk-assessment process, banks must also differentiate their pricing according to credit risk. Traditionally, many Asian banks have not done so. Loan pricing was usually governed by the existing cost of funds and the relative bargaining power of the corporation in the market. Sub-economic pricing was justified for the sake of an important relationship, despite the lack of systems for measuring and tracking relationship profitability.

In addition to incorporating the cost of funds (based on the appropriate inter-bank rate) and operating costs, banks will need to take into account two other elements in their loan pricing. First, there is a risk cost associated with the expected loss on the credit. A strong credit appraisal and rating system is clearly a prerequisite for assessing this. Banks will need to institute systems to estimate default probabilities for each of their rating classes, and measure expected losses on each loan, taking into account tenor, collateral, and any covenants. Second, the bank must factor in the cost of capital that needs to be held against the loan. This will vary by expected loss estimates. Since risk-based pricing will be new territory for many Asian banks, the initial pricing models are likely to be approximate. Care needs to be taken to monitor, upgrade, and fine-tune them by collecting and maintaining databases on defaults and collateral recovery rates.

Portfolio monitoring and preemptive strikes: A critical element in cleaning up the balance sheet, too often overlooked by CEOs in emerging markets, is the cleaning up of the vast stock of "at-risk" assets. These are assets that are not yet NPLs, but are at high risk of default. In many banks, these at-risk assets may be as large or larger than NPLs, and thus pose as great or greater threat to the bank's solvency. The weaker the underwriting systems, the greater the likelihood a bank has sizable at-risk assets. At three to four times the size of capital, at-risk assets could wipe out a big part of bank equity with only a modest loss rate.

Credit portfolio review (CPR) helps CEOs by systematically rooting out and aggressively managing at-risk assets. CPR consists of "Seven Habits" that should be executed in sequence – screening, prioritizing, performance assessment, risk assessment (in three areas), strategy setting, option development, and final formulation and implementation of an account strategy. CPR techniques and tools can also be used to ferret out and fix loans that are not so vulnerable, but are perennial under-performers, that is, the loans that limp along, never earning their cost of capital.

CPR is usually managed in a centralized group, separate from the front line of the organization and reporting directly to the CEO or top credit officers. These units practice the Seven Habits and execute the account strategies crafted after the review. These strategies could include loan restructuring, as well as the financial or business restructuring of the borrower.

CPR generates value in three ways. First, through preemptive strikes, it can help a bank to avoid major losses in the future. At one bank in North Asia, the screening criteria detected 80 percent of loans that ultimately went bad two years later, and 87 percent of loans that went bad one year later. Having this type of early warning system can give a bank a chance to exit, restructure, or reduce exposure before the loan defaults. Second, CPR reduces the overall losses on loans that do go bad. At another bank, losses on NPLs caught early by CPR screening were about 30 percent less than losses on NPLs that were not identified early. Third, CPR uncovers loans that are stable but generating poor ROE. These are the perennial "value destroyers" hiding in the loan book. Through CPR, they are flagged and either upgraded or shed. Upgrading or shedding such loans ensures the most productive deployment of financial and human capital.

McKinsey has been working with clients in Asia to set up specialized units to handle CPR. The overall impact has been substantial. Through its CPR program, one bank shed a vast amount of highly problematic credits, allowing a "write-back" of provisions equal to $45 million and avoiding additional provisions of $15 million. In another case, a CPR program for just 30 of a bank's most vulnerable accounts is expected to add $60 million to the bottom line over three years, thanks to losses avoided and earnings from upgrading. The earnings boost alone was $10 million.

CPR must be institutionalized to ensure that the impact is sustained over time. This involves integrating CPR into the decision-making processes, structure, and performance-based pay systems of the bank.

NPL management: Many Asian banks need to take a more aggressive stance in managing their NPLs. Although some banks are beginning to deal actively with this problem, many still lack either the dedicated workout unit or, if they have set one up, they have not given it the necessary human and financial resources or organizational priority. More than any other factor, the success of dealing with NPLs will make or break the future of many banking institutions, determining whether the bank has options on future growth opportunities, including consolidation, or whether it will be left behind by competitors, and ultimately become one of the institutions consolidated.

Banks in Asia that have already implemented an NPL management program often have raised recovery rates by an additional 10–20 percent of original book value of the bad loans. Such action by banks across Asia could mean up to

$100 billion in incremental value preservation. In China, one bank raised its recovery rate to 55 percent, much higher than the country average of 20 percent. This yielded nearly $600 million in value, about half in cash.

5 Empower systems to drive and manage performance

The above initiatives will only be effective if they are matched by activity and behavioral changes in the corporate banking unit and reinforced by performance management systems. The instrument for generating the desired behavioral changes and aligning the incentives of the front line and the credit group with the profit focus of the broader bank is the performance management system. That system must evolve to focus on metrics linked to bottom-line performance and have personally meaningful consequences for good and bad performance.

There are several fundamental elements in the traditional performance management system that must change. The first is the development of the right performance metrics and the process for building those metrics into budgets. At present, performance metrics reinforce a volume and credit mindset, and there are few if any built-in incentives to cross-sell. Budgets – and thus evaluations and bonuses – are also based largely on volume targets, with little or no consideration given to asset quality or risk. At one bank in North Asia, an RM's evaluation gives a 20 percent weighting to profits before provisions and a 2 percent weighting to asset quality. This creates an incentive to get any loan approved, rather than getting quality loans approved. In some cases, the performance of the credit underwriting group is also based in part on the volume of credit extended, undermining their ability to review loans objectively.

The second key part of the performance management system is performance monitoring, which is done through a combination of review sessions, reporting, and IT systems. For example, scorecards can be developed using key metrics – growth in loans, fee income, and assets under management, for example. Individuals or branches can be reviewed and ranked according to their performance relative to their peers or other branches. Weekly, monthly, and quarterly reviews of plans and priorities by unit heads and the sales force team also provide important methods of assessment and coaching.

MIS systems that provide this information and regularly update it also ensure the transparency and objectivity of performance evaluations. Of particular importance are MIS systems that can measure account performance and profitability. Risk management systems should be integrated into the MIS programs so that provisions, or their absence, can be appropriately reflected in performance reviews. Transfer pricing schemes must also be designed so that the contributions to account profitability made by different groups – product specialists, relationship managers – can be properly measured. For banks that do not have strong MIS systems to start with, simple tools can be used during the transition, with performance-based compensation introduced in select, high-priority areas as a starting point, and as catalyst for change in the broader organization.

Compensation schemes should reinforce the performance ethic and differentiate between high and low performers. In one bank, the average evaluation score for account officers was 93 out of 100, despite the fact that the bank was barely making a profit and NPLs were threatening its solvency. If the CEO is going to ask for the front line to make special efforts, then he or she must be ready to give out meaningful rewards or penalties as warranted. Performance-based pay schemes tied to budgets and loan performance can generate powerful incentives to boost sales and minimize credit risk.

THE CHALLENGES – AND BENEFITS – OF MOVING AHEAD

While banks know what needs to be done, actually doing it will be difficult. There are internal challenges to contend with, as well as external ones. Much has to change inside the banks, and reform programs are inherently fraught with hazards. Abandoning the old obsession with volume and market share and acquiring the profit mindset will require a fundamental shift for corporate bankers that will take a great deal of time to play out. Performance incentive schemes must be revised, and some longstanding relationships ended. Resistance to such moves will be stiff.

Any bank will also find it difficult to make the necessary organizational changes and secure the top talent it needs. To execute every element of the strategic plan and operational program discussed above – customer segmentation, product development, risk management – will require highly skilled managers and staff. Some will have to be imported from outside the bank or outside the market. Assuming the talent can even be found, it will take substantial effort to integrate them into the bank's operations and culture.

The external market will also make the transition difficult. Adopting a fundamentally rational pricing approach – pricing credit relative to risk and capital deployed – in an irrational market means sacrificing market share to competitors willing to under-price. Pricing may have to be adjusted even higher once Basel II capital adequacy requirements are implemented, though less so for high-quality credits. If the mindset shift away from volume and toward profits is not made, banks will find it very difficult to give away market share, as unprofitable as it might be to defend it.

Rational pricing and reducing exposure to low-performing or problematic accounts may also encounter resistance from the public sector. Regulators and policymakers may fear the political and social costs, as well as loss of face, if high-profile corporations cannot access sufficient credit or are declared non-performing and cut off. At the behest of the Tokyo government, Japanese retailer Daiei has been bailed out twice by major banks despite its having continuing, severe financial problems. Tacit and not-so-tacit political pressure may make it hard for banks to base decisions solely on objective facts and to protect their shareholders.

Despite these challenges, however, banks have little choice but to begin the process of transition, or else significantly scale down business. With 60–70 percent of their asset base tied up in corporate banking – a good part of it already damaged by non-performance – banks cannot afford to continue generating sub-market returns on their corporate books. They need the earnings flow of this asset base to generate capital for growth (and provisions), and to deliver reasonable returns to shareholders. The retail growth engine will help, but it is no panacea. For many banks, that business will take some time to seed and expand. And in some markets, such as Hong Kong and South Korea, retail banking is not a bed of roses, given problems such as rising credit card delinquencies.

The good news is that some banks have already successfully made, or are making, the transition they must undergo. Taiwan's Chinatrust Commercial Bank, which consistently outperforms the market, has successfully shifted its focus away from large corporations and more toward small and medium-sized businesses. Doing so has taken several years and required much internal retooling. Chinatrust began by first determining which segments were the most profitable and then rebalancing financial capital and organizational resources across the different segments.

In India, one leading bank has achieved similar success, but with a distinctive set of tactics. First, the bank now focuses on the top 200 customers in its corporate portfolio, selected on the basis of total wallet size, growth potential, competitive intensity, and the bank's ability to serve them. Second, it has invested in an MIS system that lets it assess the profitability of each individual customer. It tracks the top 30 clients daily, using this information to devise account plans and prepare for client meetings. Third, it has focused product development efforts on developing cash management offerings, and it has used this superior product to distinguish itself in the marketplace. As its reputation in this niche has spread, it has gained some pricing power on its core credit products and an entry point that may lead to new relationships. While it has hit bumps along the way, this institution now has a "solutions-centric" business model in its corporate bank.

It can be done. For successful banks, the first-mover payoff is worth the near-term pain for two reasons. It restores profitability to their corporate book by moving into the lucrative segments *before* their competitors. And those who move first can beat rivals to the exit on questionable accounts and avoid the earnings collapse or losses that would most likely have happened.

* * *

The overarching message of this book – the importance of acquiring a profit mindset – is perhaps more relevant in corporate banking than in any other banking business. The corporate bank constitutes a large part of the asset base of most banks across the region. In the past, the business has been profitable. However, a series of changes in the marketplace and economic shocks, including market liberalization and the financial crisis of 1997, has undercut the business and led to persistent value destruction for most players. Yet we believe that restoring profitability is eminently achievable. The problem is not the business, it is the business model. By altering strategy and remedying inherent weaknesses in operations, many players can successfully make the leap forward and seize an advantage over their competitors that they can sustain for years to come.

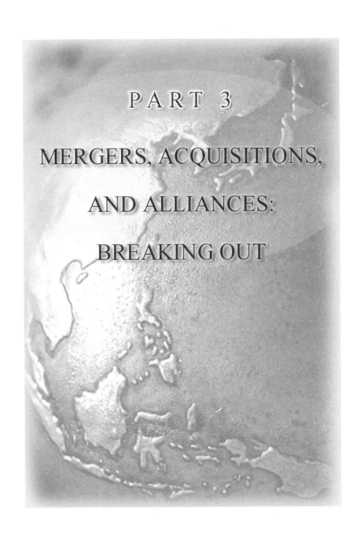

PART 3

MERGERS, ACQUISITIONS,

AND ALLIANCES:

BREAKING OUT

13

Domestic Consolidation: Better Safe Than Sorry

S o how big do I need to be safe," asked the CEO, throwing up his hands. That was 1999, when the frustrated executive was running the third-largest bank in his country. He wanted to know what would be the minimum size for his institution to survive. Today his bank is now part of the largest player in the market – and he is no longer at the helm.

What would have been the appropriate answer to the CEO's question? Is it possible to set a benchmark for minimum scale in absolute dollars or relative market share terms that could apply to all markets? Much depends, we believe, on the specific dynamics of the market as defined by competitors. A benchmark is not enough. Domestic banking mergers, acquisitions, and alliances (MA&A) is a skill that involves strategy, recognizing opportunities, and tactics. It is a strategic tool that, when used properly, can position a bank for long-term success.

Underlying the question of size is the fundamental economics that drive banks to build scale. Larger banks are more competitive and in a better position to acquire smaller institutions. This universal logic will eventually reshape the Asian banking landscape. Yet certain hurdles are in the way. First, there is a limited market for corporate control and sellers are often not driven by economics. Second, the transaction process lacks transparency and may be marred by bad debt issues. Third, even after closing a deal, capturing synergies in

Asian banking, particularly in costs, has been very difficult. More successful role models will have to emerge before widespread consolidation reshapes the markets.

Meanwhile, we will see some deals motivated by the need to acquire distinctive skills. We will also see mergers to broaden scope, as some financial institutions seek to expand their services to attract more customers and generate new marketing synergies. These deals will probably be peripheral to the fundamental consolidation process, which mainly addresses banking fragmentation.

Plainly put, Asia needs fewer banks – and consolidation eliminates banks. Good consolidation should produce fewer, but better banks that are leaner, more robust and more skilled. Examples of bad consolidation abound. The mistakes are buried in the many large, bloated institutions that saw little, if any, improvement in their skill levels or cost structures – size without the corresponding benefits of scale. This is nothing more than "half-survival." It is bad for the banks and ultimately bad for the sector as a whole.

FEWER, BIGGER, BETTER

At a recent meeting of local bankers, an official from the Hong Kong Monetary Authority was asked about the future of the city's banking industry. "Fewer, bigger banks," he growled. That could have been a rallying call for regulators across Asia. The Asian economic crisis of 1997 left piles of non-performing loans (NPLs) throughout the region and exposed the fundamental weaknesses of the banking systems. The sector, which had funded the economic miracle of the 1980s and 1990s, became increasingly inefficient at allocating capital to business risk. Some policymakers were shaken by the apparent fragility and the obvious fragmentation of their domestic banking systems. They concluded that the many state- and family-owned banks were simply not robust enough in the light of the significantly higher regional macroeconomic and financial risks.

As a result, many regulators steadily increased the pressure on banks to merge. In most counties, this has been limited to stirring up free market forces while applying a combination of capitalization ratio and absolute capital requirements. In some markets, merger and acquisition regulations were adjusted to facilitate transactions. In others markets, regulators have been draconian. Bank Negara Malaysia mandated the merger of over 50 local banks in 1999 to form 10 groups around so-called "anchor" institutions that were handpicked. Some flexibility was allowed when it came to determining which banks went under which anchor, but the forced march was concluded quickly.

Regulator pressure for consolidation has been fairly consistent across Asia. The real trigger has been financial distress. In the most troubled markets such as Malaysia, Indonesia, and Korea, regulators have driven consolidation more overtly, using both the carrot and the stick. While injecting large amounts of government capital to support the banking sector, they have also set tough capital requirements. With a privatization program and sales to approved bidders, the Seoul government whittled down the list of commercial banks in Korea from 26 players to slightly more than a dozen in four years. There have been significant reductions in the other two markets as well.

Meanwhile, the Monetary Authority of Singapore adopted a less forceful but equally effective approach, prodding local banks to combine. The merger in 1998 of government-linked Keppel Bank and family-owned TatLee Bank and the takeover the same year of state-owned POSBank by DBS Bank, also government-controlled, triggered a consolidation wave that cut the number of domestic players from seven major players to just three large institutions by 2001.

STILL TOO MANY BANKS

Despite the consolidation in certain markets, Asian banking remains fragmented. This is not unique to the region, but reflects a global trend. Except in certain business lines such as investment banking, markets around the world are typically marked by the same level of fragmentation. The top 50 listed institutions accounted for only 53 percent of global banking profits in 2000. The leading 10 banks captured 15 percent of profits. In comparison, the top 10 automakers made 64 percent of the profits in their industry, while the 10 biggest oil companies earned 52 percent of petroleum sector profits. In 2001, all Asian banks outside Japan among the top 1,000 in the world accounted for less than 10 percent of global banking profits (see Exhibit 13.1).

So why is banking – particularly in Asia – so fragmented? Are there fewer benefits of scale relative to other industries? We will demonstrate that the fundamental economic case for scale through consolidation is clear and applies well to Asian markets. Though underlying growth in most of the region's markets makes consolidation for cost savings less likely, volatility arising from banking sector distress is a far more compelling motivator. Asian banks will eventually reap the benefits of scale, though many institutions feel a lot of pain along the way. To understand the dynamics of bank consolidation in the region, let us first examine the economies of scale.

THE QUEST FOR ECONOMIES OF SCALE

Can a regional or global benchmark be calculated to ascertain the required level of scale for survival? Many have tried to come up with a magic number.

Exhibit 13.1 Share of global banking profits – Asia ex-Japan

$ million

Market	1996	% of total	2001	% of total	CAGR (%)
Hong Kong	6,835	3.6	7,649	2.3	2
Malaysia	5,005	2.7	2,506	0.8	−13
Taiwan	3,764	2.0	1,733	0.5	−14
China	3,373	1.8	3,945	1.2	3
Singapore	2,297	1.2	1,982	0.6	−3
Thailand	2,295	1.2	1,893	0.6	−4
Indonesia	1,985	1.1	1,277	0.4	−8
Philippines	1,736	0.9	275	0.1	−31
Korea	1,337	0.7	4,317	1.3	26
India	265	0.1	1,361	0.4	39
Asia (ex-Japan)	25,519	13.5	22,992	6.9	−2

Source: Bankscope; central banks; McKinsey analysis

Some have attempted to determine a market share threshold above which a bank is "safe." There is evidence in certain Asian markets – notably Southeast Asia – that, on average, banks with more than a 10 percent market share enjoy better profitability and market multiples than smaller institutions (see Exhibit 13.2). Still, any general correlation between size and performance cannot be established. Besides, in markets such as Taiwan and China, the 10 percent benchmark simply does not work.

Industry analysts have attempted to pinpoint the minimum asset base required to support certain infrastructure investments. These calculations indicate that $5 billion in assets are needed to support annual IT maintenance spending of between $15 million and $20 million. But this proposed guideline does not reflect reality. Asian banks typically spend less than their US and European counterparts on systems. Moreover, margins vary widely across markets, making a benchmark based on average return on assets difficult to apply.

Though an interesting intellectual diversion, trying to answer the question of absolute survivable scale misses the point. Required scale is defined by the dynamics of the market in which each bank operates. There is a local benchmark, but the segments of the banking sector that are regional or global, such as investment banking, demonstrate that local scale is enough only for as long as barriers keep outsiders from competing. The answer then is simple. You need enough scale to reap more economic benefits than your

Exhibit 13.2　Correlation of scale and performance

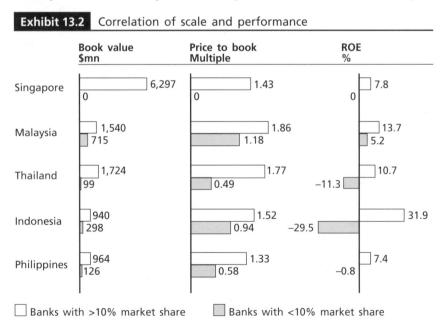

Source: Bloomberg; company reports; McKinsey analysis

competitors. When two hunters flee from an angry bear, for one to escape a mauling, he need not outrun the bear, only the other hunter.

Increasing size benefits banks in three ways:

Scaling up the platform: Domestic competition forces banks to increase investment in IT, distribution, and marketing, which needs to be spread over a large operating base. Although Asian banks generally make lower platform investments relative to Europe or the United States, increasing customer sophistication is changing that. Driving more business through scalable fixed-cost investments will over time yield better margins. Processing scale comparisons demonstrate that doubling the volume of your credit card and mortgage businesses produces savings of 32 percent and 20 percent, respectively, in most markets.

Leveraging skills and attracting talent: Skill and talent synergies are crucial as markets develop, demanding greater product and service differentiation. Banks in Asia have typically provided basic transactions and savings facilities to consumers and collateral-based lending to large corporations, but are now moving to a more service-oriented business model. As a result, the quality of management and staff becomes key. The larger and more established players will attract the best talent, provide the best services, and outperform the sub-scale players. This has already happened in more mature markets such as Hong Kong.

Bulking up financial muscle: There are also advantages that come with a larger balance sheet. A more robust capital base allows a bank to better absorb volatility, while the resulting improvement in creditworthiness means lower funding costs through deposits. A structural funding advantage is one of the best competitive edges to have. This is best illustrated in Hong Kong, a market with several large players and a set of smaller family-owned banks. The large banks enjoy substantially cheaper deposits – by up to 50 basis points. Their superiority is also reflected in the market valuations of banks relative to size (see Exhibit 13.3).

Further, on the question of whether scale can be calculated locally or globally for an institution to win, there are two aspects to this issue: first, the level of scale benefits available, and second, whether that level is sufficient for an institution to compete. The benefits of expanding banking platform, skills, and financial clout can accrue at a local, regional, or global level. Capturing them is a key strategic priority wherever a bank may be on the scale curve. For the overwhelming majority of Asian banks this means increasing domestic scale within a national market, as this is where competitive pressure is the strongest.

So how does domestic consolidation play out? At a conceptual level it follows a simple, brutal logic. Bigger banks derive more economic benefits and are more profitable than smaller institutions. Their market value reflects

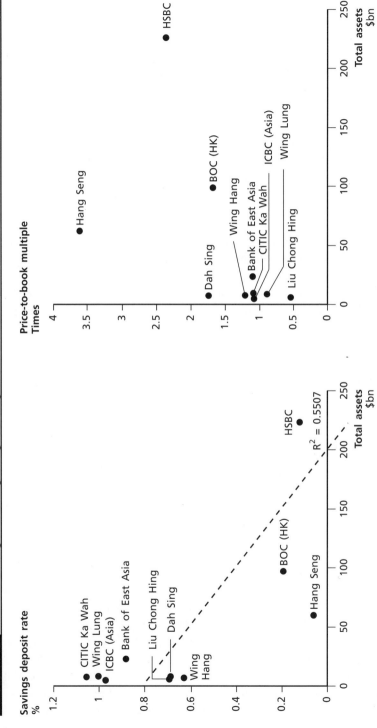

Exhibit 13.3 Scale advantages in Hong Kong banking

Source: Bankscope; Datastream; McKinsey analysis

this advantage. They are awarded better multiples on their book of business, which in turn gives them the currency to buy smaller players and integrate these targets to generate scale synergies. This pattern was illustrated in several US regional markets and in Europe during the late 1980s and early 1990s. Between 1989 and 1993, Chicago-based Bank One Corporation maintained a dedicated acquisition team that executed a total of 46 takeovers, practically one every month. Over that period, Bank One's assets grew from $27 billion to $80 billion, a 200 percent increase.

We have yet to see a similar expansion in any of Asia's markets, though most are fragmented enough to allow for such plays. The reason: There are hurdles to domestic consolidation that must be overcome.

No Easy Path

In an unprecedented move to drive domestic consolidation, the Malaysian government decided in 1999 to designate six "anchor banks," into which all the 58 local financial institutions (commercial banks, merchant banks, and finance companies) would be merged. Several banks, including RHB and Arab-Malaysian Banking Group, fiercely resisted this edict. While paying lip service to the plan by entering into discussions with various parties, both fought hard to preserve their independence and to obtain the "anchor bank" status themselves. Eventually, the government had to back off from designating only six anchor banks and extended the merger timeline by nine months. Reversing its original forced-merger policy, Bank Negara Malaysia Governor Ali Abul Hassan Sulaiman commented, "It's all up to the banks. We will leave it up to them but we want to see as much consolidation as possible." With this change of mind, 10 anchor banks were eventually formed, with RHB, Arab-Malaysian Banking Group, Hong Leong Bank, and EON added to the list. The plan managed to take out some of the marginal players from the banking landscape, but failed to build a small stable of potential champions.

Singapore offers another cautionary consolidation tale. After many years of preaching by the government and a first step with the acquisition of POSBank, DBS initiated a hostile bid for Overseas Union Bank (OUB), the fourth-largest bank. OUB had been working hard to preserve its independence, including exploring strategic alliance options with foreign partners, and was not at all pleased with DBS' unsolicited attention. Taking the opportunity of DBS' hostile bid, United Overseas Bank (UOB) offered OUB a friendly merger and won the ensuing takeover battle to become (combined) the second largest bank in the market. In its zeal to accelerate the domestic consolidation process advocated by the government, DBS eventually drove its target into a rival's arm, producing a more powerful competitor, but no clear winner.

There are certainly lessons in the Malaysia and Singapore experiences, but the need to consolidate and build banks with the scale to play a meaningful long-term role is clear. Yet with the economic and regulatory pressures in place, what is really inhibiting the consolidation of Asia's banking markets?

For domestic consolidation to create shareholder value, banks face three broad challenges: to press transactions that are driven by sound economic rationale; to avoid indigestion from unforeseen problems in the target's books; and to quickly extract synergies from a merger or acquisition to pay for the deal. Against this backdrop, five issues stand in the way of consolidation: unwilling sellers, many of whom are driven by non-economic factors and motives; the presence in several markets of big, poorly performing banks next to smaller, better ones; persistent bad loan problems serious enough to negate scale synergies; opaque due diligence processes; and difficulties achieving synergies, particularly in cost saving.

Unwilling sellers: "I know what to do," a bank chairman once said in exasperation. "The trouble is that nobody else seems to know what they should be doing – and I can't do everything by myself!" Fair enough. The economic logic of consolidation requires smaller players – the "consolidatees" – to recognize their scale disadvantage and relinquish control to the larger consolidators. This has worked particularly well in economies with a healthy market for corporate control, meaning that ownership is bought and sold regularly as shareholders apply pressure to management to deliver competitive returns. Asia does not have a well-developed market for corporate control. Hostile transactions are extremely difficult, if not impossible, to execute.

In Asia, many owner-shareholders of family-controlled banks are attached to their businesses far more deeply than a "value-maximizing" chairman would be. They are therefore willing to stick it out even in the face of returns well below the cost of equity. Their tenacity is driven by a combination of succession concerns – what will my eldest son do if we aren't running the bank? – and worries about losing face on selling out. Also, there is the persistent short-term volatility in the markets that often hides fundamental shifts in competitiveness. So many Asian bankers have "seen bad times before" and are well accustomed to gritting their teeth through yet another difficult period. A buyer at the doorstep is regarded as a cyclical opportunist rather than a godsend offering a way to preserve some of the shareholders' dwindling capital value.

State-owned institutions form another large group of Asian banks, accounting for 50–60 percent of banking assets in Taiwan, China, Indonesia, and India. They are obviously more susceptible to government influence than private-sector counterparts. The social concerns perceived to be associated with bank mergers have proved a great a hurdle for consolidation among large state-owned banks. Various priorities that are not value-driven have slowed the consolidation process. As a result, mergers are more often the result of distress and failure, rather than moves undertaken by strong players aiming to lock in winning positions.

Big and ugly, small and beautiful: Domestic consolidation typically involves larger, better banks taking over smaller, weaker ones. Yet in Asia, many big institutions that should be reaping the benefits of scale are in fact the market laggards in service, innovation, and financial results. In mature markets, niche or product winners are usually small players that enjoy higher valuations than large rivals. Without the benefits of scale, these dynamic best-in-class competitors have simply performed better. Examples of such banks include Chinatrust Commercial Bank in Taiwan, China Merchants Bank in China, and Malaysia's Hong Leong Bank (see Exhibit 13.4). Large banks with poor skills lack the credibility to be consolidators, while the small players often do not have the appetite to move on the big boys.

The bad debt trap: Much of the regulatory pressure to consolidate has been driven by the desire to reduce bad debts. But in many cases the medicine can be as deadly as the disease. In 2002 NPLs accounted for up to 24 percent, based on unofficial estimates, of the average balance sheets of Asian banks. NPLs have probably been the single biggest inhibitor of M&A banking deals in the region.

Exhibit 13.4   Performance of bigger vs. smaller banks in select Asian markets

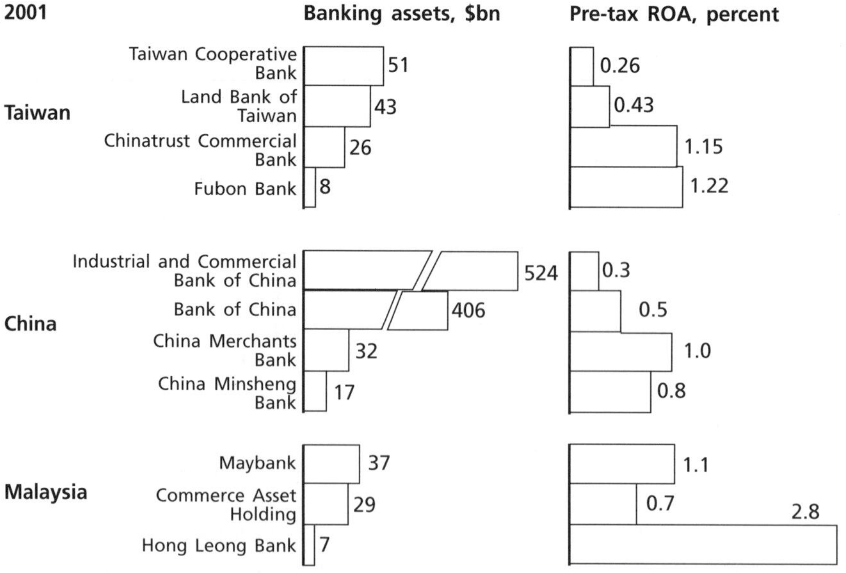

Source: Bankscope; annual reports

The issue of course is that any economic benefit to be derived from consolidation could be wiped out by bad debts in an acquisition target's portfolio. Take the example of Taiwan, where several large poorly performing banks compete with smaller, more nimble competitors. Global benchmarks indicate that a merger between domestic players would have an average synergy potential of 15–35 percent of the target's net present value. These would come mainly from consolidation of branch networks, headquarters savings, and IT consolidation, particularly in retail banking. These synergies could be entirely displaced by loan losses from NPLs, which in Taiwan's large State-owned banks are estimated at over 15 percent of total loans. Under such circumstances, the only possible trigger for consolidation would be for the State to guarantee potential buyers' portfolio losses as the Korean government has done.

Problems of valuation and due diligence: The warning "buyer beware" applies as much to Asian banking M&A as anywhere else. Typically, the purchasing bank keenly eyes its target's portfolio of retail customers with ambitious plans to generate revenue synergies by cross-selling its products to them. More often than not, most deposits turn out to be badly priced, loss-making corporate accounts. Once pricing is adjusted to market levels, these deposits quickly disappear, dashing any cross-selling hopes.

M&A in Asian banking requires more careful due diligence than in the United States or Europe. Paradoxically, it is less likely to happen. The less transparent operating environment in the region means that in some cases a due diligence review is the first time the target bank conducts a comprehensive, independent evaluation of its problematic exposure. Further complicating the process is the culture of secrecy in which many Asian banks operate to protect client interests.

If creating revenue synergies is the aim of an acquisition, then each source of potential upside must be tested. So besides looking at asset quality, risk management, NPLs, and the cost base, a buyer must screen the target's customer roster. There are two areas to examine: the quality of the customers and the sales capability in either party to identify and cross-sell; and the reliability and richness of the available customer information and how easy it is to access. Often, if a bank meets one set of criteria, it falls short on the other. In many cases, external market research and careful due diligence are required to obtain an accurate valuation.

When valuing revenue synergies, buyers must also take into account customer attrition, estimate the uptake of new products, and assign appropriate risk discounts to future revenue streams. Cost synergies on the other hand are more within the purchaser's control, and could therefore be calculated with more certainty and "paid for" through acquisition premiums. As in all markets, of course, deal fever and ego drive up acquisition prices.

Still, the average premium paid for domestic bank acquisitions in Asia between 2000 and 2002 was 26 percent, compared to 31 percent in the United States. This may be attributed in part to lower confidence in the due diligence process in Asia.

Difficulties in capturing synergies: "Firing people is so un-Asian; we can't assume redundancies," an Asian bank CEO recently declared in the midst of a meeting to value an acquisition target. He had his reputation to consider. "I'm unlikely to go down in history as the guy who created the most value even if that's exactly what I do. But with those numbers, I will certainly go down in history as the guy who fired the most people."

In Asia, cost-saving synergies are hard to generate. Though legal barriers to laying off staff are limited or inexpensive to overcome, the social contact in many societies is tough to break and few managers move from one company to another. Korea is the one Asian market where management has been able to cut jobs systematically. But this was done only after bitter confrontation with labor unions. After holding hostage the then president of Kookmin Bank, Kim Sang-hoon, in his office for 36 hours in December 2000, unionists forced the postponement of merger talks between Kookmin and Housing & Commercial Bank. The two banks eventually restarted negotiations and concluded an agreement.

Some institutions have had to rule out redundancies to close deals. In Taiwan, Cathay Financial Holding Company promised no layoffs for two years and offered generous severance packages for long-serving employees when it took over United World Chinese Commercial Bank in 2002. Such an undertaking could easily wipe out synergy value. No other buyer in Taiwan has made as deep a commitment.

Fortunately for banks in Asia, cost-saving synergies actually matter less in the region than in mature markets. In many cases they are not the most valuable driver of domestic mergers. High growth in emerging economies often makes boosting revenue more important than reducing costs. In any case, Asian banks have lower operating costs than their American and European counterparts. The average bank cost-to-income ratio in Asia is around 46 percent compared to over 70 percent in Europe (see Exhibit 13.5).

Though the income component of the cost-to-income ratio primarily drives this phenomenon due to higher margins, it nevertheless stresses the relative importance of revenue-enhancing synergies. These arise from re-pricing portfolios to the better benchmarks of the two merging parties, improving combined cost of funding if one of the players enjoys such an advantage, and the cross-selling of products from one institution to the other's customers. A typical Asian deal may have as much as 70 percent of its estimated potential synergy on the revenue side (see Exhibit 13.6). But bear in mind that real bank integration never takes place without ruffling some

Exhibit 13.5 Cost to income ratios* of Asian banks vs. US and European banks

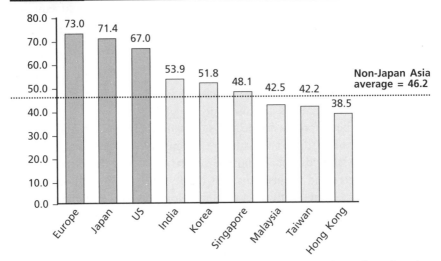

* Weighted average of top 10 banks in all markets except Malaysia (top 5) and Singapore (top 3)
Source: Bankscope; annual reports

Exhibit 13.6 Sources of synergy in domestic consolidation

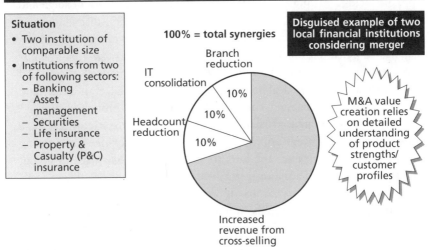

Source: McKinsey project experience

feathers. Just the perception that one side or the other has been slighted or disadvantaged is enough to scupper a deal.

These considerable hurdles stand in the way of the full-scale domestic consolidation that economic logic and regulatory momentum would dictate.

Not only do these obstacles make deals difficult to cut, but more importantly they also make it difficult for transactions that do go through to create value for both parties. The trouble and risks involved, as well as the reluctance of certain owners to sell, are reflected in the huge gaps between asking price and offer price that usually emerge. This is all part of Asian M&A, exacerbated by lurking bad debts, vendors in denial, and uncertainty about the real value of a merger. Since the financial crisis in 1997, some agreements have been concluded, based on contingent pricing formulas. However, in many instances, price differentials are too wide to resolve.

There have been too few models of successful domestic consolidation in Asia to clear the path for a wider reshaping of the regional banking landscape. This should perhaps not be surprising. Given the difficulties of executing mergers and acquisitions that create value, the logical option for many banks may in fact be to resist consolidation pressures and maintain the status quo.

<hr>

Let's get together: Key factors for a successful merger

Skittish sellers, bad debts, and a complex competitive landscape make most domestic banking M&A negotiations in Asia rather messy. Typical pitfalls include casting the net too wide during the discussion stage and the tendency – somewhat related – to confuse general discussion and institutional goodwill with a sound business case. In transactions, losing sight of the deal rationale and compromising elements essential to value creation are the key risks. Winners are those who systematically screen and prioritize targets, solve deal breakers early, and, above all, craft a clear and compelling business case at the very start and follow through with it.

Screening and prioritization: Winning in domestic M&A is a combination of strategy and opportunity. Setting priorities and revising them when necessary are the keys to success. Most Asian banks accept that consolidation is a major factor in their market, but few have a well-defined strategy for what to do or how to react. Given that the consolidation process unfolds over several years, banks must review its options regularly – at least twice a year, for serious players. An understanding of how the landscape is shifting will help determine tactics and the appropriate approach to acquisition targets.

Making the business case: A good business case explains the market context for bringing two institutions together, clearly articulates a vision for the new entity, estimates the value creation potential, and spells out transaction issues and principles. Some banks engage in too many fruitless discussions, wasting time. What is needed is a disciplined, structured approach.

Upholding deal rationale and avoiding deal fever: The key to moving from discussion to transaction is to maintain the integrity of the deal's rationale and to ensure that the essential levers for value creation are not inhibited by the merger structure. "Deal fever" is a well-known affliction. To clinch an agreement in the heat of the moment, buyers may agree to pay a premium not backed by an economic or strategic rationale.

Value-creation potential should not be sacrificed just to conclude an agreement. But the risk of this happening in Asia is high, given the importance of saving face in negotiations and the immaturity of the M&A markets. Typical compromises include delaying or restricting cost-reduction measures, maintaining sub-scale brands, agreeing not to close branches, or accepting a less-than-optimum post-merger management structure. The key is to distinguish between face-saving concessions made to manage perceptions and relationships, and those that actually destroy deal value.

CONSOLIDATION OUTLOOK

Still unresolved is the question of whether domestic consolidation will be good or bad – and how the process will pan out over the rest of this decade. Good consolidation yields stronger, more capable banks, while bad consolidation creates bigger institutions that perform poorly. A worthwhile merger should result in improved skills and capabilities; leaner cost structures; more solid capital bases; and better, more differentiated products. The signs of failure are: a fatter portfolio of bad loans and a bloated organization that is unable to compete. Bad consolidation only leads to more rigidity in the banking sector.

How likely is it that good consolidation will take place across Asia in the coming years? To answer this, it is useful to classify the region's 11 markets according to when and why consolidation will occur. CEOs of local banks would do well to understand the dynamics shaping their respective markets and be prepared to act.

Korea and Malaysia: Battle for market leadership

In these two markets, consolidation driven by heavy-handed government influence is likely to be succeeded by bank-led consolidation for commercial motives. The initial spate of consolidation pushed by regulators after the

1997 financial crisis dramatically redefined the structures of both markets. The number of commercial banks shrunk by more than 20. The combined market share of the top five players by banking assets increased from 45 percent to 65 percent in Korea, and from 36 percent to 54 percent in Malaysia.

Banks have begun to reap the benefits of scale, with the survivors jostling for market leadership. This is pushing others to consider participating in a second round of mergers to stay competitive. Consider the case of Korea, where the top five banks in 2001 had average ROEs of 15.3 percent, considerably higher than the rest of the field whose relative market power has weakened. In both these markets, a bank CEO should seek out the best partner from among the few remaining candidates.

Singapore, Taiwan, and Hong Kong: Struggle for survival

Medium-term survival is the key driver for consolidation in these product-saturated, over-banked markets. Singapore has been the leader in this group, largely to the credit of the government, which foresaw the need for bigger and stronger banks after the 1997 crisis. It is down to just three major players. Taiwan is beginning to get into the act, with a few mergers since 2001, though some 50 banks still serve the population of 22 million. Roughly half may disappear in the short to medium term. Hong Kong is likely to be the laggard, but the 30-plus banks there will inevitably come to the painful conclusion that not all can withstand the increasing competition.

Most banks in all these markets are sub-scale institutions. Prior to 1997, Hong Kong and Singapore banks thrived, thanks in part to clubby cartels that kept pricing attractive. But deregulation and liberalization have unleashed new competitive forces that have put pressure on small players. Taiwan and Hong Kong banks, in particular, are suffering, as their old manufacturing bases have been eroded by the migration of low-end industries and services to China. In both Hong Kong and Taiwan, consolidation is crucial if their leading banks are to be of sufficient scale to fund expansion into the mainland. Foreign banks will need to have at least $20 billion in assets to be allowed to enter the Chinese market in 2007.

India, Thailand, Indonesia, and the Philippines: In need of reform

These markets are extremely fragmented, crowded, and long due for consolidation. In each, between 60 percent and 90 percent of players have asset market shares of less than 5 percent, or assets under $5 billion. True shareholder accountability that might trigger mergers is lacking. In addition, astronomical levels of NPLs at many banks have been an obstacle.

India is slightly ahead of the others. When the central bank introduced financial reforms in the early 1990s, nine new private-sector banks were launched between 1992 and 1998. The era of consolidation was heralded when one of these new players, HDFC Bank, acquired Times Bank in 2000. The next year, ICICI Bank bought the Bank of Madura. Financial reforms are expected to play out over the rest of the decade. Consolidation is set to continue as competitors fight for survival in a liberalizing market.

The other three markets will lag. Except for a few isolated changes since 1997, market structures have remained largely the same. In the years leading up to 2010, local banks are unlikely to move without the government applying pressure through stricter capital adequacy requirements or more foreign competition. While the rationale for consolidation is obvious, the timing of it is not.

China and Japan: Break up the giants

China and Japan are a paradox. Mega-banks are so inefficient that, to improve their performance, they should be broken up into smaller, more profit-minded and transparent entities. Still, there are more than 100 city commercial banks in China and more than 120 regional banks in Japan that are small, with assets below $5 billion each. These players are likely to merge among themselves or be swallowed up by mid-sized players. But in both markets, this consolidation is not likely to happen soon due to the lack of external pressure and banks' preference for the status quo. Indeed, Japan has gone the opposite direction in recent years: The bloated monoliths have become even bigger.

Mizuho Bank, the largest bank in Asia in 2003, is an excellent case of what may be called a "merger by stapler." Enormous economic pressure for banking sector reform led to the coming together of Dai-Ichi Kangyo Bank, Fuji Bank, and the Industrial Bank of Japan to create Mizuho. However, little effort was made to integrate the management of the three banks. The original institutions maintained their separate identities and allegiances among staff. Where integration was implemented, it failed spectacularly. On the day the new merged bank was launched, the ATMs did not work.

Regional trends: Holding companies and limited consolidation among local leaders

While consolidation will be driven mainly by local market circumstances, there are two trends that cut across the region. The first is the formation of multi-business holding companies. In many economies, banks are allowed to put banking, insurance, asset management, and securities operations under one tent. Banks seeking to generate more customer business by offering a broader array of products are pushing this horizontal consolidation, which is the primary driver of bank-related M&A in Taiwan.

The second regional trend is the consolidation among local leaders wanting to build sufficient scale to fund growth abroad. This may occur without prompting broader consolidation. There are signs that banks in several markets from India to Taiwan may be considering such moves.

TURNING THE TABLES

Consolidation is often assumed to involve the takeover of a small bank by a big one. Developments in Asia suggest that the reverse could also be true, particularly if the smaller player has the aspirations and skills to act.

Korea's experience shows that sub-scale competitors can gain the initiative and turn the tables on larger rivals. Hana Bank's story is a remarkable example. In 1998, Hana was the tenth largest in the country with about 4 percent of total banking assets. It had a respected brand and a good reputation as a retail player with a strong base of affluent customers. Boram Bank was just one position behind Hana, with a 3 percent share of total assets. The merger of the two banks was one of the first in the market, requiring arduous negotiations involving several rounds of talks with trade unions. It produced the seventh-largest Korean bank under the Hana name. One year later, Germany's Allianz Group took an 11.8 percent strategic stake in the new entity. When Seoulbank went for sale in 2002, Hana was no. 5 in the market and the only domestic bank approved by the Korean government into the final round of bidding, having demonstrated its merger skills and established itself as a credible consolidator. It won, combining with Seoulbank to create the third-largest player in the market.

Taiwan provides another interesting case study. In the early 1990s, 17 new banks emerged to put up stiff competition for the legacy institutions. The new banks were much smaller but more professionally managed, with better quality products, and more robust credit processes. By unleashing the new attackers, the government put pressure on the poor-performing banks to accept consolidation. The new institutions have begun to buy the older state-owned ones. The acquisition in 2002 of TaipeiBank, no. 10 in the market, by the financial holding company of Fubon Bank, no. 20, was the first deal of this kind.

The above examples suggest a potential course for mid-sized banks pondering how to survive in a consolidating market. To pull off a good merger requires an understanding of the dynamics at play, the determination to lead the consolidation process, and the discipline not to overpay.

❋ ❋ ❋

The fundamental factors motivating banks to seek to build scale and the pressure from regulators will continue to drive domestic consolidation. Almost every bank and banker in Asia will be affected. Many may even experience two or more mergers or acquisitions over the coming decade. The hurdles peculiar to Asia – unwilling sellers, inadequate due diligence, and difficulties in generating synergies – will make the process slow and spasmodic, but the overall direction is clear. Many banks may see consolidation as an opportunity to hide from the tough restructuring and reforms. But the winners will welcome it and regard M&A as a way to ensure success.

14

Cross-Border M&A: Buyer Beware

When DBS Bank acquired Dao Heng Bank of Hong Kong in June 2001, Philippe Paillart hailed the purchase. "Dao Heng and DBS together effectively create the first Asian regional bank, one with a strong presence in the two key Asian banking centers," the Singapore bank's then CEO told reporters. "The combination will bring good things to all customers. We will combine knowledge, know-how and technology, and continue to have a firm focus on serving banking customers locally and across borders."

Who would have doubted the reasons for Paillart's exuberance? After all, DBS already had subsidiaries in the Philippines, Indonesia, and Thailand, while Dao Heng was one of Hong Kong's leading family-owned banks. "We have very similar visions and goals," asserted Randolph Sullivan, Dao Heng's CEO, at the same press conference. "We will move quickly to realize maximum benefits." Such optimism of course is to be expected after a deal is sealed and the champagne starts to flow once the long, hard negotiations are over. And over time, DBS may well reap the strategic benefits of this acquisition. But whenever a major cross-border merger or acquisition is concluded in Asia, the same questions always keep coming up: Are such cross-border merger and acquisition (M&A) deals inevitable in the region's financial sector? Do they benefit shareholders? Are they a real strategic imperative, or simply another alternative tool for inorganic growth?

These are issues being hotly debated in the executive suites and boardrooms of financial institutions across the globe. While Asian M&A is a potentially important accelerator in the development of overall strategic growth, these banking cross-border deals will be a viable strategic option for a few players under very select commercial circumstances. Standard Chartered Bank, for example, successfully transformed its market position in the rapidly growing Indian market by buying ANZ out of its longstanding ANZ Grindlays franchise. While many players will consider a cross-border M&A deal in the coming decade, most banks will not have an appropriate strategic rationale, nor will they be equipped to execute it well. Those tempted to try should be wary lest they be seduced into making what could be a costly mistake.

Consider the following factors. First, capturing value from cross-border transactions remains difficult. Typical acquisition premiums of about 20–30 percent are rarely justified by the value created.[1] While cross-border synergies are difficult to calculate, analysts estimate that they typically are no higher than around 10 percent and are driven primarily by management skill transfer, rather than direct and immediate bottom-line impact from cost savings.[2] This is quite different from domestic bank consolidation where cost-reduction synergies in infrastructure and head count can often justify the premiums paid. Second, the debate as to whether cross-border banking M&A in and of itself can create value is still raging. Given the diverse set of banking markets in Asia, cross-border deals are much more complex than domestic ones and less likely to succeed. The Asian context adds a third layer of difficulty, given family ownership constraints, regulatory hurdles, and inherent value perception gaps on top of typical cross-cultural issues such as language barriers. Consequently, while cross-border transactions have fundamentally redefined market structure and competitive positioning in other industries such as the automotive sector, this has not yet happened in Asian banking.

Still, provided the acquirer has a compelling strategic rationale, carefully identifies appropriate targets where it can truly add distinctive value, and pays heed to Asia-specific deal-structuring considerations, this buyer may indeed have the wherewithal to execute value-creating, cross-border deals. We believe, however, that cross-border M&A will remain a tool for only a few and is not a strategic imperative for most.

---

1 Based on McKinsey analysis of 2002 takeover premiums: 31 percent of target's market capitalization on average in the United States and 22 percent in Europe.
2 Analyst estimates reported in *The Banker* (June 2002) and *The Wall Street Journal* (December 2002).

Cross-border M&A may be justified for:

- *Global foreign banks* entering a large, attractive, and deregulated market (typically one in North Asia) where skills can be transferred to add substantial value to the target banks;
- *Leading local financial institutions* facing saturated domestic markets that are expanding into markets with a natural geographic affinity – Singapore banks entering into Malaysia, for example – or where there is inherent convergence and cultural affinity such as Hong Kong, Taiwan and mainland China, whose economies are becoming increasingly integrated;
- *International mono-lines*, or single-product competitors such as in consumer finance players purchasing portfolios from which they can capture value by employing substantial expertise and skills, and leveraging centralized IT networks and processing centers;
- *Private equity players* who can buy into distressed assets "cheaply" as nations, governments, and banks in Asia continue to restructure.

To support these postulations, we will look first to cross-border transactions in the past and what trends they indicate for the future. We then assess why and where cross-border banking M&A may be able to create value within the Asian context. Finally, we evaluate the evolution of cross-border M&A in European banking and the Asian insurance sector to cull lessons for banks in Asia. We define cross-border M&A transactions as *strategic* acquisitions of either influential minority or majority equity stakes in Asian financial institutions by either strategic or financial investors from another country.

FIVE TRENDS IN ASIAN BANKING M&A

Prior to the 1997 Asian financial crisis, cross-border acquisitions in the region were rare for various reasons, including regulatory constraints, tightly held family ownership structures, and significant market uncertainty regarding the inherent value of underlying assets. The economic turmoil and persistent banking sector problems in Asia have created momentum for selected players seeking to create value by taking cross-border stakes in domestic financial institutions. Despite this, cross-border transactions continue to represent a small portion of total overall Asian M&A activity (see Exhibit 14.1) in volume and amount. Moreover, a large number of transactions have involved relatively small stakes with undisclosed values, falling outside our definition of a strategic acquisition.

Cross-border transactions to date can be classified according to a number of core themes or trends. They have been geographically concentrated in

Exhibit 14.1 Increased financial sector M&A activity in Asia since 1997

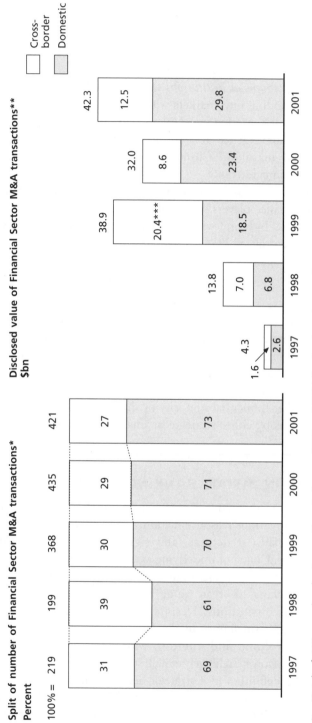

Split of number of Financial Sector M&A transactions*
Percent

Disclosed value of Financial Sector M&A transactions**
$bn

Cross-border

Domestic

*   Total of 497 cross-border transactions between 1997 and 2001 in the 11 Asian markets covered in this book
** Total disclosed value does not account for transactions where deal value is not announced
*** Includes Japan Leasing–GE Capital deal, valued at $7 billion

Source: Bankscope; central banks; McKinsey analysis

North Asia, marked by a few large landmark transactions, characterized by the emergence of strategic "options-seeking" players, involved in the sale of distressed assets, or have involved the market entry of mono-line players.

Let us consider each of these five trends.

Geographic concentration in North Asia: Japan has historically accounted for 36 percent of the total disclosed value of cross-border M&A activity in Asia (see Exhibit 14.2). As the world's second-largest market, Japan has been an investor priority. The "Big Bang" financial sector reform launched in late 1996 included the full liberalization of foreign exchange transactions. This led to a plethora of cross-border alliances and acquisitions as the prospect of cut-throat competition led Japanese players to look to foreign partners for the expertise they lacked.

There has been a noticeable lack of any significant cross-border activity in the Southeast Asian markets. This is not surprising as most are still recovering from the 1997 crisis and continue to be over-populated with financial institutions. Even today, the Malaysian market has 10 local banks, while Thailand has 13. There are 45 domestic banks in the Philippines, 33 of which have an asset market share of less than 1 percent. In Indonesia, 130 out of the 148 local banks each have less than 1 percent of total banking assets. Clearly, these markets are still in need of domestic consolidation.

Meanwhile, in China, investors and financial institutions have been clambering to establish a presence. This emerging giant, with the potential to be the next economic superpower, is likely to overtake Japan as the key market for cross-border M&A in the coming decade. Nevertheless, cross-border M&A activity in Korea and Japan, especially with respect to distressed assets, is unlikely to diminish as the restructuring of the financial sector in both economies will continue for the foreseeable future.

Few large landmark transactions: Although few in number, cross-border transactions tend to make headlines for their significant dollar value and their ground-breaking strategic intent. DBS Bank's acquisition of Dao Heng in 2001 for over $5 billion had been the biggest cross-border bank acquisition in Asia outside Japan up to that time. GE Capital's purchase of Japan Leasing in 1999 attracted attention both for the $7 billion price paid and the ill-fated condition of the seller, Long-Term Credit Bank of Japan. While both these transactions grabbed significant analyst, investor, and media attention, whether they created real value remains an open question. There will surely be more such high-priced deals over the coming decade.

Emergence of strategic "option-seeking" players: Recently, strategic players have made acquisitions to gain a foothold in new markets. In Taiwan, Citigroup purchased a minority stake in five of Fubon Group's product lines to solidify its domestic position and use it as a launching pad for further regional growth. In India, Standard Chartered Bank acquired Grindlays Bank

Exhibit 14.2 Financial sector cross-border M&A concentrated in North Asia

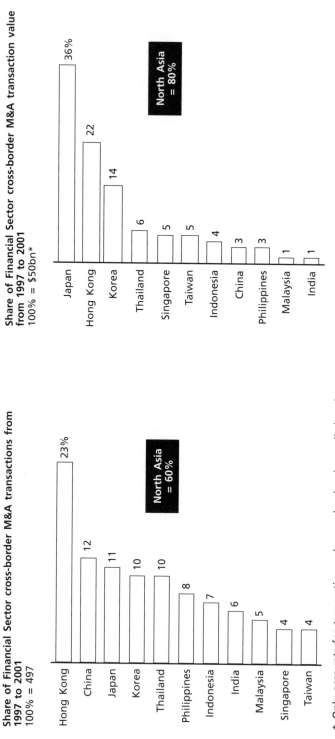

Share of Financial Sector cross-border M&A transactions from 1997 to 2001
100% = 497

Hong Kong 23%
China 12
Japan 11
Korea 10
Thailand 10
Philippines 8
Indonesia 7
India 6
Malaysia 5
Singapore 4
Taiwan 4

North Asia = 60%

Share of Financial Sector cross-border M&A transaction value from 1997 to 2001
100% = $50bn*

Japan 36%
Hong Kong 22
Korea 14
Thailand 6
Singapore 5
Taiwan 5
Indonesia 4
China 3
Philippines 3
Malaysia 1
India 1

North Asia = 80%

* Only accounts for transactions where value has been disclosed

Source: Thomson Financial Securities Data Company (SDC); *M&A Asia*; McKinsey analysis

from ANZ for $1.34 billion, or 2.3 times book value, to establish its foothold in the attractive affluent consumer segment. Standard Chartered Bank also tried unsuccessfully to buy two banks in Indonesia – Bank Bali in 1999 and Bank Central Asia (BCA) in 2002.

In China, where foreign ownership limits are more stringent, minority stakes in local banks offer strategic players considerable "option value" ahead of full deregulation. The International Finance Corporation (IFC), the private-sector investment financing arm of the World Bank Group, has taken minority stakes in the Bank of Shanghai, Nanjing City Commercial Bank, and Xian City Commercial Bank. In early 2002, HSBC also bought into Bank of Shanghai, paying $65 million for an 8 percent stake. The London-based global institution became the first foreign commercial bank to acquire an interest in a Chinese domestic bank. Citibank followed suit in early 2003, purchasing 5 percent of Shanghai Pudong Development Bank. Not willing to be left behind, Singaporean banks are also positioning themselves for when the mainland fully opens to foreign competition in 2007. In Dao Heng, for example, DBS now has a platform for capturing China capital flows.

Meanwhile, there have been several option-creating cross-border deals in Korea. In 1999, Internationale Nederlanden Groep, known as ING, bought 10 percent of Housing & Commercial Bank, or H&CB. The following year, Germany's Allianz formed a strategic alliance with Hana Bank, in which it took a 12.5 percent stake. In 2001, BNP Paribas of France bought a 4 percent share in Shinhan Financial Group, one of Korea's leading financial institutions. In each of these cases, the foreign player took a minority stake in the local bank to cement a relationship. But the real value creation is supposed to come from the formation of strategic joint ventures in businesses such as bancassurance or asset management, to which both partners would contribute their best skills and capabilities.

The use of minority stakes as a way to enter a market and create option value is likely to continue and could even increase. It allows investors to gain local knowledge and to position themselves for future expansion, while lowering upfront risk.

Sales of distressed assets: In markets such as Japan, Korea, and more recently, China, regulators have recognized the value of private equity investors and have begun to encourage these financiers to take over and recapitalize some of the more distressed banks. The primary motive has been to reduce the need for government-led bailouts and to stimulate the transfer of required skills to the local players, including the expansion of their product scope (see Exhibit 14.3).

Private equity activity has predominantly been in North Asia. Examples are numerous: Newbridge Capital's purchase of a controlling stake in Korea First Bank in 1999 after months of on-again-off-again negotiations;

Exhibit 14.3 Financial sector cross-border M&A by type

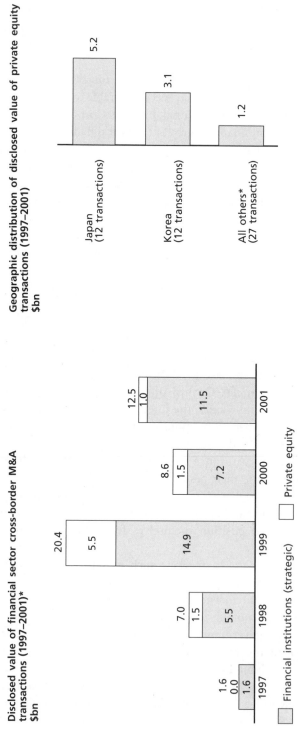

Disclosed value of financial sector cross-border M&A transactions (1997–2001)*
$bn

Geographic distribution of disclosed value of private equity transactions (1997–2001)
$bn

Japan
(12 transactions)   5.2

Korea
(12 transactions)   3.1

All others*
(27 transactions)   1.2

1997   1.6 / 0.0 / 1.6

1998   7.0 / 1.5 / 5.5

1999   20.4 / 5.5 / 14.9

2000   8.6 / 1.5 / 7.2

2001   12.5 / 1.0 / 11.5

Financial institutions (strategic)   Private equity

* India, China, Taiwan, Hong Kong, Singapore, Thailand, Indonesia, Philippines, Malaysia
Source: Thomson Financial Securities Data Company (SDC); *M&A Asia*; McKinsey analysis

Goldman Sachs' $500 million investment in a 17 percent share of Korea's Kookmin Bank in 1999; the leveraged buy-out also in 1999 of Long-Term Credit Bank of Japan by a consortium led by Ripplewood Holdings LLC; Cerberus Capital Management's acquisition of 5 percent of Nippon Credit Bank, now know as Aozora Bank, in 2000 and its subsequent investment to raise its stake to about 60 percent; the Carlyle Group's acquisition of 41 percent in KorAm Bank in 2000; and Lone Star Funds' acquisition in 2001 of Tokyo Sowa Bank, now Tokyo Star Bank.

Private equity investors have found it much more difficult to enter some of the other Asian markets. This may be explained by their smaller size and reduced attractiveness; greater uncertainty about the quality of assets; and governments that have been less welcoming of foreign non-strategic investors, preferring instead to focus on domestic consolidation. Still, Indonesia's recapitalized BCA attracted significant private equity interest when the government put its 51 percent stake up for sale in early 2002. A number of consortiums of strategic and financial investors combined to bid for what was arguably Indonesia's banking crown jewel. BCA ultimately fell into the hands of US financial investor Farallon Capital for $531 million.

Mono-line players building Asian business slivers: While private equity investors have participated in many high-profile, high-value transactions in Asia, strategic mono-line players have been the major buyers in the region. Their total dollar investment and participation in an increasing number of transactions are a sign of their long-term commitment to build pan-Asian franchises. This select group of strategic players has focused its efforts on particular product lines, rather than full-scale mergers, as a way to gain scale and leverage its core skills. GE Capital's acquisitions of consumer finance companies – including United Merchants Finance in Hong Kong, SRF Finance in India, Sindo Finance in Korea, and both Koei Credit and Lake Co. in Japan – well illustrate this wave of activity. Standard Chartered Bank purchased Chase Manhattan Bank's credit card operations in Hong Kong for a total of $1.3 billion, or 4.5 times net asset value, to solidify its position in unsecured lending in a market that in the past offered attractive margins. But the recent rise in personal bankruptcies in Hong Kong has hampered performance.

Historical themes will typify future Asian cross-border M&A activity. The nature and type of activity discussed above will persist. Driven by the emergence of China, cross-border M&A activity will be focused in North Asia. In Korea and Japan, the continued restructuring of the financial sector will be the catalyst. Despite the lack of activity to date, more transactions in other Asian markets can be expected over the long term as a result of market saturation post-domestic consolidation, and further liberalization. The most significant participants in Asian cross-border activity to date – the strategic investors especially the mono-line franchises – will continue to dominate M&A in Asia. Yet even as existing foreign players strengthen their positions, new entrants such as BNP Paribas, Fortis, Capital One, and MBNA could seek to establish a presence, especially in some of the larger, more lucrative markets where margins remain more attractive than back in their home markets.

While the themes we have outlined above are likely to play on, we maintain that only select categories of players should even consider cross-border M&A as a strategic tool. More importantly, only a handful of deals will make strategic sense and thus lead to value creation.

THE STRATEGIC RATIONALE IS PARAMOUNT

An acquirer must set out a convincing strategic rationale for conducting a cross-border transaction. A McKinsey study of about 360 domestic and cross-border M&A deals in the United States and Europe in the late 1990s that were larger than $500 million indicated that, on average, only half succeeded. The measure of success was whether returns were greater than expected (vis-à-vis relevant indices). The study also found that acquirers achieved success not because of convenient P/E ratios, relative size formulas, innovative deal structures, accounting gimmicks, or market dominance. They succeeded when there were fundamental value-creation opportunities that could be expediently realized between the buyer's and the target's businesses. In other words, the keys were a compelling strategic rationale and rapid integration.

Acquirers must remember that Asian market conditions add a degree of complexity. Typically, in healthy markets, corporate control is regularly bought and sold as shareholders apply pressure on management teams to deliver competitive returns. In general, this is not the case in Asia. In addition, takeover moves that may be perceived as hostile are virtually impossible to launch, given the regulatory barriers. Finally, family owners are often unwilling to sell, with value perception gaps and family wealth transfer remaining significant obstacles.

But sound strategic rationales for cross-border M&A transactions do exist. These include:

- *Exploiting attractive economics of Asian markets*: Margins prevalent in Asian markets are far superior to those in more developed markets. For example, average credit card margins in Hong Kong and Singapore are between 1,000–1,300 basis points versus 600 basis points in Europe and as low as 300 basis points in the United States. Similarly, mutual fund fees are typically 300–400 basis points higher in most Asian markets than in the United States and Europe.

- *Creating growth options*: After the 1997 financial crisis, there has been significant government- or market-led domestic consolidation (a 50 percent reduction in the number of banks in Malaysia; a 36 percent reduction in Indonesia; a 33 percent reduction in Thailand). The saturation point is even more marked for the Singapore market, where three large local institutions and a series of world-class foreign players are targeting the same set of attractive customers in an environment with increasing margin pressure. Players in such markets must create new avenues to growth.
- *Diversifying risks*: Geographic expansion could allow banks to diversify risk. A McKinsey study of European banks suggests a potential 30–40 percent reduction in credit risk as a result of reduction of exposure to single counter parties, to individual geographic areas, and to individual industries. This diversification of credit risk is a significant opportunity that shareholders might find difficult to exploit within a single market.
- *Increasing market clout*: Being able to offer the value proposition of a stronger, regional institution, potentially achieved through mergers and acquisitions will be essential to attract, develop and retain top talent, and win the battle for institutional investor flows.
- *Exploiting economies of scale:* Cross-border acquisitions could create opportunities for the centralization of processing and back-office operations, achieving economies of scale, and lower and more competitive cost positions compared to other home-market competitors.
- *Preempting competitors*: Since the number of potential attractive targets is in some cases very limited, every transaction reduces the number of possible partners. In China, for example, only a handful of non–state-owned banks have tolerable NPL levels.
- *Leveraging skills to a new geographic market*: Financial institutions that have built skills and expertise in particular products such as bancassurance, asset management, private banking, and consumer finance have the opportunity to leverage these skills and transfer them to customers in new markets. A clear skill advantage is likely to be the most critical element for cross-border acquirers to recapture the value of their up-front acquisition premiums.

Technically speaking, the reasons for cross-border transactions make sense. But we believe they make sense only for four categories of players: global foreign banks entering large, attractive markets where skills can be transferred to add substantial value to the target banks; leading domestic financial institutions or Asian regional winners facing saturated domestic markets expanding into markets with a natural geographic and cultural affinity; mono-line players purchasing portfolios where they can employ substantial focused expertise and skills to add value; and private equity players purchasing "cheaply" into distressed assets as economic restructuring in Asia continues.

Global strategic players and regional powerhouses are poised

For strategic investors, Asia remains a very attractive market for its sheer size, but more importantly for its significant growth potential. Moreover, as discussed earlier, margins obtainable in Asia far exceed those of many developed markets.

Natural acquirers will be global and regional powerhouses already with a market presence that derive a substantial portion of their profits from Asia. In 2001, Standard Chartered Bank generated 91 percent of its profits from Asia, compared to 47 percent for HSBC, and 21 percent for Citibank. These institutions will thus continue to be dominant forces in future cross-border M&A transactions, leveraging their superior skills, experience, and presence in Asia as they move to solidify their positions through selective acquisitions in untapped markets.

For example, HSBC has yet to establish a significant foothold in Korea and Japan. This could perhaps be achieved through a purchase of distressed assets in these markets. Standard Chartered Bank, for its part, is likely to continue to search for targets in Southeast Asia following its two failed attempts to acquire banks in Indonesia.

The attractive margins in Asia will also attract other global players like BNP Paribas and ING to establish or strengthen their Asian presence. Already these newer entrants are combining strategic alliances with acquisitions for this purpose; for example, in Korea. Players such as global insurance giant AIG are also exploring opportunities to enter into the broader banking space in the region through product slivers, including bancassurance, unit trusts, and credit cards.

Domestic market leaders must earn the right to play in the region

Asian players must first earn the right to play. The Asian financial industry is still emerging from a period of financial crisis. Financial indicators – NPLs, capital adequacy ratios, and ROEs – have yet to return to healthy levels in many Asian markets. While domestic consolidation has occurred, many of these emerging larger banks remain relatively weak. In addition, with changing customer preferences, the entry of foreign players, and the emergence of technology, most Asian banks are badly equipped to face this changing and increasingly liberalized landscape.

Therefore, despite tempting reasons to embark on a cross-border M&A program, incumbent domestic banks with regional aspirations will first have to earn the right to play in cross-border M&A. Over the rest of this decade, only a handful will. To do so, they must have achieved a leading position in the domestic market measured by assets and market capitalization; developed inherently superior and exportable skills ranging from proprietary credit scoring to customer relationship management (CRM); and attained significant market reputation to attract talent and capital flows. Only once a local incumbent has fulfilled these requirements will it be in a good position to participate in the pan-regional expansion game. Such a bank will have developed a true skill-based advantage that it can bring to new markets to create additional value. Very few of the top players in each Asian market meet these criteria today (see Exhibit 14.4). This is measured by total market capitalization – the necessary acquisition currency – and market share of domestic assets, a secured leadership position at home, to afford international expansion.

Among the banks that appear in Exhibit 14.4, Korea's Kookmin Bank seems to have managed to narrow the gap with respect to scale, scope, and skills, and appears poised for regional expansion. The development of exportable skills will be the key to unlocking value in any potential future cross-border transactions for such players.

A second potential candidate, DBS Bank, the largest bank in Southeast Asia with over $80 billion in assets, has already embarked upon a regional expansion plan that employs cross-border M&A as a tool. DBS has acquired controlling stakes in Thailand's Thai Danu, Hong Kong's Kwong On Bank, and a 21 percent stake in Bank of Philippine Islands controlled by the Zobel family of Ayala Corp. With the acquisition of Dao Heng, DBS ranked as one the top five banks in Hong Kong by assets. Despite the Singapore bank's aggressive cross-border M&A activity, it is clear that it has not yet reaped the full benefits of its strategy. But if the synergies do materialise, and DBS develops the capabilities to strengthen the franchise of its acquisitions, then it would have built a powerful platform for future expansion and acquisitions, and benefited from having been a "first mover" in regional M&A.

Where might cross-border M&A make sense for Asian banks in the years ahead? We see three areas but are not excluding other possibilities as long as a clear strategic rationale exists:

Banks in saturated domestic markets: For historical and cultural reasons, Singapore banks have a natural link with the Malaysian market. Therefore, with a saturated domestic market, an acquisition in Malaysia would be a natural next step, provided the 30 percent foreign ownership limit that

Exhibit 14.4 Domestic dominance could become "acquisition currency"

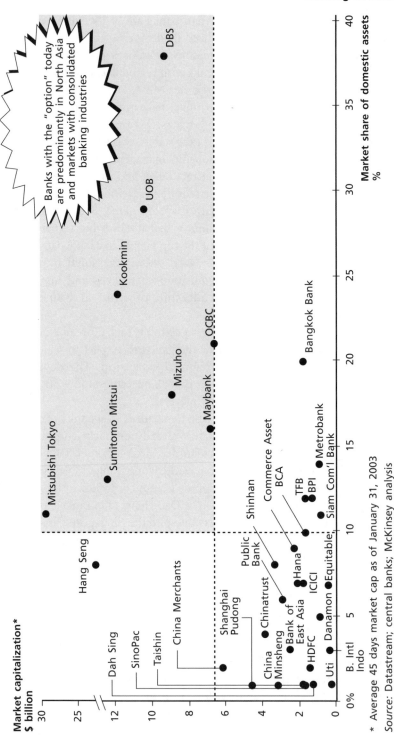

Banks with the "option" today are predominantly in North Asia and markets with consolidated banking industries

Market capitalization*
$ billion

Market share of domestic assets %

* Average 45 days market cap as of January 31, 2003
Source: Datastream; central banks; McKinsey analysis

existed as of early 2003 is relaxed. Malaysia would be especially compelling for OCBC or UOB, given that they already have full banking licenses, an extensive branch network, and a growing customer base across the causeway.

Similarly, Hang Seng Bank and the Bank of East Asia face a saturated Hong Kong market. For them, an acquisition of, or at least a minority stake in, a Chinese bank would be a natural maneuver with the increasingly porous border between Hong Kong and the mainland, and their cultural affinity. In addition, both these banks meet the $20 billion asset threshold required by Chinese regulators to enter the China market once it is fully opened to foreign competition in 2007.

Indian banks may also have the opportunity and aspirations to expand outside. Given their relative size in the Asian context, the most likely markets for expansion would be Southeast Asia. Indian banks that have learned how to effectively and efficiently serve the retail mass market may be able to export these skills to other developing economies. For example, in its capacity as a financial institution as well as an astute investor, ICICI could take a stake in a small bank in one of the Southeast Asian markets, after it consolidates its position in its home market.

Markets where there is inherent convergence: Hong Kong, Taiwan, and China are markets that are converging commercially, socially, and economically. Hong Kong and Taiwan banks have an advantage over other foreign strategic players, as they can leverage their insider knowledge, common Chinese business practices, and cultural affinity, to better position themselves in the eyes of regulators and potential targets, thus easing their entry into China. Taiwan financial institutions such as Chinatrust, Fubon, and Taishin, for example, could employ a "follow-the-client" strategy in China to begin with, providing seamless banking products and services to these customers who themselves expand to tap the local market in the mainland.

Asian mono-lines expanding across Asia: Japanese consumer finance companies that have mastered their business model and developed deep exportable skills would have the wherewithal to expand abroad through selected M&A deals. These players could focus on markets where lending margins will remain attractive for the foreseeable future and where market entry is not prohibited or limited. Likely targets include Hong Kong, Taiwan, and Korea.

International mono-lines make for formidable competition

International mono-lines will continue to be key drivers of cross-border M&A activity across Asia. Those already in the region will aim to strengthen their foothold and then perhaps expand to other Asian markets where their presence is minimal. Those seeking to take a first step in the region will focus on the more attractive, larger markets in North Asia and product lines or businesses where profit margins continue to be attractive such as unsecured lending, and where value-added exportable skills may be employed, such as credit scoring, risk management, and collections.

International mono-lines that already have strong Asian franchises, such as GE Capital, Cetelem, and Fortis, will continue engaging in cross-border M&A transactions much like the foreign powerhouses described above. These mono-lines will be able to derive value from such deals as their skills are truly exportable and far superior to those of most domestic incumbents.

Private equity investors can provide bridging and ensure skill upgrade

Private equity players will remain significant contributors to cross-border M&A activity. Distressed assets will always be attractive to these financial investors who are able to buy in relatively cheaply as economies, corporations, and banks in Asia continue to restructure.

While most financial investors actively work to create value for the target institution – Newbridge's bringing in new management to Korea First Bank, for example – many end up merely as a source of capital and thus act as bridge financing, or else, they seek to arbitrage assets that are currently undervalued by the market. In such a situation, they add little value in terms of management skills and sector experience. After a period of time, usually between three and five years, they seek to monetize their investment by selling to another financial institution, either local or foreign.

In Korea, the trend has been to sell back to surviving domestic institutions. As such, the financial investors that invested in distressed assets post-1997 will soon be looking to monetize their investments. In June 2002, Goldman Sachs reduced the 10 percent stake in Kookmin Bank that it acquired in 1999 (its original 17 percent share was diluted after Kookmin's merger with H&CB) to about 7 percent, netting a return of over 300 percent.

In most cases, governments that encouraged private equity players to enter their markets were seeking investors that could transfer management expertise, financial discipline, and sector knowledge to the respective financial institutions. Before these private equity investors would have been allowed to invest, they would have had to convince the relevant regulatory authorities of the value that they could contribute and transfer to these banks. This was one of the key deciding factors in the sale of BCA. Standard Chartered Bank submitted a business case to upgrade BCA's skills and capabilities, as did winning bidder Farallon Capital, which led a consortium that included Deutsche Bank.

Private equity players will expand their geographical focus and increase their participation in non-distressed situations where they can apply the local knowledge they have recently gained. These investors have yet to tap many Asian markets, including those where financial assets could benefit from the transfer of skills, knowledge, and talent by this class of investors. China seems to be on the radar screen for many such players. Its portfolios will eventually expand beyond North Asia to other liberalizing economies where governments are increasingly more welcoming, especially as the positive effect private equity investors have had in markets such as Korea is widely publicized.

LESSONS FROM ASIAN INSURANCE AND EUROPEAN BANKING

With Asia's liberalizing market environment, cross-border M&A banking activity will increase. As of early 2003, only two Asian markets – China, and Malaysia – restricted foreign players from acquiring majority control of local banks. To gauge how cross-border banking M&A may play out in Asia, we have looked at the Asian insurance industry, which has seen greater cross-border M&A activity, and at Europe, where cross-border M&A in banking started to take root in the 1990s with the arrival of the European Union.

Foreign insurers: "Plant and pounce" strategies

For foreign banks, the 1997 financial crisis and the subsequent lifting of restrictions on ownership in many economies presented new entry opportunities. For many overseas insurance companies in Asia, the crisis represented a chance to deepen already established positions. In fact, many foreign insurers pounced. A select group has successfully achieved leadership positions in Asian markets by either making acquisitions to enter markets or taking minority stakes on which a bigger presence was built through subsequent acquisitions (see Exhibit 14.5). Analyzing the approaches of foreign insurers to Asia provides insights into the likely evolution of cross-border M&A in banking.

In mature markets such as Japan, Korea, and Taiwan, where there are no ownership restrictions, foreign insurers have made large-scale acquisitions, rather than take small stakes in joint ventures or limited greenfield operations. The life insurance markets in these countries are mature and dominated by entrenched local players who command considerable market shares. Only through big, bold acquisitions have foreign insurers been able to instantly obtain the scale required to compete. For example, prior to its acquisition of Alica Life in 1987, AIG had no market presence in Korea.

Exhibit 14.5 A few select foreign insurers have achieved leadership positions in Asia via cross-border acquisitions

Foreign insurers	Years established in Asia	No. of markets with presence	Markets entered via M&A
AIG	In Shanghai since 1919	13 – Japan, Korea, Taiwan, China, Hong Kong, Vietnam, the Philippines, Thailand, Malaysia, India, Singapore, Indonesia, Sri Lanka	• Entered Korea via acquisition • Entered India via JV • Made subsequent acquisitions in Thailand, Indonesia, and Taiwan to strengthen positions
Prudential UK	In Singapore since 1931	12 – Japan, Korea, Taiwan, China, Hong Kong, Vietnam, the Philippines, Thailand, Malaysia, India, Singapore, Indonesia	• Entered Japan, Taiwan, Korea, and Indonesia via acquisitions • Entered Malaysia, India, China, and Thailand via JVs • Made subsequent acquisitions in Malaysia and the Philippines to strengthen positions
ING/Aetna	In Taiwan since 1988	10 – Japan, Taiwan, Korea, Hong Kong, Malaysia, China, India, Indonesia, Thailand, the Philippines	• Entered Malaysia, Taiwan, Hong Kong, and Indonesia via Aetna acquisition • Entered China, India, and Thailand via JVs
Allianz	In Thailand since 1992	9 – Japan, Korea, Hong Kong, the Philippines, China, Malaysia, Indonesia, Taiwan, Thailand	• Entered Taiwan, Korea, and Malaysia via acquisitions • Entered China, Japan, Thailand, the Philippines, and Indonesia via JVs • Made subsequent acquisitions in Thailand to strengthen positions
Manulife	In the Philippines since 1901	8 – Japan, China, Vietnam, Hong Kong, the Philippines, Taiwan, Singapore, Indonesia	• Entered Japan, Singapore, and Indonesia via JVs, and then subsequently increased JV stakes • Made subsequent acquisitions in Indonesia and Taiwan, and set up JV in China to strengthen positions
AXA	In Malaysia since 1975	8 – Japan, China, Hong Kong, the Philippines, Thailand, Malaysia, Singapore, Indonesia	• Entered Japan and Hong Kong via acquisitions • Entered Malaysia, China, Thailand, and Indonesia via JVs

Source: Press releases

Prudential plc made a similar splash when it acquired Young Poong Life in 2001, instantly propelling the UK insurance group into a top 10 position in the Korean market. Also that year, Prudential used the same strategy to enter the highly competitive Japan market, acquiring Orico Life. In Taiwan, Prudential bought Chinfon Life from the family-owned parent group that had come under severe financial pressure. In general, foreign insurers have leveraged a downturn in the mature local markets into an outright buying opportunity, a chance to pounce.

In the less mature Asian markets, foreign insurers have deployed a "plant-and-pounce" strategy. Here, the primary barrier to entry has traditionally been foreign ownership restrictions. A number of foreign players have effectively used small equity stakes in joint ventures (JVs) with established local players to overcome ownership barriers and rapidly climb the learning curve. Later, when the opportunity presents itself, the foreign partners have leveraged their initial "plant" to then "pounce" and secure market position.

This approach is perhaps best exemplified by Prudential, which took gradual steps to build a leading position in Malaysia. Prudential first launched a joint venture with insurer Berjaya in 1989. Over the next nine years, Prudential introduced new skills into the joint venture. This led to improved agent productivity and the market's most productive sales force. In addition, the venture launched new innovative offerings, including the first unit-linked products. Prudential transferred its effective customer segmentation skills to its partner. With its expertise, Prudential gradually assumed management control and by 1998 obtained majority ownership.

Similarly, AIG invested $1 million in Nan Shan Life, when Taiwan was still an emerging insurance market. In 1996, AIG increased its stake to 40 percent and finally to 94 percent two years later. Over this time, AIG established a network of 320 offices and 40,000 agents, and is now perceived as a local player. Interestingly, Prudential and AIG have both used somewhat similar strategies in Indonesia, making acquisitions to strengthen initial market footholds.

In markets such as Malaysia, only a few new insurance operating licenses are available. Elsewhere, for example Indonesia, resources such as trained agents are finite or scarce. In these places, entry via a joint venture or through the purchase of a minority stake makes sense. This would also be the best course when the foreign insurer either lacks local knowledge or has not identified an appropriate acquisition target. This creates considerable "option value" without having to make a large-scale bet on an uncertain future.

Successful foreign insurers have typically applied a systematic approach to entering Asian markets. Whether going for an outright pounce or a plant-and-pounce strategy, players from outside the region have aggressively built on their initial entry by bringing world-class skills to their partners.

Successful foreign competitors have demonstrated a clear strength in introducing innovative and customized products, improving distribution and marketing, and enhancing systems. AIG, for example, increased premiums in Japan by 15 percent in 1999 even as the market was shrinking. It managed this through extensive new product development, agency and sales force recruiting and training, and improving operating efficiency. After acquiring Chinfon in Taiwan, Prudential tripled the number of agents in the first 12 months and pioneered the launch of unit-linked products.

Banks considering cross-border M&A in Asia would be well served by adopting similar "plant-and-pounce" strategies. As non-performing loans (NPLs) continue to haunt banks in the region, outside banks may be better off by first developing an insider's view, initially through minority stakes. When a market downturn hits, they will then know whether it makes sense to pounce. There will be opportunities where an outright pounce makes sense, but players who take this more aggressive approach must be confident that they have sufficient resources to inject superior skills into their acquisition targets. The experience of cross-border M&A in European banking suggests that the ability to inject new skills and capture synergies will occur in markets that are close geographically and share a cultural affinity.

European cross-border M&A: "Second home markets"

Europe, like Asia, consists of countries that because of their geographic proximity can come together as a single economic bloc, though it is made up of countries with distinct identities, cultures, and languages. The integration of Europe has advanced significantly under the European Union, which, through policy and legislation, has quickened the pace of deregulation, introduced a single currency, and harmonized taxation and legal procedures, resulting in an environment where cross-border transactions can be conducted with greater ease. While Asia has no equivalent common market, some of the fundamental factors that have driven cross-border banking M&A in Europe are present in the region. One is domestic market saturation. The growth of financial institutions within each market is increasingly limited due to domestic consolidation. Another factor is increased cross-border trade, which requires banks to expand their operations to meet their customers' demands.

In Europe, these macroeconomic forces significantly increased the number of cross-border transactions between 1991 and 2001 – with the share split roughly doubling (see Exhibit 14.6).

On closer inspection, although cross-border activity rose dramatically, many transactions have been restricted to neighboring countries. "Real"

Exhibit 14.6 European banking mergers: 1991–2001

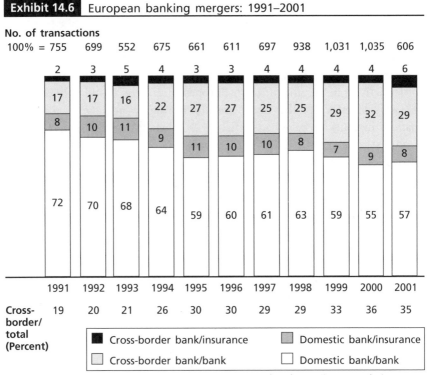

No. of transactions

100% =	755	699	552	675	661	611	697	938	1,031	1,035	606

	1991	1992	1993	1994	1995	1996	1997	1998	1999	2000	2001
Cross-border/total (Percent)	19	20	21	26	30	30	29	29	33	36	35

- ■ Cross-border bank/insurance
- ■ Domestic bank/insurance
- □ Cross-border bank/bank
- □ Domestic bank/bank

Source: Thomson Financial Securities Data Company (SDC); McKinsey analysis

intra-European deals have yet to materialize. An analysis of 61 major European banking deals from 1990 to 2001 indicates that 50 were domestic. Of the remainder, eight involved what may be called a second home market, or a market with similar economic characteristics and cultural identity – a Swedish bank acquiring a Norwegian one, for example. The balance were broader geographic cross-border transactions, say, a British buyer and a French target.

The propensity for cross-border transactions to be second-market deals has resulted in the forming of sub-regional banks, rather than truly pan-European players. An illustration of this is the formation of Nordea, the financial services group in the Nordic and Baltic region. Finland's Merita first merged with Sweden's Nordbanken in 1997. Two years later, MeritaNordbanken acquired Norway's Christiania Bank and then in 2000 merged with Denmark's Unidanmark to form Nordea.

HSBC has attempted to lay the foundations to become a truly pan-European player with its acquisition in 2000 of Crédit Commercial de France (CCF). Widely regarded as one of the best managed banks in France, CCF seemed to fit neatly into HSBC's strategy of building its presence in Europe in lucrative business areas such as private banking and asset management. HSBC's purchase in 1999 of Republic New York and Safra Republic Holdings was consistent with this approach.

Although the forces that drive cross-border activity, including a liberal fully deregulated market, have existed in Europe for a while, true cross-border activity in pursuit of a pan-European franchise is still very much in its early stages. Only the brave are attempting to achieve it. European financial institutions have had difficulty establishing and defining clear and strong strategic rationales for embarking on a cross-border M&A transaction, especially as such deals usually involve paying a significant premium. The "second home market" strategy is a safer bet and a reasonable first step for most aspirants in pursuit of cross-border opportunities in Asia.

A FEW GOOD PLAYERS

In Asia's liberalizing market environment, the need to meet growth expectations and the personal agendas of CEOs will drive an increase in Asian cross-border M&A. But true value creation will remain difficult and will be limited to a handful of players in a few markets.

The European experience suggests that it is uncertain whether a true pan-regional player can emerge through M&A. Perhaps the European trend of expanding to a second home market may be the best option for most Asian acquirers to grow cautiously. The insurance experience in Asia indicates that select players can use M&A to catapult themselves into leading positions in certain markets. But this approach has been limited to players such as AIG and Prudential plc, which have the inherent skills, financial expertise, and management bandwidth to take such bold moves. Research has shown that premiums offered on takeover bids remain significant – about 30 percent in the United States in 2002, and 20–40 percent in Europe between 1995 and 2001. Other studies have indicated that M&A deals, both domestic and cross-border, in the United States and Europe have about a 50 percent success rate. Analysts estimate that synergy value from cross-border deals is about 10 percent, making them difficult to justify on financial grounds alone.

While a compelling strategic rationale may exist, many would need to come together in concert to allow for real economic gains. There are four categories of players that will have the capability and the relevant strategic imperative to conduct pan-Asian plays over the next decade. As discussed above, these will be the global strategic players and select regional powerhouses such as Citibank, HSBC, and Standard Chartered Bank; international mono-lines including GE Capital, Cetelem, American Express, and MBNA; private equity players such as Newbridge Capital and Carlyle Group; and Asian incumbents aspiring to be regional winners.

For the Asian incumbents, cross-border M&A will be limited to players that have earned the right to play, by narrowing the scale, skill, and scope gap with the global big boys to emerge as local winners. They may be helped by domestic consolidation. Current frontrunners in this category include Kookmin Bank of Korea, the Singaporean banks, and market leaders in Hong Kong and Taiwan. This is not to say that others will not qualify. After all, Kookmin has emerged as a contender in just two years. What is important is for incumbents to carefully execute moves that build on their natural strengths, cultural affinity, or geographic proximity.

Cross-border M&A remains a hotly debated issue, one of the top five agenda items in board meetings and senior management conclaves around the world. Asian financial institutions must determine if cross-border M&A is a game they wish to play. Most that jump in are likely to fail. But those that take the plunge must ensure that they are equipped to face the many challenges required to be successful, and to derive the appropriate financial and strategic value. Our experience suggests that any participant looking to pursue cross-border M&A in Asia must undertake a very systematic and well-structured approach (see sidebar below). This special tool is not for everyone. Buyer beware!

Key factors for success in cross-border M&A in Asia

- *Identify a clear strategic rationale*: Avoid being seduced by "flag-planting" and proceed with extreme caution, leveraging developed skills that are truly exportable to other markets. Entry into new markets does not guarantee value creation in light of the acquisition premiums paid. Further, this strategic rationale must be executed in a systematic manner to avoid partner conflict, poor target selection, over-paying, and the mistiming of market entry.

- *Identify early and constantly monitor potential targets*: Acquisition targets should be carefully screened and limited to only those institutions that can truly benefit from the transfer of the buyer's superior skill set. Acquirers should constantly monitor the movements of potential targets so as to pounce when the opportunity arises. Watch out for family ownership changes, capital raising initiatives, and regulatory changes. In addition, buyers should leverage local experience and networks to gain intelligence and develop a robust value proposition to out-maneuver rivals competing for valuable targets.

- *Involve local regulators*: In most cases, a buyer can simplify and expedite the M&A process by making it clear to local regulators that the broader local banking sector would benefit from the acquirer's entry through the transfer of skills that would upgrade the banking game. This is especially true in markets such as China where cross-border M&A activity is an increasingly important regulatory issue.

- *Develop a clear business plan for the acquisition*: Prior to entering into actual negotiations, acquirers should develop a robust business case for the acquisition that clearly defines goals, required actions, timing, performance targets, and post-merger integration plans. In some Asian markets, such as Indonesia and Malaysia, the regulator may get involved in reviewing this business plan.

- *Partner with other investors to leverage expertise and spread the risk*: By working early on with a strategic investor, such as a private equity player that participated in the first wave of cross-border transactions, a new entrant could benefit from the veteran's experience. Moreover, such a partnership could help in managing total exposure and risk in the first stages of a cross-border investment.

- *Be discriminating in structuring an acquisition*: Given the inherent complexity of harnessing value out of deals in Asia, an acquirer should aim to structure acquisitions in such a way that it is able to assume a strategic stake through the single largest shareholding, management representation, or other means. Hence, the buyer would have control, or at least have the option to ramp up its investment to take a majority stake so long as certain milestones are met. In addition, creative earn-out structures, put and call options, and other instruments will help bridge the perceived valuation gaps and protect the acquirer's interests.

- *Ensure sufficient management bandwidth and resources*: An internal team dedicated to, and accountable for, the M&A transaction and with clear roles and responsibilities will ensure that issues do not fall through the cracks. This group should be in place from the due diligence stage to post-merger integration. Members would likely assume some of the management positions in the target bank. Having such a team in place could prevent disasters. For example, after a three-month due diligence period, Standard Chartered Bank's M&A team uncovered financial irregularities that led it to pull out of a bid for Indonesia's Bank Bali.

- *Apply a systematic approach*: Acquirers should formulate a road map for its cross-border M&A activity. This plan should cover the exact target geographies in order of priority; the types of potential acquisitions and likely candidates in each market; the mode of acquisition; and the relevant deal-breakers for each possible transaction. This will ensure that a deal will not be in conflict with existing or future partnerships, and that the acquirer will be able to move quickly should a target suddenly become available. Buyers that fail to set out a road map could engage in haphazard transactions, resulting in overpayment, the selection of partners that conflict with future targets, and the mistiming of entry into specific markets. A road map is particularly important in situations where an acquirer enters a new market with a minority stake, intending to build upon it later. A miscalculation in identifying the first target will not only ruin the chances of increasing the initial investment, but could also preclude the acquirer from forming partnerships with subsequent targets.

15

International Alliances: Not for the Faint-Hearted

"This joint venture is more than just about insurance. We believe it is a partnership that will enable us to become a complete and reliable financial planner for all our customers. I have no doubt that we will be able to chart new horizons."

Amirsham A. Aziz,
Managing Director of Maybank, at the signing ceremony for the Malaysian bank's bancassurance joint venture with Dutch–Belgian group Fortis,
8 February 2001

"Joint ventures are like an annuity for us. The partners are back every couple of years, asking us to help renegotiate or terminate the joint venture because of conflicts."

Senior partner at a leading international law firm

For the CEO of any bank in Asia, deciding whether to forge an international alliance can be a dilemma. The hope is that a foreign partner would provide the critical competitive edge the domestic bank needs to reshape its business mix and boost market position. While an alliance might help both sides address strategic challenges, structuring and negotiating a deal can be extremely difficult. The track record of partnerships is poor: The majority fail to deliver on the high expectations and are terminated only after the parties involved put in a lot of energy and time.

Is the upside worth the effort and compromise needed for an alliance to succeed? On first consideration, the answer would be yes. Forming an alliance – any tie-up ranging from a simple distribution agreement to an equity-based joint venture – should be a core element of the strategy of any domestic bank. But getting it right requires careful attention and highly skilful handling of every stage of the partnership, from design to execution.

After "fixing" high non-performing loan (NPL) ratios and strained balance sheets following the 1997–98 financial crisis, some domestic banks in Asia have shifted their focus to pursuing growth opportunities by attacking the most attractive customer segments with innovative offerings. Banks used to compete mainly on price, but the requirements for success have multiplied. Players must develop new skills, upgrade services, invest in technology, and broaden their scope to include complex products such as wealth management and personal loans. They need strategies to enable them to withstand increased competition from foreign banks and specialists. For these reasons, many Asian banks are forging alliances with foreign players. The thinking is that an alliance would provide the domestic partner with world-class skills and capital, while the overseas party would enter the market at a lower cost. Together, they could generate new businesses more quickly and build volume faster than if each were to work alone.

When properly designed and structured, a tie-up can have a significant upside. For example, the Nikko Securities–Citigroup alliance – Nikko Salomon Smith Barney – is the market leader in investment banking in Japan. The joint venture combines Nikko's customer access and Salomon's best practice products and links to international markets.

Yet few alliances meet the strategic objectives of both parties and become clear competitive successes. From past experience, we predict that most will fail to deliver. Japan's experience provides fertile ground from which to learn. The majority of cross-border alliances in banking, asset management, and securities that were launched between 1996 and 1999 neither created value nor had any material impact on the market. Many have already been terminated.

It takes more than the right partner for an alliance to succeed. Designing and managing a partnership can often be more complex and time-consuming than closing a merger and acquisition (M&A) transaction. An alliance is not a one-off deal. It is all about painstakingly building a new business jointly with a partner. In contrast, the core issues in a merger or takeover are the target's strategic fit and the purchase price. While the challenges are also significant, a buyer with management control is typically better able to respond to problems than is a partner in an alliance.

On the other hand, a partnership offers more design freedom than an acquisition or merger. This can be both a blessing and a curse. An alliance may be comprehensive and include all components of a business – or it may be narrowly framed. Both parties must choose the appropriate business design, taking into account factors in the target markets. The right ingredients must be in place to enable the alliance partners to deal with changing conditions. But the risk of getting the design wrong is high. Globally, two-thirds of all major alliances are terminated within eight years.

In the rest of this chapter, we analyze the three waves of alliances in Asia since 1996 and offer a perspective on why partnerships provide a compromise arrangement that allows both parties to capture growth. We also review the types of alliances that are popular and propose an approach to making negotiations a success.

THREE WAVES OF ALLIANCES

Historically, strategic alliances have accounted for 60–70 percent of the transactions in the financial sector in Asia (see Exhibit 15.1). More so than acquisitions, they have been a key way for most institutions to expand in the region. Some foreign players such as Dutch–Belgian group Fortis and France's Cetelem have used alliances almost exclusively to grow their Asian operations. They have dedicated executives scouting for partnership opportunities. Once in an alliance, they leverage their global network and resources to transfer skills and operational know-how to their domestic partners.

There have been three waves of alliances since 1996, each in different geographies, driven primarily by market-opening opportunities: in Japan in 1996, in the rest of Asia after the regional financial meltdown in 1997–98, and in China since its accession to the World Trade Organization (WTO) in 2001. These waves have taken place in different business lines, from investment banking and asset management in Japan during the bull market of the mid-1990s, to retail banking elsewhere in Asia after the crisis.

First wave: Japan between 1996 and 1999

After Japan's "Big Bang" financial services deregulation in 1996, many foreign investment banks and asset managers rushed to penetrate the world's second-largest market after the United States. The result: a slew of alliances in asset management, retail brokerage services, and investment banking, as illustrated by Exhibit 15.2.

The objectives of these alliances were to match the foreign players' sophisticated investment product manufacturing skills, and access to global markets with the domestic partners' distribution networks. The link-ups have yielded limited positive results so far, with the exception of a select few such as the Nikko Securities-Salomon Smith Barney and the Nippon Life-

Exhibit 15.1 Bank alliances in Asia

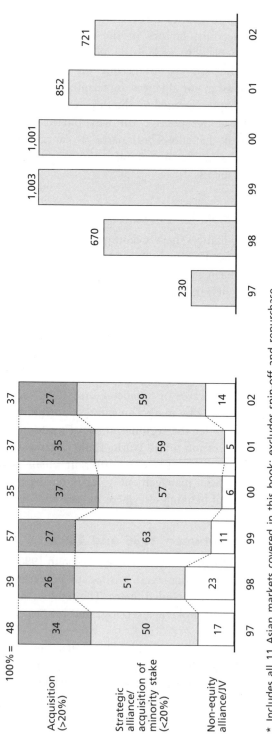

Number of cross-border bank transactions in Asia*

Number of press articles on banking alliances in Asia

* Includes all 11 Asian markets covered in this book; excludes spin-off and repurchase
Source: Thomson Financial Securities Data Company (SDC); Factiva; McKinsey analysis

Exhibit 15.2 Examples of alliances in Japan between 1996 and 1999

Date	Alliance	Business scope
Investment banking		
Jul. '97	Long Term Credit Bank of Japan, Swiss Bank Corp	Investment banking, asset management and private banking
May '98	Nikko Securities, Salomon Smith Barney	Investment banking, trading, and research for corporate and institutional investors
Sep. '99	Nomura Securities, Wasserstein Perella	M&A advisory services for Japanese corporations
Brokerage		
Jul. '97	Softbank, E*Trade	Online brokerage service
Dec. '98	Tokio Marine, Charles Schwab	Retail brokerage service
Asset management		
Jun. '97	Nippon Life, Putnam Investments	Pension fund management and investment products
Sep. '98	Dai-Ichi Kangyo Bank, JP Morgan	Retail investment trust business
Dec. '98	State Street Bank, Mitsui Trust & Banking	Master trust and custody services in Japan
Aug. '99	Sanwa Bank, Morgan Stanley	Asset management
Sep. '99	Meiji Mutual Life Insurance, Dresdner Bank	Asset management

Putnam Investments alliances. These rare successes underscore how well-designed alliances can be powerful partnerships.

Take Nikko Salomon Smith Barney, an innovative tie-up that turned into one of the leading investment banks in Japan. Both parties were looking for a way to enhance their capabilities and competitive strengths. Nikko – now known as Nikko Cordial Securities – was struggling to build its investment banking capabilities to compete with local competitors that were taking a growing share of domestic deals. It also had no way to compete for lucrative international transactions. In the mid-1990s, revenues were down as Japan's equity markets stagnated. Nikko's own stock was under pressure. Salomon, meanwhile, had a reasonable business in Japan mainly centered on its strength in fixed-income products. But it had far less scale and market power than rivals such as Goldman Sachs or Merrill Lynch.

In 1998, Citigroup – Salomon's parent – boldly committed all of its wholesale operations in Japan to a joint venture with Nikko. While Citigroup held a 49 percent stake, both parties had equal board representation. "It must be a Japanese company," Junichi Arimura, Nikko's President and CEO, insisted during negotiations with Citigroup Chairman Sandy Weill and his team.[1] Citigroup also acquired a 7 percent minority stake in Nikko Securities, thereby strengthening the Japanese firm's capital base. By 2002, Citigroup had raised its share in Nikko to 20 percent.

The alliance turned out to be a powerful combination – Citigroup's product strength and global network with Nikko's customer access, deal-sourcing, and domestic placement capabilities. It has outperformed all the independent American investment banks in Japan. The venture's share of equity issues topped the league table at 36 percent in 2001, while its net profit for the year to March 2001 doubled to $287 million, at a time when other American investment banks such as Merrill Lynch and Goldman Sachs were struggling with a net profit of $31 million and net loss of $102 million, respectively. Nikko Salomon has kept the top spot in the league tables for equity issuance since 1999, while performing consistently well in M&A too. Citigroup's success led many Japanese and foreign brokers to review their strategies. "Many are wondering if the Nikko Salomon Smith Barney tactics could be copied," said one foreign banker in May 2001.[2]

Another success story is the Nippon Life-Putnam Investments alliance. Each partner complemented the other well, creating a profitable business. In the mid-1990s, Nippon Life (often referred to as 'Nissay' for short in Japan) was looking to improve the performance of its international assets, particularly in institutional fund management. It wanted a semi-exclusive partnership that would be cost-effective and provide more direct access to fund management skills that could potentially be used in other areas of its business. For its part, Putnam wanted to tap a large pool of funds in Japan, without having to make a substantial investment in infrastructure. And it aimed to make the business profitable early, even if scale was limited.

Nippon Life and Putnam set up a 50–50 joint venture with a narrow scope. It is mainly run by Putnam, which provides marketing support to Nissay's channels for the American partner's products. The core of the

---

1   "Merging Markets: Travellers, Nikko Union is Many Things: Easy is Not One of Them." *Wall Street Journal*, May 19, 1999.

2   "NSSB Set to Outstrip US Banks in Japan," *Financial Times*, May 11, 2001.

alliance structure is the split responsibilities. Nippon Life raises funds directly from its existing business and coordinates its distribution channels with the joint venture (JV), while the actual fund management is handled by Putnam through its operations outside Japan. Leveraging heavily on the parent companies' capabilities, this low-cost partnership turned a profit in only its second year. By 2002, it had over $10 billion in funds under management.

These two successes are the exception rather than the rule in Japan. Most players have been burned by their experience with alliances and are now retrenching operations. Many of the partnerships listed in Exhibit 15.2 were ended within their first three years. The difficult stock market environment since 2000 explains some of the failures. However, many were due to design faults.

Consider these examples. Nomura Securities and Wasserstein Perella terminated their alliance in September 2000, just one year after signing an agreement. Nomura figured that it had successfully grasped the skills it needed from Wasserstein Perella and no longer required a partner. Swiss Bank bought out Long-Term Credit Bank of Japan's (LTCB) stake in the two joint ventures they created in September 1998, one year after their agreement, because LTCB was in financial distress. Dai-Ichi Kangyo Bank bought out JP Morgan's stake in their mutual fund joint venture less than two years after its creation when each went through major domestic mergers (Morgan with Chase Manhattan and Dai-Ichi with Fuji Bank and Industrial Bank of Japan to form Mizuho Bank). Their new situations led to changes in strategy and conflicts of interest that were too tough to overcome for an alliance that was already taking more management time than was justified by the meager business flow.

Second wave: Post-crisis Asia

Since the Asian crisis, most alliances have been structured around retail banking products – primarily in consumer finance such as credit cards and unsecured personal loans, and in bancassurance (the selling of insurance through bank channels). Exhibit 15.3 lists some examples.

For the domestic player, the primary objective of such alliances is to be able to offer innovative products by leveraging the foreign partner's best-in-class skills. The local partner expects to build the critical competitive advantage it needs to emerge as a winner in its market. Most of the tie-ups in this wave have been structured around product-focused joint ventures or distribution agreements.

In consumer finance, some tie-ups have been successful at accelerating the growth of the domestic partner. State Bank of India (SBI), one of the largest banks in its home market, wanted to develop its credit card operations

Exhibit 15.3   Examples of alliances in Asia (excluding China and Japan) since 1997

Date	Alliance	Business scope
All business lines		
May '00	Citigroup, Fubon Financial Holdings (Taiwan)	Broad strategic partnership, entailing Citibank's taking a 15% stake in Fubon's five financial services businesses (property and casualty insurance, life insurance, asset management, securities, and banking)
Consumer finance		
June '98	GE Capital, State Bank of India (India)	Credit cards and financial consultancy services
Feb. '00	GE Capital, Bank Mandiri (Indonesia)	Credit cards
Oct. '01	Thai Farmers Bank, Cetelem (Thailand)	Consumer finance
Dec. '01	Shinhan, Cetelem (Korea)	Consumer finance
Bancassurance and asset management		
Apr. '97	Prudential plc, ICICI Ltd (India)	Life insurance
Mar. '98	AXA Group, Krung Thai Bank (Thailand)	Life insurance
Dec. '98	Standard Chartered Bank, Prudential plc (regional)	Insurance services, launched PruCard and alliances to sell life insurance
May '00	Maybank, Fortis (Malaysia)	Bancassurance
Jan. '01	Hana Bank, Allianz (Korea)	Bancassurance and asset management
Jul. '01	DBS, Aviva (Singapore)	Life and general insurance
Dec. '01	Shinhan, Cardif (Korea)	Bancassurance
May '02	Kookmin, ING (Korea)	Life insurance
Aug. '02	Cardif and State Bank of India (India)	Life insurance

and better penetrate its customer base, but lacked the credit-scoring skills and risk-based pricing to make an aggressive push through its extensive branch network. GE Capital, for its part, aimed to expand its credit card operations by leveraging its credit-scoring system and state-of-the-art back-office and processing capabilities. The SBI–GE Capital alliance was an immediate success, with SBI selling more than half a million cards within the first year of operation.

We have also seen successful alliances in bancassurance. UK insurance group Prudential's partnership with Standard Chartered Bank is a good example. In December 1998, the two companies entered into a 12-year venture, structured primarily as a distribution agreement, with Prudential providing extensive support to the bank's sales channels. In addition to designing the products and providing full technical support including underwriting skills, administration, and IT systems, Prudential also sent dedicated, well-trained financial service consultants to Standard Chartered branches. The combination has been extremely effective in penetrating Standard Chartered Bank's customer base, particularly in products such as mortgage insurance that are easily bundled with banking services. Prudential has since successfully rolled out similar partnerships with Standard Chartered Bank in Singapore, Malaysia, and Taiwan, and with Bank Bali in Indonesia and ICICI Bank in India.

Many product-distribution alliances have had initial success. As a result, foreign players have been replicating the model widely. But the jury is still out on whether these partnerships create enduring value for the parent companies. Are the domestic players simply using the alliances to build new capabilities? Will they jettison their partners in a few years, keeping the customers and future profits for themselves? Or are these joint ventures "Trojan horses" for foreign players who focus on the most attractive customers and product segments, only to skim this cream off their local partners' businesses later? Success depends on how such alliances have been designed and structured. The acid test for the domestic banks is whether they would be able to protect and control their customer bases over the long run.

Third wave: China since 2001

Since China's accession to the WTO and recent deregulation of foreign ownership, overseas players have been racing to forge alliances with, or acquire minority stakes in, Chinese banks. No credible institution can afford to ignore what will become one of the world's largest financial markets over the next decades. A key aim is to be better positioned to capture opportunities in personal financial services. Several alliances and acquisitions have been structured in retail banking, insurance, and securities, as illustrated in Exhibit 15.4. We anticipate many more over the coming years.

An alliance is an attractive way for foreign players to get around heavy restrictions on renminbi deposit-taking and lending. Recent rule changes mean that foreign banks can acquire up to a 25 percent stake in the most attractive joint stock and private commercial banks. An alliance allows a Chinese bank to leverage its skills and brand to develop its retail banking franchise. China's retail market is limited – retail assets typically account for less than 10 percent of the total assets of large banks – and many retail products have yet to take off. As a result, in some partnerships, the foreign player has taken management control of specific product lines that could be highly lucrative. For example, at the end of 2002, Citibank purchased a 5 percent stake in listed Shanghai Pudong Development bank for $72 million, with an attractive option to increase stake to 24.9 percent in 2008. The American bank was to set up and run credit card operations for its Chinese partner.

Exhibit 15.4 Examples of alliances in China since 2001

Date	Alliance	Business scope
Banking		
Nov. '01	HSBC, Bank of Shanghai	HSBC takes an 8% stake in Bank of Shanghai
Dec. '02	Citibank, Shanghai Pudong Development Bank	Citibank takes a 5% stake in Shanghai Pudong; credit cards
Insurance		
Oct. '01	Fortis, Taiping Life	Fortis takes a 24.9% stake in Taiping Life
Jul. '02	HSBC, Ping An Insurance	HSBC takes a 10% stake in Ping An
Securities and investment banking		
Mar. '02	BNP Paribas, Changjiang Securities	Securities brokerage
Dec. '02	Credit Lyonnais Securities Asia, Xiangcai Securities	Securities brokerage
Asset management		
Jan. '02	Prudential plc, Harvest Fund Management	Fund management
Jan. '03	China Merchant Securities, ING	Mutual funds

Given the regulatory constraints and market environment, alliances and joint ventures are an attractive option, if not the only one, for a foreign player to break into China. The crucial issue is timing: Should an investor go in now with a joint venture or wait until regulations are clearer and more control is allowed? Some players such as Citigroup and HSBC are following a two-track strategy to hedge their bets. In addition to strategic alliances with Chinese financial institutions, they are pursuing organic growth by gradually opening their own branches. The key advantage is to gain real market insight through early exposure to the retail renminbi business before it is fully open to foreign competition in 2007. This knowledge could easily be leveraged for their own operations later.

Foreign financial institutions with a conservative attitude might rule out getting in early through a JV, preferring to follow a more gradual approach. A McKinsey survey of some 30 joint ventures in China in non-financial sectors shows that about half are under-performing and unprofitable.

The control issue remains a difficult hurdle in framing any partnership. Most Chinese companies want to retain management of their operations and are not very transparent, even to foreign partners. "Your alliance in China is safe as long as it loses money," quips a top executive of one global bank with long experience in the mainland. Are the risks and uncertainty too high for any business model to be profitable? No one has the answer, but one thing is certain: In China, alliances are not for the fainted-hearted.

CONSIDER THE ALLIANCE OPTION

Even though our analysis of these three waves of alliances in Asia since 1996 shows that the track record of these tie-ups is mixed, we still consider a partnership an attractive option if both the domestic and foreign players complement each other, creating clear competitive advantages to build new businesses and accelerate growth. In addition, partnerships can be less risky than either a greenfield operation or acquisition. Let us consider those two alternatives.

Greenfield opportunities are few

For both domestic and foreign players, there are few greenfield opportunities worth considering because of the long-term commitment and investment required to make them work. Most new enterprises take up to a decade, or longer, to turn into true winners. The challenge for the local player is to develop organically the necessary skills to offer innovative services and products. This takes time, with no guarantee of success. To move away from the traditional banking model to a more sales-oriented, customer-focused approach, a domestic bank must hire managers with the right skills and expertise, typically acquired during stints at foreign banks such as Citibank or highly innovative local institutions.

But the pool of talent is limited in Asia, with competition sharp for the best and brightest. As a result, attracting the right people could be costly. Moreover, acquiring new skills and implementing the changes required is a long and arduous process in any organization resistant to change. An alliance provides an attractive way for a domestic bank to surmount these hurdles. It means access to the foreign partner's talent pools and training facilities. The local bank can use the alliance as a means of generating the necessary internal momentum for change, particularly in its sales force.

All things being equal, many foreign players prefer to grow organically in Asia because this enables them to control the customers and avoid any potential hidden liabilities that could arise in an acquisition, such as exposure to unattractive corporate portfolios. But the greenfield option is viable only when certain conditions are met. There must be a market for new products or services, with attractive growth rates and the opportunity for the foreign player to have direct access to customers. While few opportunities may satisfy these requirements and the risk-return balance for a greenfield operation is increasingly unattractive, several players have succeeded in pursuing this approach in Asia. Citibank, for example, has created a robust retail franchise across the region, focusing on affluent customers with its CitiGold products. Similarly, Aeon and GE Capital have built highly successful consumer finance businesses in Hong Kong and other markets.

In most cases, large incumbents still dominate and control customer access. The large investments required to acquire customers and the competitive difficulties entailed can be real deal-breakers for new players trying to break into existing markets. Another problem with the greenfield play is regulation, particularly in markets which have not yet fully opened to foreigners, as was the case in most of Asia before the crisis. The approval process can be long and tedious. For these reasons, foreign players have typically shied away from placing the big bets required in a greenfield investment.

Acquisitions can be expensive

In markets with ownership restrictions such as Malaysia and China, strategic alliances through the acquisition of minority stakes are the only option for the foreign player. In places fully opened to outsiders only recently, there are either very few attractive franchises for sale or the risks associated with buying distressed banks are too high.

In many Asian markets, there are few appealing acquisition targets because most family-owned financial institutions are reluctant to cede control for cultural or sentimental reasons. The few that have been put on the block were sold at extremely high prices. In 2001, for example, Singapore's DBS Bank acquired Dao Heng Bank in Hong Kong at a price-to-book multiple of 3.3, at a time when listed banks in that market, with the exception of HSBC, were trading at a multiple of 1.4. Because of the high premium required to make a purchase, it may be difficult for other foreign players to extract enough synergies to create value from their acquisitions.

Distressed banks could be potential acquisitions for foreign investors. In Japan and in Korea, for example, the government has organized auctions in the hope that invited foreign institutions would buy weak banks, recapitalize them and turn them around. But many potential buyers have walked away because of the high risks and hidden liabilities in the banks' loan portfolios. In September 1999, HSBC backed off from buying a controlling stake in Seoulbank because of a disagreement over the value of the Korean bank's loan portfolio. Carving out the risks related to NPLs, as the Carlyle Group did when the American private equity fund acquired a controlling interest in Koram Bank in 2000, may not be feasible. Realistically, only the limited number of players that already have a large presence in the region are in a position to assess the potential risks of a purchase and dedicate enough resources to revitalize a major bank. For most of the others, focusing on building new businesses without having to deal with legacy problems is the preferred strategy.

Alliances are an attractive compromise

If prospective partners complement each other well, an alliance offers clear advantages. First, the time needed to launch a venture's products in the market can be cut down since partners leverage existing assets or know-how. The domestic partner can easily and speedily access critical skills. Coming out with innovative products and services quickly is a key success factor in Asia because customers often take to new offerings fast.

Second, because set-up expenses and investments are shared, the cost of launching an alliance is usually relatively low. The venture can tap the skills, networks and facilities of its parents. This is a key advantage in businesses where clear economies of scale are needed. A credit-card processing platform, for example, usually requires a minimum of one million active cards to break even. GE Capital can leverage its regional credit card platform across multiple partnerships in several countries. This means that its partners enjoy much lower processing costs than if they were to build their own operations.

Alliances are difficult to pull off because of the shared control. For this reason alone, before entering any negotiation, prospective partners should reflect on whether the tie-up they are contemplating is really the best option for them. They should weigh the potential upside against the time and effort they would need to put in to make the partnership work. Should they decide to push ahead, both parties must pay careful attention to the design of the alliance if they are to maximize the chances that the partnership will succeed.

The devil is in the details: Key alliance design points

Strategic rationale: There has to be a compelling one. Too often prospective partners get caught up in an initial idea and do not stop to ask why they should forge an alliance and what are the real benefits.

Material impact: An international bank must consider whether an alliance could become successful enough to have a material impact on the performance of its whole operation. For all the pain and time needed to manage it, an alliance may offer only negligible returns.

Partner selection: Choosing the wrong partner can naturally lead to a strained relationship and frustration. Assessing the real value of what each party brings to the table may be difficult when it comes to "intangibles" such as a brand name, but taking the time to do so is critical.

Balance of power: While a venture may start out with the partners' roles in balance, this frequently changes. An alliance must have a degree of flexibility to ensure that shifts in market conditions do not jeopardize the business model.

Exit strategy: Alliances do not last forever. Parties should agree on how a venture would be wound up. Otherwise, should the relationship fall apart, one partner could end up without benefits or be locked out of some markets.

DESIGNS FOR SUCCESS

With the variety of options available, choosing the right design for an alliance is a major challenge for prospective partners. The key is to select the appropriate structure, given the strategic objectives of both parties. The two sides should come to an agreement on critical issues such as the business scope, management control, and the ownership of customers. Let us look at the rationale for alliances in two business lines – bancassurance and consumer finance – and consider examples of design models that players have adopted.

Bancassurance: Deciding the overall alliance structure

Bancassurance is expected to become as prevalent in Asia as it is in continental European markets such as Spain, France, and Italy, where more than half of new insurance products are sold through bank branches. In Hong Kong and Singapore, the most liberalized markets in Asia, bancassurance already accounts for 15–20 percent of new insurance product sales. In most of the other markets where regulations are gradually allowing bancassurance, there has been strong initial growth.

Because customers tend to prefer a financial services provider that can deliver a wide range of products, there are attractive opportunities for a bank-based financial holding company. A bancassurance offering increases product scope and reinforces the bank's wealth management value proposition. Bancassurance also provides attractive economics. Banks generate additional income streams either from distribution fees or underwriting income, while the insurer reduces distribution costs by not relying exclusively on an expensive agency sales force.

The potential for bancassurance tie-ups across Asia is significant, and provides a major opportunity for domestic banks. The strategic rationale for designing bancassurance alliances between a domestic bank and a foreign insurer is strong. First, banks rarely have the required skills and systems to run an insurance company effectively, particularly in the areas of product design, underwriting, and claims management. There is a clear advantage for a bank to enter into a partnership with a player that can transfer its know-how. Second, the foreign player can leverage its bancassurance experience to develop a successful business model to avoid one major pitfall: providing the same offering as the one for the traditional agency sales force. This usually does not work. A customer on a bank branch visit is normally unwilling to spend the required time to understand complex insurance products. A successful bancassurance operation requires a simplified offering that is linked to banking products, an effective marketing and sales approach, and the necessary IT systems.

How both parties complement each other indicates the way in which responsibilities should be split. Typically, the bank focuses on marketing, sales, and possibly the management of the assets, if the bank has the necessary skills and infrastructure. The insurer provides the product design, underwriting, administrative support, and claims management.

When structuring a bancassurance partnership, the critical issue for the domestic bank is to select the right business model. Every insurer with bancassurance experience will propose its own model, each with different implications. There are three basic models to consider for an alliance (see Exhibit 15.5). The correct choice depends on the level of integration between the bank and the insurer.

Exhibit 15.5 Potential bancassurance models

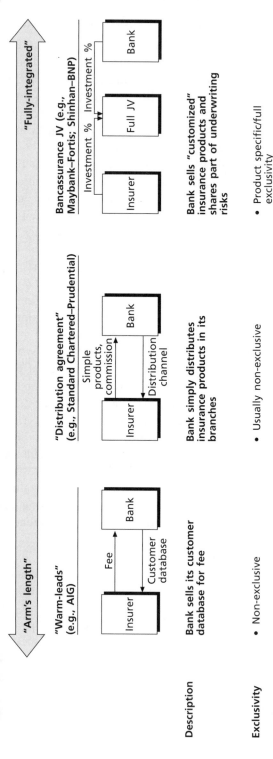

"Arm's length" ◄──► "Fully-integrated"

	"Warm-leads" (e.g., AIG)	"Distribution agreement" (e.g., Standard Chartered–Prudential)	Bancassurance JV (e.g., Maybank–Fortis; Shinhan–BNP)
Description	Bank sells its customer database for fee	Bank simply distributes insurance products in its branches	Bank sells "customized" insurance products and shares part of underwriting risks
Exclusivity	• Non-exclusive	• Usually non-exclusive	• Product specific/full exclusivity
Value-sharing • **Bank**	• Fee per warm-lead	• Distribution fees • Asset management fees	• Distribution fees • Asset management fees • Part of underwriting profit
• **Insurer**	• Underwriting profit • Distribution profit	• Underwriting profit	• Underwriting profit

Source: Press releases; McKinsey analysis

The "warm-leads" model: For a fee, the bank lets the insurer target sales to potential buyers from among its account holders. The insurer's sales force pursues the leads. The arrangement is usually non-exclusive, meaning that the insurer may have similar agreements with several banks. This model is typically used by insurance companies with good operations and strong brands, such as AIG. The partnership has little impact on the bank, with the exception of the fee income received. Such an alliance is relatively simple to arrange, with the value of each lead the main issue to negotiate. The bank could lose control over its customer base because the insurer would "own" the customers to whom it sells insurance products. That could eventually hurt the bank, as the insurer is likely to target the most attractive customers and could then cross-sell competing financial products to them. If a bank selects this model, it has to address potential conflicts of interest that may arise throughout the life of the partnership.

The distribution agreement model: The bank becomes another distribution channel for the insurer, which provides sales and systems support, but keeps full control over insurance-related operations. As in the case of the Standard Chartered Bank alliance with Prudential, product sales are done by tellers or a dedicated sales force. The advantage for the bank is that it can earn steady fee income without having to commit much capital. In 2001, for example, DBS Bank received an upfront payment of S$71 million, or $38.2 million, as part of a 10-year bancassurance partnership agreement with UK-based CGNU, now known as Aviva. Further payments are possible if DBS meets performance requirements.

To make such a partnership a success, the domestic bank has to assess the insurer's ability to contribute. A good knowledge of the local market, an extensive training program for bank staff or the dedicated sales force, and the necessary IT systems are critical to penetrating the bank's customer base effectively.

The bank also has to consider three issues. First, as with the "warm-leads" model, customer ownership could be an issue as the bank's customers become the insurer's after sales occur. Second, the type of products offered could potentially result in conflicts of interest between the bank and the insurer. For example, selling "hot" products with attractive returns could be extremely favorable for the bank, as it would increase distribution fee income. But these products might be unprofitable for the insurer. The two parties would have to ensure that they have a mechanism in place to deal with such a discrepancy. Third, the interests of the insurer and the bank may diverge over exclusivity. The insurer would clearly favor a non-exclusive partnership that would make the bank a third-party provider with an offering that would not be unique.

The joint venture model: A joint venture (JV) can be set up as a dedicated bancassurance vehicle, as in the case of the Maybank-Fortis and Shinhan-BNP Paribas partnerships. This approach integrates and aligns the interests of the bank and the insurer, as both parties have to put up capital and split the total economics of the business. Such a partnership is usually exclusive. A JV provides better customer ownership protection for the local bank. Client data is usually owned by the joint venture, not the foreign partner. The bank should set terms in the agreement to protect itself in case of a change in ownership or the termination of the venture.

The structure of a JV has implications for the bank partner's economics and on the time it takes to get products to the market. Cash flows in the early years of a venture are typically negative because distribution costs have to be written off. For this reason, the bank or financial holding company has to be comfortable with consolidating losses during the first few years. It is therefore critical for both sides to agree on the pace of business growth and on how long it should take for the venture to break even.

As the JV has to develop new bancassurance operations, it is important to consider the time necessary to obtain a license, build the IT platform, design the products, and train the sales force. If the foreign partner has no presence in the market and no license, it could take a while before the venture gets into gear. Other factors affecting the timing of a launch include the complexity of the business model, the dedicated on-the-ground resources available, and the effectiveness of the insurance partner in transferring skills from its global headquarters. In deciding with whom to set up a venture, the bank should compare what potential partners have to offer in these areas.

All three of these models can create value, but each requires different trade-offs. The partners should select the right type of alliance based on their overall strategic objectives and their ability to implement a particular plan successfully.

Consumer finance: Structuring control and value creation

Across Asia, consumer finance represents a significant opportunity. Both credit cards and unsecured personal loans remain under-penetrated, while margins are attractive. Historically, most players have pursued a "land-grab" growth strategy, providing a generic offering to customers. But it now takes more effort to succeed. Domestic banks need to develop highly sophisticated skills quickly, especially as default levels rise in many markets.

Effective risk-based credit-scoring and customer segmentation skills are critical to targeting the most attractive customers and making profits as competition intensifies. Innovative products, tailored to specific consumer segments, are increasingly important in acquiring customers. In Indonesia, for example, Bank Mandiri has had enormous success with the air miles credit card program it developed jointly with GE Capital. State-of-the-art processes for everything from credit card and loan applications to debt collection are also essential.

Alliances are therefore a very appealing option for domestic banks, as these partnerships leverage the skills and infrastructure of established consumer finance players. These tools include risk-based credit-scoring systems, customer segmentation and data-mining, and the processing platform. If the complementarity between partners cuts across the whole range of the consumer finance business, an alliance can create significant value.

The major difficulty is to structure the partnership in a way that ensures an effective transfer of skills to the local bank, while giving the foreign player enough control to preserve a sustainable balance of power over time. Here are two examples of alliances with differing approaches to management structure (see Exhibit 15.6).

Non-exclusive joint venture: In December 2001, Shinhan Bank and the Korean subsidiary of France's Cetelem set up a 50–50 consumer finance joint venture to provide unsecured personal loans to Shinhan's customers. Cetelem contributed its product design and credit-scoring system, while Shinhan brought its customer base and distribution network. Cetelem retains full control over its platform – the IT system and credit-scoring process – through its fully owned subsidiary, while Shinhan has joint control over the operations of the venture to facilitate the transfer of skills. The alliance, however, is not exclusive. In its business model, Cetelem leverages its local platform through multiple partnerships to gain critical mass. For example, in Thailand, it has an agreement with about 400 vendors, including discount stores and retailers, as well as a partnership with Thai Farmers Bank, the third-largest commercial bank in the country. Shinhan accepted Cetelem's terms in exchange for the opportunity to develop a broad partnership and platform across several business lines, including bancassurance and asset management.

Shared control: GE Capital and the State Bank of India structured a novel deal that affords each partner full management control over specific elements of their businesses. The partnership is structured around two joint ventures. The first, in which SBI holds 60 percent, is responsible for marketing and customer acquisition, while the other, 60 percent of which is controlled by GE Capital, handles credit approvals and back-office processing. To ensure that the two ventures effectively coordinate operations, the partners put in place service agreements and a dispute-resolution mechanism.

In the two partnership structures described above, the mono-line players maintain strong control over their systems and know-how. This raises the

Exhibit 15.6   Addressing the control issue in consumer finance partnerships

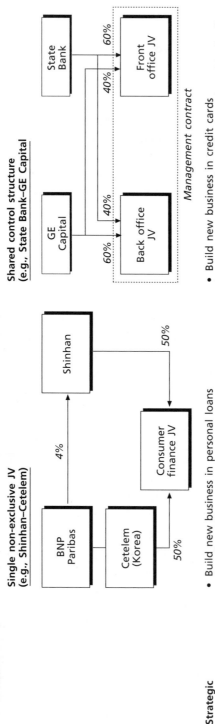

Single non-exclusive JV
(e.g., Shinhan–Cetelem)

BNP Paribas — 4% → Shinhan

BNP Paribas / Cetelem (Korea) — 50% → Consumer finance JV ← 50% — Shinhan

Shared control structure
(e.g., State Bank–GE Capital)

GE Capital — 40% → Front office JV ← 60% — State Bank

GE Capital — 60% → Back office JV ← 40% — State Bank

Management contract

Strategic objectives
- Build new business in personal loans
- Transfer skills

- Build new business in credit cards
- Leverage GE Capital credit approvals and back-office system

Design rationale
- Part of global platform partnership between BNP Paribas and Shinhan Bank
- Non-exclusive joint venture so that Cetelem can leverage its platform with other distributors (e.g., Carrefour)

- Two JVs created to ensure full control by each party of key elements of the business system

Source: Press releases; interviews; McKinsey analysis

question of how a domestic bank can open this locked "black-box" to access the skills it needs.

From our experience, "learning by doing" is the most effective way of transferring skills, even if the tools and systems remain fully under the control of the foreign player. The domestic bank must ensure that the overseas partner provides enough training support and that the bank's staff receives direct exposure to the operations. For example, they need to participate in credit risk analysis, be part of the monthly risk management meeting, and review the customer relationship management and segmentation tools. The domestic bank should also consider sending staff to the foreign partner's head office during the period when the joint venture operations are being set up. To ensure that such training programs are implemented as part of the partnership agreement, the domestic bank must explicitly state early in the negotiation that the transfer of skills is one of its key strategic objectives.

NEGOTIATING ALLIANCES

The negotiation of a partnership is not a one-off transaction, but a business-building effort. It is more important to focus on designing a partnership that will work over the long term, rather than on winning short-term advantages that would not matter if the alliance is not a success. The bank should be represented by executives who are skilled at negotiation and who have a detailed knowledge of operations. Talks should not be led by a dealmaker who prefers to conclude a broad agreement first, leaving operational details for underlings to wrap up later. Often, a partnership fails to take off because the nuts and bolts of the alliance have not been completely sorted out early.

To negotiate and design alliances that are competitive and meet the strategic objectives of each partner, both parties must follow the following four-step approach: confirm the alliance's strategic rationale, jointly frame the key terms critical to the business case for the partnership, resolve potential deal-breaking issues, and carry out rigorous negotiations in stages.

Confirm the strategic rationale

Since designing an alliance is a complex task and the success rate of partnerships is low, the rationale for a tie-up must be compelling. There should be a clear consensus on strategy within the organization to avoid embarrassment during negotiations. But before moving forward, each party must be sure that an alliance is the best option to achieve its strategic objectives. Many corporations enter into negotiations without making the effort to articulate their goals, the business case for a partnership, and the problems and issues that need to be addressed. Few bother to ask why an alliance is needed. Indeed, many partnerships should never have been born in the first place.

Frame key terms jointly

When developing the business case for an alliance, prospective partners should together frame the terms of an agreement on the basis of the following eight "building blocks" (see Exhibit 15.7):

Aligned aspirations: The two parties need to agree on what would make the partnership a success. The definition of success should include both partners' objectives – financial goals such as sales volume and profitability, the expected time-to-market period, and any intangible benefits such as the transfer of sales skills.

Shared market perspective: Both parties must have a common understanding of the market and the opportunity they are pursuing. They should agree on product growth potential, product profitability, customer targets, and competitive dynamics. A shared perspective is a strong foundation for building a joint business plan.

Shared economic impact assessment: Prospective partners should understand the value the alliance would create. Both sides must be fully aware of their commitments, as well as the value of each party's contribution to the partnership.

Shared responsibilities: Both parties should map out all key processes in the business model. They need to decide how responsibilities are to be split to maximize the success of the venture.

Partners' contributions: The prospective partners must have a detailed understanding of what resources, systems, and know-how each will contribute. These contributions need to be synthesized into the total value of contributions to the alliance by each partner.

Governance principles: To be successful and sustainable, an alliance must be designed to allow it to respond to changing market conditions and future uncertainties. An agreement should put in place the right governance principles and processes so that the alliance can evolve and adapt. Not all details can be agreed up-front. Built-in constraints that are not necessary for long-term success could jeopardize the future of the partnership.

Skills transfer: If the transfer of skills is a strategic objective of one party, the two partners need to define the mechanisms required to do it effectively.

Time-to-market period: Partners must agree on the time needed to develop the new business. The length of the time-to-market period depends on the business model and what each partner is contributing.

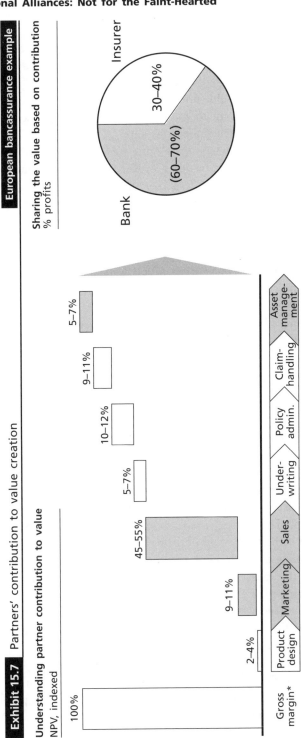

Exhibit 15.7 Partners' contribution to value creation

European bancassurance example

Understanding partner contribution to value
NPV, indexed

Sharing the value based on contribution
% profits

Source: McKinsey analysis

Resolve potential deal-breaking issues

In any negotiation, potential deal-breaking problems or contentious "zero-sum" issues are bound to arise. They should not be put off to one side, but be confronted and resolved to the mutual satisfaction of both parties. Otherwise, an alliance could run into trouble later. Several areas need special attention if both sides are to minimize the chances of a serious dispute arising that could threaten the partnership:

Value-sharing arrangements: Value can be extracted within the partnership, through joint venture profits, for example, and outside it, through royalties, distribution fees, cost allocations, or funding costs. When negotiating financial arrangements, it is crucial to avoid any value-sharing "myopia." Transparency is essential to ensure the fair sharing of value.

Governance terms: Both parties should precisely set out governance terms and principles, including voting and veto processes.

Exclusivity and non-competition clauses: Agreement should be reached on exclusivity and competition issues to resolve or prevent conflicts of interest or constraints over the long run.

Termination arrangements: Partners should agree on how to wind up an alliance so that both sides are properly protected. For example, they might adopt mechanisms that ensure that the domestic bank keeps its customer base and the foreign player retains its know-how. They might also agree on a formula to value the partnership at the time of termination.

Carry out rigorous negotiations in phases

The negotiation process should be rigorous and conducted in phases (see Exhibit 15.8).

Phase 1 – Partner selection and validation of the business case: The choice of partner must be based on strategic criteria and not purely on relationships or cultural fit. The domestic bank should validate the business case for the alliance and bring to the fore deal-breaking issues early. The parties should consider signing a non-binding memorandum of understanding (MOU) at the end of this phase. The MOU is critical to establishing over-arching business principles and securing the commitment of both sides. But prospective partners should be careful to minimize any damage to their credibility in the market should the partnership not materialize. Hyping a partnership in the press too early can be risky.

Phase 2 – Detailed business planning and final negotiation: The objective is to transform the business case into a detailed business plan that includes financial targets and a roadmap for implementation. In parallel, legal arrangements should be negotiated. At the end of this phase "definitive

Exhibit 15.8 Negotiation Process

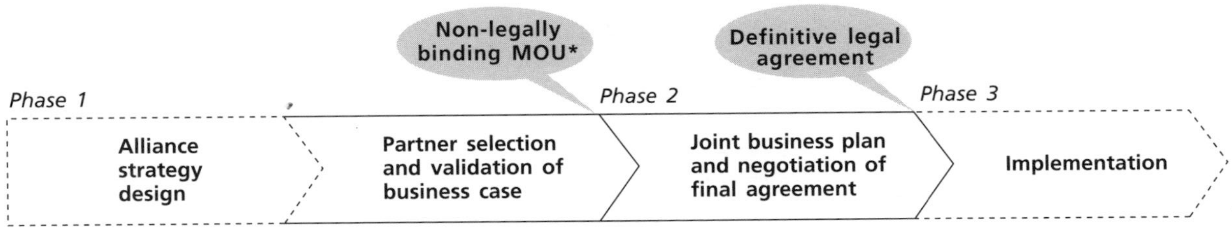

Phase 1

Phase 2

Phase 3

Non-legally binding MOU*

Definitive legal agreement

Alliance strategy design

Partner selection and validation of business case

Joint business plan and negotiation of final agreement

Implementation

- Both parties' aspirations
- Market overview
- Partnership economics
- Business model and processes
- Partners' contribution
- Governance principles
- Transfer of skills mechanism
- Time-to-market

- Value-sharing arrangements
- Governance terms
- Exclusivity/non-competition clauses
- Termination arrangements

- Detailed joint business planning
- Detailed implementation plan

- Final negotiation of partnership legal agreement

Business case

Zero-sum partnership issues

* Parties to consider whether it is in their interests to sign the MOU

Source: McKinsey analysis

agreements" are usually signed, which define the final terms and closing arrangements for the launch of the alliance.

Phase 3 – Implementation and execution: Partners set the business plan in motion and launch the venture.

International alliances in Asia are extremely attractive for both domestic and foreign banks. They can create significant upside when properly designed and structured. But only a few are happy. Partnerships are much more difficult to negotiate and execute than an acquisition or a greenfield operation. Two elements are crucial to ensure that a potential alliance is designed to create value for its two parent companies. First, each partner should articulate a rational strategy that identifies an alliance as the best option before engaging in any exploratory negotiations. Second, before starting any talks, both sides must have a solid understanding of the business case for the partnership and its operational implications. Those who fail to take these two crucial steps will waste a lot of energy and time on an alliance that may be promising at the outset, but only ends up in tears.

DATA SOURCES FOR GEOGRAPHIC MARKET CHAPTER PROFILE PAGES

MACROECONOMICS/SOCIOECONOMICS/BANKING MARKETS/CAPITAL MARKETS

Annual reports of financial institutions
Asian Demographics
Bank for International Settlements
Bloomberg
Central banks (all Asian markets)
Council of Labor Affairs & Government Pension Fund (Taiwan)
Cris Infac (India)
Datamonitor
Datastream
Directorate of Insurance, Ministry of Finance (Indonesia)
Economist Intelligence Unit
Global Insight
Government statistics (all Asian markets)
InfoBank Magazine (Indonesia)
Insurance Commission (the Philippines)
International Monetary Fund
Japan Consumer Credit Industry Association
Japan Tariff Association
Korea Financial Supervisory Service
Lafferty
Life Insurance Corporation (India)
Mandatory Provident Fund Schemes Authority (Hong Kong)
National Council of Applied Economic Research (India)
Nikkei Annual (Japan)
Office of Insurance Commissioner (Hong Kong)
Securities Investment Trust & Consulting Association (Taiwan)
Sigma Report (all Asian markets)
Singapore Central Provident Fund Board
Singapore Housing Development Board
Stock exchanges (all Asian markets)
Taiwan Life Insurance Association
The Investment Trusts Association (Japan)

Thomson Financial Securities Data Company
World Federation of Exchange

FINANCIAL LANDSCAPES

Almanac of China's Banking and Finance
Bankscope
Bank for International Settlements
BusinessWorld (the Philippines)
Business On-line (Thailand)
Central banks (all Asian markets)
Centre of Monitoring Indian Economy
China Statistical Yearbook
Federation of Bankers' Association of Japan
InfoBank Magazine (Indonesia)
Indonesian Financial Statistics
Korea Financial Supervisory Service
KPMG Banking Survey (Hong Kong and Singapore)
Manual for Regulations of Bank (the Philippines)
Quarterly Banking Report (the Philippines)
Rating Bank 2001 (Indonesia)
Taiwan Ministry of Finance

INDEX